The Teaching of Physical Skills

The Teaching of Physical Skills

Annie Clement
Cleveland State University

Betty G. Hartman
Professor Emeritus, Kent State University

WCB Brown & Benchmark
PUBLISHERS

Madison, Wisconsin • Dubuque, Iowa

Book Team

Executive Managing Editor *Ed Bartell*
Editor *Scott Spoolman*
Production Editor *Ann Fuerste*
Art Processor *Brenda A. Ernzen*
Visuals/Design Developmental Consultant *Marilyn A. Phelps*
Visuals/Design Freelance Specialist *Mary L. Christianson*
Marketing Manager *Pamela S. Cooper*
Advertising Coordinator *Susie Butler*

Brown & Benchmark

A Division of Wm. C. Brown Communications, Inc.

Executive Vice President/General Manager *Thomas E. Doran*
Vice President/Editor in Chief *Edgar J. Laube*
Vice President/Sales and Marketing *Eric Ziegler*
Director of Production *Vickie Putman Caughron*
Director of Custom and Electronic Publishing *Chris Rogers*

Wm. C. Brown Communications, Inc.

President and Chief Executive Officer *G. Franklin Lewis*
Corporate Senior Vice President and Chief Financial Officer *Robert Chesterman*
Corporate Senior Vice President and President of Manufacturing *Roger Meyer*

Cover and interior design by Ellen Pettengell Design

Copyedited by Karen Dorman

A Times Mirror Company

Library of Congress Catalog Card Number: 93–74108

ISBN 0–697–14802–5

Printed in the United States of America by Wm. C. Brown Communications, Inc.,
2460 Kerper Boulevard, Dubuque, IA 52001

10   9   8   7   6   5   4   3   2   1

Contents

Preface

The Teaching of Physical Skills is written for the professionals and students, graduate and undergraduate, in elementary education, physical education, and sport management. They include instructors, supervisors, and students preparing to teach, coach, or instruct in chartered schools, health spas, corporate fitness programs, and recreational environments.

The distinguishing feature of the text is that instruction is dictated by the needs and skill level of the learner. Content is organized under a hierarchy of movement with emphasis on commonalities of movement and sequential progressions from simple to complex. Instructors use the hierarchy and progressions to identify where the learner is on the learning continuum and to select the next best skill for instruction.

The consumer of *The Teaching of Physical Skills* will acquire an understanding of fundamental movements and motor patterns, thus showing learners how complex skills are created. This understanding will enable the tennis or volleyball professional, for example, to analyze basic or fundamental movements of elite athletes to correct errors. At the same time the elementary teacher can use the text to plan activities using basic skills most often found in traditional sports.

The hierarchy of movement was originated by the authors and other members of the Ohio Guide for Girls Secondary Physical Education Committee. Members were Shirley Babitt, Lucille M. Burkett, Patricia K. Fehl, Sally F. Murphy, Lois E. Wood (deceased), and Margaret E. Love. Dr. Betty G. Hartman was director and Dr. Annie Clement was editor. The hierarchy of movement is based on the premise that the ability to execute fundamentals and patterns is requisite to success in learning specialized sport skills. Further, it suggests that a number of fundamental skills are common to nearly all sport and physical activity organizations. With the advent of computer graphics as the primary vehicle for learning physical skills, an understanding and appreciation of commonalities will be a must.

Commonalities in game strategy and rules are also identified. Knowledge of the commonalities will enable participants to recognize the same skill in a number of sports. This will enhance participants' capacity to enjoy many sports as spectators. Existing computer technology will enable a person, schooled in the commonalities of human movement, to create new and different games.

Part I provides the content of physical activity. Part II explains why the content was selected and how it is to be used. The hierarchy of movement, or the content of physical activity, uses nutrition, physiology, biomechanics, psychology, and sociology as the underlying bases. Law is also presented in a comprehensive manner.

Part III discusses how to use parts I and II in the learning environment. Visual analysis, a teaching and learning technique, is presented in a unique manner in *The Teaching of Physical Skills*. Instructors are encouraged to use their knowledge of biomechanics as they view the progress of their learners. Participants learn how to view physical activity, internalize what they have seen, and coach themselves. Details of the creation of theory within the text is contained in the introduction.

▶ Acknowledgements

We are grateful to Lynn Howell for the photographs in the book and to the Cleveland State University students who posed for the pictures.

Annie Clement, Ph.D., J.D.
Betty G. Hartman, Ph.D.

Introduction

An instructor of physical skills has a wide choice of jobs and a varied array of careers. Instructors may be employed by public or private agencies; by schools—elementary, middle, secondary, or collegiate; by community centers; by agencies catering to one or more sport or activity, such as spas, racquet clubs, dance studios; by corporations and businesses; or by professional teams. They may be self-employed or employees of a business. They may be called teachers, instructors, coaches, activity specialists, or professionals, and their learners may be identified as students, professional athletes, clients, or corporate participants. Instructors, whether they work with a dance student or a football player, require a knowledge of human movement and physical skills. They also need to know where their particular teaching area fits within the total scheme of physical activity. The purpose of this text is to provide such information.

This book identifies the content of physical activity. Although a few books—written explicitly for elementary school physical educators—have defined content, statements of content appear to cease when the needs of youth have been met. Curriculum sources and texts available to middle, secondary, senior high, corporate, or sport specialists have failed to define the content of physical activity. Content in this text is described from beginning to advanced and organized by means of a hierarchy of movement. Skill acquisition or level of performance, rather than age, is used to determine content selection.

This hierarchy of movement uses fundamentals, combinations, and patterns common to all physical activity. Order (progression, sequence) is imposed with the idea that the learner will be proficient in all fundamentals, combinations, and patterns before working on a specialized skill. This is based on the premise that the ability to execute fundamentals is requisite to success in the learning of physical skills. No sport skills books of which the writers are aware stress the role of fundamentals and patterns in skill development. A few texts on specific sports are beginning to trace special-ized sport skills to motor patterns. However, this is the first text that deals with a range of sports and all fundamentals, combinations, and motor pat-terns requisite to the acquisition of sports skills.

Fundamentals, the simple form of movement, involve changes in body position sufficient to permit classification. Beginning forms of walking, run-ning, tossing, jumping, and hopping are among the fundamentals included in the text. They are movements in which the learner executes broad gen-eral actions in space with one or more body parts. The movement is not goal-oriented. These skills are to be learned before sport skills are taught. The idea of acquiring fundamentals and patterns prior to learning specific sport skills is contrary to the philosophy of some coaches. These coaches advocate learning and practicing only those skills used in a particular sport. A pass in basketball, for example, may be taught for the purpose of direc-tion and distance for the receiver. However, when the passer's throwing pattern is faulty, the success of the basketball skill is nebulous. Combina-tions involve the combining and integrating of fundamentals. Patterns repre-sent movements organized so that the timing of each body segment, the amount of force exerted, and the space utilized is vital to the execution of the skill. Consistency and quality are important to the creation of successful patterns.

Specialized skills give direction to the fundamentals and patterns as they are adapted to meet the needs demanded by specific sport, dance, and swimming situations. An overarm throw pattern becomes a tennis serve or a softball throw from the outfield. Pulling and pushing fundamentals become swim strokes. Pivots and the ready position become dance techniques. Im-parting force may be dribbling with feet (soccer) or hands (basketball).

Although most sport, dance, and swimming skills are derived from run-ning, kicking, throwing, or catching, little effort has been made to inform students of the derivatives of these fundamental skills. In the traditional ap-proach to the learning of sports, the student is reintroduced, time after time, to such fundamentals as kicking and throwing. Seldom does a student un-derstand that an overarm throw pattern, for example, exists in the tennis serve, the volleyball smash, and the throw for distance.

Activity organizations are the structures or methods for using physical skills in a social situation. Sports, dance, and swimming form the subsys-tems for organizing human movement content and are employed primarily to deal with socialization.

Organizational forms classify all sports according to the method used in scoring or winning. They replace the traditional emphases on team, individ-ual, and dual sports. The organizational forms have been identified as placement, convergence on a goal, target, and self-dominated. These titles or categories were selected following a comprehensive analysis of how each activity is viewed from a scoring standpoint or an aesthetic form. Tennis and volleyball represent placement; field hockey and soccer are examples of convergence on a goal; golf, archery, and fencing represent target activities; and gymnastics, modern dance, and synchronized swimming are self-dominated activities. Organizational forms also identify the commonalities of rules, strategy, and aesthetic forms for each category. The strategy and theory of rules sections of this text, for example, codify the elements of all activities into a common set of understandings. Such information will enhance the participant's knowledge of game play and strategy and will enable performers to transfer knowledge of a known sport to an unknown sport. This transfer may be as an active participant or as a spectator.

▶ Human Movement

Human movement—what the body does—is the basis of content. How the body moves, how the body appears in space, the actions that the body takes, the position the body assumes—all of these constitute the content. As the authors searched for a means of making the understanding of the content easier to express, they focused on what the body could do to display content and formulated the hierarchy of movement (Hartman and Clement 1971, 5).

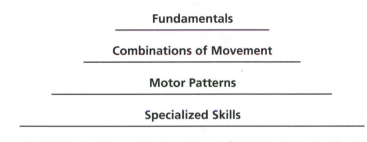

Fundamentals

Combinations of Movement

Motor Patterns

Specialized Skills

Sport, Game, Dance, Swimming, and Activity Organizations

With the advent of schema theory (Schmidt 1975; Kerr 1978; Schmidt 1988), the hierarchy takes on an even greater importance to the professional in physical activity. Kerr (1978) notes that "schema theory proposes that the motor programs we store are not specific records of the movements to be performed, rather, they are a set of general rules to guide performance. . . . If what is stored is a schema, or set of rules, for baseball overhand throwing, for example, we can understand why the outfielder can always throw accurately to second base regardless of where on the field, or how, the ball is caught" (15–16). Schema theory supports the development of "a general base of motor activities in the elementary grades prior to developing more specific sports skills" (Kerr 1978, 17).

Support for the commonalities approach is also found in the literature in Arend's (1980, 4) plea for the need to meet prerequisites to achieve efficiency: "These prerequisites provide the 'tools' to engage in more complex behavior and, those offered here, are carefully derived from an examination of what the end product of 'motor control and strategy' might actually entail. It is critical to realize that the end product of efficiency is not merely a sum of the individual prerequisites, but rather, a functional integration of the prerequisites in service of goal-directed adaptive movement."

This text has been created to bring a system of organization, delivery, and evaluation of physical activity to those persons beyond the infant stage. Research and observation suggests that many people have not learned or will not learn fundamentals and motor patterns at a young age; therefore, it is appropriate to deal with the learning of human movement from fundamentals to specialized skills and from beginner to advanced for all ages. It is inappropriate to say that children will learn to run, walk, skip, and that adolescents will learn basketball, softball, soccer, and dance. All persons will learn fundamentals and motor patterns prior to learning sport skills.

Previously, professionals accepted the fact that students would be able to execute certain movements at specific ages. With the exception of a few skills in which maturation plays a major role, experience is crucial to skill development—learning of movement skills occurs on a continuum; age is meaningless. A beginner at six or at sixty is required to learn specific movements before progressing to more difficult or refined movements. Students in third or eleventh grade must learn the overarm throw pattern before they can execute a successful tennis or volleyball serve. Each must be challenged by a lesson planned so that the learner will derive the greatest satisfaction in acquiring the skill.

For the physical activity professional to program and organize the movement needs of learners, it is imperative that the content be identified and clearly delineated, and that samples of program implementation be made available. It may come as a surprise to some readers that the content is not basketball, volleyball, tennis, etc. The content is the fundamentals, combination of movement, motor patterns, and specialized sport and dance skills.

Because of variations in movement experiences of today's activity participants, instructors should be able to identify movement deficiencies. Such deficiencies, if not corrected, will inhibit learning. Also, media such as water, air, and land require adaptations in the application of movement fundamentals. Given a background in fundamental movement understandings, the transfer of common elements through experience and application will enhance the learning of new movement forms.

Part I of this text provides the content of physical activity. Part II explains why the content was selected and how it is to be used. Chapters on physiology, nutrition, biomechanics, psychology, and sociology provide the underlying bases for the hierarchy of movement, or the content of physical activity. In Chapters 9 and 10, an explanation of the need for physical activity and a basis for the content are provided. Chapters 11, 12, and 13 on biomechanics, psychology, and sociology guide application of the content in physical activity. They explain how physical activity is to be used. Effort is made throughout the text to provide examples of these concepts in teaching physical activity.

Each chapter includes a comprehensive reference list and the bibliography at the end of the book can be used to obtain additional information on all the subjects presented. Readers are encouraged to relate the principles identified in Part II in their teaching. Whenever a scientific explanation, based on physiology, nutrition, biomechanics, psychology, or sociology, is the appropriate reason for presenting the activity, the learner should be informed of this reason. Although explanations need to be tailored to the learner's level of knowledge, the learner's lack of familiarity with the information is not considered a reason for ignoring theoretical and scientific content in teaching. Persons working in chartered schools may wish to integrate this learning with learning in science and social studies. Those working with adults may be pleasantly surprised by the level of understanding of these concepts among many members of our society.

Part III illustrates how to apply Parts I and II in the learning environment. It includes a comprehensive presentation of evaluation and visual analysis. The results of evaluation and visual analysis enable the teacher to determine where the performer is within the learning hierarchy. Given this information, the instructor is ready to establish learning goals and to identify specific objectives.

Content, taken from the hierarchy, is then identified and sequenced for the learning environment. For certain specialists, learning will occur in a physical education classroom; for others, it will occur in a spa or sport club. Lesson plans and activity sequences will be provided for each setting; however, emphasis from time to time will be placed on the physical education classroom.

The content is structured in an effort to show the instructor how to organize human movement or how to enable the performer to "learn to learn" physical skills. As learners acquire skill, they become aware of what their bodies are doing. They also become aware of how similar movements will enable them to pursue an activity never tried before. Sequential learning is apparent. The learner acquires kinesthetic acuity and a visual picture of the correct form. Visual and kinesthetic pictures enable learners to use acquired fundamentals, combinations, and motor patterns to pursue new and unfamiliar activities.

Effective learning occurs when a student has had adequate time to acquire the initial feel of the movement (fundamental), sufficient experience to be able to repeat the action with the proper timing of body segments (pattern), and success in executing the skill with a target in mind (specialized sport skill). A practice progression or sequencing of activities, based on contemporary motor learning theory, is recommended:

- Alone
- Side by side
- Paired

- In opposition
- Complementation
- Competition
- Situational play
- Sport, dance, and swimming

The practice progression begins with a learner attempting the fundamental, combination, motor pattern, and specialized skill using a wall or individually allocated space. This environment is maintained until the learner acquires a modest level of success. The second step in the learning progression, referred to as side by side learning, enables two persons of approximately equal skill to share a common space and to recognize the differences that are inherent in the movements of another person. An example is a learner throwing a ball to the wall and a second learner catching the ball from the wall and throwing it back to the wall so that the first learner can catch the ball. Learners in this setting become aware of the skills of another and at the same time concentrate on the development of their own personal skills.

Play at the wall becomes more advanced as the players play an object back and forth so that they are conscious of the performance of another; now they are engaging in paired play. When ready, they may discontinue the side by side paired play and move to play in opposition. Play opposite another may be throwing and catching. At this stage the ability of the other performer to throw hard, soft, straight, or at an angle becomes apparent. Performers now throw so that their partners can catch the object; they are no longer free to concentrate only on their own personal skill or their ability to throw the object as hard as possible.

The level of complementing another in play is reached when one person practices with another in such activities as tennis or volleyball. Performers in a tennis setting, for example, will have the net person hitting forehands and backhands to their partner at a pace that will enable the partner to perform to the best of the partner's ability.

Only when students have successfully learned efficient form and are able to play with and to complement another person's movements are they encouraged to begin to compete. Competition means that the performer places an object where another player, the opponent, will have difficulty succeeding. When the other person becomes an opponent, as occurs in tennis, volleyball, or soccer, effort is exerted to place the playing object beyond the opponent's capacity to handle it.

Situational play or minigame settings highlight the methodology of handling large groups. Again, complementary and competitive plays are contrasted.

Situational play, taken from observations of the informal play of young adults and professional and collegiate practice sessions, influences the progression into full game play.

An individualized approach to learning encourages the teacher to work with participants in small groups until skills are acquired, to match students with others of similar skill until confidence is gained in the activity, and, when skill and confidence have been demonstrated, to introduce a complex game or subgame. It is further assumed that all persons will be able to execute all fundamentals and motor patterns. Success will also exist when participants acquire a wide range of specialized skills.

Land, sea, and air are other dimensions that are considered as the program is structured to meet the needs of the learner. All persons are to be prepared to control their bodies and execute a wide variety of human movement skills on land, in the water, and in the air.

Two unique features of Part III are a brief description of legal liability and a risk management outline to be implemented in program design and curricular planning.

Once instructors know what a learner can and cannot do, they are ready to use the resources and guidance provided by Part III to organize learning experiences for long or short periods of time, for beginners or elite performers, for adolescents or seniors.

The text has been written for the physical education teacher (primarily the middle school, junior high, and senior high teacher), the coach of beginners, the club professional, the health spa employee, the corporate fitness director, and the senior citizen activity specialist. A comprehensive understanding of the essentials of human movement and the foundations on which they have been established is important to anyone working in the human movement area.

The importance of this approach to the sport and dance professional is exemplified by Jack Groppel (1989) in *The Science of Coaching Tennis* and Clarkson and Skrinar (1988) in *The Science of Dance Training*. They draw on the research gleaned from the foundational area of biomechanics, exercise physiology, motor learning, and nutrition to help the tennis and dance professional succeed with people of all ages. In recent years two sports, gymnastics and basketball, have used biomechanics; tennis has used sport psychology. No one source, however, other than Groppel has addressed the foundational areas in general.

This text not only provides the foundation of human movement but an understanding of the fundamental skills and motor patterns common to sports in general. It also identifies the commonalities of skill and the understanding essential in transferring the knowledge obtained in one sport, dance, or swimming activity to another.

▶ Summary

The text is divided into three parts. Part I is the content or framework of physical activity. The hierarchy of movement serves as the broad organizing structure of the framework. Fundamentals, combinations, and motor patterns are addressed. Specialized sport skills, dance, and swim organizations are demonstrated.

Part II provides theory, philosophy, and the results of research on which the program of physical activity is based. Physiology, nutrition, biomechanics, psychology, and sociology are used to explain components of the framework of physical activity (Part I) and to guide content selection and program implementation (Part III).

Part III also enables the reader to use the framework in organizing learning experiences.

The unique aspects of the text are:

- a learning progression that includes fundamentals, combinations, and motor patterns prior to the acquisition of specialized skills
- a commonality approach to the organization of sport, dance, and swimming
- a progression in learning physical skills based on progress rather than age
- human movement skill instruction based on mechanical, psychological, and sociological principles
- methodologies influenced by the level of skill as well as the age of the learner
- application of legal concepts in the planning and design of programs

▶ References

Arend, Susan. (1980). Developing the substrates of skillful movement. *Motor Skills: Theory into Practice, 4*(1), 3–10.

Clarkson, Priscilla M., and Skinar, Margaret. (1988). *The Science of Dance Training.* Champaign, Illinois: Human Kinetics.

Groppel, Jack L. (1989). *The Science of Coaching Tennis.* Champaign, Illinois: Leisure Press.

Hartman, Betty, and Clement, Annie. (1971). *Ohio Guide for Girls' Secondary Physical Education.* Columbus, Ohio: Ohio Department of Education.

Kerr, Robert. (1978). Schema theory applied to skill acquisition. *Motor Skills: Theory into Practice, 3*(1), 15–20.

Schmidt, R. A. (1975). A schema theory of discrete motor skill learning. *Psychological Review, 82,* 225–260.

Schmidt, R. A. (1988). *Motor Control and Learning.* Champaign, Illinois: Human Kinetics Press.

Status of Physical Activity

This text is based on an approach to understanding the structure of a subject, in this case physical activity, and a model of the hierarchy of human movement. Both were designed originally for the Ohio Guide for Girls' Secondary Physical Education (Hartman and Clement 1971) and later refined as presented in chapter 1. Jerome Bruner's *The Process of Education* served as the inspiration for creating a formal way of looking at the teaching of human movement. *The Process of Education* is a report of a conference in which thirty-five leading scientists, scholars, and educators met to "examine the fundamental processes involved in imparting to young students a sense of the substance and method of science" (Bruner 1960, 7). Results of their deliberation charted a course that caused educators to define the structure of subjects. The conference report stated that "grasping the structure of a subject is understanding it in a way that permits many other things to be related to it meaningfully. To learn structure, in short, is to learn how things are related" (Bruner 1960, 7). Bruner's work also recommended the presentation of general conceptual ideas rather than the learning of isolated elements.

An examination of instruction in human movement skills of the late 1960s suggested to the authors that two models were readily accepted by Americans for the organization of content in physical skills and two systems existed for learning physical skills: movement education and sport.

▶ Movement Education: Content

Movement education, a system traced to the work of Rudolf Laban, took hold in the United States following two Anglo-American Seminars sponsored by the University of Michigan in 1956 and 1966. The seminars were based on the concepts of Laban as applied in elementary, secondary, and collegiate physical education in England. As a result of the seminars, American teachers conducted extensive observations in the British schools. Participants in the seminars and other professionals adopted the British approach to teaching human movement skills in as pure a form as was possible in a transfer of content from one continent to another. They imported British texts (Cope 1967; Laban 1963; Layson and Mauldon 1965; Mauldon and Redfern 1969; Pallett 1965; Russell 1961, 1965; Ullman 1960, 1966) to be used as the basis for instruction.

Laban divided the body into parts and developed movement directions for the use of the body parts in space. Time units were developed to guide the teacher's observation of body action and flow. All the elements were combined in an effort graph. Four motion factors—weight, time, space, and flow—were considered necessary for the understanding of effort in movement.

The evolution of movement education can be traced back another generation to Delsarte's influence on Laban. Delsarte, as reported by Brown and Sommer (1969), took the trinity as a model and suggested a unity of mind, body, and spirit as the concept of man. He explained movement as a combination of:

1. tension-relaxation, balance, and form
2. force, form, design
3. eccentric, concentric, and normal motions

Delsarte's body zones were:

1. head—concentric, mental, and intellectual zone
2. upper torso and arms—the normal, emotional, moral, and spiritual zone
3. lower torso and legs—the eccentric, vital, and physical zone

Delsarte also identified an order of movement as:

- Opposition—any two parts of the body moving in opposite direction simultaneously and the force used to overcome gravity
- Parallelism—simultaneous motion of two body parts in the same direction
- Succession—the fluid wave-like motion that passes through the whole body or through parts of the body

His nine laws of motion included:

- altitude
- motion
- direction
- velocity
- extension

- force
- sequence
- form
- reaction

Many of Delsarte's definitions were expressed in the emotion felt while moving and had little relationship to scientific connotations assigned to such definitions in contemporary United States programs.

Rudolf Laban, influenced by Delsarte, began to evolve a new terminology as he worked with his students and followers. When Laban, a native German, was forced to leave Germany and the people with whom he had shared his thinking, he found it essential to write and share his ideas with the public. His initial works, prepared prior to 1940, were presented when he was nearly sixty years of age. Laban's works, significantly expanded through the editing of Lisa Ullmann (1960, 1966), also provided a unique approach to visual observation of human movement and to the identification of the inner feeling of movement expressed for his purposes as "quality."

▶ Movement Education: Process

Problem solving, a process for applying the principles of movement education, must be credited to John Dewey and to the British open classroom. The use of a verbal cue that permits students to interpret a task and to move according to their personal capacity is the process. Instead of giving a direct command requesting that all performers move in a certain way, the verbal cue gives performers the opportunity to select, from an array of possibilities, the movement that is best for them. Students are expected to be able to identify when they are in a particular learning sequence and what they are capable of executing. They must also recognize which movement will give them a personal challenge while not placing them at risk. This methodology enables the teacher to transfer certain risks to the students. Students are aware of the many skills available and are expected to execute a skill that is a challenge but not beyond their capacity.

Most of the early movement educators in the United States, in a zealous missionary spirit, failed to realize that they were not only introducing a new system of human movement but an entire new approach to learning in general: the open classroom. A number of physical educators successfully introduced the program in schools across the United States while others, failing to transfer the entire program, did force physical educators to examine their thinking and touched off an era of change within the physical skill profession. It should be noted that physical educators were far more successful in applying the principles of the open classroom than were other American educators who attempted to use the system for other subjects.

▶ Movement Education in General

Modern movement education is best exemplified by the works of Sheila Stanley (1977), Marion Sanborn (1978), Bette Logsdon (1984), and Kate Barrett

(1984). These people were influenced by Laban and the British authors. In some cases they chose to ignore the American system; in other cases their work became eclectic. Movement education has had substantive impact on schoolchildren participating in such programs, and on dance and gymnastics in general. Nearly all the impact has been on young people and the teachers of young people. Movement education has not influenced the teaching of most coaches, dance studio instructors, junior and senior high school teachers, corporate or spa instructors, or senior citizen activity specialists.

Paralleling Laban's work, in time, were many American leaders in kinesiology and mechanics. Halsey and Porter (1958), for example, evolved an interdisciplinary approach to human movement in the following themes:

1. anatomical and muscular concerns
2. elements of physics expressed as force, balance, motion, and leverage
3. study of kinesthesis or control of the body

Ellfeldt and Metheny (1948), Metheny (1965), Scott (1964), H'Doubler (1966), and Broer (1960) each designed a method of dealing with the concept of kinesthesis at the same time that Laban was working with quality. As a result of Laban's failure to publish his ideas in their formative stage, none of these American authors were able to profit from his thinking prior to their writings. Scott's (1964, 375) definition of kinesthesis as the "sensation through which one is aware of position and movement of the total body or its segments" parallels Laban's concern with the feel of the body, or quality.

▶ Sport: Content

Sport is the model that many American physical educators have used for programming human movement activities. Elementary schoolteachers, who consistently use lead-up games and direct all activity toward specific sports, have selected this approach. They concentrate on the development of skills of the game of basketball, softball, square dance, etc., just as they would present them to a group of elite athletes. They then place learners into a game or form (dance) setting as soon as possible. If the full-blown game is not a viable option, they make use of the numerous books of minigames that have been created to enable learners with limited skills to enter game play.

Secondary physical educators usually think of their program as the teaching of many different sports and the presentation of each sport as a single set of isolated elements or skills. The authors perceive that the majority of middle and junior high school physical education programs in this country consist of six- or eight-week segments devoted to various sports such as basketball, volleyball, softball, soccer, and track. They also believe that the average student participant does not recognize the elements common to these sports. Sport professionals and college instructors appear to be pressed into the same teaching approach.

Physical skill learning in America has also been traced to specific sports, notably those sports that appear on television or in other media. Teachers in the schools have made every effort to build on the learner's acquaintance with the media in an effort to inspire enjoyment in the learning environment. As a result of this approach to instruction, a large segment of the population has had little or no assistance in human movement. Even though they may have command of the fundamentals related to a particular sport, they do not have command of a range of fundamentals. A skilled basketball player may be totally unable to control a ball with his or her feet, to enter a distance running event, or to swim in deep water. He or she is motorially deficient and no different than the sixth-grade student who reads at the level of a senior in high school and possesses the mathematical skills of a second-grader.

▶ Sport: Process

The process most often used in the sport approach is the direct method, or the explanation of the movement according to a predetermined prototype of how the skilled athlete moves. Little thought is given to the learner's developmental level, previous learning in physical skills, or genetically endowed capacity. Instructors often demonstrate the skills and encourage learners to copy the demonstration. In the learning of a specific sport skill, teacher time is usually dedicated to correcting the skill until each performer is moving according to the prototype. On occasion, the prototype is the performance of an outstanding, elite athlete and may or may not conform to the best practice from the standpoint of the physics of the body or the individual's human movement skills.

▶ Program Delivery

Process, or how the program is delivered, is a component in the movement education and sport programs. Mosston (1966, 1972) has provided physical educators with the most comprehensive discussion of teaching styles available. From command to discovery, the teacher is provided with specific "how to do it" applications for a continuum of styles: command, task, reciprocal, small group, individual, guided discovery, and problem solving. He suggests that the style selected is based on the needs of the individual, with a dependent person requiring the command style and an independent person needing problem solving.

▶ Contemporary Models

Movement education and sport are the two models identified as constituting physical education programs. Jewett and Bain (1985), in contrast, describe curriculum in physical education as constituting seven different models: developmental education, humanistic physical education, fitness, movement education, kinesiological studies, play education, and personal meaning.

Developmental education uses a multiactivity program of games, sports, dance, and exercise to accomplish such broad educational goals as competence, individuality, socialization, and integration. This model assumes that development will occur through games and sport and that individualization is not necessary.

The *humanistic physical education* model "shares the developmentalists' commitment that physical education should contribute to the total well-being of the individual, but stresses the unique qualities of each human being" (Jewett and Bain 1985, 50). Student self-esteem, actualization, understanding, and interpersonal relations are primary. For example, the assumption is that "how a person feels is more important than what he knows" (Hellison 1973, 4).

Fitness has been one among many objectives of physical education programs. Today some programs place a primary focus on fitness. The conceptual framework in health-related fitness programs consists of cardiorespiratory function, body composition, flexibility, and strength. Activities that will foster the development of these components make up the program.

Movement education was described earlier. Jewett and Bain note that the strength of the movement education program is in its "effort to integrate and interrelate the content of games, dance, and gymnastics and to provide a logical bases for progression in these areas" (Jewett and Bain 1985, 60). They also note that the teacher in the movement education setting must be able to observe and analyze movement. Both of these tenets are incorporated in the content and process recommended in using the hierarchy of movement in this text.

The *kinesiological studies* model has been used by MacKenzie (1969) and Lawson and Placek (1981). Lawson and Placek (1981) identify the model as a blend of performance skills and experiences in sport, exercise, and dance with knowledge about performance derived from the foundational fields of physiology, kinesiology, psychology, and others.

Play education teaches one to play and makes play voluntary but not frivolous. The purpose of the program is to acquire skills so that one can engage in play at higher levels. Play programs may provide intrinsic or extrinsic rewards. When intrinsic reward or the purpose of movement is for the joy of moving, the program is classified as the *personal meaning* model. Twenty-two purposes identified under three major headings—fitness, transcendence, and performance—constitute the model. (For detailed descriptions of these models, see Jewett and Bain 1985, 41–89.)

Cratty discusses various classifications of sport made by sport psychologists based on psychological demands. He notes that the "classifications may clarify the demands and stresses a particular sport places on participants" (Cratty 1983, 110). The following are also mentioned: aesthetic expression in figure skating, free exercise, gymnastics, and dance; body contact in football and wrestling; steady hand-eye coordination in archery and shooting; total mobilization of energy in weight lifting, shot putting, and discus throwing; and endurance in running and swimming (Cratty 1983, 11, 12). Movements involving the anticipation of the movements of another are also discussed by Cratty and include indirect aggression of sports using a net (volleyball and tennis), direct aggression (American football and wrestling), and parallel effort (golf and bowling) (Cratty 1983, 12–13).

▶ Recent Changes

The past five years have seen changes in physical education influenced by the National Association for Sport and Physical Education, a twenty-five-thousand-member professional organization representing teachers of physical skills. In their massive project, they have developed a two-prong thrust to the improvement of teaching physical skills. Quality is the focus of the Outcomes Project described in detail in a series of articles entitled "Quality Daily Physical Education" (Loughrey 1987), "Justifying Physical Education" (Seefeldt 1987), and "Physical Education Outcomes" (Franck 1989). These articles provide a series of programs and lists of characteristics that identify program quality. The Outcomes Project, as described in a workshop presented at the Alliance Convention in Boston in 1989, identifies the physically educated person as one who:

- *has* sufficient skill to perform a variety of physical activities
- *does* participate regularly in physical activity
- *is* physically fit
- *knows* the benefits, costs, risks, and obligations of physical activity involvements
- *values* the role of regular physical activity in the maintenance of a healthy lifestyle

These characteristics are covered in depth in Part III.

A recent study that may have a significant impact on the future of physical education and physical activity reports that there is ". . . a strong, graded and consistent inverse relationship between physical fitness and mortality in both men and women" (Blair et al. 1989, 2395). This means that people who exercise live longer. Further, the study suggests that moderate levels of activity, such as walking, play a significant role in increasing longevity.

▶ # References

Barrett, Kate R. (1984). Educational games and educational dance. In Bette Logsdon (Ed.), *Physical Education for Children: A Focus on the Teaching Process.* Philadelphia: Lea and Febiger.

Blair, Steven N., Kohl, Harold W., Paffenbarger, Ralph S., Clark, Debra G., Cooper, Kenneth H., and Gibbons, Larry W. (1989). Physical fitness and all-cause mortality, a prospective study of healthy men and women. *Journal of the American Medical Association, 262*(17), 2395–2401.

Broer, Marion R. (1960). *Efficiency of Human Movement.* Philadelphia: W. B. Saunders.

Brown, Margaret, and Sommer, Betty K. (1969). *Movement Education: Its Evaluation and a Modern Day Approach.* Reading, Massachusetts: Addison-Wesley.

Bruner, Jerome. (1960). *The Process of Education.* New York: Vintage Books.

Cope, John. (1967). *Discovering Methods in Physical Education.* London: Thomas Nelson and Sons, Ltd.

Cratty, Bryant J. (1983). *Psychology in Contemporary Sport.* Englewood Cliffs, New Jersey: Prentice Hall.

Ellfeldt, Louise, and Metheny, Eleanor. (1948). Movement and meaning, development of general theory. *Research Quarterly,* Washington, DC: AAHPER, 264–273.

Franck, Marian. (1989). *Physical Education Outcomes.* Reston, Virginia: NASPE.

Halsey, Elizabeth, and Porter, Lorena. (1958). *Physical Education for Children.* New York: Henry Holt.

Hartman, Betty, and Clement, Annie. (1971). *Ohio Guide for Girls' Secondary Physical Education.* Columbus, Ohio: Ohio Department of Education.

H'Doubler, Margaret N. (1966). *Dance, a Creative Art Experience.* Madison, Wisconsin: University of Wisconsin Press.

Hellison, D. (1973). *Humanistic Physical Education.* Englewood Cliffs, New Jersey: Prentice Hall.

Jewett, Ann E., and Bain, Linda L. (1985). *The Curriculum Process in Physical Education.* Dubuque, Iowa: Wm. C. Brown.

Laban, Rudolf. (1963). *Modern Educational Dance.* London: MacDonald and Evans.

Lawson, H. A., and Placek, J. H. (1981). *Physical Education in the Secondary Schools.* Boston: Allyn and Bacon.

Layson, J., and Mauldon, E. (1965). *Teaching Gymnastics.* London: MacDonald and Evans.

Logsdon, Bette (Ed.). (1984). *Physical Education for Children: A Focus on the Teaching Process.* Philadelphia: Lea and Febiger.

Loughery, Tom (Ed.). (1987). Quality daily physical education programs. *Journal of Physical Education, Recreation and Dance, 58*(6), 34–64.

MacKenzie, Marlin M. (1969). *Toward a New Curriculum in Physical Education.* New York: McGraw-Hill.

Mauldon, E., and Redfern, H. B. (1969). *Games Teaching.* London: MacDonald and Evans.

Metheny, Eleanor. (1965). *Connotations of Movement in Sport and Dance.* Dubuque, Iowa: Wm. C. Brown.

Mosston, Muska. (1966). *Teaching Physical Education, from Command to Discovery.* Columbus, Ohio: Charles E. Merrill.

Mosston, Muska. (1972). *Teaching: From Command to Discovery.* Belmont, California: Wadsworth.

Pallett, G. Doreen. (1965). *Modern Educational Gymnastics.* New York: Pergamon Press.

Russell, Joan. (1961). *Modern Dance in Education.* New York: Frederick A. Praeger.

Russell, Joan. (1965). *Creative Dance in the Primary School.* London: MacDonald and Evans.

Sanborn, Marion. (1978). *Elementary School Physical Education.* Columbus, Ohio: Ohio Department of Education.

Scott, M. Gladys. (1964). *Analysis of Human Motion.* New York: Appleton-Century-Crofts.

Seefeldt, Vern (Ed.). (1987). Justifying physical education. *Journal of Physical Education, Recreation and Dance, 58*(7), 42–72.

Stanley, Sheila. (1977). *Physical Education: A Movement Orientation.* Toronto: McGraw-Hill.

Ullman, Lisa. (1960). *The Mastery of Movement by Rudolf Laban.* London: MacDonald and Evans.

Ullman, Lisa. (1966). *Choreutics by Rudolf Laban.* London: MacDonald and Evans.

The Hierarchy of Movement

Part I explains the hierarchy of movement and describes each area in depth. Fundamentals and patterns, from simple to complex, are analyzed. They serve as the bases for the specialized sports skills used in sports, dance, and aquatics.

Specialized sports skills for twenty activity organizations, including sports, dance, and aquatics, draw from the fundamentals and patterns in creating learning sequences.

A new method for looking at games, sports, dance, and aquatic organizations is used in identifying commonalities of rules, strategies, and play.

The Content of Physical Activity

The content of physical activity consists of all the ways a person can move. This massive array of content has been organized as described in chapter 2 under the hierarchy of movement.

Fundamentals

Combinations of Movement

Motor Patterns

Specialized Skills

Activity Organizations

The Hierarchy of Movement

1. orders the content of physical skills.
2. provides a progression in the acquisition of physical skills with fundamentals the easiest and specialized skills the most difficult.
3. eliminates the repeated teaching and reviewing of the same movement in one sport after another as one movement is often the basis for many specialized skills.
4. fosters the transfer of movements and movement knowledge from activity to activity. The performer is no longer asked to learn a skill such as throwing before learning every sport in which it is included.
5. enables the learner to be aware of how and when skills transfer to new activities that they may wish to pursue at a later date.
6. provides a system for "learning to learn" or "learning to teach oneself" physical skills. It is a system to be used in teaching oneself new movements.

Fundamental movements or changes in body position include walk, run, ready position, jump/hop, land/stop/fall, swing, strike, toss, kick, push, pull, lift, catch/trap, spin/turn/twist, curl/bend, and roll.

Motor patterns include underarm, overarm and sidearm throws; horizontal and vertical jumps; and sprint and distance runs. Combinations are the execution of two or more fundamentals in sequence. They are found in nearly all organized physical activities. Movements within aerobic dance, for example, are primarily combinations.

Specialized sport skills are the refinement of fundamentals, combinations, and patterns into movements designed to meet specific purposes. The activity organization in which the performer will use the movement dictates the purpose.

Activity organizations provide the framework for the ultimate enjoyment of physical activity. Each organization has an objective and, in most cases, a rather complex system of rules, strategies, and theories for achieving the objective. Movement now has purpose.

Historically, activities have been classified as sport and art forms, with the major reason for the classification attributed to collegiate, scholastic, and professional sport organizations. Dance, synchronized swimming, and, on occasion, gymnastics have been referred to as art forms, while basketball, volleyball, and tennis are considered sports. Also, sports are classified as individual, dual, or team. This classification appears to be based solely on the number of participants in an activity; no other commonalities are readily identified.

Another system devised to classify human movement was the open/closed system. The system was devised by Poulton (1957) and refined by Knapp (1963) and Robb (1972). It is based upon the performer's response to factors operating in the movement environment. Closed movements are planned sequences of movement repeated in the same manner every time. They are predetermined routines. Open movements are movements executed in response to the movement of others. They are used to react to the movement of others. Performers in open movement know many different movements and strategies; they do not, however, know the actual movement that they will execute until the opponents begin to make their play. Gymnastics, figure skating, and archery represent closed movements; basketball, fencing, and tennis favor open movements.

One of the unique features of this book is the activity organization model, a system for classifying activities. This system was created by the authors to organize physical activity. The model emphasizes commonalities of the activities from the perspectives of methods of scoring, equipment, environment, strategy, and rules.

▶ Activity Organization Model

The activity organization model arranges human movement according to methods of scoring or the means of gaining success. The model enables the learner to identify and compare commonalities found in scoring, strategy, and choreography. Learners are able to identify similarities and differences among activities, thus increasing their knowledge of sport. Movements, rules, strategies, and choreography are described in such a way that a performer proficient in a sport such as basketball or an art form such as synchronized swimming would recognize the known elements in all other activity organizations. In addition to enabling performers to recognize commonalities in these activities, the model will enable spectators to understand and appreciate a wide range of sports.

The activity model has four distinct categories. The characteristics of each include not only skill but strategy, rules, and other factors that influence success. The organization categories are:

- Placement
- Convergence on a goal
- Target
- Self-dominated

Placement sports include badminton, racquetball, table tennis, tennis, and volleyball. Convergence on a goal activities use the body with or without an implement to manipulate an object into a goal. They include basketball, field hockey, soccer, and water polo. Target activities include archery, bowling, fencing, golf, and softball. Self-dominated activities include all forms of dance, gymnastics, ice skating, skiing, swimming, and track.

Professionals planning a comprehensive human movement program will include activities from each of these categories in order to enable the participant to acquire a comprehensive vocabulary of movement (see table 3.1).

▶ Placement

The goal or primary objective of placement sports is for the performer to place the playing object (i.e., ball, shuttle) in a position on the playing surface that will prohibit the opponent from returning the object. Also, players succeed when the placement enables the opponent to contact the object and fail in making a successful return. Scoring or the opportunity to control the game and score in the future is achieved by placing the object where the opponent either cannot reach it or if reached cannot return the object successfully. Placement sports tend to be ones in which either the hand or an implement serving as an extension of the hand is used for contacting the object. The sports tend to make use of a net or the walls of the playing court.

▼ **TABLE 3-1**
Activity Organization Model

PLACEMENT	CONVERGENCE ON A GOAL
Badminton	Basketball
Racquetball	Field hockey
Table tennis	Soccer
Tennis	Water polo
Volleyball	

TARGET	SELF-DOMINATED
Archery	Dance
Bowling	Aerobic
Golf	Folk
Fencing	Modern
Softball	Gymnastics
	Ice skating
	Skiing
	Swimming
	Regular
	Synchronized
	Track

Characteristics of Placement Activities

Playing Environment

1. The playing environment includes a net or a wall. When a net is used, players are located on either side of it and no physical contact is expected. When the sport has a wall as part of the playing environment, performers employ a system that permits one player to play the object followed by the next player in a continuous rotation.

2. The size of the court determines the use of equipment and number of team members. One or two people using implements are often housed on fairly large courts whereas activities involving only the use of the performer's arms and hands (e.g., volleyball) accommodate large groups in smaller spaces.

Strategy

1. The objective or means through which a player scores is achieved by placing the playing object so that it cannot be reached by the opponent. Placement must be away from the opponent.

2. Overarm and underarm throw patterns are found in nearly all placement sports.

3. Shuttle running and slides are used to move the body forward, backward, and sideward in play. The size of the court is a factor in whether the run is a shuttle or a sprint.
4. Many stopping and starting movements are used.
5. Due to the confined space in most of the activities, spins are often used to reduce the distance of strokes.
6. The use of the implement and the quality of the projectile are influenced by court size.

Rules
1. Boundary areas exist and are identified by lines and walls in most placement activities, and the table surface in table tennis.
2. Serving is usually rotated either by game or by so many points or a side out within a game.
3. Volleyball is unique in that the ball can be played by more than one player before it goes over the net, thus requiring team strategy on each play.

▶ Convergence on a Goal

The purpose of activities organized into this classification is to use the body with or without the aid of an implement to manipulate an object into a goal to score. Activities include basketball, field hockey, soccer, and water polo.

Characteristics of Convergence on a Goal Activities

Playing Environment
1. The number of players on the team and the nature of the equipment influence the dimensions of the playing field. As the number of players increases and the equipment includes an extension of the body, the playing area tends to increase in size.
2. Goals are at either end of the playing area; however, the size of the goal areas differ, ranging from the confined space of basketball and water polo courts to the larger areas provided in field hockey and soccer. Basketball, water polo, and soccer require the use of the body to shoot a basket or kick a goal. Field hockey uses a piece of equipment as an extension of the arm to increase the force of the body in driving the object across the scoring area and through the goal.
3. Teams consist of fairly large groups of individuals, with a team of five being the smallest and twenty-three the largest.

Strategy
1. Running and swimming are the primary skills requisite to successful performance in the convergence on a goal category. The performer is required to move long distances on the court or playing field (pool) before he or she can concentrate on scoring.

2. Kicking or throwing an object are the principle means through which a performer scores. Performers are to be proficient at kicking or throwing from a distance and at close range.
3. Knowing when to throw or kick is as important as knowing how to pass in front of the person who is to receive the pass.
4. Persons receiving the object in a pass should move toward the object as they prepare to receive it.
5. Movement of opponents dictate and influence the decisions made. The playing object is to be watched at all times.
6. Each team member is responsible for offense or defense. The offense members are primarily responsible for scoring whereas the defense player's major role is to protect the goal or prevent the opponents from scoring. These responsibilities change as the possession of the object moves from one team to the other.
7. Offensive strategies are based on:
   a. a desire to find the shortest route to score;
   b. the use of a quick alternate plan to deceive or mess up the thinking of opponents.
8. When reaching scoring territory, the performer attempts to get the shot off rapidly.

Rules

1. Offensive or severe body contact is considered a foul. When a foul occurs, the opponent receives some type of a free advantage. In basketball it may involve a chance to score, and in field hockey an unguarded pass may be obtained.
2. Play is initiated at the center of the court. After a team scores, play is initiated from the end line or the center of the court. A jump ball, bully, or cross sticks usually starts the game.
3. Violations result in an advantage for the opponents; fouls result in an opportunity for opponents to gain advantage in scoring or favorable play.

▶ Target

The primary means of scoring in target activities is based on successful contact with a target or designated spot. Targets may be subcategorized as stationary and moving. They may be further defined by whether the participant established the target or whether it was predetermined. Stationary or static targeting includes archery, bowling, and golf. Moving or dynamic targeting includes fencing and softball. Softball is unique because it combines target (scoring by putting someone out) and placement (throwing or hitting to a spot). For this discussion, softball will be treated as a target sport.

Static target activities use few fundamentals and patterns whereas the dynamic target sports make use of a wide array of fundamentals and patterns. Archery, bowling, and golf each start with a specific position based on the fundamental ready position. Each then relies on another fundamental for action. Archery uses the pull, bowling uses the walk and underarm throw, and golf, a swing.

Characteristics of Stationary or Static Targets

Playing Environment
1. The size of the playing area defines the limits of the target.
2. Static performers tend to be a great distance from the target.

Strategy
1. Kinesthetic acuity or knowledge of what the performer's body is doing is essential to success. The performer needs to visualize the best movement pattern before executing the move.
2. Precision and concentration are required to reach the target.
3. Knowledge of the characteristics of the surface upon which one is playing is essential. In golf and softball, for example, weather, geography, and texture of an area can change radically from one spot to another and from one playing area to another. Archery, bowling, and fencing provide a common surface on which to operate.

Rules In Static Activities
1. In golf, archery, and bowling, a performer's position in play cannot be changed by an opponent.
2. Rules respect the individual's need to apply skill without annoyance from an opponent.
3. The target or where the performer achieves success is stationary.

Characteristics of Moving or Dynamic Targets

Playing Environment
1. Dynamic performers are close to the target.
2. The target is moving; the performer must make contact.
3. Softball uses a target for scoring by putting someone out.

Strategy
1. The performer must sense the actual and potential movement of an opponent and make decisions based on that information.
2. An individual makes every effort to disturb opponents.

Rules in Dynamic Activities

1. The game starts with opponents as equals.
2. In fencing, when an opponent is touched they are scored against. Absence of score means no win or no higher number of touches against someone.

▶ Self-Dominated

Only one person is involved in self-dominated activities. The individual either follows a predetermined routine or creates one of his or her own.

Dance:

- Aerobic
- Folk
- Modern
- Square
- Ballroom
- Gymnastics
- Skating
- Skiing
- Swimming
  - General
  - Synchronized
- Track

Characteristics of Self-Dominated Activities

Playing Environment

1. Persons usually perform by themselves. On occasion, two or more people may join together and present a predetermined routine. This often occurs in dance and synchronized swimming.
2. Specific floor, rink, mat, or pool space may be dedicated for competition; however, it is seldom identified for noncompetitive performances.

Strategy

1. Closed systems of movement are used in self-dominated organizations.
2. Balance is a primary element in acquiring the skills essential to most of these organizations.
3. Movements in self-dominated activities are established traditional skills (movements created by the performer) or a combination of traditional and created movements.
4. Performance involves precision, timing, creativity, and the ability to replicate the performance of another.
5. A composition has a beginning, a middle, and an ending.
6. The theme of the composition conveys the idea or purpose of the presentation to the audience.

7. Unity, continuity, transition, variety, and repetition are elements of the composition.
8. The speed events of swimming, skating, skiing, and track require efficiency in starts, pacing within the event, and finishing with a burst of speed.

Rules

1. Most movements are predetermined or copied. Detailed descriptions of stunts exist. Competition is controlled by trained and certified judges.
2. Precise, controlled movements tend to be rewarded in competition.
3. Creativity is rewarded in certain forms of competition.
4. In aerobic dance and other activities in which competition seldom occurs, rules are established to provide a safe environment for the performers. They include warm-ups and cool-downs as well as the use of progressions appropriate to the performer.
5. Square dance and folk dance have their own sets of rules or forms of movement.
6. When music is used, the type selected may affect scores in competition.

References

Knapp, B. (1963). Skills in Sport, the Attainment of Proficiency. London, England: Routledge and Kegan.

Poulton, E. C. (1957). On prediction of skilled movements. *Psychological Bulletin, 54*, 467–478.

Robb, Margaret D. (1972). The Dynamics of Motor-Skill Acquisition. Englewood Cliffs, New Jersey: Prentice Hall.

Fundamental Movement

Fundamental movement (see table 4-1) describes changes in body position sufficiently distinct to permit classification. The execution of the movements are seldom goal-directed or focused on a particular purpose. Instead, they are the basis for the development of the goal-oriented movement found in specialized skills. Emphasis is placed on the gestalt of the movement or the tracing of the action in space. Timing, reaction to others, and other fine motor points are not important at this stage. Can learners trace the picture of the movement with their body parts? That is what is important.

Each fundamental movement is a word picture. A jump, for example, describes an action in which a performer places his or her feet on the ground in a certain way. The action of the movement is most important in its initial instruction. Examples and descriptions are provided in this chapter to enable the instructor to gain a clear concept of the action. Mechanical principles are used to illustrate the movements.

▼ **TABLE 4-1**

Fundamental movement

Walk	Kick
Run	Push
Ready position	Pull
Jump/hop	Lift
Land/stop/fall	Catch/trap
Swing	Spin/turn/twist
Strike	Curl/bend
Toss	Roll

▶ Walk

A walk (see figures 4-1 and 4-2) is a series of balance and loss of balance motions or a series of weight transfers from one foot to the other as the individual moves through space. One foot moves forward ahead of and slightly to the side of the other foot, with the heel of the forward foot touching the ground or landing before the toe of the opposite foot pushes off. The person pushes or exerts force against the ground or the floor in order to initiate each step. The resistance of the floor or ground provides the force necessary to move the body forward. This action is best explained by Newton's third law of motion—for every action there is an equal and opposite reaction. A soft surface, such as snow or sand, will require more force from the body in walking or pushing off from the surface than will a hard surface such as a hardwood floor. Force will be lost in pushing the soft surface down; force will not be lost in contacting the hard surface. Legs move alternately in the walk between a supporting and swinging phase while the shock of landing is absorbed by the knees. Arms are moved in opposition to the leg swing in order to facilitate the forward momentum of the body and to maintain balance or to counterbalance the rotation of the trunk. In placing each foot down, the most efficient position is to have the toes pointed straight ahead. In walking, the body segments—head, shoulders, hips—are aligned, one over the other. Body weight as a whole is shifted forward from the ankle. The head is held up with eyes focused straight ahead.

Various activities alter the position of the body in walking. The flutter kick used in swimming the front crawl includes the swing phases and the coordination of the walk. Body position in swimming dictates that force be applied to the water by the surface of the legs rather than the bottom of the feet, as occurs in walking.

Also, carrying an object may alter a person's walk as he or she has to compensate for the weight of the object by making it part of the total body weight. Speed is increased in walking by moving the center of the body forward and by increasing the length of the stride.

The backward walk is a new movement; it does not parallel the sequence of the forward walk. In the backward walk, the weight transfer precedes the leg lift; however, the leg is placed on the supporting surface a short time later. The nature of the formation of the foot, with a large base of support forward and a limited base to the rear, provides the rationale for the difference in mechanics.

▼ **FIGURE 4-1**

Mature walking pattern—lateral view. Key features are heel-strike, "double knee lock," and coordinated arm swing. From R. L. Wickstrom: *Fundamental Motor Patterns,* 3rd edition. Philadelphia, Lea & Febiger, 1983. Reprinted with permission.

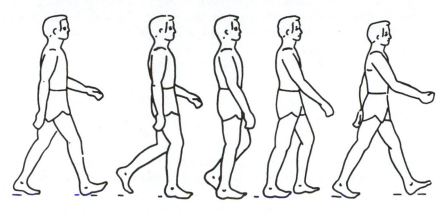

▼ **FIGURE 4-2**

Mature walking—posterior view. Dynamic base is narrow and arm opposition is reflex-controlled. From R. L. Wickstrom: *Fundamental Motor Patterns,* 3rd edition. Philadelphia, Lea and Febiger, 1983. Reprinted with permission.

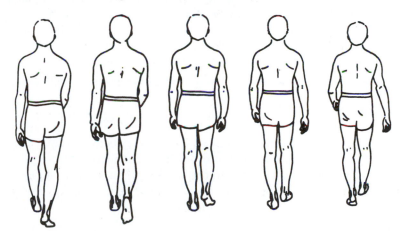

Principles

1. Stability and the capacity to lose stability are key factors in walking.
2. Gravity aids in overcoming the inertia of the body as the body is moved forward from a stable position.
3. Walking is linear motion brought about by the rotary motion of the hips and legs.

4. In walking, each foot is placed directly ahead of and under the center of gravity of the body. Placement of the feet outside the center of gravity results in a sideways movement of the body, often referred to as a "duck walk" (Broer and Zernicke 1979, 177).
5. When walking up or down a grade, the center of gravity is adjusted to the grade; the body leans backward while descending and leans forward while ascending.
6. Momentum provides a continuous flowing pace in walking.

▶ Run

Running is an exaggerated form of walking and results as the performer attempts to increase speed. The major difference between walking and running is that in running, the body is moving in space for a long period of time with no support from either foot and at no time are both feet in contact with the ground. In walking, there is no period of moving in space because one foot is in contact with the ground at all times. To increase speed, the runner exerts greater force in the extensor muscles of the driving leg and foot against the resistive surface, and the leg swings forward and starts back as the ball of the foot is placed on the ground. The body is then pushed into the air toward the next step. In landing, the foot strikes the ground under the center of gravity. Absorption of force by bending the knee is essential to successful landing and is used to build momentum as the leg extends for the next step. The arms are moved in opposition to the legs to facilitate forward movement and balance similar to the movement found in walking. As the legs move faster, the arms also move faster.

Principles

1. The greater the distance through which a body segment (knee and leg) moves, the greater the momentum or force generated.
2. Body alignment is balanced with the trunk upright, as in walking.
3. In the run, the leg swings faster and the knee bends sooner, thus shortening the lever and increasing angular velocity, and moving the body with less effort.

▶ Ready Position

A position of readiness or stability is required for numerous activities. Such a position exists when a person places the feet shoulder distance apart and aligns the knees, hips, shoulders, and head directly over one another. A relaxed bend or slight flex at the knees assists the person in being ready to move and ready to either absorb or give force.

The balanced ready position is focused in the direction in which the performer either expects to receive force or to give force. It may be a forward-backward stride position or a side to side position.

Principles

1. Balance is enhanced by body alignment.
2. Stability or balance is improved by placing the feet shoulder width apart, thus increasing the size of the base of support.
3. Stability is enhanced by bending the knees to lower the center of gravity.
4. Position will be directional according to where the performer is to apply or receive force.

▶ Jump/Hop

Jump and hop are actions that project the body from a standing position into the air. The body moves into the air until the upward projection of the body equals the force of the pull of gravity. Following the moment of suspension in midair when the forces are equal, the body returns to the ground. A jump occurs when the force is initiated with one or both feet on the ground and the body returns to the ground on both feet. A jump may be executed to gain height or to gain distance. It can also be used to move forward, backward, or sideward. The arms play a major role in determining whether the person is jumping for distance or for height. When jumping for distance, the arms swing forward; when jumping for height, the arms swing up. A jump for height begins in a balanced ready position. The hips, knees, and ankles are flexed in a crouched position, with the arms forcefully thrusting the body into full extension. The body assumes a vertical alignment with the head held upright, the toes pointed, the knees over the feet, and the hips over the knees until the feet are ready to land. Upon landing, the knees flex to absorb the force as the feet make contact with the landing surface. In the horizontal jump, the arms lead the body forward with the lower body flexing and extending in the desired direction. Following takeoff, the lower body flexes at the hips, knees, and ankles in order to rapidly bring the lower body in line with the upper body.

The jump requires that the body be off the ground for a longer period of time than that required for the run. Body strength is essential to the achievement of this longer period of elevated time off the ground.

Stepping down from a platform or object is also a jump (Wickstrom 1983, 65–68). The person distributes weight over both feet, allows the body to move into the air, bends the knees, and stabilizes the body equally over both feet. As the feet make contact with the new object, the body straightens, particularly at the knees, to increase the distance that the body moves as it absorbs the jar or force of landing.

The hop is similar to the jump. The hop is the movement executed when the force production and landing is on the same foot. The other leg is bent but does not participate in the movement. The hop requires that the body weight be shifted over the hopping foot. In the jump, the body weight is over both feet; in the hop, the body weight is shifted and balanced over the one hopping foot. Balance and strength play essential roles in hopping. Considerable strength is needed to support the body weight over one rather than both feet, and kinesthetic acuity and balance are necessary to center the body weight over the hopping leg.

Principles

1. All principles involving projectiles affect the body during the jump and hop.
2. Sufficient force must be produced in order to overcome the inertia of the body.
3. The magnitude and direction of the force at takeoff determines the path of the body.
4. Force for takeoff is produced by a quick contraction of the leg extensor and by the lifting of the arms in the arm swing. The greater the ankle, knee, and hip bend (crouched position) within anatomic limits, the greater the force upon extension.
5. The angle of takeoff is a major difference in the jump for height and the jump for distance. For height, the takeoff is up, while distance is best obtained if the angle of takeoff is approximately 45 degrees.

▶ Land/Stop/Fall

Land or landing is what the body does as it returns to the ground, to an object, or to the water after it has been projected into the air. Usually it follows a jump, hop, or dive. Generally, the body maintains an erect position and is returned to the ground with the balls of the feet making initial contact. As the feet contact the landing surface, the ankles, knees, and hips bend or give in order to absorb the force of impact. The distance through which each joint moves increases the body's capacity to absorb force or to decelerate. Landing in water differs from landing on a hard surface because the body passes through the surface of the water.

The stop is a method of absorbing force that occurs following running or walking. A runner moves his or her feet into a forward stride position, bends the knees, and leans the body backward to establish balance. A hop may be added prior to taking the stride position in an effort to halt forward momentum by transferring the forward momentum to an upward motion, thus gaining balance rapidly.

A fall or loss of balance of the body is much like landing, except that in landing the person has control over the body.

Principles

1. To increase stability, maintain a base of support about equal to shoulder width.
2. Distance and time are the major factors in deceleration and absorption of force. Distance is accomplished in landing by increasing the bend at the ankle, hip, and knee. The same actions also consume a greater amount of time.
3. Making use of padding, sand, or other soft textures applied to the body or to the landing surface also reduce the shock of landing.

▶ Swing

Swing is a movement of the arm or leg in any direction permitted by the joint involved. The arms and legs may swing freely in forward-backward movements as a result of their location in the respective sockets. Both the arms and legs may swing out or away from the body, and the arms can rotate full circle in the shoulder joint. The legs, as a result of the construction of the hip socket, are not permitted the full circle rotation.

Principles

1. Gravity assists the body in swing movements.
2. The limitation or the potential for action within a joint plays a major role in the use of swings.

▶ Strike

Striking is the use of a body part—head, hands, knees, feet—to impart force to an object. The object that is struck may be stationary or moving. A stationary object requires an application of force sufficient to overcome its inertia and to permit it to travel the distance the performer desires. When contact is made with a moving object, sufficient force must be imparted not only to cause the object to travel the desired distance but to reverse the direction in which the object is currently moving or was moving toward the performer. The distance and the direction of the object struck is influenced by the amount of force applied to the object and the point or location of the application of the force upon the object.

Principles

1. The longer the striking lever, the greater the speed and range of motion.
2. The point of application of force influences the direction to which the object will move. If the force is applied directly behind the center of gravity of the object, the object will move straight ahead. If the force is applied below the center of gravity of the object, the flight will be up. If the force is imparted above the center of gravity of the object, the object will move down.
3. All principles of projectiles apply to the object that is struck.

▶ Toss

The toss is a series of arm movements used to impart force to an object that upon release will move into the air as a projectile. Motion is transferred from the body to the object.

Principles

1. Momentum is increased as the distance through which the arm moves is increased.
2. Point of release influences the direction in which the object will move.
3. Momentum built up within the body is transferred from the body to the object at the time of release.
4. A stable base of support and a weight transfer will increase the momentum built up within the body.

▶ Kick

The kick is also a form of striking or imparting force. In this instance, the leg imparts the force to an object. With the knee and ankle flexed, the leg flexes as far back in the hip joint as the joint will permit while continuing to maintain balance. The hip joint is extended forward, followed by the extension of the knee and ankle just before contact is made with the object. Either the side of the foot or the top of the foot may be used as the driving wedge, or contact point, in kicking. The body may kick an object for height or for distance. Body alignment, coupled with the direction of the backswing of the leg, determines the direction the kicked object will move. The flutter kick is also a swing from the hips but a controlled limited swing. In this case, the water serves as the resistance.

Principles

1. The longer the backswing, the greater the momentum imparted to the object. (Caution: Note the need for balance.)
2. Force is applied to the object so that the object moves into the air at the angle most efficient to permit the greatest flight distance.
3. Sharp, quick, forceful, flat kicks by the side of the foot usually provide the greatest force.

▶ Push

Push is an application of force by the body or by a body segment used to move an object. The arm may push a ball into action, or the entire body may be aligned behind an equipment dolly to move the object across the room. The person about to push an object determines the weight of the object, the resistance of the surface upon which the object rests, if applicable, and the direction in which the object will move. The body part or parts involved in pushing are aligned directly behind the object and centered in line with the object's center of gravity. In pushing, the feet are placed in a forward stride position with the toes pointed toward the object. The body assumes a flexed position, bending at the knees and hips, in an effort to develop momentum and to gain maximum efficiency.

Principles

1. If the object to be pushed is heavy, maximum efficiency in terms of body stability and placement of the center of gravity is employed.
2. The direction of force is applied in line with the desired direction of the movement. When an object is pushed below its center of gravity, the object will move up as well as forward; when pushed above its center of gravity, the object will move down as well as forward.

▶ Pull

In pushing, the performer's center of gravity was placed behind the object and in line with the object's center of gravity; in pulling, the performer maintains a position ahead of the object and draws the object toward his or her body. Performers may also employ a rope or some other device as an extension of the body to increase efficiency. If, for example, the individual pulling wishes to relieve surface friction she or he will place a rope on the object and pull it forward and slightly up. While the activities included in this text seldom draw upon pulling with the use of a rope to relieve surface friction, the technique is often employed in moving equipment.

The majority of movements through the water employ a pulling motion. The hand, cupped to offer a greater area of resistance against the water, applies force and pulls against the water, permitting the body to move forward or backward. Pulling is also used in climbing activities. Here the arms are used to pull the lower part of the body up an object. In rope climbing, the legs are folded around the rope to secure the lower part of the body while the arms are used to pull the body to a higher level.

Principles

1. To decrease friction, pull an object upward and forward. An object can also be placed on wheels or on some other material to decrease its friction.
2. Once the object is put in motion, it should be continued in motion. Greater force is required to overcome inertia or put the object in motion than to maintain the object in motion.
3. The optimal angle of pull for any muscle is 90 degrees.

▶ Lift

Lifting or picking up an object is an example of pushing and pulling in a vertical rather than a horizontal plane. The performer determines the weight of the object and the purpose to be achieved prior to executing the lift. In lifting, the body moves as close to the object as possible and uses the largest muscle group (hips and legs) to exert the necessary force. The width of the stance is balanced. The spine is straight with all bending occurring at the knees. Effort is made to balance the weight of the object.

Principles

1. To maintain stability the body assumes a forward-backward stride position.
2. A person should be able to lift approximately one-half his or her own weight.

▶ Catch/Trap

Catching is using body parts to receive an object. The object is gathered with the hands; at the same time the hands, wrists, arms, and body are moving backward in an effort to absorb the force or decelerate the speed of the object. A similar action is found in trapping or absorbing the force of a ball with the feet. The object can also be stopped by using the entire body to absorb the force of the object. In these situations, the initial contact may be with any body part. The object is allowed to roll off the body as the force of the object is absorbed. The faster the object is moving, the greater the distance the body must move in order to absorb the force. A backward-forward stance enhances the body's ability to absorb force. The body should be positioned directly behind or beneath the oncoming object.

Principles

1. The greater the distance over which the body moves, the easier it is to decelerate or absorb the force of the object.
2. The stability of the body enhances the body's capacity to receive the force. Stability can be increased by enlarging and lowering the base.

▶ Spin/Turn/Twist

A spin is a rotation of the body around the long axis of the body. A turn is also a rotation around the long axis of the body and is accomplished by a series of short steps. The arm and one foot provide the impetus for the spin; both feet provide the impetus for the turn. In a twist or a pivot, one foot is used for balance while the other foot provides the force to rotate the body. A twist is a movement in which the feet assume a position and then rotate at a 90- to 180-degree angle to reverse the feet and body position. The body stays in a balanced position while the arms provide the force necessary to rotate the body.

Principles

1. The body is usually in an extended position in the execution of these skills.
2. Balance and the maintaining of balance is essential. In a spin and a turn, the balance is on one leg, similar to that of a hop; in a twist, the body weight or balance is maintained over both legs.

▶ Curl/Bend

A curl is the bending of the body toward the center of the body. All joints are flexed so that the body shape resembles a ball. There are various degrees of bending and curling essential to carry out certain tasks. The tighter the curl, the faster the body will move in a roll; the greater the body extension, the slower the body will move in a roll.

Principles

1. The head is to be part of the body shape in a curl.
2. A tight curl requires a high level of flexibility.
3. The tighter the curl, the greater the speed and range of motion; the greater the body extension, the lesser the speed and range of motion.

▶ Roll

A roll is the rotation of the body parts around either the longitudinal or transverse axis. A roll can occur in an extended or a curled position. A forward roll is executed by curling the body tightly and taking the weight on the hands and shoulders. Rolls may be used for safe landings in falls or as part of gymnastic and swim techniques. Rolls may be forward, backward, or sideward.

Principles

1. A roll is a rotation around a body axis.
2. The body may be in a stretched or curled position.

▶ References

Broer, Marion R., and Zernicke, Ronald F. (1979). *Efficiency of Human Movement.* Philadelphia, Pennsylvania: W. B. Saunders.

Wickstrom, Ralph L. (1983). *Fundamental Motor Patterns.* Philadelphia, Pennsylvania: Lea and Febiger.

Combinations of Movement

A combination of movement (see table 5–1) is the selection of two or more fundamental movements and the execution of the movements in sequence. As in fundamentals, the combination of the movements is not employed to achieve a specific goal or purpose. Emphasis is on the act of learning to execute the combinations of movement.

Many movements used in dance, particularly aerobic dance, and in basic exercise programs are combinations. A few are sampled and described in this chapter. Although effort has been made to provide combinations essential to the professional, no effort has been made to assume that the list is comprehensive.

Additional challenges are provided to students when two or more movements are combined. As these skills are acquired, students are encouraged to place attention on timing or fluidity from one movement to the next.

▼ **TABLE 5–1**

Examples of movement combinations.

COMBINATIONS	FUNDAMENTALS
Hop kick	Hop, kick
Flea hop	Step, hop
Leap	Hop from one foot to the other foot
Gallop	Walk, hop from one foot to the other foot
Skip	Step, hop
Dribble	Push with hands, tap or push with feet
Passing	Pushing, catching
Movement through water	Pull and kick

▶ Hop/Kick

The hop kick, a popular dance combination, includes a hop on one foot while maintaining the erect body in place. The lifted leg or the nonhopping leg kicks either to the front or side. To maintain balance the arms are extended out from the shoulders in the direction in which the force is exerted.

Principles

1. The body is aligned with one body segment over the other.
2. Arms are extended at shoulder height for balance.

▶ Flea Hop

A flea hop consists of a step to the side followed by a hop and a complete stop.

Principles

1. Body alignment is essential.
2. Arms are extended in a forward, back, opposition pattern for balance during the hop.

▶ Leap

Eckert describes the leap as a "specialized version of the run with the take-off being made from one foot and the landing on the alternate foot" (Eckert 1987, 195). Leaping is a hop, a jump-like, or an aerial movement in which the body weight is transferred from one leg to the other. As in the run, the body is suspended in air as the weight transfer occurs. The leap may be executed forward, backward, or sideward. The backward leap, like the backward run and walk, differs considerably from the forward leap (see chapter 4).

Principles

1. Strength is required to execute the hop.
2. Arms are used for balance. Opposition and direction of force must be considered in arm position.
3. Balance is best maintained when arms are extended at shoulder height.

▶ Gallop

The gallop is a combination of a walk and a leap on one side of the body. Balance beyond that of a hop is essential to the development of the skill. It may be executed forward, backward, or sideward.

Principles

1. Balance is to be maintained over the base of support.
2. The body is extended upward to obtain the feeling of suspension for as long as possible.

▶ Skip

A skip is a combination of a step and a hop on the same foot. Balance, at a level beyond that required for a hop, is essential to the development of the skill. It can be executed forward, backward, sideward, or as a turn.

Principles

1. Transfer body weight to the skipping foot to maintain balance.
2. Keep arms in line with body force and extended at shoulder height.

▶ Dribbling with Arms and Hands

Dribbling or imparting force with body parts is a combination of pushing and catching or controlling the object. It may be executed by the arms and hands or the legs and feet. When a ball is controlled by the hands, it is usually referred to as bouncing the ball. The hands push the ball toward the floor by pressing hard on top of the ball. The ball immediately leaves the hands and moves as directed in the push. When striking the floor or an object, the ball rebounds at an angle of approximately ninety degrees or equal to that at which it was pushed. The ball may be pushed straight down or forward a short distance. It may be pushed hard or soft or some pressure in between. If the objective of the performer is to maintain contact or control over the ball, the ball is to be pushed straight down so that the performer can stand still and maintain control of the ball. If the performer's objective is to move forward with the ball, the ball is to be pushed forward so that the performer can walk along with the ball and obtain control of the ball as it rebounds from the floor.

Principles

1. The amount of force on the push will determine the time and force of the return.
2. The direction of the push will influence the direction of the rebound. Angles are not technically equal; however, they are approximately the same.

▶ Dribbling with Feet

When imparting force with the feet, a step, followed by a push by the inside or outside of the foot, will be executed. It is usually called dribbling. The force of the push is important because all movement will be forward or sideward, unlike the situation in hand contact where the movement of the object is up and down. The amount of force and the direction of force is controlled so that the performer can maintain contact with the object.

Principles

1. The force of the push determines the speed at which the object will move and thus the speed at which the performer will need to walk or run to maintain contact with the object.
2. The direction of the push on the object will influence the direction of the object.

▶ Passing

Passing is a combination of imparting force or pushing and catching, and it requires two or more people. Passing uses the imparting forces of bouncing or dribbling mentioned previously. However, it differs in that the location and position of the catcher influences the amount of and direction of the force. If the catcher, or trapper in soccer, is opposite the performer, the direction will be forward; if the catcher or trapper is to the side, the direction will be sideward. If the catcher or trapper is stationary, the performer directs the ball straight to the catcher. If the catcher or trapper is moving, the performer estimates the point at which the catcher or trapper will receive the object. The amount of force placed on the object is influenced by the distance between the performer and the catcher or trapper and the capacity of the catcher or trapper to control a fast-moving object.

Principles

1. Direction of pass is determined by desired ultimate location.
2. Speed of the object or the amount of force applied is influenced by distance to be covered and skill of the receiver.

▶ Movement through Water

Many movements in water are a combination of pulling by the arms and kicking in various positions by the legs. Leg kicking movements are executed in the water to obtain a pushing movement against the water. Forward movement in the water is a result of pushing against the water at an appropriate angle. At the same time the arms usually pull through the water to force the body forward.

Principles

1. The body is most efficient in the water in a prone position. Holding the head high above the water is inefficient and will tend to cause the feet to sink.
2. The pull through the water is an action-reaction with the body moving in opposition to the direction of the pull.

This chapter contains merely a sample of possible combinations. It should, however, guide the professional in selecting and presenting combinations that will enhance a performer's skills.

▶ References

Eckert, Helen. (1987). *Motor Development*. Indianapolis, Indiana: Benchmark Press.

Motor Patterns

A motor pattern is a sequence of movements organized such that the timing of each body segment, the amount of force exerted, and the space utilized is vital to the successful execution of the skill. Once the path of action is known by the learner, the quality (soft, hard, slow, fast) takes on importance. Quality of movement, for example, determines whether a walking pattern is a strut or an amble. Laban and his descendants (Ullmann 1960) identified human movement not only as something that could be visualized and described as a picture but also in terms of its quality.

Consistency in form upon repeated executions is another means of differentiating fundamentals from patterns. In a pattern, the body traces an exact picture or predetermined sequence of movements, whereas freedom to utilize the body in a number of different ways characterizes the mode of expression in a fundamental. Learning a fundamental is acquiring a general idea of the movement. In learning the toss, for example, the performer learns to apply force to an object and to release it. In the pattern throw, an advanced form of the fundamental toss, each body segment involved in the movement receives specific attention. The timing of each body segment is important. The throwing action is viewed by isolating each of the joint segments. Success or failure of the throw is determined by the performer's ability to allow each joint segment to build upon the movement of the previous joint segment. Ultimately the throw is to be executed in such a way that power results from the momentum of the first joint segment flowing into the second joint segment.

Patterns (Anderson 1979) often become the basis for the specialized skills that are introduced in chapter 7. Learners need to be able to execute the patterns prior to attempting to acquire the specialized skill. Learners also need to appreciate the value of a pattern such as an overarm throw in learning a variety of sport, dance, game, and swim skills.

▼ **FIGURE 6-1**
Selected motor patterns.

Throw
    Underarm throw
    Overarm throw
    Sidearm throw
Run
    Sprint
    Distance
Jump
    Standing long
    Vertical

▶ Throw

"Throwing and striking differ from other methods for moving objects in that as maximum velocity is reached, the object is released and it then continues to move without further impetus from the body" (Broer and Zernicke 1979, 253). Speed and direction are the most important elements of the throw. Speed is developed by increasing the swing, placing the feet in a stable position, adding body segments in a continuous sequence (no hesitation in movements), and using weight transfer. Direction of the object's flight is influenced by point of release, arc of release, action of gravity on the object, size of the object, and wind.

The toss described in the fundamental skills now reaches the stage where it is recognized as three distinct throwing patterns: underarm, overarm and sidearm. Although the shoulder joint plays the same role in each throw, different patterns emerge as individual segments of the arm come into play. Factors of speed and accuracy are common to all three patterns; however, the method in which they are applied varies. One major difference is that each of the throwing patterns is executed in a different body plane.

▶ Underarm Throw

In the underarm throw the body assumes a comfortable stance and a forward-backward ready position, with the object held in front of the body and the body facing the desired direction of object flight. The throwing arm sweeps down and back as the weight shifts to the rear foot. The performer steps forward as the arm swings forward until the object is released. Release of the object is in relation to the spot at which the person wishes to direct the object's flight. The arm then follows through in the direction of the intended flight. The nonthrowing arm serves to maintain body stability throughout the throw. Figure 6-2 illustrates the underarm throw pattern and its use in the volleyball serve.

Principles

1. As the length of the swing increases, the distance through which the object is moved prior to release increases, thus increasing acceleration and causing the object to move faster at release.
2. The weight transfers from back to forward foot, increasing the force that the body is able to place behind the object at the point of release.
3. An extended arm increases the distance, thus increasing the speed.
4. The object will move at a tangent to the arc of the hand at the time of release so attention should be given to the selection of the best possible release point.

▶ Overarm Throw

The performer stands in a forward-backward stride position and brings the throwing arm down and back in a sweep, much as in the underarm throw; however, as the swing reaches its lowest point, the elbow is flexed and moved away from the shoulder joint. The elbow swings forward ahead of the forearm, and the forearm extends upward beyond the elbow at the same time with whip-like action in the wrist and lower arm. The object is released as the total body weight is transferred and as the arm is in line with the total body. Speed and distance are the reasons for selecting the overarm throw.

Principles

1. In order to maintain and increase momentum, each segment of the arm is in a continuous flow of movement. If the upper arm stops before the lower arm comes into action, momentum will be lost.
2. The release occurs at the optimum angle of efficient flight and when the hand is moving at its fastest speed.
3. Rotation of the body and weight transfer increase the distance through which the body can gain acceleration.

▶ Sidearm Throw

The body's movement begins from a ready position or a forward stride position with the object to be thrown held in front of the body. The body and shoulders rotate, the weight is shifted backward, and the dominant arm swings sideward in a horizontal arc. The arm swings forward in the same horizontal arc as the body, and the shoulders rotate back toward the target. Again, the object is released as the hand is at a point tangent to the target.

Principles

1. Body and shoulder rotation, increased length of arm swing, and transfer of body weight all contribute to an increase in the speed and range that the object will travel.
2. Release is in line with the target for accuracy.

▶ Run

Running, by definition, is the acceleration of the walk to the point where the body is propelled through space with brief periods of time in which neither foot is in contact with the ground.

Factors involved in running include stride, bounce, and pace. Jogging is a combination of short strides, bouncing motion, and slow pace; sprinting is a combination of long strides, minimal bounce, and fast pace. In jogging the entire foot strikes the ground, whereas in fast sprints only the ball of the foot may touch the ground. Sprint and distance running will be described as two separate patterns.

Sprint

The objective in sprinting (see figure 6-3) is to run at maximum velocity. Wickstrom (1983, 52) identifies the essentials of a mature pattern as:

1. The knee and ankle of the support leg bend slightly after the foot has made contact with the ground.
2. Action of the support leg at the hip, knee, and ankle propels the body forward and upward into the nonsupport phase.
3. As the recovery leg swings forward to a high knee raise, the lower part of the leg is flexed, bringing the heel close to the buttock.
4. Extension at the hip and knee of the recovery leg causes the foot to move backward rapidly and contact the ground approximately flat and under the body's center of gravity.
5. The trunk maintains a slight forward lean throughout the stride pattern.
6. Both arms swing through a large arc in an oblique vertical plane and in synchronized opposition to the leg action.

▼ **FIGURE 6-2**

Underarm throw pattern (top) and its use in the volleyball serve (bottom). Photos by Lynn Howell, Cleveland, Ohio.

▼ FIGURE 6-3

Mature pattern used in running at the sprint pace. From R. L. Wickstrom: *Fundamental Motor Patterns,* 3rd edition. Philadelphia, Lea & Febiger, 1983. Reprinted with permission.

Distance

In distance running the major objective, in addition to endurance and relaxation, is rhythm. The trunk is carried more erect than in sprinting, the knees are not raised as high, and the feet often contact the ground with weight evenly distributed from the ball of the foot to the heel. The arms are relaxed and the stride length is a comfortable one.

Principles

1. Force in running is obtained by thrusting the foot against the surface. The more efficient the angle of the foot in relation to the ground, the greater the force.
2. It takes less energy to maintain a given speed than to change the speed (Newton's first law, inertia).
3. Movement of limbs in a direction other than the desired direction will decrease efficiency.

▶ Jump

Two motor patterns identified for examination are the jump for distance and the jump for height. The jump for distance is often referred to as the long or the standing long jump, and the jump for height is called the vertical jump.

▼ **FIGURE 6-4**

Mature form in the standing long jump prior to takeoff and at landing. Before takeoff:
(a) weight moves forward as arms perform preliminary swing; (b) weight continues to
move forward as the arms start a downward and forward swing; and (c) heels are lifted,
arms swing forward and upward, and a series of propulsive forces thrust the body into
full extension. Landing: (d) legs are extended and well forward, trunk and arms are
forward in reaction, knees flex when heels contact the ground, and arms and trunk
reach forward to prevent a backward fall. From R. L. Wickstrom: *Fundamental Motor
Patterns,* 3rd edition. Philadelphia, Lea & Febiger, 1983. Reprinted with permission.

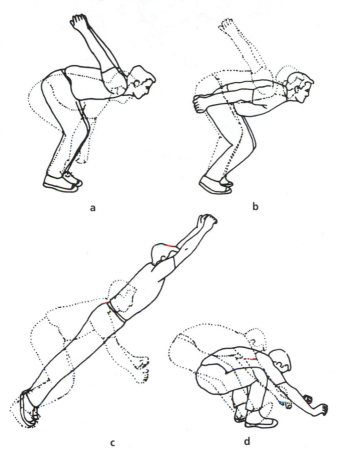

a   b

c   d

Standing Long Jump

The standing long jump consists of a preparatory crouch or tuck position
with the arms swinging backward. Arms swing forcefully forward and upward as the body extends at an angle of forty-five degrees, the most effective position for producing maximum distance upon landing. Balance is regained by bending the knees and bringing the legs under the center of
gravity while allowing the upper body to continue to lean forward. Wickstrom (1983, 83–84) identifies the body positions (see figures 6-4 and 6-5).

▼ FIGURE 6-5

Mature form in the standing long jump during flight: (a) body is fully extended at takeoff; (b) lower legs flex while trunk and arms offer a long lever for reaction; (c) knees come forward as the hips flex and lower legs continue to flex; (d) legs swing forward and begin to extend in preparation for landing, and trunk and arms continue forward and downward in reaction to the leg movement; and (e) legs are approximately straight at the knees and reach forward for maximum distance at landing. From R. L. Wickstrom: *Fundamental Motor Patterns,* 3rd edition. Philadelphia, Lea & Febiger, 1983. Reprinted with permission.

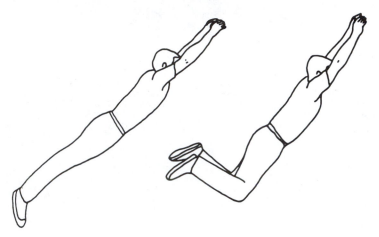

a   b

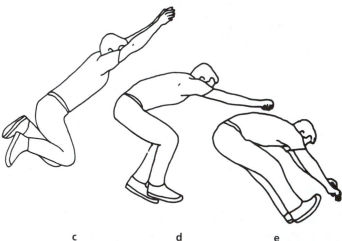

c   d   e

Vertical Jump

The vertical jump consists of a preparatory crouch in which the knees bend to allow the body to gain height for the explosive force in the jump. The arms are brought down to the knees in a relaxed position. At the moment of takeoff, the arms forcefully lift forward and upward as the body extends at the hips, knees, and ankles. The body remains in full extension until gravity brings the body back to the floor or playing surface. As the body is about to land, the ankles, knees, and hips are flexed or relaxed to absorb the shock of landing.

Principles

1. Once the body leaves a projecting surface, it will move in a predetermined path established by the angle of the projecting force and the body's center of gravity. Only when the movement of the body parts alters the center of gravity within the body can change occur.
2. Force of the body is increased by taking off from a crouched position or increasing the distance at takeoff.
3. Distance through which the arms move increases the potential for body distance.
4. Gravity is always working to bring the body down.

▶ References

Anderson, Margaret B. (1979). Comparison of muscle patterning in the overarm throw and tennis serve. *Research Quarterly, 50*(4), 541–553.

Broer, Marion R., and Zernicke, Ronald F. (1979). *Efficiency of Human Movement.* Philadelphia, Pennsylvania: W. B. Saunders.

Ullmann, Lisa. (1960). *The Mastery of Movement by Rudolph Laban.* London, England: MacDonald and Evans.

Wickstrom, Ralph L. (1983). *Fundamental Motorpatterns* (3rd ed.). Philadelphia, Pennsylvania: Lea and Febiger.

Specialized Skills

When movements are fundamentals, combinations, and patterns (presented in chapters 4 through 6), attention is on the movement itself or the path the body segments take in executing the movement. In the specialized skill stage, the movement is executed to accomplish an objective. Movement for movement's sake is the role of fundamentals, combinations, and patterns; movement to accomplish an objective is the role of specialized skill. For example, in the pattern overarm throw the performer concentrates on the action of the body. In the specialized skill overarm throw, the performer's objective is to execute a successful volleyball serve, a tennis serve or smash, or a softball throw.

This chapter defines specialized skills, discusses factors affecting the acquisition of such skills, and identifies a variety of specialized skills used in sports, dance, and swimming. The refinement of fundamentals, combinations, and patterns for use in organized settings requires the performer to make decisions about the quality of the movement. Qualities affecting movement include the motor learning concepts of control, movement sense or kinesthetic acuity, imagery or visualization, and timing. They influence the learner's decisions.

Proficiency at the specialized level is influenced by such factors as distance, point on a target or location on a playing surface unique to scoring, need to control speed to ensure success, and unique recognition of the characteristics of angles of rebound and projection.

The throw from outfield, the tennis serve, and the basketball throw the length of the court are overarm patterns that involve a target. Game situations in these sports dictate the distance over which the object will be required to move. Therefore, the fine tuning of a particular throw is governed by the rules of the game and size of the playing area.

A performer's body size, skill, and speed influence decisions about the movement sequence. When the performer has a large body, considerable strength, and an efficient throw, it may not be wise to throw for maximum distance. Throwing as far or as hard as possible may not be necessary for success in an event. The performer may need to control movement in such a way that he or she will use only one-half or one-third of capacity for maximum force and distance. Point or moment of release is another factor to be considered. The nature of the sport and the skill, size, and strength of the performer dictate specific time and direction of releases. When the object is hit rather than projected, additional factors come into play. Hitting a moving object demands a sense of timing of the oncoming object. When the throw is for the purpose of hitting a target, its success or failure is determined by whether the purpose is met (i.e., the target is hit).

Twenty activities are analyzed as fundamentals and patterns in tables 7-1 and 7-2.

Specialized Skills Based on Fundamentals

Fundamentals: Run and Walk

Nearly every activity depends to some extent on running and/or walking. Of the twenty activities selected for analysis, walk is part of all except archery; run is part of all except archery, badminton, bowling, golf, racquetball,

▼ TABLE 7-1

Fundamentals used in activities

	WALK	RUN	READY POSITION	JUMP/ HOP	LAND/STOP/ FALL	SWING
ACTIVITIES						
Aquatics						
Archery						
Badminton	X		X		X	
Basketball	X	X	X	X	X	
Bowling	X		X		X	
Dance	X	X	X	X	X	X
Fencing	X	X	X	X	X	
Field hockey	X	X	X	X	X	X
Golf	X					X
Gymnastics	X	X		X	X	X
Ice skating	X	X		X	X	
Racquetball	X		X		X	
Skiing	X	X		X	X	
Soccer	X	X	X	X	X	
Softball	X	X	X	X	X	
Table tennis	X		X		X	
Tennis	X	X	X		X	
Track	X	X		X	X	
Volleyball	X	X	X	X	X	
Water polo	X				X	

▼ TABLE 7-1—*Continued.*

ACTIVITIES	STRIKE	TOSS	KICK	PUSH	PULL	LIFT
Aquatics				X	X	
Archery					X	
Badminton	X					
Basketball		X		X		
Bowling		X				
Dance			X			
Fencing				X		
Field hockey						X
Golf	X					
Gymnastics						X
Ice skating				X		
Racquetball	X			X		
Skiing				X		
Soccer			X			
Softball	X	X				
Table tennis	X			X		
Tennis	X	X		X		
Track						
Volleyball	X	X				
Water polo		X	X	X	X	X

ACTIVITIES	CATCH/TRAP	SPIN/TURN/TWIST	CURL/BEND	ROLL
Aquatics		X	X	X
Archery				
Badminton		X		
Basketball	X	X		
Bowling				
Dance		X	X	
Fencing		X		
Field hockey	X	X		
Golf				
Gymnastics		X	X	X
Ice skating		X	X	X
Racquetball		X		
Skiing				
Soccer	X	X		
Softball	X	X		
Table tennis		X		
Tennis		X		
Track				
Volleyball		X		
Water polo	X	X		

▼ **TABLE 7-2**

Patterns used in activities

| ACTIVITIES | THROW | | | JUMP | | RUN | |
	Over-arm	Under-arm	Side-arm	Vertical	Horizontal	Distance	Sprint
Aquatics	X						
Archery							
Badminton	X	X	X				
Basketball	X	X	X	X			X
Bowling		X					
Dance				X	X		X
Fencing							X
Field hockey			X			X	X
Golf			X				
Gymnastics				X	X		X
Ice skating				X	X	X	X
Racquetball		X	X				
Skiing							
Soccer						X	X
Softball	X	X	X	X			X
Table tennis			X				
Tennis	X	X	X				X
Track				X	X	X	X
Volleyball	X	X	X				X
Water polo	X			X			

table tennis, and water polo. In nearly all the activities analyzed, walking or running is executed as described under fundamentals. Runs are fast, slow, backward, forward, and from side to side. Sometimes the knees are raised in an exaggerated position in running. The typical run and walk are described in chapter 4. The bowling walk is described as part of the underhand throw in chapter 4. The following are the stylized movements of walk and run found in skating, skiing, dance, and gymnastics.

Skating

Sculling.   Sculling involves bending the knees, turning the toes out slightly, letting the skates glide, and gaining a position of balance. The object is to find comfort or balance over the blades and to glide forward. The legs are maintained in ready position about shoulder width apart. When performers feel competent, they experiment with sculling with legs close together and with legs far apart.

Forward Stroking.   The performer begins by standing erect, with arms out from the sides for balance, and faces the direction in which she or he intends to move. Feet are placed in T position with the skating foot forward. To push off, the body weight is back, both knees are bent, and the weight is transferred forward as the forward foot glides on a flat blade. In recovery following the glide, the rear foot is brought forward and the body weight returned to both feet. This enables the performer to be ready for the next step or glide. Because the performer now has momentum, not as much glide is needed as she or he moves into the next stroke. Stroking forward is a series of pushes from one foot, followed by glides. Weight is transferred from the pushing foot to the gliding foot just as weight is transferred from one foot to the other in walking.

A speed skater's body is forward in the glide while an ice hockey glide requires a slightly more erect position. A figure skater maintains the upper body in an erect position for balance and beauty.

Stroking backward differs from stroking forward in that the construction of the body prohibits a similar pushoff. Knee and hip action, coupled with effective positioning of the toes, enables the body to push backward. The legs also move together and then apart to increase the momentum. As the performer increases the length of the stroke backward, the glide increases.

Crossovers.   Crossovers are used to move in a circle or to make corners. The forward crossover consists of pushing on the outside foot and crossing over the inside foot. The inside foot takes a small step to return the body to a balanced position. The outside foot repeats the action until the circle is complete.

Backward crossovers are essentially the same action with the body going backward. The outside foot crosses in front of the inside foot as the body moves backward. The inside foot steps into the original position for balance. The outside foot repeats the move.

Skiing

Cross-Country Diagonal.   The cross-country skiing diagonal stroke is like walking. One arm comes forward as the opposite leg comes forward. A kick or push from the rear foot enables the body to build the energy needed to push the body forward. The leg flexes as the kick begins and the leg extends into the glide. The body's center of gravity is over the kicking foot. Some people refer to this action as an explosion. The action is much like leaving the blocks in track or beginning a horizontal jump. A quicker kick or faster acceleration will produce more force.

As the skier's body moves forward, the upper body moves slightly up. This rise occurs at the time of the kick rather than during the glide. It serves to produce an action-reaction, thus increasing the forward momentum.

The ski pole is planted in line with the foot; as the pole is angled back, a distinct push is made to gain force and drive the body forward. The body weight moves forward.

The glide is the most important phase of the movement because it determines the distance and speed the body will move. The gliding leg remains flexed with the body weight on the heel of the foot and centered over the ski. With weight on the heel of the ski, the toe of the ski will be up off the snow, allowing the ski to move faster or to have less resistance.

To eliminate the need to overcome inertia or to maintain momentum, the next kick should be started before the body comes to a halt.

Cross-Country Herringbone.   The herringbone, another form of the walk, is a technique used to climb straight uphill with the skis in a V position. The V position is assumed with toes of the skis out and heels close to each other. If skis have metal edges, effort is made to maintain weight on the inside edge as the body moves up the hill.

Downhill Skiing.   Downhill skiing is allowing gravity to take the body down an incline. The angle of the incline is increased as the performer's skill improves. Equipment, including skis and poles, is used as it is in cross-country skiing. The efficient downhill skier is able to control his or her body on its descent and to make turns or stops at any time she or he wishes.

Dance
Dance includes many fundamentals, with walking and running the ones employed most often in routines. Dance steps are used in aerobics and folk, square, social, and modern dance.

Grapevine.   The grapevine is a "step to side, step behind with trailing foot, step to side, and step in front with trailing foot" (Hall 1980, 226).

Skipping.   Skipping is a combination of step and hop on the same foot. Skipping may be forward, backward, from side to side, or in a circle.

Slide.   Slides may be forward, backward, and to the side.

Gallop.   The gallop is similar to a slide with one difference: both feet are in the air at the same time. Some people call it a leap, hop. The forward foot takes a leap or long step while the back foot takes a hop or short step.

Two-Step.   The two-step, a step, together sequence, starts with the lead foot stepping, the trailing foot coming together with the lead foot, and then shifting the body weight in a step.

Polka.   The polka is a two-step with a hop. Hop, step, together, step is the sequence, with the leading leg executing a hop followed by a step; the trailing foot joins the lead foot, and then places the body weight on it. On occasion, the hop includes a heel, toe placement prior to the hop.

Schottische.   The schottische is a step, step, step, hop or a step, together, step, hop. The lead foot steps, the trailing foot steps, the lead foot steps and hops.

Waltz.   The waltz is a step, step, step sequence with the lead foot taking a big step in a direction, the trailing foot joining the lead foot in the second step, and the lead foot taking a step in place. It is often executed in a box pattern with a series of waltz steps involved in creating the pattern.

Fox-Trot.   The fox-trot begins with the feet together. The lead foot slowly steps forward, the trailing foot slowly steps forward, then the lead foot takes a quick step to the right, followed by a quick step by the trailing foot joining the leading foot.

Mazurka.   The mazurka is a step, cut, hop sequence. The leading foot steps, the trailing foot comes up to the leading foot, cuts, and takes weight onto the foot alongside the leading foot. Cut and hop are both executed by the trailing foot.

Cha-Cha-Cha.   Cha-cha-cha sequence is the forward, back step, step, step in place. The sequence begins with both feet together. The forward slow step is taken by the lead foot; the trailing foot takes a slow back step. The lead foot steps next to the trailing foot with the trailing foot stepping in place for the finish. The last three steps are quick. Cha-cha-cha is slow forward, slow back, quick together, step, step, step. This step can be modified in a crossover and is used forward, backward, and sideward.

Gymnastics

Walks and runs of a short sprint nature are often used to gain momentum as the performer moves into a leap, jump, or vault. Gymnastics stunts use a number of unique or stylized versions of the walk.

Back Walkover.   The back walkover begins in standing position, with feet shoulder width apart, and arms extended overhead. The back arches as the body moves backwards, allowing one leg to lift off the mat. As the hands touch the mat, the legs are brought over the body one at a time. The hands leave the mat just before the first foot makes contact with the mat. The stunt is completed in a standing position.

▶ **Figure 7-1**
Ready position. Photo by
Lynn Howell, Cleveland,
Ohio.

Fundamental: Ready Position

Whenever a performer is about to receive an object, he or she is to assume
a ready position with knees flexed, feet shoulder width apart, and body
aligned with one major segment over the other. Body weight is to be extended in the direction of the oncoming force in an effort to meet and successfully catch, stop, or trap the oncoming object. For example, a volleyball
player assumes a ready position in anticipation of an oncoming ball (see
figure 7-1). A tennis player assumes a similar position in waiting for the
serve.

A basketball player assumes a forward-backward, stride position in an
effort to absorb the force of the oncoming ball. Soccer and field hockey
players also assume the ready position to either trap the ball with the feet
or to stop it with the stick. Again, the body weight is in the direction of the
oncoming object.

Barnett (1983) argues that the skier, like all sport persons, begins with
the ready position and returns to the ready position, knees relaxed, feet
shoulder width apart, and body balanced over the feet, whenever possible.
The body is aligned with the knees under the hips and the shoulders directly over the feet. As the incline increases, the body position remains the
same, thus giving the notion that the body is leaning forward. There is a

slight bend at the hips; knees are flexed. Feet and skis are usually placed about shoulder width apart for balance with body weight evenly distributed over the feet. This stance is a typical beginner's stance.

In skiing, the greater the bend at the knees that can be offset by ankle or forward waist movement, the greater the stability. A lower body is a stable body; an upright or taller body is an unstable body.

Bowling

The performer stands erect with feet either together or shoulder width apart and head held high. The dominant hand is placed in the holes of the bowling ball with the ball in the palm of the hand. Fingers of the nondominant hand are placed beneath the bowling ball for balance. The higher the position used in holding the ball, the greater the effect of gravity on the ball.

Archery

The stance or ready position in archery places the feet shoulder width apart; weight is distributed equally on both feet with toes in line with the center of the target. This placement of the feet in line with each other and toes in line with the target is called the square stance. Body weight is evenly distributed and does not transfer during the execution.

In the open or oblique stance (see figure 7-2), the performer's foot nearest the target moves away from the target so that the body is a quarter turn open to the target. Although the performer is not facing the target, the body is open to the target.

Golf

In golf, the stance and aim at the target work together as the body is aligned to be sure that an efficient swing directs the ball to the target. If the position is perpendicular to the target, the face of the club is facing the target. The body—shoulder, hip, and side of the foot—is at a ninety-degree angle to the target. An open stance (moving the body ten degrees or more toward the face of the target) or a closed stance (moving the body ten degrees or more away from the face of the target) will measurably change the flight of the ball. Note when teaching either the open or closed position that the length of the swing must be altered to permit the performer to reach the intended result. Only a position that is perpendicular to the ball—a ninety-degree angle—will be discussed here.

▶ **Figure 7-2**
Square and open stances in archery.

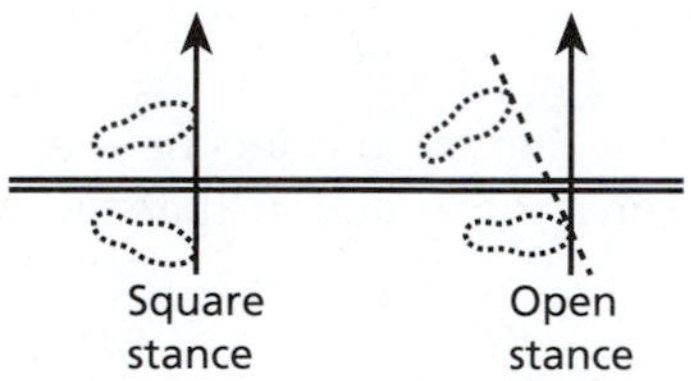

Square
stance

Open
stance

Ready position in golf includes the ready position discussed in fundamentals with a few changes. The body stands erect with knees slightly flexed. Placement of the feet hip width apart is recommended. Foot width is decreased when using the short irons.

Body weight is to be balanced directly over the feet with slightly more weight on the foot away from the target. Feet are secure, usually as a result of wearing cleats on shoes, so no slipping can occur.

Fencing

The guard or ready position in fencing is one in which the feet remain at right angles with the forward heel or the heel on the side of the dominant hand directly in front of the rear heel (see figure 7-3). The heels assume a stance shoulder width apart with knees flexed and the body in ready position. Knees are to be over the toes with body weight evenly distributed over the balls of both feet. The knees are bent a little more than in a general ready position. The position of the feet allows for both forward and sideward stability. The ready positions in general are positions that allow for either forward or sideward stability, but not for both in the same movement. The nonfoil or nondominant hand and arm remain behind the body, with the upper arm in line with the shoulder and the elbow bent so that the hand is facing the back of the head. The nondominant hand and arm position is for balance.

The foil arm is in front of the body with the lower arm and wrist chest height and the foil pointed toward the opponent's chin.

▶ **Figure 7-3**
Side view of an on guard position in fencing.
Photo by Lynn Howell, Cleveland, Ohio.

Fundamental: Swing

Swing is found in dance, field hockey, golf, and gymnastics. Swing as a fundamental is found in dance and gymnastics. Specialized forms of swing are used in field hockey and golf.

Golf

Backswing.   The golf swing is influenced by the distance the performer stands from the ball. The farther the performer is from the ball, the flatter the plane of the swing; the closer the performer is to the ball, the more upright the swing.

Width and length are two factors in the swing. The length of the nondominant arm added to the length of the club is the radius of the swing. The longer the radius, the greater the speed the clubhead can develop. Bending the arm reduces the radius, thus decreasing the potential for clubhead speed. The length of the backswing or arc determines the amount of speed in the downswing that can be imparted as force to the ball and thus determines the distance the ball will travel. Performers adjust their backswings and downswings to accommodate the amount of speed they deem essential to drive the ball a desired distance.

The swing consists of two phases, backswing and downswing. The club is aligned with the ball, with the nondominant arm making a straight line from the shoulder to the club. As the club is brought back in the backswing, the relationship of the club to the nondominant arm remains the same, thus creating as long an axis as possible. The arms and shoulders work as a unit. As the dominant arm and shoulder rise, the shoulder on the nondominant side lowers. The lower body is in a fixed position. As the club is brought back in the backswing, the pelvis and spine rotate, enabling the strong muscles of the trunk and lower extremities to come into action. The head also remains in a fixed position.

The turn continues until the back is facing the target at the highest point of the swing. The body weight has slowly shifted throughout the backswing until the weight is almost totally on the rear foot.

The downswing is the uncoiling of the pent-up energy acquired in the backswing. Gravity assists the performer in bringing the club through the downswing. The downswing should follow the same path that the club followed on the backswing.

Contact.   The club should hit the ball square, reaching maximum speed at the point of impact. The weight should be transferring or have transferred at that point. If the contact is not straight, the ball can be expected to move in the angle in which it was directed. At times, due to course layout, it may be desirable to place a spin on the ball. The spins will react the same on a golf course as they react on surfaces in other sports. A topspin will make a ball drop sooner and roll farther; a backspin will keep the ball in the air longer and make it drop at nearly a dead spot. Topspins require contact on top of the ball while backspins occur when contact is beneath the center of the ball. The farther the contact is from the center of the ball, the greater the spin. Performers should also be cognizant of the velocity and direction of the wind.

The follow-through is an extension of the downswing. As the distance of the desired ball flight becomes shorter, the performer selects a club with an increased inclination and decreases the amount of the swing. These principles are used in all driving strokes.

Field Hockey

Passes.   Passes in field hockey, usually executed while moving, use a swing from waist height or less. As in golf, the greater the distance of the swing, the greater the force. The faster the swing, the greater the force imparted. When force is favored, both hands are placed as close together on the stick as possible to increase the length of the lever and thus increase speed and range of motion. Wrist snaps are used in passes to increase the force or distance the ball will go. The more time that the stick maintains contact with the ball, the greater the force imparted. Follow-through occurs in all passes to obtain momentum from the body action. Body weight is transferred from back to front either prior to or during contact, thus increasing force. As maximum force is not always wanted, each pass makes use of a combination of these elements.

Drive.   Field hockey drives, also executed while moving, use a swing. In a beginning drive, the back foot takes the body weight and points toward the ball. The shoulders and hips turn toward the direction of the intended drive. The performer places both hands as close to the top of the stick as possible to increase the length of the lever and thereby increase speed and range of motion. A backswing is taken so that the stick is at waist height— the rules prohibit a greater backswing. The arms are straight, the wrists firm, and the weight transfers from back to front as the swing is executed. These factors increase the force that is placed on the ball at contact. Accuracy is important. The ball must be hit with the stick directly behind it. The follow-through is in the direction that the pass is intended. A topspin results from the swing described.

Fundamental: Push

Push is used in aquatics, basketball, fencing, field hockey, ice skating, skiing, and water polo. Ice skating and skiing use the push of one foot against the ground, snow, or ice to enhance the weight transfer from one foot to the other. The technique is explained in walking and running. Pushes are used in chest passes, shots, and dribbling in basketball and water polo. Push as a dribble also occurs in basketball, soccer, and field hockey.

Fencing
Fencing provides unique skills in the push area.

Lunge.   The lunge is the attack or extension of the body and weapon toward the opponent. The top of the foil is aimed at the part of the opponent where the touch is to be made. The hand and the foil precede the foot in the lunge. The forward foot reaches as far as possible with the knee remaining over the foot. The rear leg is extended with the foot remaining on the ground and weight shifted forward. The nonfoil arm is moved down for balance.

Recovery from the lunge is made by pushing the heel on the forward foot and bringing the legs together while the arms return to guard position. Balance becomes central with weight evenly distributed.

Rhythm of movement is important to the attack, retreat, and the lunge.

Attacks or Strikes.   There are four types of simple attacks: straight thrust, disengagement, cutover, and counter-disengagement.

The straight thrust is a lunge with a direct attack on the opponent. The disengagement is an attack in which the performer passes his or her blade under the opponent's blade and goes in for the attack. The performer quickly pushes the opponent's blade out of the way and attacks. In the cutover, the performer passes his or her blade over the top of the opponent's blade and comes in for an attack. Again the performer moves the opponent's blade out of position. The counter-disengagement, a more complex skill, requires that the performer read the intention or follow the blade of the opponent. "At lunge distance, one fencer passes his blade under the opponent's in order to cover in the opposite line. As he does so, he moves his arm and sword across to close the line completely" (Pitman 1988, 38–39).

Defense Skills or Parries.   Parries use the foil to protect the body or stop the advance or attack of the oncoming fencer. They may be direct or simple, circular, semicircular, or diagonal.

The direct parry is made by moving the opponent's blade out of the way. The foil is to be held at chest height with the arm bent rather than at full extension. The blade is moved laterally while keeping the point in line with the target. Movement forward is restricted to that essential to parry the blade.

The circular parry requires a complete circle of the opponent's blade, deflecting the blade and then immediately moving in for an attack. Here, the blade is moved with the fingers. The feel of the blade or kinesthetic acuity is important. Semicircular parries are the same as circular parries, except that a half circle rather than a full circle is involved. The point of the blade goes from a high to low or a low to high position. In the diagonal parry, the blade travels diagonally across the target, moving the attacking blade out of the way.

In all parries the arm is slightly bent to increase the amount of force available. The actions are executed with the fingers and wrist so that the opponent is not able to easily ascertain the performer's movement.

Basketball
Pushing is used extensively in basketball and water polo passes, shots, and dribbling.

Chest Pass. The chest pass, the most frequently used pass in basketball, is a push. A chest pass is a quick, short pass that is usually coordinated with the catch in a continuous movement. Accuracy is important. The player receives the ball and passes it to someone else without hesitating or stopping. There is continuous flow in the movement. A chest pass is executed by holding the ball in front of the chest, "the thumbs pointed toward each other and the fingers comfortably spread behind the ball. From this position, the ball is drawn backward a little as the wrists are 'cocked' before applying force to the ball in the direction of the pass" (Hay 1985, 225). The cocked wrist permits flexion, increasing the force that the wrist can place on the ball. The arm is extended and the body weight shifted forward as the ball is released. Force comes from the shift of body weight, extension of the arms, and flick or snap of the wrist. The arms extend in a follow-through in the direction the ball is expected to move. The ball is released at an angle slightly above the horizontal to accommodate the pull of gravity.

Force from the arms and wrist may be adequate to direct a short pass; longer passes will require weight transfer as well as use of the back, neck, and arm muscles. Short passes usually have a short follow-through; long passes generally call for an extension of the whole body in the follow-through.

Overhead Pass. Overhead passes, popular among tall players, are also used to get the ball to the person who is cutting in or pivoting and about to shoot. The ball is held in both hands similar to the chest pass, only in front of and "slightly forward of the head" (Hay 1985, 226). Elbows may be flexed to protect the thrower from opponents. The pass may be the same as the chest pass, with a step forward and a flex of the wrists, or the performer may move quickly, reaching up on her or his toes to gain or add force. Either the step forward or the extension on the toes needs to be so fast that it is detected by opponents only at the last second. The pass is usually directed forward and slightly downward in the desired direction. The angle of downward direction must accommodate the downward flight that gravity causes.

Bounce Pass.   The two-handed bounce pass, another push, is executed in the same manner as the chest pass, except that the direction of flight is toward the floor. A point on the floor someplace between the passer and the receiver is the spot at which the ball is expected to make contact with the floor. That point should enable the receiver to obtain the ball at waist height. The point often recommended is two-thirds the distance between the players. Spins, topspin or backspin, will have an impact on what the ball will do following the bounce. Hay (1985, 227) notes that a bounce pass usually requires greater distance and that the floor reduces the speed of the ball, thus requiring that the passer in the bounce pass exert greater force than would be required of the same person in a chest pass. He goes on to say that the increase in time of the pass and force necessary increases the chance for error in its execution.

Two-Handed Jump Shot.   At takeoff, the feet are shoulder width apart and in line with the body's center of gravity. The ball rests on the fingers or palms of the hands and is slightly ahead of the body. Total body alignment exists. The performer flexes the knees, pushes against the floor, and moves the body into the air. The longer the performer can hang in the air, the more time there is available for executing the shot. The elbow should be pointed in the direction of the hoop at the time of release. The release is usually at the peak of the jump. Eyes are on the basket at all times.

One-Hand Set or Foul Shot.   The feet take a forward-backward stride ready position close to the foul line, with the same foot as the dominant hand forward. The ball is held by the fingers below the chin or above the forehead. The shooting hand is behind or beneath the ball, with the wrist cocked. The nonshooting hand guides the ball and is placed to the side of the ball. The body flexes and extends as the ball is shot from the hands. The wrist flexes forward. Both hands extend toward the target on the follow-through. Eyes are to remain on the target at all times. Extraneous movements are to be kept to a minimum.

Lay-Up.   The basketball lay-up begins with one or more bounces (dribbles) toward the basket. The ball is taken with one or two hands from the last dribble to an above-the-head position. Following the dribble, the performer takes one step and then jumps vertically while carrying the ball high above the head. The ball is then laid against the backboard at the point of aim on the backboard. The follow-through is complete upon landing. A left-handed lay-up is released as the player jumps from the right foot; the right-handed lay-up is executed as the player jumps from the left foot.

Tip-In.   A tip-in is a push, executed while jumping, that directs the ball toward the goal. It is usually a one-hand push and makes use of either the backboard or rim of the basket.

Dribbling.   Dribbling in basketball is imparting force to the ball in a downward and slightly forward manner. The hand is on top of the ball, the elbows are extended, and the wrists and fingers flexed, pushing the ball to the floor. As the ball hits the floor, the force of the floor, often called rebound, sends the ball back to the performer. The amount of force imparted, the direction of the force, the surface of the floor, and the condition of the ball affect the rebound or bounce.

Dribbling is a skill that requires a high level of kinesthetic sense; performers dribble the ball without watching it. The dribbler maintains an upright position, sometimes low but not bent over. They must see what other players are doing and where teammates and opponents are moving. The taller the dribbler can stand and control the ball, the faster the dribbler can move. Persons who dribble effectively can dribble forward, backward, from side to side, and with either hand. Also, they can change pace to evade opponents.

Water Polo

Forehand Shot.   Water polo forehand shots are pushes executed while treading water and used when the passer is clear to face the target and throw the ball. An overarm throw is executed for a fast and accurate shot. The shot is aimed just over the heads of the opponents. Aim is toward any one of the four corners of the goal. The eggbeater or whip kick is used to support the body while the pass is executed. These kicks are described in detail in this chapter under the heading Fundamental: Kick.

Hook passes are similar to a hook shot or lay-up in basketball. They are used when a person is closely guarded and when the objective is to pass backwards.

Pop Shot.   The pop shot is executed when the nondominant hand presses slightly on the ball to make it bounce and the dominant hand grabs the ball and throws it with the fingers, wrist, and arm to make the throw look like a front crawl arm stroke. To avoid fouling by using two hands on the ball, the nonworking hand must be sculling under water at all times. This shot is used in a breakaway while swimming.

Deflection Shot.   A deflection shot or a tip-in permits the ball to bounce off any part of the body into the goal. A closed fist is prohibited by the rules.

Dribble.   When dribbling in water polo, the performer moves toward the ball in such a way that a wave is created, which pushes the ball forward. The ball continues to move about a foot in front of the swimmer. Players swim toward the ball with head up and elbows high, with an arm stroke consisting of short, rapid pulls. Dribbling is to be used only when passing is not appropriate. Passing is the preferred option.

Racquet Sports

The push or block is used effectively in racquet sports in two situations. The first situation is where the object is moving so fast toward the performer that all the performer can do is put the hand or racquet in a position that will, in effect, stop or block the object and turn it in the opposite direction. With a little thought, the performer may also position the racquet or hand such that the angle of the rebound can be controlled. This situation often occurs on the receipt of serve in those sports involving a net. A second need for a block is when a performer is either near the net or close to the playing wall, and the best action is merely to position the hand or implement such that the object rebounds off the equipment. This may, on occasion, be referred to as a volley. Blocks become pushes when the player assumes a degree of control by executing a miniswing.

Soccer

Dribble.   In soccer, dribbling is a means of advancing the ball by giving it small taps with the insides of the feet. The object is to maintain control of the ball while advancing it down the field as fast as possible. The ball is to be kept ahead of, but controlled by, the feet. It is not necessary to tap the ball on every step. The body is held erect with the eyes forward, not looking at the feet.

Field Hockey

Dribble.   In field hockey, dribbling is executed with the stick in front of the body and the left elbow bent and held slightly away from the body. An underarm throw motion is used with the hockey stick. The body weight is forward on contact. In dribbling, the player gives short, quick taps and maintains control of the ball as he or she moves down the field. Contact must be close enough to prohibit opponents from taking the ball away. Most play is on the right side of the body. This is dictated by the construction and therefore the use of the field hockey stick.

Push Pass.   The push pass is a pass reserved for short distances. No backswing is used. The performer assumes a ready position in the direction in which she or he plans to give force. As the body moves forward to the ball, the arms move a little off center of the ball and tap the ball, maintaining contact as long as possible and pushing the ball toward the intended receiver. The location of the anticipated receiver is spotted prior to contact with the ball.

Reverse Stick Push.   While hands and arms maintain a regular grip on the stick, the stick is rotated or turned over the top of the ball. The toe of the stick pushes the ball toward the intended target.

Dodges.   Dodges are used to evade a tackler and maintain possession of the ball. Three dodges often used are push to the right, left, and reverse. The momentum of the body must be maintained. The push to the right may be started "with a right dodge by angling her dribble slightly to the left to lure the opponent in that direction. Just before the tackle, she pushes the ball to the right of the opponent, runs to the left of the opponent (to avoid obstruction), recovers the ball and continues her dribble." (Barnes and Kentwell 1979, 50). The left dodge is essentially the same as the right. A left dodge is executed by lowering the stick handle and lifting the ball about six inches from the ground. On a reverse dodge, the player moves in with a reverse stick (described earlier) and merely pulls the ball away.

Skiing

Double-Pole Push.   Skiers start in a balanced position, body upright and relaxed, hips directly over feet, and weight over the heels. The hands, with poles in them, are swung up to about head level. The body flexes and the poles are brought down and planted on the ground. The drive of the body through the poles to the ground moves the body forward. The force and angle of placement used by the skier determines the speed and distance moved.

Friction from the snow and the condition of the bottom of the skis are factors in the distance of the glide.

Skate.   The skate in skiing begins with a downward pole plant. Feet are pushed to the side with a slight push to the rear. At pushoff, the body weight is transferred to the skating leg as the ski moves diagonally. Quickly the weight is transferred to the gliding ski. This push or thrust and glide is to be executed in a common rhythm. The legs may be pushed forward, or a V or greater side thrust may be used. The motion, similar to ice or roller skating, allows for a rapid thrust forward as the body weight shifts onto the gliding foot, and is followed by a return of weight to both feet for the glide. The weight is then placed over the pushing foot for the next movement.

Gymnastics

Handstand.   Carpenter (1985, 81) identifies the handstand as "a prerequisite to all other inverted movements." Starting from either a standing or stride squat position, the performer places the hands on the mat, shoulder width apart, and kicks first one and then the second leg over the hands or over the base of support. The body is stretched with the toes pointed toward the ceiling.

A handstand may be combined with a forward roll as a means of completing the movement. The head is tucked as the handstand is abandoned for the roll. The body will follow the head in the roll.

Cartwheel.   A cartwheel is a handstand in which the body moves sideways and places weight on the hands one at a time so that there is continuous movement. The stunt begins as the performer stands with feet on an imaginary line, with one foot in front of the other. The body weight is taken on the hand on the same side as the forward foot; the other hand is placed about shoulder width apart on the mat in the same line. The feet and legs are kicked up, with legs straight, and swung over the body one at a time, with the body finishing in a standing position. A run and a hurdle may be used as an approach to a cartwheel.

A roundoff is a stunt that begins the same as a cartwheel. As the legs are lifted into the air, they are straightened and brought together. When they are together, the body rotates a quarter turn. The body is brought back into a standing position.

Front Limber.   The front limber begins in a standing position. Hands are placed on the floor; legs are lifted into the air. After the body is stable in the air, the back is permitted to arch, and the legs are slowly lowered to the floor. The stunt is finished as the body is pushed up into a standing position.

Front Handspring.   A front handspring is similar to a front limber up to the stable handstand position. At that point the body is pushed by the hand and shoulders as it arches so that the performer moves rapidly into a standing position. The speed of the motion enables the hands to drive the body into the standing position. A front walkover is a limber in which one leg precedes the other as the body drops over into a standing position.

Volleyball

Setting in volleyball is a push.

Fundamental: Jump/Hop

The fundamental jump is used in nearly all activities; a number of specialized skills use jump, as described later in this chapter under the heading Pattern: Jump. Hops are fundamentals. They are incorporated into stopping and starting motions in basketball, dance, field hockey, and soccer. A classic example of a hop is found in the basketball lay-up shot. The performer drives to the basket and hops as she or he lays the ball up on the backboard. In field hockey or soccer, a hop may be used in conjunction with a run or stop as a player positions the body to receive a pass, to execute a pass, or to play the object. Hops are used extensively in dance.

Fundamental: Land/Stop/Fall

Landing means being able to absorb the force of a jump following a track event or a volleyball or basketball jump. It is the ability to absorb the force of an intentional land. Landing plays an important part in diving and jumping in the water. Ability to land is also important to skating. Skating requires the ability to execute intentional lands and landings that are not planned.

A landing occurs in basketball following a jump. Absorption of the body's force occurs as the knees and ankles bend to increase the distance through which the force is absorbed. Landing in the water in diving and swimming may involve returning to a vertical position or throwing the body to the side to increase the amount of force in contact with the water and to stop the body. Landing may be on the surface of the water, or it may intentionally take the body underwater. Because a person's weight is sufficient to pass through the water surface, the learner should approach the water surface with as small a body area as possible and in a streamlined position (Broer and Zernicke 1979, 203).

Bringing the body to a halt or stopping is important to many sports in that the body needs to be under control for the performer to either recover or project an object. This includes catching, passing, shooting, kicking, etc.

The objective in a fall is to absorb the force by increasing the distance over which the body moves as it falls. This is accomplished by giving or relaxing body segments in order to absorb as much force as possible. Effort should also be made to land on the feet, buttocks, or shoulder area for protection, rather than on the head, knees, or elbows. Increasing the area of the body that receives the force, as in rolling, is another way to dissipate force in landing.

Skiing

Stopping on skis may be in a parallel position or in a V position. A parallel stop on skis uses a skid or a slide. Considerable force and a high level of edge using the sides of the skis results in a quick stop. A combination of a high edge-set, a strong body, and well-sharpened edges allows the body to slow and stop rapidly. If time is available, the edge-set will be lower in stopping. This stop is similar to the hockey stop in skating.

In the V stop, the performer creates a V with the toes of the skis together, heels apart, and weight on the inside edges of the skis. The performer pushes on the inside edges to stop. A V stop is also used in ice skating.

Skating

Stops. Three stops are popular in skating: snowplow, T, and hockey. The snowplow stop, similar to the snowplow or V stop in skiing, requires the performer to point his or her toes toward one another, bend the knees, and place the weight on the inside edges of the skates. Arms are held out to the sides, just below shoulder height, for balance.

The T stop requires that the body weight be placed on the forward foot with the rear foot coming into the forward foot to make the T. As the rear foot comes into position, the body weight is transferred to the rear foot.

The hockey stop is performed with feet parallel to each other and perpendicular to the body or the direction of forward force. The knees are bent to absorb force and the arms are to the side, just below shoulder height, to maintain balance.

Falling.   Falling is inevitable in learning to skate. Therefore, the performer is encouraged to learn to fall. A successful fall is one in which the performer is able to completely relax and absorb the force of the body in the fall. The length of the slide and the amount of body surface on the ice are factors in reducing the severity of the fall. As the fall takes the performer close to the ice, the performer falls sideways with knees bent and arms extended to reach the ice first. As contact is made, the seat and side of the body slide along the ice. Following the slide, the performer rolls over onto the knees, moves into a crawl position, and stands up.

Gymnastics

Stopping or absorbing force by using the hips, knees, and ankles is the usual method of completing a stunt in gymnastics. The patterns of horizontal and vertical jump are used in gymnastics.

Fundamental: Kick

Kicks are found in dance, soccer, swimming, and water polo. They are used in soccer for passing, tackling, shooting, and goalkeeping. Kicks are used in water polo and synchronized swimming to sustain and support the body's upright position and as part of the stroke technique in swimming. In dance, kicks are made to the side, front, or back.

Soccer

Passing in soccer sends the ball to a teammate by means of a kick. The inside, outside, or instep of the foot may be used.

Inside-of-the-Foot Pass.   The inside-of-the-foot pass is used for short distance passes, shooting, and clearing the ball from the goal. As more surface of the foot is used, accuracy and control increase. The foot remaining on the ground is pointed toward the target. The kicking foot is brought out and back with knees and toes pointed out or at a ninety-degree angle to the ball. The ankle joint is locked as the foot is drawn back and brought forward, contacting the ball. With the body held erect, and the arms and hands in a balanced position, the passing leg moves back with the knees and toes at a 90-degree angle to the ball. The leg comes forward with the flat surface on the inside of the foot placed directly behind the center of the ball. The leg comes forward with acceleration, hits the ball, and follows through. The passer uses as great an area of the side of the foot as possible and maintains contact with the ball in the pass for as long as possible.

Outside-of-the-Foot Pass.   The outside-of-the-foot pass is used when the performer is moving rapidly "without breaking running stride, to pass to the side and to curve the path of the ball" (Thomson 1980, 25). The body is erect and the outside of the foot is flat, with the toe pointed in. The body is aligned directly behind the ball. The kicking foot is lifted with the toe extended downward and rotated inward. The knee is inward and the ankle is locked. The heel is lifted up toward the body for a swing. The outside of the foot makes contact with the center of the ball. The leg and foot swing back and follow through in a quick-snapping continuous motion. This is a movement that is difficult for the opponent to observe in time to react.

Instep Kick.   The instep kick is used to shoot for goal and to pass for long distances. The performer's body is aligned behind the ball. The performer's leg is brought straight back with the foot placed beneath the ball. As the leg extends and follows through, the ball is raised up and off the ground and forward into the air. The placement or the contact point of the foot on the ball determines the ball angle and direction of flight. The force and speed of the leg at the moment of impact determines the distance the ball will move. The kick is executed rapidly with a quick backswing and follow-through.

Swimming

Flutter Kick.   The purpose of the flutter kick is to balance the body in swimming. The performer, swinging the legs at the hip joint and allowing the toes to point and the ankles to extend, kicks up and down in the water. The top of the foot pushes the water in the down movement and the bottom of the foot pushes the water in the up beat or movement (American Red Cross 1981, 47).

Whip Kick.   The whip kick is executed in a prone position. The knees are allowed to drop down, hip width apart, with knee caps pointing toward the bottom of the swimming area. Feet are flattened with toes pointing away from the body. The knees are separated, about shoulder width apart, and the feet and lower legs circle to the outside as far as the body will permit. The thighs do not move a great deal during the stroke; movement is in the lower legs.

Eggbeater Kick.   The eggbeater kick is performed with the body in an erect sitting position (see figure 7-4). Head, shoulders, and spine are in a straight line. The knees are forward of the body, forming a ninety-degree angle with the trunk. With the knees as far apart as possible, the legs are lowered from the knees toward the bottom of the swimming area. The kick is executed as each foot makes as large a circle as possible using the rotation at

▼ **Figure 7-4**

Eggbeater kick. From *Coaching Synchronized Swimming,* 2nd Ed. (p. 74) by M. Swan Forbes for United States Synchronized Swimming, 1989, Champaign, IL: Leisure Press. Copyright 1989 by United States Synchronized Swimming. Reprinted by permission.

the knee as the axis for the circle. The performer should "reach as far as she can forward, sideways, and backward, while still maintaining the ninety-degree angle between her thighs and trunk" (Forbes 1989, 74-75).

As the performer travels forward with the eggbeater, the knees are lowered, creating a ninety-degree angle between the lower and upper legs, thus allowing the feet to push the water. When the performer moves backward, the knees and feet are in front of the body kicking the water in front of the body. To move to the left or right, the lead leg is positioned beneath the body, as one would position a leg for hopping or balancing on one foot. The other leg is to the trailing side of the body. The kicks are executed as they are in the stationary position (Forbes 1989, 92).

Fundamental: Pull

Pulls are used primarily in aquatics, including water polo, and in soccer, archery, and field hockey.

Field Hockey

Tackle.   A tackle is a means of taking the ball away from an opponent. The tackler player, keeping the stick low and the flat side of the stick facing the ball, reaches in with a long sweep or pull and takes possession of the ball, dribbling it away. The body position is generally a forward-backward stride. A player may place the stick in only one hand to tackle the ball. This use of one hand on the stick increases the distance the body can lunge. Tackling may also be done with a reverse stick.

Soccer

Front Block.   The front block is an inside pass that puts the ball between the legs of the opponent. As soon as the pass is executed, the performer moves around the opponent and continues dribbling the ball in the desired direction.

The block tackle may also be an inside-of-the-foot pass used to move the ball away from the opponent.

Swimming and Water Polo

The standard strokes that enable the performer to move through water in swimming and water polo are the front crawl, back crawl, elementary backstroke, sidestroke, and breaststroke.

Floating.   Floating is influenced by buoyancy, gravity, and density of the body in the water. Gravity forces the body toward the bottom of the swimming area; buoyancy is an upward force created by the water that tends to support the body at the surface. Density is the relationship of the weight of the body to the weight of an equal amount of water.

A performer learns to float by extending his or her body on the surface of the water. Prior to floating, a novice learns how to stand up or right the body in the water. Swimmers will practice picking their feet off the bottom into a tuck position and returning their feet to the bottom. As they feel more comfortable in the water, they begin to assume a front layout position and return to a standing position. Back floating is executed next. Back floating is easier than front floating because the head is out of the water and the performer does not have to worry about breathing. Righting the body or standing up is more difficult than with the front float.

Front Crawl.   In front strokes, a swimmer is encouraged to place the head in the water for efficiency and to breath at certain key times in the stroke. (See page 94 for description of stroke.)

The principle of inertia is important in swimming. A body at rest will remain at rest; a body in motion will remain in motion. The kick is used to put the body in motion.

Elementary Backstroke.   In the elementary backstroke, the arms start with the hands at the sides of the body. Slowly the hands move up the sides of the body to the shoulder; then the wrists rotate outward, allowing the fingers to point away from the body. The arms are fully extended away from the body and at approximately head height. With arms straight, the hands pull down toward the sides of the body.

The stroke is coordinated as follows: Hands come up the sides of the body with feet held straight and together. As the hands begin the outward rotation, the legs bend at the knees, then drop, and the feet rotate out in a whipping action. The legs straighten and come together as the arms are pulled to the sides. The body pauses or rests as it glides, following the stroke. As the momentum decreases, the stroke is repeated.

Back Crawl.   The straight arm is brought out of the water with the palm down. As the arm is lifted through the air, the palm of the hand turns to the outside. The arm reaches as high as possible and is placed in the water directly above the shoulder. Once in the water, the elbow bends toward the bottom of the swimming area as the arm sweeps through the water and pushes through the final phase. Arms rotate with one arm out of the water while the other arm is completing the water phase of the movement. A continuous flutter kick accompanies the arm motion.

Sidestroke.   As a result of the extensive use of the glide, the sidestroke, popular among adults, is considered a resting stroke. The stroke includes a leg scissors kick coordinated with an arm action so that the body remains on its side and the head is held above the water.

A sidestroke is begun with the body on the side, legs straight and together, underarm stretched above the head, and upper arm to the side of the body. The kick begins with the legs together and knees bending; the legs move apart with the top leg forward and the under leg back. Legs are straightened at the knees to form a V in the water, with the top leg forward and the bottom leg back. Legs are brought together, toes are pointed, and the body assumes the original position for the glide. The legs bend, move apart, and squeeze together in the working or power phase of the kick.

The arms begin with the underarm stretched tall beneath the head and the upper arm resting on the side of the body. As the knees bend and the legs come up, the top arm sweeps down into the water to about shoulder level and recovers under water, returning to its original position. The upper arm comes up and in front of the body just below the surface of the water. The hands pass at chest height as they return to their original positions.

Arms and legs start moving at the same time. While the legs are engaged in the work phase, the arms move toward each other. As the legs come together, the arms stretch to their original positions.

Breaststroke.   The arm movement for the breaststroke starts with the body prone and the face floating in the water. The "propulsive action of the arms starts by positioning the hands so that they are angled slightly downward and the palms are turned outward to about a 45-degree angle to the surface of the water" (American Red Cross 1981, 64). The hands and arms are then pressed down as the head comes up for a breath of air.

Fundamental: Lift

Lifts occur in field hockey, dance, gymnastics, and water polo.

Field Hockey

Scoop.   In the field hockey scoop, the ball is picked up by the stick and thrown. The body assumes a ready position of a forward-backward stride with the right foot forward.

Flick.   The field hockey flick is a combination of the push pass and the scoop. The performer is in a ready or stride position with the right foot forward. The ball is picked up by the stick and lifted or forcefully projected forward and into the air. The ball in flight can be dangerous. The direction must be kept low.

Dance

Lifts in dance can be forward or to the side.

Stride Leap.   The stride leap is a large running step. The performer steps and lifts the leaping leg upward into the air in front of the body. The rear leg is extended as the front leg reaches the ground. Various body shapes or poses can be executed to vary the step. They include a stag leap that is a bending of one knee while the body is in the air, and a scissors leap in which the first leg into the air is the first leg back on the floor.

Fundamental: Catch

Catching or collecting is found in basketball, field hockey, soccer, softball, and water polo. The concept of catching or receiving an object is used in many sports. It is called catching in basketball and water polo, and trapping in soccer and field hockey. Catching is receiving an object and absorbing the force of the object. To reduce the chance of an interception, the person catching the object moves toward it for the catch. The passer is to anticipate the movement of the receiver, and place the object where the receiver is expected to be at the time of the catch. Speed and flight of the object, speed of movement of the receiver, and the number and placement of defensive players affect the successful catch. The receiver gives with the hands and arms by flexing the elbows and leaning the torso back to dissipate the force.

Basketball

Catching is a primary skill in basketball. If closely guarded, "the receiver should catch the ball with the palm of one hand under and the palm of the other on top of the ball. This grip enables the offensive player to withstand more easily the force of a slap or to move the ball away from the direction of a slap" (Cooper 1987, 55).

The person throwing needs to know what the receiver is capable of handling from the standpoint of force and placement. Will the receiver be able to pull in a high pass? Can he jump for a pass over his head? Can she catch a ball and bring it down?

Catching may also be intercepting an opponent's pass. Here the receiver leaps into the anticipated path of the thrown ball and attempts to receive it.

Ideally, a ball is caught or intercepted at chest height in front of the body. A ball may, however, be caught while above the head, to either side, or in front of the body. It may also be caught high or low. Also, one may deflect the oncoming pass and put it into a dribble.

Field Hockey

Fielding. Fielding is receiving the ball in field hockey. It is catching the object with an implement. To stop the ball, the performer aligns the body with the path of the oncoming ball and moves to meet the ball. The stick is placed on the ball and moved back toward the body as the force of the ball is absorbed. The performer becomes conscious of angles at this point and attempts to deflect the ball slightly forward in fielding. The speed of the oncoming ball must also be determined. A fast ball requires a greater reach with the stick than a slow ball, as the length of the reach will increase the time the stick has in dissipating the velocity of the ball. Balls are received from the front, back, or sides. The ball, if high in the air, may be stopped by a hand. This action is merely a block and a drop of the ball.

Soccer

Receiving a Ball. Receiving a ball in soccer is like catching, except the foot and leg are used to absorb the force and stop the oncoming ball. The entire body or any segment of the body is employed to absorb force in the stop. As the ball makes contact with a body part, the body gives to absorb the force. The greater the distance over which the object moves, the greater the amount of force dissipated.

To receive a ball, a player needs to determine in which direction the ball is moving, align his or her body in the perceived direction, and move forward to meet the ball. The receiver is balanced to receive the ball. The ball may be stopped by using the foot to wedge the ball against the ground.

Collecting/Stopping/Trapping. Collecting, stopping, or trapping the soccer ball makes use of the entire body, not just the legs and feet. The head, chest, abdomen, or thigh, or inside, outside, or instep of the foot may be used to collect a ball in the air. The body segment selected for the action is moved toward the ball to make contact. The body segment is aligned as close to a ninety-degree angle as possible prior to making the contact to enable contact to be in direct line of the flight of the ball. Immediately upon contact, the body segment is withdrawn so that the ball drops directly to the ground. If the moment of contact is too long, the ball will bounce off the body segment, thus reducing the chance for the performer to obtain and maintain control.

Trapping is another method for stopping the ball. The performer moves into the direct line of flight or roll of the ball, moves forward to meet the ball, uses a body surface to contact the ball, gives with the body to absorb the force of the ball, and controls the ball in play. Ball control has a great deal to do with the performer's understanding of the amount of give or relaxation that must occur in order to bring a particular ball under control.

The ball may be trapped by placing the sole of the foot on top of the ball and bringing the ball to a complete stop. Also, either side of the foot may be used to stop the ball.

Volley. Volleying in soccer is allowing the ball to rebound off body parts. The technique is the same as collecting, with one major change. At the moment of impact, the body part remains firm and the object rebounds off it. Alignment of the body part as the ball comes into contact is important because the ball will rebound at an angle nearly equal to the angle the ball was moving at the time of impact. The performer decides what the angle should be.

Heading. In heading, the performer stands in a balanced or ready position facing the oncoming ball. The body is moved forward to meet the ball with the contact occurring on the forehead. The head is to hit the ball; the ball is not to hit the head. The body continues forward after contact, as a follow-through. It is important that the entire body, especially the neck and shoulders, be maintained in a firm position upon contact and follow-through. As the ball comes toward the performer, the body weight is brought back to the rear foot. The entire body moves forward with the weight shifting to the forward foot and the entire body slanting forward as the head strikes the ball. Neck muscles are to be firm and the chin down upon contact. Headed balls may be directed straight ahead as described or the side of the forehead may be used to head a ball to the side. Soft soccer balls should be used when heading is first introduced.

Softball

Catching the ball in the air and on the ground (fielding) are important to softball. In catching, the performer tracks the ball and assesses the speed and direction of its flight and spins. After determining the path of the ball, the body moves into the path in a ready position. Eyes are focused on the ball. As the ball moves toward the performer, the performer moves forward to meet the ball, shifts the body weight forward, and reaches out to catch the ball. At the moment of contact, the performer moves the arms and hands back to increase the distance in dissipating the force of the ball while moving the entire body back to further absorb the force of the ball. As the ball is caught by the hand that has a glove, effort is made to squeeze the ball and to cover it with the noncatching hand. The follow-through of a catch is a throw.

Fielding.   The fielder moves directly behind the ball, assesses the speed and direction of the ball and the spins and friction caused by the turf over which the ball is moving. The hands, gloved or not, are placed directly in front of the body. The body moves forward to receive the ball and transfers the body weight back immediately upon contact. When the catcher bends low, the forward-backward motion is less than when the catcher is standing.

Fundamental: Turn

Turns are used in nearly all sports and forms of physical activity. A few of the specialized turns are highlighted.

Basketball

Pivots, or the placing of the body weight on the balls of the feet and turning, is often used in basketball.

Skating

Skating turns are easy turns. To turn right, one pushes off the left foot and transfers weight to the right foot, centering the weight of the body over the right foot. To turn left, one pushes off the right foot, transferring and centering weight over the left foot.

Skiing

Telemark Turns.   Telemark position is assumed when the performer bends both knees and centers the body weight directly over the skis. The heel of the forward foot is down and the ball of the rear foot is over the ski, heel up. The rear thigh drops straight down. The downhill hand is held low and back for balance. The uphill hand is pointing downhill pulling the body toward the fall line (Barnett 1983, 38).

Telemark position in movement is, on occasion, compared to bicycling. The turning of the bicycle is determined by the two wheels; the turn of a telemark is determined by the front and back legs and feet. In the turn, position must be held, with the front foot and hands used to turn the skier.

A telemark turn is executed by moving the rear ski forward in front of the front ski. The edges of the skis are flattened. The body is moving in the direction of the new turn. The arm of the forward moving foot comes forward as the body turns.

Downhill Turns.   Two types of downhill turns are popular—stem and parallel. To execute a stem turn, a performer starts with skis parallel. One ski is moved into a V by placing the body weight on the inside edge of the ski. The toe of the ski is pointed in the direction the performer wishes to move.

Most of the body weight is transferred to the ski that has been put in the V or that is making the turn. Near the completion of the turn, the other ski is brought alongside the first ski and body weight is balanced between the two skis.

In parallel skiing, skis are fairly close together, edge control is on the same edge for both feet, and body weight is evenly distributed over both feet. The turn is executed by changing the direction and edging of both feet at the same time. To move both feet at once, there needs to be a moment of unweighting, described by Sanders (1979, 16) as "a quick hop upward, a quick bend of the knees to drop the seat downwards, or by skiing over rough terrain."

The turn is finished with a skid that is controlled by the amount of edge placed on the skis. Carving, a second method of control, occurs when the skier travels in the direction the skis are pointing without slipping to the side. Carving usually makes a larger turn than other methods of turning.

The principle of stability is primary in skiing. Up-down balance or un-weighting permits the performer to lose balance in order to change directions. The stable position, following unweighting, allows the performer the opportunity to use the force of the body to skid or to carve a turn or to bring the body to a stop.

The arms and poles play a roll in turning. They are held in front and to the side of the body. The primary purpose of the ski pole is to maintain balance when unweighting. Usually the downhill pole is planted a foot or more ahead of the feet. For slow radius or short turns, the pole is planted close to the feet. The upper body and shoulders should remain forward and not be affected by the pole plant. The body unweights at the time of pole plant. The body returns to stable position with the poles following through in a natural sequence. No effort is required to remove the pole from the planting position.

Skiing involves a series of turns, one to the left and the next one to the right, as the performer moves down the hill.

Fundamental: Roll

Rolls may be forward, backward, or from side to side. They may be executed in the tuck, pike, or extended positions.

Gymnastics

Forward Roll.   In the forward roll, the body is flexed or bunched with the feet and knees together and the hands shoulder width apart. Carpenter (1985, 73) recommends that the performer lifts his or her hips by straightening the knees as the head is brought to the chest. The arms lower the back of the head (not the top) and the shoulders to the mat.

The performer's arms reach forward as soon as the shoulders lift from the floor. The performer's weight is shifted forward to the feet to arrive at the starting position.

Forward rolls may be completed with any one of a number of positions or poses. They may also be modified to start with a close tuck, a straddle, or an arabesque.

Backward Roll.   The backward roll begins with a squat to the ground, with feet together. The body is kept in a ball by holding the chin on the chest during the roll. The performer moves backward, with the hips hitting the mat first, followed by the middle of the back. As the back contacts the mat, the hands are placed on the mat near the ears, with thumbs toward the ears. The feet come over the head as the hands push. The body weight shifts to the feet, and the performer is in a balanced squat position ready to stand.

The backward roll may be adapted to finish in a straddle or half-straddle position. It may also be started in a straddle position.

Fundamental: Strike

Striking occurs in field hockey, soccer, and softball. The hockey stick contacts the ball in field hockey whereas the foot plays a similar role in soccer. Both sports require that performers be able to assess the direction and speed of the ball and be able to align their bodies behind or alongside the ball, thus enabling them to engage in continuous play. The ball is stopped and stroked in a particular direction. Most of the time the ball will have to be received or controlled prior to being directed.

Softball

The fundamental strike is the basis for the specialized skill of batting in softball. The bat grip is a firm handshake grip, with the hands close together; the dominant hand is on top. The size of the bat enables the performer to spread the fingers slightly apart.

To receive the pitch, the performer aligns the side of the body with the side of home base in one of three stances: square, open, or closed. In a square stance, the feet are parallel with the plate; in an open stance, the foot nearest the pitcher is back (see figure 7-2); in a closed stance, the foot farthest from the pitcher is back.

In batting, the performer assumes a position with feet shoulder width or more apart and knees slightly bent. The bat is held at shoulder height, away from and to the rear of the body. The performer steps forward, turning the hips toward the ball as the swing starts. The bat is swung through the ball with the body moving forward as contact is made. The follow-through takes the bat to the opposite side of the body. Head position should be stable throughout the action.

▶ Patterns in Specialized Skills

Patterns include three distinct throwing patterns, two jumping patterns, and two types of runs. The throwing patterns are the overarm, sidearm, and underarm throws. Runs are either distance or sprint; jumps, either vertical or horizontal.

Pattern: Throw

Throwing patterns occur in aquatics, badminton, basketball, bowling, field hockey, golf, racquetball, softball, table tennis, tennis, volleyball, and water polo. An activity may require only one throwing pattern or all three throwing patterns. Aquatics, for example, requires the use of only one pattern, the overarm throw, whereas the participants in badminton, basketball, softball, tennis, and volleyball employ all three patterns.

Throwing patterns are used to accomplish four distinct types of movement. First, they may be for a body action that conveys meaning in dance or moves the performer through the water. A second use may be to project an object, such as a ball, in a desired direction. Usually an object placed in the hand is thrown with the hand releasing the object at the time of greatest momentum and optimum angle of release.

Third, a body limb may be used as an implement to strike an object. In volleyball, for example, the player's hand, wrist, and arm become the implements used in striking. Fourth, an implement as an extension of the arm and hand may be used in striking an object. Tennis and badminton are examples of the fourth application. Throwing patterns that require the gripping of an object to be projected or the gripping of an implement for striking are addressed next. A discussion of striking follows.

Gripping an Object

A number of activities employ a pattern of throwing in which an object, resting in the performer's hand, is projected into space. The object may be gripped by the hand or hands with the muscles of the hand supporting the weight of the object, or by the fingers with the fingers supporting the weight and controlling the object. In softball, control of the ball is maintained by gripping the ball with the fingers, usually the thumb and two or three fingers. The number of fingers is related to the performer's size. The fingers are placed across the seam of the softball; the thumb is placed on the opposite side. Grasping the ball in the fingers frees the hand to employ a wrist snap in throwing. Wrist snaps are used to impart spin on the object or ball.

The basketball is gripped with the fingers or with the fingers and the palms of the hands in throwing. Fingers are used to project the ball short distances whereas the fingers and palms of the hands are used in long distance throws. In water polo, the performer places one hand under the ball, lifts it to clear the water, and moves into the throwing pattern. If possible, the ball is grasped with the fingers.

The bowling ball grip is unique in that in tenpin bowling, the fingers are placed into holes in the ball. The dominant hand is used; fingers are placed in the holes with the ball resting in the palm of the hand. Fingers of the nondominant hand are placed beneath the bowling ball for balance. The higher the position used in holding the ball, the greater the effect of gravity on the ball.

Gripping an Implement as an Extension of the Body

Badminton, fencing, field hockey, golf, racquetball, table tennis, and tennis use racquets, paddles, clubs, or sticks as aim extensions that must be gripped. With the exceptions of field hockey and golf, there is a degree of similarity among the grips in these sports, particularly among the grips recommended for beginners. The three universal grips—eastern, continental, and western— are used at all levels in tennis, racquetball, and badminton. Equipment may be gripped by the fingers or by the whole hand. Generally the heavy tennis racquet is gripped in the hand, and the light badminton racquet is gripped in the fingers, with emphasis on the forefinger and thumb.

Eastern Grip.　The eastern grip, often referred to as the handshake grip, is the easiest for beginners to acquire and the one most often used in tennis. While a teammate is holding the racquet by the head, the performer shakes hands with the grip of the racquet. The fingers are wrapped around the handle and spread comfortably as the grip is tightened. The V formed by the thumb and first finger is over the flat part of the handle (figure 7-5). The object is to hit the ball with a racquet face that is near vertical, thus enabling the performer to meet the ball squarely.

The eastern backhand grip requires that the fingers be rotated from a forehand grip one-eighth turn toward the midline of the body. The racquet face remains perpendicular with the surface of the court as the stroke is executed; contact is made with a vertical racquet. Eastern grips are most valuable in games where there is adequate time to change grips from forehand to backhand. Racquetball players often use the eastern forehand and backhand grips in learning the game.

Continental Grip.　As players improve and find that their opponents allow them far less time to change grips, they usually move to a continental grip and play all balls with the same grip. Some net play in tennis and many advanced skills in racquetball demand a switch to the continental grip. As the pace of play increases, performers do not have adequate time to change grips.

The continental grip requires a one-eighth turn toward the midline of the body from the position used in the eastern grip. The hand is placed on top of the racquet, thus opening the racquet face slightly (see figure 7-6).

▼ **Figure 7-5**
Eastern grip: Right and left hand grips. Photos by Lynn Howell, Cleveland, Ohio.

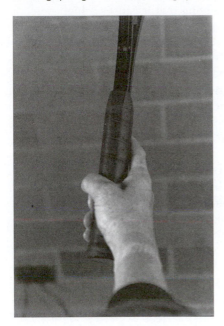
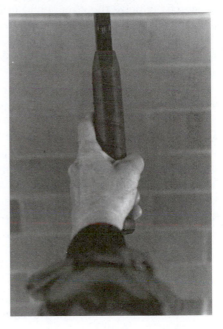

▼ **Figure 7-6**
Continental grip: Left and right hand grips. Photos by Lynn Howell, Cleveland, Ohio.

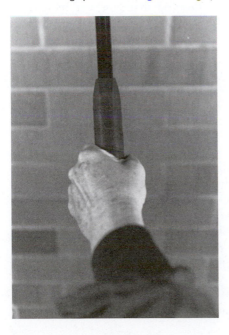
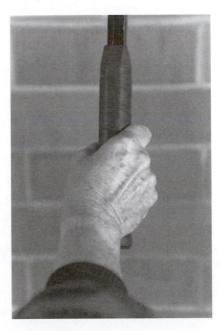

Because this grip is used for both backhand and forehand strokes, it is no longer necessary to change grips. A number of contemporary teaching professionals criticize the continental grip, saying that it causes a high percentage of errors and that these errors occur most often in hitting balls above waist height. In spite of the criticism, many top-ranked British and Australian tennis players have used the continental grip successfully. Today it is most often used on faster surfaces.

The continental grip is a popular grip for the serve because it permits a greater range of wrist action allowing for a variety of strokes. Murphy and Murphy (1975) suggest that in tennis the beginning performer start with the eastern grip on the serve and move to the continental grip as the serve reaches an intermediate level. Changes in the serve, from a flat to a twist, are also the result of grip change. The ball toss and the overarm throw racquet swing usually remain the same, while the contact between the racquet and the hand on the grip create the various spins and changes of ball flight. Tennis players are advised to use an eastern grip for forehand and backhand strokes and a continental grip for net play, volleys, overheads, lobs, drops, and serves.

Western Grip.   The third grip is the western grip, executed by turning the hand on the racquet from the continental grip another one-eighth turn toward the midline of the body. The racquet is placed in the palm of the hand with the fingers spread tightly over the racquet handle. The palm is behind the racquet as the racquet swings forward. When the ball bounces high, as occurs on clay courts, the grip enables the performer to make an easy contact; when the ball bounces low, the grip makes it extremely difficult for the performer to return a shot. The advantage of the western grip is the amount of top spin that can be placed on the ball.

Effect of Equipment Size, Shape, and Weight on Common Grips

Tennis racquets are fairly heavy. The distance that the object must travel is great and the object hit is heavy. Therefore, the grip is firm, very firm at contact, and provisions are made between strokes for the racquet to rest in the nondominant hand so that the player may relax and prepare for the next stroke.

Badminton racquets are much smaller and of lighter weight than tennis racquets; however, they possess a fairly long shaft. The lighter racquet enables the performer to use wrist action to increase the distance through which force is applied. Badminton players usually learn the continental grip first. They use the grip because it not only facilitates wrist action but allows them to control the racquet with their fingers rather than with the palm of the hand and the fingers. The finger control increases the player's ability to execute a wrist snap.

Badminton grips may be changed from forehand to backhand as described earlier. Badminton also employs a frying pan or panhandled grip that is used for playing close to the net. The performer grips the racquet just as he or she would a frying pan. The grip allows the performer to stroke on either side of the body.

Racquetball players employ the eastern, continental, and western grips. Although they are encouraged to use an eastern grip, they are also taught to control the racquet in their fingers. Allowing a little distance between the first and second fingers is recommended for the best position on the racquet. Many racquetball players use the eastern forehand grip for all strokes because most of the returns are forehand shots. The forehand is favored for drives, serves, and volleys. This is in contrast to tennis, where the performer moves to a continental grip for those strokes.

Table Tennis Grips.   Table tennis players grip the paddle so that they have control of the implement but hold it sufficiently loose to maintain maximum wrist control. A number of styles are used in holding the paddle; the horizontal attack, horizontal defense, and vertical defense are pictured in figures 7-7, 7-8, and 7-9.

The table tennis grip referred to as the penholder grip places the paddle handle between the thumb and index finger with the remaining three fingers used to support the paddle. Grips are changed for forehand and backhand strokes, or one grip is used for both strokes. When only one grip is used for backhand and forehand, only one paddle face is involved; the same side of the paddle strokes balls on both sides of the body. This is possible because all strokes are executed in front of the body; such form is not possible if the body rotates a quarter turn prior to striking the ball.

▼ **Figure 7-7**
Horizontal attack in table tennis. Photos by Lynn Howell, Cleveland, Ohio.

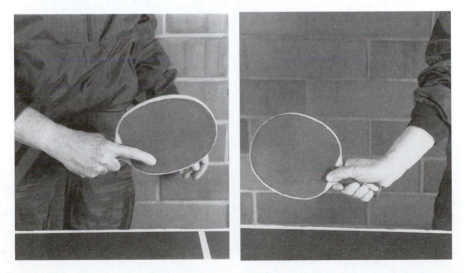

▼ **Figure 7-8**

Horizontal defense in table tennis. Photos by Lynn Howell, Cleveland, Ohio.

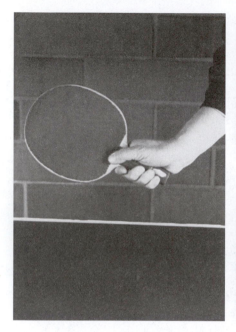

▶ **Figure 7-9**

Vertical defense in table tennis. Photo by Lynn Howell, Cleveland, Ohio.

Field Hockey, Fencing, and Golf Grips.   Field hockey, fencing, and golf require grips unique to the equipment. A hockey stick is flat on one side and round on the other. The rules permit only the flat side of the stick to be used in moving the ball. A player holds the stick in the right hand with the flat side of the stick facing left. (There is no such thing as a left-handed or left-sided stick. It is perceived by experts that the nature of the stroke enables the left-handed person to do as well as the right-handed person.) The performer places the left hand at the top of the stick and shakes hands with it. The right hand is placed below the left hand on the stick with the fingers wrapped around the stick. "The lower the right hand is placed, the more control the player has over the stick; the higher the hand is placed, the more natural is the running position for the body" (Barnes and Kentwell 1979, 11).

In fencing, the proper (right or left) French foil is held in the dominant hand with the wider side on the top and bottom. Foil grips differ for right- and left-handed fencers. The last joint of the thumb is placed on top, one-half inch from the guard. The second joint of the forefinger is placed on the bottom of the handle in opposition to the thumb. The thumb and forefinger guide and control the foil with the rest of the fingers gripping the foil. The hand is then rotated so that the knuckle of the thumb is at two o'clock (Bowers 1985, 16). The grip is light and firm so that it can be manipulated as rapidly as possible.

Golfers may use three different grips: interlocking, overlapping, or baseball. "The variations in the three grips relate to the way your two hands contact each other on the club handle. With the baseball grip, all eight fingers are wrapped around the club handle, with the index finger of one hand merely touching the little finger of the other hand. The interlock grip is named because the index finger of one hand interlocks with the little finger of the other hand, thus neither finger is actually in direct contact with the club. The overlap grip gets its name because the little finger of one hand overlaps the index finger of the other hand" (Ewers 1989, 18). The importance of the grip is noted by Bunker and Owens (1984, 17) in stating that "rotating your hands as little as one quarter inch can cause the face to open enough for a 40 yard slice!"

Striking with the Body as the Implement

Striking may occur with the body used as the striking implement. In volleyball, the hands, wrists, and lower arms are the striking implement. A volleyball player may use an open or a closed hand position in striking. An open hand is often used by the server who wishes to gain control rather than to use maximum force. Greater control is obtained by permitting the fingers to direct the ball to a specific location or to place a spin on the ball. A closed hand position enables the performer to place greater force on the ball. Volleyball players usually use the closed hand position when contacting a low ball. Low one-handed strikes may be combined with a dive and roll.

Volleyball rules permit the ball to make contact with the hand, wrist, or arm. Two-handed contacts are preferred in volleyball because of the need for maximum force and distance. The large court and heavy ball sometimes require the force of the entire body to move the ball the length of the court. The weight of the ball also demands considerable force to redirect the flight of the ball and return it with the speed essential to score. Volleyball players usually use their entire bodies or two hands in play because they have adequate time to get into position. The size of the volleyball court and the number of players provides time for the performers to determine where the ball will be and to align the body directly behind the ball.

Volleyball players make two-handed contacts with both the open and closed hand positions. All overhand passes and sets are made in the open position, with the hands held above the wrists at shoulder height in front of the body. The fingers and palms of the hand form a cup. As contact occurs, effort is made to avoid holding the ball in the cup. The object is to strike rather than to absorb the force of the ball. The set may be made from a low or a high position, and the pass may be made in any direction. In the back set, for example, the hands make contact with the ball as the player's back is rapidly arched so that the ball will continue on over the player's head to the person receiving the set.

Pattern: Overarm Throw

The overarm throw pattern is probably the most heavily researched movement of all the fundamentals, combinations, and patterns. Although it may not appear as often in sport as do certain other fundamentals and patterns, it is by far the most complex movement. Atwater (1967), Broer (1971), Wickstrom (1983), and others have discussed the commonalities of the overarm throw in sport skills.

Aquatics

Front Crawl Overarm Throw.   An overarm throw pattern, without the rotation for projecting an object, is the swimming crawl arm stroke or body movement that occurs above the surface of the water. The prone body position causes the performer to lift the elbow out of the water. The lower arm follows above the surface of the water as the arm extends. The hand is placed in the water and pulls back under the long axis of the body, creating an action-reaction of the water and the body. As the arm pulls down the vertical axis of the body beneath the surface of the water, the water forces the body to move forward. The arm recovers near the waist and repeats the modified overarm throw. As one arm is pulling through the water, the other arm lifts the elbow out of the water and reaches forward. The flutter kick and a breathing system, employing a turn of the head to catch a breath of air each time the elbow lifts on the selected side, completes the front crawl.

Overarm Throw of Projected Object

The overarm throw pattern is used to project a handheld object in basketball, water polo, and softball.

Basketball Overarm Pass.   The overarm basketball pass is the overarm throw pattern without modifications. As basketballs are heavy and difficult to control in this pattern, the pass is used only for long distances such as the length of the court. The pass is usually used when the performer is in the open—not heavily guarded—and has sufficient space to execute the throw.

Water Polo Overarm Pass and Shot.   Water polo uses the overarm throw in the forehand and layout passes and in the forehand and skip shots. The forehand pass and shot and the skip shot are executed while the body is either treading water or using the eggbeater kick, and when the passer is clear to face the goal. The overarm pass is a fast and accurate pass aimed just over the heads of the opponents. To pass in water polo, the performer places the hands under the ball, lifts the ball to clear the water, and brings the ball behind the head. The performer either passes or presses down hard on the ball so it will bounce from the surface of the water to the receiver. The overarm shot is aimed toward any one of the four corners of the goal. The skip shot is a powerful overarm throw in which the ball is targeted to bounce off the surface of the water into the goal.

The water polo layout pass differs from other passes because it is a ball thrown just as the swimmer moves onto his or her back. "To make a layout pass while dribbling the ball, the ball carrier rolls onto his back while pushing the ball ahead to keep it at an arm's length away. As the roll to the back is completed the ball is picked up from below and thrown in one continuous motion" (Cicciarella 1981, 14).

Basketball and water polo basket shooting may employ the overarm throw; however, analysis of most passes and shots in both sports suggests they are pushes rather than throws.

Softball Overarm Throw.   In softball, the overarm throw is used in throws for distance and speed. It is frequently used in throws from the outfield, from the shortstop, and from third to first base. The softball overarm throw is the throw described in chapter 6. In softball, as in basketball and water polo, the throw has a target, so the performer eyes the target and steps in the direction of the target as he or she executes the throw. The performer assesses the distance to the receiver and determines the amount of force that is used. The following is a checklist, taken from Potter and Brockmeyer (1989), for analyzing the throw.

Overarm Throw with the Body as the Implement—Striking

Throwing is a less difficult skill to acquire than striking; therefore, the performer should be able to throw the ball accurately and successfully before learning to strike. There are two types of striking. The object to be struck may be tossed by the performer or the performer may be about to make contact with an object that has been driven by another player or moving object, or has rebounded from a wall or stationary object. Success in striking requires that the performer be able to sense the position and speed of

▼ **TABLE 7-3**

Checklist for analyzing the throw

PREPARATION PHASE

THE THROWER'S

_____ grip on the ball is with two fingers across one seam, and the thumb on the opposite side of ball on a seam.

_____ feet are in staggered stride, the throwing side foot back.

_____ weight is on back foot.

_____ glove side is toward throwing target.

_____ arms are both extended, glove is pointed at target, and ball hand is away from target wrist cocked . . .

EXECUTION PHASE

THE THROWER

_____ steps in direction of throwing target with glove-side foot.

_____ starts ball forward by leading with throwing side elbow.

_____ makes sure ball hand trails elbow until shoulders are square to throwing target.

_____ forcefully rotates throwing-side forearm forward toward target, passing through vertical.

_____ keeps wrist cocked and the throwing hand and elbow high, the ball passing by the head.

_____ forces body weight forward by driving off back foot.

_____ has fingers directly behind ball, snaps wrist and releases ball toward target.

_____ has glove hand low.

FOLLOW-THROUGH PHASE

THE THROWER

_____ takes full weight on glove-side foot.

_____ drives throwing-side shoulder forward and down.

_____ brings throwing hand down past glove-side knee.

_____ brings throwing-side foot forward and shifts weight into balanced position.

Note: From *Softball: Steps to Success* (pp. 28-29) by D. L. Potter and G. A. Brockmeyer, 1989, Champaign, IL: Leisure Press. Copyright 1989 by Leisure Press. Reprinted by permission.

either a tossed ball or a ball that is traveling through the air after being hit by an opponent or following a rebound from a wall. The performer's body is aligned behind the moving object. Ability to sense the speed and direction of such an object is a prerequisite to making successful striking contact.

Incoming Flight of Object in Striking

Another factor to consider when preparing to strike is the flight of the object about to be contacted. Is the object on its way up in flight? Has the object just reached the spot at which the projected force of the object is equal to gravity (often referred to as the dead spot)? Or is the object on its way down? Objects on the way up tend to continue in an upward flight after contact; objects on the way down tend to continue the downward flight after contact; and objects at the dead spot are influenced only by the direction of the force at the time of contact. Performers about to strike an object should consider:

1. direction and speed of current object flight
2. desired direction and speed of object's flight after projection

Volleyball.   In volleyball, the hand, moving in an overarm throw pattern, becomes the striking implement. Contact with the object usually occurs as the striking arm and hand reach their greatest height in the pattern and the object to be contacted is immediately above or slightly in front of the body. When the ball is to be contacted above the head and the desired trajectory is either straight for distance or a downward flight, the overarm throw pattern is emphasized. Volleyball players use the overarm throw in the serve and in the spike.

When the goal in the overarm throw pattern is to strike the object as hard as possible with a downward trajectory, a wrist snap is executed at the moment of contact. To gain height prior to forcing the ball down, the volleyball spiker will take a jump prior to the strike, thus forcing her or his entire body weight down on the ball. When the goal is to project a lengthy downward flight, the performer strikes the object with a forward stroke rather than a downward stroke and eliminates or reduces the wrist snap. Contacts are controlled and executed in the direction of the desired flight of the object.

Performers executing a volleyball serve will usually strike the ball straight forward, placing no downward direction on the ball, to ensure that the ball will clear the net. In fact, volleyball players will extend the arm upward but will avoid using a complete extension (see figure 7-10). Softball players, using the same movement, will throw a ball with an upward flight in order to achieve the distance desired. Volleyball players should also consider the force required to achieve the desired arc of flight. The desired flight will dictate the point at which contact is made and the direction of flight given the object. Moment of contact is the same as moment of release and is to be viewed accordingly by striking performers.

▶ **Figure 7-10**
Overhand volleyball
serve. Photos by Lynn
Howell, Cleveland, Ohio.

Volleyball players use the overarm throw pattern most effectively in the serve called the floater. The floater is a soft, straight, forward contact with the ball. The ball merely floats; contact is momentary. Volleyball players also employ the overhand spin, which results in a fast-dropping ball. An open hand contact or a wrist snap can be used to apply the spin. The same open hand contact or wrist snap can be used to place a spin on an overhead stroke near the net. If the objective is to direct the ball by spin rather than by smash, an open hand will be used. (See the discussion of spin in chapter 11.)

Striking with a Paddle or Racquet. Once a racquet is placed in the performer's hand, the overarm throw pattern becomes an important skill. It influences the serve in tennis and all overhead position play in racquet sports. Whenever a performer wishes to hit the ball down as rapidly as possible, it becomes the best method. In situations where downward flight is preferred, a player may rush forward toward the net or the wall to hit the object while it is above the head so that he or she has the opportunity for the downward flight.

In the overarm throw pattern, there is a tendency for the person throwing or striking to hit the object in a downward fashion as the distance is reduced. The action, the strength of the movement, and the pattern remain the same until the final thrust. In the final thrust, the force is applied downward as it occurs in a volleyball spike or a tennis smash.

When the player wishes to make contact with an object that is above the head and shoulders, the overarm pattern becomes a natural. In a number of cases the overarm spike and the overarm serve draw upon the same pattern; however, the movement of the body prior to striking differs considerably. The full swing learned in the stationary position or the position of serve is now shortened and executed as the performer moves into position for contact. The performer no longer has the luxury of tossing the ball to the ideal location; she or he must be capable of assessing the location of the object and of moving the body into the best position for contact.

If a performer is hitting a self-tossed object, she or he must execute an efficient toss and be able to provide a toss that can be controlled. If the overarm throw is to be used in a smash, the performer moves so that the object is directly above his or her body at the time of execution. The location for contact in an overhead smash and an overhead serve are the same; body positioning for an overhead smash and for an overhead serve differ. The body can be moved into position for the smash, whereas the server's toss accommodates the location of the body.

The smash is a popular overhead stroke in tennis and racquetball; the ceiling shot is used in racquetball. In these skills, the performer is able to read the flight of the oncoming ball and to sense the elements of weight transfer and follow-through. Badminton makes use of a modified overarm throw, which is nearly a sidearm throw, in the round-the-head stroke and a regular overarm throw in the overhead clear.

The volleyball serve and spike require a common overarm throw pattern; however, the volleyball serve from the baseline includes a weight transfer and a tossed ball, whereas the spike from the net is often executed following one or two steps and a jump to meet a ball traveling toward the performer at a high rate of speed. The volleyball server directs the ball forward while the spiker directs it downward. A volleyball overhand shot from midcourt will cause the performer to make use of a combination of a forward and a downward application of force. This discussion is also applicable to the tennis serve and the smash at the net. In light of the fact that the tennis net is close to the ground, there is no longer a need for a two-step approach and jump prior to contact.

Once a successful overhead stroke has been acquired, it must be tailored to the situation. Where do you want the object to land? Should it be driven down as fast as possible, as in a tennis smash? Should it be driven with a little less force and considerable wrist snap, as in a badminton smash? Should it be hit softly and forward, as in a volleyball floater serve? Should it be hit hard forward, as in a racquetball stroke? Contact, whether it includes wrist snap or downward force of the racquet arm, dictates where the object moves. On occasion, effort will be made to camouflage contact to the opponent. Movement of the body and racquet after contact is in the direction of the placement.

Badminton players are adept at camouflage by executing the clear, drop, and the smash in the same manner so that the opponent is not able to distinguish the selected stroke until the shuttle is hit.

Equipment as an Extension of the Arm.   The use of a racquet as an extension of the arm alters the overarm throw in a number of ways. When the arm is extended with a racquet, the timing of the stroke contact must be altered to allow for the arm extension or distance. The player visualizes a ball tossed so that it is at the middle of the racquet face when the extended arm and racquet are about to make contact.

In volleyball, the ball is tossed so that the optimum time for contact occurs at the height of the body's extension; the optimum time for contact in the tennis serve is the same. The difference between the volleyball and the tennis serve is the length of the tennis racquet. The length of the tennis racquet requires the performer to account for the racquet length in adjusting for the ideal point at which ball contact is to be made.

Pattern: Sidearm Throw

The sidearm throw pattern is used in badminton, basketball, field hockey, golf, racquetball, softball, table tennis, tennis, and volleyball. Softball and basketball use the sidearm throw basic pattern. The sidearm throw pattern is found in all forearm racquet sports strokes, and a modification of that pattern on the nondominant side is used for backhand strokes. It is also the stroke most often used in volleys, chops, and drop shots. The movement may be a throw, a strike with a part of the body used as the implement, or a strike where the body grips an implement.

The sidearm is used in self-dominated movements in dance. It is used, on occasion, as an implement in volleyball. The sidearm stroke in volleyball is usually a desperation shot and is often accompanied by a dive and roll. The sidearm pattern is popular in throwing activities and as a means of extending the arm in racquet and paddle activities.

Softball
The sidearm throw in softball is a basic pattern. It is used for quick releases, usually in the infield. It is used more often with advanced players because it is a difficult skill to acquire and thus less accurate than the overarm throw.

Water Polo
The water polo roundhouse shot is a sidearm throw in which the body rotates to face the goal and is extended throughout the throw and follow-through. It is used close to the goal.

Racquet as an Extension of the Arm in Sidearm Pattern
All racquet and paddle sports—badminton, tennis, table tennis, and racquetball—use the sidearm pattern as a primary skill in game play. Racquetball and table tennis also use the pattern for certain types of serves.

The movement in the overarm throw was in a forward-backward plane; the sidearm throw pattern is in a side-to-side plane or a side rotation. The movement is initiated with the side of the body to the wall or net. A swing is taken one-quarter or more distance back, usually straight back with no loop, with the racquet or paddle facing parallel to the playing surface. Performers bring the racquet back as far as possible on the dominant side (see figure 7-11). A higher backswing loop is often added when the racquet is lightweight.

Most racquetball and badminton players use a backswing loop; however, it is not uncommon to find such a loop in a tennis player's repertoire. The feet are usually placed shoulder width apart. The playing object is contacted at the midpoint of the body or off the forward foot. As the performer becomes more advanced he or she may alter grips, stance, and distance of follow-through in order to vary strokes. Most players, using strung racquets and balls, will also use wrist action to place spin on the ball. Paddles tend to prohibit the application of spin unless the performer can control the paddle with the fingers.

When the performer wishes to stroke an object on the nondominant side of the body, or backhand, he or she turns to the opposite side of the

▼ **Figure 7-11**

Tennis forehand drive. Photos by Lynn Howell, Cleveland, Ohio.

playing area and executes the swing exactly the way he or she executed the forehand. If the performer is using an eastern grip, the grip can be changed to a backhand grip by turning the hand a quarter turn toward the body. If the performer is using a continental grip, there is no need to change the grip.

The two-hand backhand in tennis, a sidearm stroke on the nondominant side of the body, is similar to batting in softball. Both hands are placed on the implement. The implement is drawn back on the nondominant side. Body weight is rotated or thrust forward just before the arm swing occurs. Both hands grip the racquet in the follow-through, much as they would retain contact with a bat.

The sidearm stroke may be used as a serve or as a means of beginning informal play. The stroke may begin with the object being bounced to the floor and the stroke executed on the bouncing object. At other times, the performer will be expected to contact an oncoming object. The performer will be required to assess the position of the ball or object in relation to body position. Assessment will need to be made as to whether the oncoming force will be with the performer, as in racquetball, or in opposition to the performer, as in most other sports. In situations where something other than maximum force is dictated for a successful return, the performer will decrease the swing, face the net to decrease body rotation, and bend the elbow, thus decreasing the effort of the back, neck, and shoulder muscles.

Some sports will require reading the bounce from the playing surface, and others will require a sense of object trajectory and flight.

Pattern: Underarm Throw

An underarm throw pattern exists in specialized skills in badminton, basketball, bowling, racquetball, softball, tennis, and volleyball. Basketball and softball use the underarm throw pattern with no modifications. In basketball it is used as a handoff, an infrequently used skill. In softball, underarm throws are used in pitching and for throws while a person is running or moving toward a target. It is the recommended skill for use in instruction and for use in the infield where the performer is moving toward a target. The underarm throw pattern is used frequently in volleyball and racquet sports. It is often used as a lob and is emphasized in badminton and volleyball as a serve. The height of the net coupled with a lightweight shuttle and a rule that demands that the racquet head be below the player's wrist requires an underhand serve in badminton. The goal of the lob, whether it be a serve or a stroke, is to hit the object as far into the back court as the size of the court permits.

Objects in the air to be struck by an underarm stroke are often those that have moved very low and are about to be saved. Only when the game dictates that a lob will be the best stroke do most sport players permit the object to move so low that only an underhand stroke can be used. The purpose of a lob is to move the object high into the air to avoid a net or close players.

Volleyball makes use of the underarm stroke in a unique fashion by combining the two arms as a single implement and by executing the underarm pattern in front of the body. Because the arms are in front of the body, the force for the underarm action is created by bending the knees and lowering the body. It is a total body action.

The volleyball forearm pass is one of the basic volleyball skills. It is used to receive a serve, to dig the opponents' spikes, to set the ball to a teammate, or as a bump in desperation to get the ball over the net. Underhand passes or digs make use of both hands so that the hands combine to make one instrument for applying force. The ball is not played with open hands in the underhand position. Although there is no rule to that effect, most officials believe that the ball cannot be clearly hit using an open hand. Underhand passes are executed with a clenched fist, with both thumbs on top, or with curled fingers. The clenched fist is the most popular.

When receiving a serve, the body must be aligned directly behind the anticipated flight of the object. The body is held in a stride position with feet shoulder width apart and with one foot slightly ahead of the other in order to give forward direction at the moment of contact (see figure 7-12). Direction and speed of the ball will create a situation in which the performer is forced to make body adjustments.

▶ **Figure 7-12**

Volleyball forearm pass.
Photos by Lynn Howell,
Cleveland, Ohio.

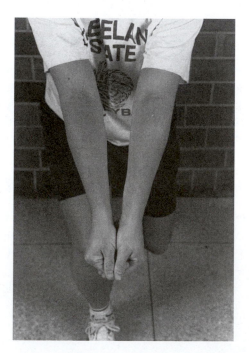

Bowling—The Four-Step Approach

The four-step approach, a combination of walk and underarm throw, is a series of steps taken in a straight line that allows the performer to gain momentum prior to delivery. The performer starts by facing the bowling pins squarely. Eyes are fixed on the pins or on a target in the alley. The distance required for the approach is paced off so that the performer can determine where to start the steps. Martin, Tandy, and Agne-Traub (1986, 16) note that "(1) speed is not the essential factor, (2) you are going to progress at a moderate pace rather than 'charge' toward the foul line, and (3) you will prepare to 'roll' the ball instead of 'throwing' it." The performer steps forward on the foot on the dominant side and at the same time brings the ball forward and down to the dominant side of the body for the backswing of an underarm throw. Gravity assists the body in bringing the ball down. The maximum use of gravity and the heavy ball increase ball velocity. As the next step of the foot on the nondominant side of the body occurs, the ball is brought back and down in the backswing. On the third step, the backswing is completed. The fourth step includes a slide, as the dominant hand swings forward in the underarm throw and releases the ball. Follow-through occurs as the throwing hand moves up toward the head. The velocity acquired by the body in the approach is transferred to the ball in the swing and release.

Pattern: Run

There are two types of running—distance and sprint. Running is used in basketball, dance, fencing, field hockey, gymnastics, ice skating, soccer, softball, tennis, track, and volleyball. Water polo replaces running with a flutter kick for use in mobility as the performer moves around the pool. The large playing areas of soccer and field hockey demand longer periods of running that are classified, along with track, as distance running. Dance, gymnastics, fencing, soccer, field hockey, basketball, softball, and tennis require considerable sprint running. Players are expected to move rapidly to advance the playing object or to gain a desired position prior to receiving the playing object from another person. Field hockey requires a high level of comfort in running with an implement, the stick. Adrian and Cooper (1989, 602) note that in field hockey, "the performer must learn to use the same mechanics as do sprinters, with the exception that the performer runs under control, at about 80 percent maximum speed. This control is necessary because it enables the player to change direction, using maximum agility in response to movements of other players and the ball."

Softball uses sprint running to achieve maximum speed in the short distance from one base to the next. Run of a sprint nature is also found in dance, gymnastics, and in various track events. Sprints used in dance and gymnastics usually consist of a number of steps executed prior to a stunt, a leap, or some other movement. The only distance or sprint run that requires a specific start is the track start. Fencing movements, rapid forward and backward, are of such short duration that they may be called a sprint.

Start for Run

The purpose of the start is to attain optimum acceleration in the beginning or to run out of the blocks at full speed. Inertia is overcome by causing the body to apply maximum force against the blocks. The distance between blocks determines the type of start: bunch, or feet close together (about 11 inches); medium, or feet about 16 inches apart; and elongated, or feet about 26 inches apart. The greater the distance between the blocks, the greater the need for an application of force. The greater the potential for application of force, the greater the strength needed to apply the force. Therefore, the bunch or medium starts are the ones most often used.

Set Position

Blocks are placed so that the athlete has a 90-degree angle at the front of the knee and a 110 to 120-degree angle in the back of the knee. This results in a position with hips slightly higher than the shoulders (see figure 7-13).

In the start, hands are placed in front of the body, slightly wider than shoulder width apart. Fingers and thumbs are in a high bridge position; shoulders are above and slightly ahead of the hands. Arms are straight.

For good starts, a sprinter must:

1. cue on moving the hands and arms as quickly as possible in reaction to the gun
2. push back against the blocks
3. drive out; the direction of applied force should be out and up, not up and out; that is, the athlete should move the hips quickly from the starting position to a running position
4. run out of the blocks; do not jump out (Gambetta 1981, 60)

As the performer's speed improves, greater attention is given to the use of the arms. The strength of the arms in the movement will serve to increase the speed of the run and relax the body. Arm strokes are vigorous and rapid. Upper and lower arms form a right angle to one another, and arms move backward and forward in opposition and in line with the direction that the runner is moving.

Runners are to maintain maximum speed beyond the finish line and to lunge forward right at the finish line.

Distance Running

Distance running is divided into middle and long distance. Mile, half-mile and quarter-mile are middle distance runs. In middle distance running, endurance becomes an important factor.

▼ **Figure 7-13**

Track start position. Photos by Lynn Howell, Cleveland, Ohio.

Pace becomes important as the running distance increases. To maintain a continuous time, runners will be forced to move faster as they negotiate the curves.

Form in distance running is considered individual; however, there are certain concepts of efficiency, including relaxation, that will enhance performance. A major objective is to conserve energy. Most distance runners have a short stride, low knee lift, and an easy, relaxed arm action. An easy, relaxed rhythm is important.

Distance runners land on the balls of the feet, drop the soles of the foot to the ground, transfer the weight forward, and push off at the toes for the next step. At the point of pushoff, the body's center of gravity is over the foot.

Arms continue to play a role in balance in endurance running. They usually remain close to the waist.

Sprint Running

In sprinting, speed is the primary factor. The distance runner needs speed, endurance, and the ability to use energy effectively over a longer period of time. Sprint running usually consists of short bouts of all-out running, often followed by limited activity. Sprints may be forward, backward, or from side to side.

As the runner moves into sprint position, the body is fairly erect, not leaning forward. The erect position permits the legs to follow through efficiently; however, some runners have trouble with the position and choose to maintain their center of gravity forward at all times. Arms aid the body in applying force.

Fencing Attack/Retreat.   In fencing, forward movement is referred to as advancing and backward movement as retreating. The advance is accomplished with a heel, toe walking step, with the forward foot and a slide of the rear foot. Body weight is distributed equally to both feet. The head is held erect and still; changing head position affects balance. Short, quick steps are recommended. The weight is maintained on the balls of the feet, and the rear foot is used as the driving force. Fencers maintain distance so that the performer can just touch the opponent at full lunge.

Pattern: Jump

Jumps are vertical and horizontal. Dance, gymnastics, and track use both vertical and horizontal jumps. Also, basketball, softball, volleyball, and water polo use vertical jumps.

Vertical Jump

Vertical jumps are used in volleyball, basketball, and water polo to accomplish similar objectives. In volleyball and basketball, the performer may be blocking the ball with a jump. In volleyball, the performer may be smashing the ball, whereas in water polo, the jump is used for thrusting the body above the surface of the water to enhance a shot for goal.

The vertical jump is used in the volleyball spike. It allows the body to gather momentum prior to striking the object. Whether one approaches a vertical jump with a series of steps, a short run, a hop, or no prior movement is determined by the distance involved in the movement.

Vertical jumps are important in basketball. Players assess their personal velocity, the amount of force needed to project their bodies, and the desired angle of takeoff for jumps involving shooting, blocking, and rebounding. Water polo players use a kick under water to project the body above the surface. This enables them to execute in the water the same skills used in basketball.

Bouncing on a Trampoline. Bouncing on a trampoline is a form of jumping and landing on a stretched surface. It is similar to bouncing on a springboard. As the feet make contact with the bed of the trampoline, they are shoulder width apart. A regular jumping movement causes the body to be projected into the air. The legs come together as the body is projected. The body is turned on the trampoline by executing a twist. As the body is projected into the air, one hand is raised into the air and above the head while the other is brought close into the body. The body turns in the direction of the extended hand. The same movement can be done to turn the body all the way around.

Drop on a Trampoline. Drops on trampolines begin with a vertical jump. They include the knee, seat, back, and front. Each of the skills is executed so that the body assumes the position in the air, drops to the trampoline in the pose, rebounds into the air, and returns to a standing position.

Vaulting in Gymnastics. Reuther boards are usually used to enhance the vault or jump in gymnastics when the jump is used as a preliminary to a stunt on equipment. The spring of the board provides an added force to the approach. The board is to be contacted with feet shoulder width apart, legs fairly straight, and body weight over the balls of the feet.

Fosbury Flop. The Fosbury Flop, although described as a jump, can also be called a back dive over the bar. The performer has a predetermined starting mark and knows the length and speed for the first step. She or he also knows where to begin the curved approach. The performer approaches the jump running as fast as possible while maintaining control of the body. The jumper approaches the takeoff in an arc and turns during the last three to five steps so the body leans away from the bar as the takeoff heel is placed. Hips are kept under the shoulders and the upper body is straight. The jumper is coached to look at the target mark during the straight strides. Shortly before the heel is placed, the jumper is to look up at the crossbar.

Dance.   The vertical jump in dance may be forward, backward, in place, sideward, or diagonally. Jumps can also include a twist and be for a quarter, half, or full turn. Jumps can occur with legs split, legs together, or legs forward in a lunge. Arm position can vary from alongside the body to out from the shoulders or over the head.

Ice Skating.   The vertical jump in ice skating is an integral part of a number of advanced ice skating stunts. Because of the narrow blade on the skate, balance becomes a key factor in the success of the jump.

Hopping.   Hopping, a form of jumping on one foot, can occur in place and with the nonhopping leg in various poses, either forward, back, up, or down. The hop may also include a kick. Arms are generally held out to the sides to maintain balance.

The flea hop is a series of hops from side to side with one arm forward and the other arm to the hopping side.

Leaps.   Leaps, vertical jumps from one foot to the other, may be forward, backward, sideward, or diagonal.

Horizontal or Long Jump

A pit or a very good mat is necessary for this stunt. A quick, continually accelerating run is executed as the performer moves into an upright position. The takeoff is from the preferred foot with a leg-hip extension and an upswing of the free leg and arm.

The hitch kick or "running in air" is the style most often selected for the long jump. The takeoff foot is immediately under the center of the body, and the free leg is driven as high as possible with the body held erect. Arms are used to further lift the body into the air upon takeoff.

Many specialized skills based on fundamentals and patterns are found in sport. Table 7-4 provides a list of specialized skills identified in the sports and activities selected for analysis in chapter 8.

▼ **TABLE 7-4**
Specialized skills used in activities

ACTIVITY ORGANIZATION	SPECIALIZED SKILLS
Aquatics	
Swimming	Front crawl
	Back crawl
	Elementary backstroke
	Sidestroke
	Breaststroke
Synchronized	Dolphin
	Ballet leg
	Somersault
	Tuck
	Pike
	Somersub
	Kip
	Swordfish
	Eggbeater kick
	Strokes
Archery	Shooting
	Stance
	Placing arrow in bow
	Draw
	Anchor
	Aim
	Release
Badminton	Drives, forehand/backhand
	Serve
	Overhead clear
	Drop shot
	Underhand clear
	Underhand drop
	Smash
	Round-the-head shot
	Hairpin
Basketball	Passing
	Chest
	Bounce
	Overhead
	Overarm
	Handoff
	Catching and receiving
	Dribbling
	Shooting
	Lay-up
	Set shot
	Jump shot
	Free throw
	Guarding
	Faking/feinting
	Rebounding
	Cutting
	Screens

▼ **TABLE 7-4—*Continued.***

ACTIVITY ORGANIZATION	SPECIALIZED SKILLS
Bowling	Throwing the ball
	Stance
	Approach
	Backswing
	Release
	Follow-through
Dance	
Aerobic	Flexibility exercises
	Steps
	Grapevine
	Run
	Jumping
	Hopping
	Leaps
	Skipping
	Slide
	Gallop
	Knee lifts
	Kick, ball change
Dance steps	Two-step
	Polka
	Schottische
	Waltz
	Fox-trot
	Mazurka
	Cha-cha-cha
Gymnastics dance steps	Stride leap
	Body wave
	Toe stand
	Arabesque
	One leg balance
Fencing	Advance
	Retreat
	Lunge
	Attack
	Parry
Field hockey	Dribbling
	Passing
	Shooting
	Receiving or topping
	Tackling
	Dodging
	Push stroke
	Reverse stick push
	Scoop
	Flick
	Lunge
	Jab
	Fielding
	Dodges

ACTIVITY ORGANIZATION	SPECIALIZED SKILLS
Golf	Drive
	Putting
Gymnastics	Forward roll
	Backward roll
	Handstand
	Cartwheel
	Front limber
	Back walkover
	Bouncing on trampoline
	Drop on trampoline
	Vaulting
	Balance beam
Ice skating	Falling
	Stops
	Snowplow
	Hockey
	T
	Strokes
	Sculling
	Forward
	Backward
	Crossover
	Forward
	Backward
	Edge control
Racquetball	Drives, forehand/backhand
	Serve
	Drive
	Lob
	Crosscourt
	Overhead
	Lob
	Drop shot
	Volley
	Smash
	Ceiling shot
Skiing	
Cross-country	Cross-country diagonal
	Double pole
	Skate
	Turns
	Skating
	Telemark
	Herringbone
Downhill	Downhill skiing
	Turns
	Stem
	Parallel
	Stopping
Soccer	Passing
	Inside of foot
	Outside of foot

▼ **TABLE 7-4—*Continued.***

ACTIVITY ORGANIZATION	SPECIALIZED SKILLS
	Receiving and controlling
	Wedging
	Running and dribbling
	Tackling
	Kicking
	Inside drive
	Goalkeeping
	Hands
	Falling
	Catching and throwing
	Heading
Softball	Throws
	Overarm
	Sidearm
	Underarm
	Catching or fielding
	Running
	Pitching
	Hitting
Table tennis	Drive, forehand/backhand
	Push
	Block
	Chop/spin
	Lob
	Loop
	Slash/kill
	Smash
Tennis	Forehand
	Backhand
	Serve
	Lob
	Smash
	Volley
Track	Start
	Running
	Hurdling
	Distance
	High jumps
	Fosbury Flop
	Long jump
Volleyball	Serve
	Overhead
	Underarm
	Sidearm
	Forearm pass
	Bump
	Set
	Dig
	Spike
	Block
	Overhand pass/back set

ACTIVITY ORGANIZATION	SPECIALIZED SKILLS
Water polo	Strokes
	Kicks
	Eggbeater
	Whip
	Dribbling the ball
	Catching the ball
	Passing
	Forehand
	Hook
	Layout
	Backhand
	Push
	Shooting
	Forehand
	Pop
	Push
	Roundhouse
	Skip
	Deflection

▶ References

Adrian, Marlene, and Cooper, John. (1989). *Biomechanics of Human Movement.* Indianapolis, Indiana: Benchmark.

American Red Cross. (1981). *Swimming and Aquatic Safety.* Washington, D.C.

Atwater, Anne E. (1967). *What Film Analysis Tells Us about Movement.* Midwest Association of Physical Education for College Women, French Lick, Indiana.

Barnes, Mildred J., and Kentwell, Richard G. R. (1979). *Field Hockey, the Coach and the Player.* Boston: Allyn and Bacon.

Barnett, Steve. (1983). *Cross-Country Downhill.* Seattle, Washington: Pacific Search Press.

Bowers, Muriel. (1985). *Foil Fencing.* Dubuque, Iowa: Wm. C. Brown.

Broer, Marion R. (1971). *Individual Sports for Women.* Philadelphia: W. B. Saunders.

Broer, Marion R., and Zernicke, Ronald F. (1979). *Efficiency of Human Movement.* Philadelphia: W. B. Saunders.

Bunker, Linda E., and Owens, DeDe. (1984). *Golf: Better Practice for Better Play.* Champaign, Illinois: Leisure Press.

Carpenter, Linda Jean. (1985). *Gymnastics for Girls and Women.* West Nyack, New York: Parker Publishing.

Cicciarella, Charles F. (1981). *The Sport of Water Polo.* Boston, Massachusetts: American Press.

Cooper, J. M. (1987). *Basketball: Player Movement Skills.* Dubuque, Iowa: Wm. C. Brown.

Die, Ding Shu, Fang, Wang Lian, Zuo, Zhu Quing, and Lu, Yuan Hai. (1981). *The Chinese Book of Table Tennis.* New York: Atheneum, 29-30.

Ewers, James. (1989). *Golf.* Glenview, Illinois: Scott, Foresman and Company.

Forbes, Margaret Swan. (1989). *Coaching Synchronized Swimming Effectively.* Champaign, Illinois: Leisure Press.

Gambetta, Vern. (1981). *The Athletics Congress's Track and Field Coaching Manual.* Champaign, Illinois: Leisure Press.

Hall, J. Tillman. (1980). *Dance! A Complete Guide to Social, Folk and Square Dancing.* New York: Books for Libraries, a Division of Arno Press.

Hay, James G. (1985). *The Biomechanics of Sports Technique.* Englewood Cliffs, New Jersey: Prentice-Hall.

Martin, Joan L., Tandy, Ruth E., and Agne-Traub, Charlene E. (1986). *Bowling.* Dubuque, Iowa: Wm. C. Brown.

Murphy, Chet, and Murphy, Bill. (1975). *Tennis for the Player, Teacher and Coach.* Philadelphia: Saunders.

Pitman, Brian. (1988). *Fencing.* Witshire, England: The Crowood Press.

Potter, Diane L., and Brockmeyer, Gretchen A. (1989). *Softball, Steps to Success.* Champaign, Illinois: Leisure Press.

Sanders, R. J. (1979). *The Anatomy of Skiing.* New York: Random House.

Thomson, William. (1980). *Teaching Soccer.* Minneapolis, Minnesota: Burgess.

United States Professional Tennis Association. (1984). *Tennis, A Professional Guide.* New York: Harper and Row.

Wickstrom, Ralph. (1983). *Fundamental Motor Patterns.* Philadelphia, Pennsylvania: Lea and Febiger.

Activity Organizations

Activity organizations are the structures through which the fundamentals, combinations, patterns, and specialized skills are processed for use at advanced levels. Once the performer has acquired a range of specialized skills, an environment is provided that will enable the performer to use the skills. The environment may be a sport or an art form. Sports and art forms are games or events based on sets of carefully constructed rules and strategies that dictate the means through which the performer succeeds or fails in the event. Movement becomes purposeful. The objective is to win or to perform a series of movements according to criteria. Sport organization is based on ritualization, rules, and performance criteria. For example, the sports of basketball and field hockey have detailed rules and playing strategies. The art forms of swimming, gymnastics, and dance require the performer to achieve a predetermined performance criteria.

The classification of activity organizations—placement, convergence on a goal, target, and self-dominated—are based on observed commonalities of equipment, playing environments, strategy, and rules.

In this chapter the organizations are analyzed for commonality and discussed in detail. Lists of skills described in traditional sport books were provided in chapter 7 and should be consulted. A bibliography is provided at the end of the book should you wish to obtain greater detail on any one sport or activity. Although considerable effort has been made to address a wide range of activity organizations, the group is not comprehensive.

▶ Placement

The primary objectives in placement activities are the placement of the playing object, a ball or shuttle, in a location that will prohibit the opponent from returning the object. The placement of the playing object determines whether a particular player or team will score or will be able to obtain the privilege of serving and scoring in future play. Placement sports use the hand, or a racquet or paddle as an extension of the hand, in contacting the object. Many of these sports use a net or a wall as part of the playing court:

- Badminton
- Racquetball
- Table tennis
- Tennis
- Volleyball

Discussion of their organization includes:

1. Equipment
2. Playing environment
3. Strategy
   a. Skills
   b. Starting the game
   c. Receiving the serve
   d. Game play
4. Rules
   a. Starting the game
   b. Receiving the serve
   c. Game play

Equipment

Within the placement category are sports that employ various implements, from the small paddle of table tennis to the large racquet of tennis (see table 8-1). Volleyball is unique in using the hands and arms as the striking implement.

▼ **TABLE 8-1**
Sports and their striking implements

SPORT	EQUIPMENT
Badminton	Lightweight, strong racquet Shuttlecock, which has a tiny rubber ball on the end of a plastic or feather structure
Racquetball	Strung racquet
Tennis	Large, fairly heavy strung racquet Rubber ball with lots of bounce
Table tennis	Paddle and a white plastic ball
Volleyball	Large round ball

Playing Environment

Playing environments in placement sports have one of two principal characteristics: a net or an enclosed playing area (see table 8-2). By enclosing the playing environment, walls—front, side, and in some cases, back—become part of the official playing area. For example, racquetball is played in an enclosed area, does not have a net, and uses the walls of the enclosure as part of the official court. Volleyball, tennis, badminton, and table tennis use nets as a means of separating teams, are not enclosed, and do not require performers to remain within the playing area while executing a stroke. Table tennis is unique in that the entire game is played on a table rather than being played on a court. The performer's feet never make contact with the playing surface. The performer is outside, beneath, and above the surface at all times.

A tennis court is the largest of the courts in placement sports, with dimensions of seventy-eight feet by thirty-six feet (see figure 8-1). The center of the net is three feet above the ground; it is three-and-one-half feet above the ground at the posts. The court is used by two players in singles and by four players in doubles.

▼ **TABLE 8-2**
Environmental commonalities of placement sports

	NET	OPEN COURT	HAND	FRONT WALL	PADDLE/RACQUET
SPORT					
Badminton	X	X			X
Racquetball				X	X
Table tennis	X	X			X
Tennis	X	X			
Volleyball	X	X	X		

▼ **FIGURE 8-1**
Tennis court.

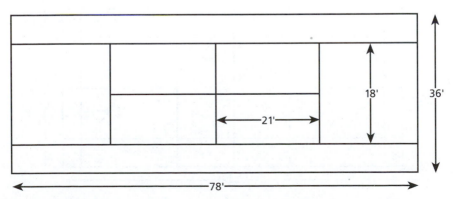

Volleyball, the only placement sport that has a fairly large team, six players, is played on a court slightly smaller than a tennis court (see figure 8-2). The volleyball court is sixty feet by thirty feet. Although it is shorter than a tennis court it is almost as wide. A net, eight feet for males and seven feet four-and-one-half inches for females, is stretched across the center of the court.

A badminton court is twenty by forty-four feet or about one-half the size of a tennis court (see figure 8-3). A net of two-and-one-half feet is stretched across the court at a height of five feet one inch.

Table tennis uses a table nine feet by six feet that stands four feet six inches off the floor. The table is subdivided by a six-inch net. The net extends beyond each side of the table by six inches. Only one table marking exists. It is a center play line used in serving in doubles. Players stand on the floor outside the table during play.

▼ **FIGURE 8-2**
Volleyball court.

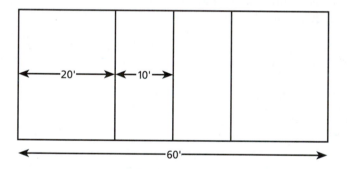

▼ **FIGURE 8-3**
Badminton court.

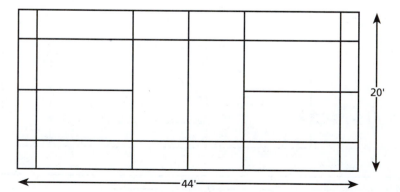

Racquetball is played on a handball court. The back wall is required to be a minimum of twelve feet high. Racquetball may also be played on one- and three-wall courts; however, most of today's games are played on the traditional four-wall handball court.

Volleyball and badminton use a net that is strung above the playing surface. Although all net sports may prompt the use of an overhand smash, only those sports whose nets are fairly high encourage opponents to block the smashes.

Commonalities Related to Equipment and Facilities

The size of the playing surface, the use of the body as an implement in play, the type and size of the equipment used, and the object and number of players influence the movements and strategies most effective in game play.

Effect of Court Size on Players and Equipment

1. As the court increases in size, the number of players tends to increase. This is most noticeable in tennis and badminton. As the number of players in doubles increases, so does the size of the court.
2. When the court is large and there are few players, participants have to run, rather than sidestep, to cover the court space. When the court is small, players tend to use fast, short steps or glides in moving around the area. The need for endurance training in running or the development of flexibility and fine footwork are factors influenced by court size.
3. The size of the court influences the equipment. As the court increases in size from badminton to tennis, the racquet increases in size and the light shuttle gives way to a sturdy ball.
4. Nets are used in these games to maintain distance between opponents.
5. When paddles are used, usually only two persons are permitted on the same side of the playing area. When only hands and arms are used, in volleyball for example, a large group can be accommodated.

Strategy

Skills

1. The overarm and underarm throw patterns are the primary skills used in placement sports.
2. Throwing patterns are often used in striking. Striking is contact with an object that has been projected by a force other than the force used in striking. That force may be either human, an opponent or material, or a wall or floor.
3. The volleyball serve and spike use the same overarm throw pattern; however, the volleyball serve from the baseline includes a weight transfer and a tossed ball, whereas the spike from the net is often executed

following one or two steps and a jump to meet a ball traveling toward the performer at a high rate of speed. The volleyball server directs the ball forward while the spiker directs it downward.

4. In a volleyball overhand shot from midcourt, the player applies a combination of forward and downward force. The same application of force is used in the tennis serve and smash at the net. Due to the fact that the tennis net is close to the ground, there is no longer a need for a two-step approach and jump prior to contact.

5. In the fundamentals and patterns explanations, the performer's objective was to gain maximum force from the body in executing a movement. In tennis, for example, the performer's side is turned toward to the net and his or her arm is extended in the forehand and backhand. Now, the amount of body rotation to the side is dictated by the distance the performer expects the object to travel. When the maximum body force is beyond the level of force desired or danger exists that the object, when struck or thrown, will go out of bounds, the performer decreases the amount of force and controls the object by placing a spin on the object at the time of contact.

6. The amount of backswing increases as the object is stroked for greater distance (i.e., forehands and backhands from the baseline). The length of the swing decreases as the object is stroked for shorter distance.

7. Force is reduced by:
   a. decreasing the length of the swing
   b. decreasing the speed of the swing
   c. facing the net while executing strokes, thus eliminating body rotation

8. Force can also be controlled with the use of a topspin. Topspins direct the object's flight down, causing the object to meet the surface sooner than it would on a regular stroke. Some players put topspin on all balls to maintain control.

9. Control of body strength is important in placement sports. If the entire arm is used as a lever, as occurs in tennis, the performer keeps the arm relaxed but straight, employing the large muscle masses of the neck, back, and shoulders. When that same performer picks up a racquetball racquet, he or she needs to be conscious of controlling his or her strength. Control can be accomplished by keeping the elbow fairly close to the body in a stroke, thus eliminating the use of the large muscles of the shoulder and back. When the elbow is brought close to the body, the position permits only the forearm and the wrist muscles to operate at maximum capacity.

10. Underarm swings are used as lobs to provide change of pace, to serve, or to move the object to the back court. Lobs landing in the front court or near the net give the opponent an opportunity for a smash. Such lobs are to be avoided.

11. Sliding and shuttle running movements dominate play, with performers seldom permitting one leg to cross in front of the other. Slides are from left to right or front to back. In situations where rapid movement is required, performers will often hop from the slide into the next action.

12. Placement sports, confined to small areas, use quick changes of direction and constant shuttling movements; they do not provide opportunities for distance or sustained running.

13. Eyes are to be focused on the object at all times.

14. Nets ensure safety by permitting players to acquire a level of skill before they are pitted against opponents in close quarters. Sport skills are learned in the net area, individually practiced at the wall, and played against opponents on the wall or court.

15. The elements of placement activities are easily acquired by learning a game that requires only the use of the hand(s). A progression that takes the learner from the hand to a small paddle, to a racquetball racquet, and finally to the full-size tennis racquet, is preferred.

16. The addition of a wall creates a need for strategies to accommodate the angles that balls can be played.

17. The direction of flight of the object coming over the net or the angle at which the ball moves from a wall influences a performer's movement decisions.

    a. Lines of interception in net sports include the concept of rushing the net to enable a player to shorten the distance through which the object may travel.

    b. Lines of interception in wall play operate on the same principle, thus allowing the performer to reduce the angle by rushing toward the wall for the shot.

    c. In up-back play, the person near the net is expected to hit the shots coming over the net, thus reducing the angle of the flight.

18. An object rebounds from a wall at relatively the same angle that it was thrown toward the wall. This assumes a hard, flat-surfaced wall, a hard object, and no spins. When spins or wall texture exist, the angles will change accordingly. Information regarding potential object flight can be obtained from watching the opponents and other persons play. (Detailed discussions are found in chapter 11.)

Starting the Game

All placement games begin with a serve. Although the type of serve may vary—underarm serves are considered defensive and overarm serves are considered offensive—most players believe that the server, at the moment of serve, is in control of the game. The server holds the edge as the only person who knows where the ball or shuttle will be placed; how it will be served—hard, soft, spin (if spin, what spin and its direction); and where the server will move immediately after the serve. The server is also in charge psychologically because everyone else can only guess as to what will take place. The server should make every effort to exploit this advantage.

Serve—Defense or Offense. Serves are classified as defensive or offensive. The classification is usually determined by whether the serve is executed in an overarm or underarm pattern and whether the placement of the served object is in the back or foreground of the opponent's court. Badminton's underarm serve is required by rules. Also, it must land in a specific area of the court. A volleyball serve, in contrast to badminton, tennis, and table tennis, may land at any spot on the court as long as it is within the boundaries. Racquetball uses an underarm pattern in the serve; however, the small size of the ball and the small and lightweight racquet cause the underarm pattern to take on an aggressive form.

- Table Tennis: Until the Chinese began to influence table tennis, the serve was considered defensive. The defensive serve was used primarily to put the object in play. It was not expected to be an ace or an automatic point. Today, the new table tennis serve is expected not only to put the object in play but to challenge the opponent in returning the object. Placement and the use of varying speeds create a difficult return. Finesse, timing, and varied flight increase the challenge.
- Volleyball: The volleyball underarm and sidearm defensive serves are executed using deceptive tactics in an effort to place the ball in different locations. These serves may be executed with such force that the speed of the ball will prohibit the net opponents from blocking the shot and will make it difficult for the back court players to execute a successful underarm set. Sidearm serves are effective crosscourt shots, particularly if they are so well disguised that their direction is not readily noticed until the object is in flight.
  The volleyball overarm throw pattern or offensive serve is executed to create an ace or an automatic point. The server either expects to win the point or set up a weak return. An overhand arm position is used to force the flight of the ball toward the back court in volleyball.
- Badminton: Badminton has four typical serves: short, flick, drive, and high. The two most frequently used serves are the short serve, hit to just drop in the front service court, and the high serve, hit deep into the opposition's service court. Doubles play tends to use the short serve.
  On the short serve, the shuttlecock reaches its highest point before crossing the net, thus eliminating an opportunity for the opponent to smash the shuttle back into the server's court. The server executes the shot so that the opponent will be forced to hit the shuttle into the air to get it back over the net. Placement, speed, and varying flights are important elements of the short serve. High, long serves are hit as far into the back court as possible. Placement plays an important role here also.

- Racquetball: Racquetball has five principal serves: drive, Z, jam, lob, and overhand. One objective for all these serves is to keep the receiver deep in the back court while the server protects center position. Another objective is to force the opponent to play the ball on the run and/or cause the receiver to run as far as possible in the court space. The soft and hard serves are planned to hit the front wall, maybe a side wall, and the back court, whereas the Z serve hits the front wall, side wall, opposite side wall, and back court. The drive serve, an offensive play and the most popular serve, is used primarily on the front wall. Variations in speed and placement, including spins and slices, are keys to successful serving.

  According to Fabian (1986, 13), "the purpose of the Z-serve is to keep the receiver in back court, neutralize his/her power by preventing a full-arm swing, and limit his/her effectiveness and return by forcing the receiver to play the ball waist high in a corner."

- Tennis: The best tennis serve is the classic ace or big game technique. A tennis net permits a downward flight for only the tallest performers; however, a reasonably hard forward flight can be acquired by most performers. To encourage players to be on the offense, the rules of many of these sports give the performer an opportunity to make two attempts in serving prior to losing point or side-out. Tennis servers have two opportunities to serve within bounds. Most tournament players expect to win their own serve points and expect that their opponent will win when the opponent serves; thus, a chance to win the match is based upon breaking the opponent's serve. Three types of serves are used: flat, slice, and twist. Major differences in executing these serves involves the grip and the racquet swing.

Locations of Players.   The location of the server and receiver on the court play a major role in the serve. Badminton players execute the serve while standing in a specific predetermined location. No part of the body may be outside the defined area. Tennis, racquetball, and volleyball players execute the serve from behind a designated line. Volleyball and tennis players use an overarm serve and have a line requirement at the rear of the playing area. Racquetball players use an underarm serve and begin behind a line halfway up the court.

Served balls or shuttles are often required to land in specific locations. Volleyball and table tennis players use the entire court as a playing area. Tennis and badminton serves must land in a court diagonally across from where the serve was executed. Badminton, unlike other net sports, and like the wall sports, finds opponents standing fairly close together at the time of the serve. As a result of this proximity, they are well aware of the stance, position, and racquet swing of the opponent. The ability to disguise strokes is important to the success of the serve.

Receiving the Serve

Successful receipt of the serve is a combination of anticipation, body position, and concentration. Knowing the skill level and specific characteristics of the opposing server and using that knowledge to select the most appropriate position for receiving the serve will enhance the receiver's chance for success.

The serve is an offensive tactic, and the server is expected to chart the course of play. A receiver can look at the return of the serve as a defensive play and merely attempt to return the object to the required area in order to maintain play. Or the receiver can become an offensive receiver and take charge of the game as he or she returns the serve. The receiver's options are to miss the object altogether, merely return it, or aggressively take over the game plan. Beginning players focus on a defensive strategy of being able to accept the serve and return it, whereas advanced players use offensive strategy to take over the game.

Whether the return of the serve will be offensive or defensive relates to the

- amount of power the server puts on the object
- ability of the server to strategically place the object
- skill of the receiver in reversing the server's strategy

Volleyball's three-touch rule on the return of the serve, for example, allows the receiver who does not receive an ace to turn the strategy from defense to offense. The three-touch rule means that the ball may be played three times on the return. The receiver accepts the ball and sends it to a setter. If the receiver can successfully make the transition and is able to convert the speed of the ball so that the setter can place an effective set for the spiker, the receiving team has become the offensive team. In placement sports at the beginning level, it usually requires a weak serve to enable a receiving team to reverse the strategy on the return of the serve. The following points of strategy should be considered as one prepares to successfully return a serve.

1. The server is in control. The receiver is ready to guess at what will occur. The guess is influenced by traditional game theory and knowledge of peculiarities of the server. The distance between the server and the receiver provides the receiver time to analyze the opponent's execution and strategy. This is true of all strokes.
2. Traditional game theory in placement sports suggests that:
   a. the server will drive the serve back to keep an opponent as far back in the court as possible. In racquetball, the player's body is stationed in the center of the court to take the object on the fly and avoid being driven to the back court.

b. when the designated placement for the return of the serve prohibits the "way back" tactic, such as that needed for a ball bounce prior to the return of the serve in tennis, or when the goal is to locate the playing object in the rear of the designated box, effort is made to vary object speed and placement.

c. when possible, the object is driven low. An exception to this strategy is found in badminton where the shuttle is so light that it does not follow a typical trajectory in its downward flight.

d. servers will attempt to follow an aggressive serve by rushing the net.

e. servers return to the center area in racquetball. Note that there is a tendency for a wall court server to return to the middle of the playing area, whereas net court players, with the exception of badminton players, will rush the net. A badminton player usually assumes a center court spot similar to those identified in the wall court sports.

f. volleyball, with its team of six players, uses a unique set of plays for the return of serve. Selection of the play is related to the strength of the server.

A strong serve is followed by a typical one, two, three or receipt, set, and spike play, whereas a weak serve is converted to a set and smash or just a smash. The server, following delivery of the serve, is expected to pick up a regular court position.

g. objects are served to nondominant sides or to any weaknesses the receiver(s) may have.

3. Knowledge about opponents include the following:
   a. what the server usually does
   b. receiver's weaknesses
   c. server's strengths
   d. shots that are most successful

4. Signals peculiar to the situation should be identified.
   a. Is the server standing in the traditional spot for serve? Note that racquetball players have a repertoire of serves and will seldom execute the same serve twice in a row. Server's position might provide a clue as to what serve is about to be executed.
   b. Is server's execution traditional?
   c. In volleyball, the formation of players may provide clues.

Position. The receiver assumes ready position when accepting a serve. Ready position includes:

1. Body facing forward.
2. Balanced body stance with feet shoulder width apart, knees flexed, and body ready to move in any direction. In racquetball's small court, the receiver takes a wide stance in an effort to use the body to cover the space.

3. Preparing to execute a backswing or to run as soon as the object is contacted by the server. Anticipate the movement—forward, backward, or sideward.
4. Knowing the stroke the receiver will use as the opponent executes the serve.

Footwork, movement of hips, and center of gravity of the body are all factors that a player views and takes into consideration when competing against an opponent across a net.

1. If the racquet or paddle is swung downward, expect backspin.
2. If the opponent faces the net, expect a crosscourt on return.
3. If the opponent's side is to the net, anticipate either a crosscourt or down-the-line shot.

Determine What You Will Do to Receive the Object.
1. Get to the location or shift the body appropriately.
2. Take a preliminary position for hitting.
3. If the sport is a partner or group activity, note the backup role of the partner when the opponent fails to execute play as anticipated.
4. In volleyball, the receiver operates as a single receiver would in other sports. The receiver is designated by the spot to which the ball is traveling.

Carry Out the Actions.
1. First, maintain the playing object in play.
2. Plan a strategy on the return of the serve so that one can anticipate the next shot.
3. Attempt to change the server's pace.
4. Know where your returned object should land. Practice until accuracy for that predetermined location becomes high.

Game Play
1. Basic rules in nearly all game play are to:
   a. determine where the opponent will place the object at the moment the opponent makes contact with the object. Player's position on court, grip, use of racquet or paddle, position of feet and hips, and swing provide clues about the opponent's execution.
   b. run or move as fast as possible to where you anticipate the object is being directed. Move on the balls of the feet with sliding, quick movements. Avoid bouncing.
   c. stop the body, if possible, before executing a stroke.
   d. hit the object from a stationary position using mechanically efficient form.

2. The concept of center court territory is used in racquetball. A player is to return to the center following play. This is considered the best court position.

3. An aggressive player forces the object downward in play; a defensive player sends the object into the air.

4. Aggressive net sport players rush the net, striking the playing object down as early in the play as permitted by the rules. For example, the receipt, set, and spike of a volleyball permits a team to turn the return into an offensive smash or winning point.

5. Hard, fast-moving drives are used to force players to either run long distances across the court to make contact or to make contact while moving backward or in an unbalanced position. When an opponent is not in a favorable position for a return but hits the object in desperation, the object will often go into the air, thus creating an opportunity for the opposition to smash the object. In volleyball, such a situation is created by a set of plays by one team. In the other sports, one player orchestrates a set of plays in executing a single shot. Each side is looking for a weak return that can be converted into a spike or smash and a score.

6. Placement of the object where it cannot be reached is the ultimate method of scoring. The object also may be directed to a spot where no team member is located, may be sent to a team member's known weakness, or may be tipped just out of reach of all team members.

7. Players may strive to fatigue opponents by merely returning the ball rather than planning a strategy that would bring the point to a close. Although this strategy is not considered good, on occasion it may be effective.

8. Force the opponent to move out of an effective position, thus causing either a weak return or enabling the aggressor to locate the second shot before the opponent can return to a good position.

9. Keep the opponent running or out of position at all times.

10. Drive the opponent to back court with deep, fast shots, providing an opportunity for the aggressor to rush the net.

11. Lobs may be used to drive opponents away from the net whereas drop shots are used to encourage opponents to move up to the net or wall.

12. Vary strokes in speed, direction, and tempo.

13. In doubles play, players should consider placing the object or ball between opponents.

14. Smashing or hitting the object down is an offensive tactic; blocking or hitting the object up is considered a defensive tactic.

Winning.   Placement games are won because one side or team has the ability to locate or place the object with such accuracy and speed that the opposing side or team either cannot return the object or can only return the object in a weak manner, thus becoming vulnerable to the next round of play. Offensive or serving sides or teams lose because they cannot serve successfully, place shots accurately, tire players, or fine-tune placement strategies. A performer is wise to plan a winning strategy and to execute it as soon as feasible.

1. Keep the object in play rather than risk an unknown shot.
2. Hit balls deep in the back court.
3. Use a variety of shots and placements. When the opponent rushes the net, counter with straight, down-the-line shots. Returning crosscourt shots enables the net player quicker access to the shots. One reason for rushing the net is to enable the player to shorten the distance for obtaining crosscourt volleys before they bounce. Approach shots executed on the way to the net should be returned down the line.
4. Take the ball on the volley, which gives the opponent less time to prepare and react, thus making it easier to catch the opponent off guard.
5. Rush the net and smash when feasible.
6. Know opponents' strengths and weaknesses. Create a game based on that knowledge.

Rules

Starting the Game
Prior to starting play, one side or team tosses a coin or spins a racquet or paddle while the other side or team calls the choice. The side winning the toss or spin has a choice of:

- serving first
- not serving first
- end or side of the playing court
- requiring the other side to make the choice

The side or team losing the toss shall have a choice of the remaining alternatives.

Scoring.   The major distinctions in scoring are the game point systems, the employment of a technique called setting, and the number of points that one side must achieve to win. Three different game point systems are used in the five sports. Tennis uses a four point system, numerically referred to as fifteen, thirty, forty, and game. This system requires that the winner be ahead by two points, as does a number of other sports. Tennis also differs from other placement sports in that a deuce-add arrangement is employed. When a tie occurs at forty to forty, and the serving team scores the next point, it is called *advantage in;* if the receiving team scores the next point, it is called *advantage out*. The winner of the advantage must also gain the next point. If the score becomes tied again, it returns to deuce and the entire process is repeated.

Volleyball and women's badminton require a score of fifteen points in each game, whereas men's and doubles badminton, racquetball, and table tennis require twenty-one points. Badminton allows a team to set a match at a specified time. The set is usually established at five when the score is three points from a game-winning situation and three when the score is two points from a game-winning situation. Whether the game is set or not, it is won by a single point in badminton and racquetball. All other placement sports—tennis, table tennis, and volleyball—require the winning side to be ahead by two points.

A match usually consists of two out of three games except tennis, where the winner scores either two out of three sets or three out of five sets. A tennis set is won when a player obtains six or more games and beats the opponent by at least two games.

Number of Serves. Another distinction among placement sports is the number of times a player may serve for a single point. Badminton, volleyball, and table tennis permit one opportunity for the server to produce a successful serve. Racquetball and tennis allow two attempts to achieve a successful serve. Except in tennis and table tennis, the server is the only one who can score. A loss of the opportunity to serve is not scored to either team and the serving object goes to the opposing team, allowing them to serve and score. This is referred to as a side-out. Tennis players designate a server for an entire game, rotating servers at the beginning of each new game. Table tennis rotates servers at the completion of each five points. In tennis and table tennis, either team may score as a result of the serve and rally.

The Serve. All placement sports start the game with a serve. Rules dictate the location of the server and, on occasion, the location of the receiver. Location of the server combined with the position of the net or wall markings may also dictate the type of serve. In volleyball, tennis, and table tennis, the server puts the ball into play from behind the back line of the court. In tennis and badminton, the serve is directed diagonally to a box located in the front half of the opponent's court. In table tennis doubles, the serve is directed to the entire diagonal court, whereas in volleyball and table tennis singles, the rules permit the ball to land anyplace in the court. Served objects are also directed diagonally in badminton but the server serves at midcourt.

In badminton, a singles player initiates the serve in the right court when the server's score is zero or an even number, and in the left court when the server's score is an odd number. A successful server rotates the serve from right court to left court until the serve is lost. In doubles play, the second server serves from the next regular court. Rotation occurs following the failure of the first server. When the serve returns to a side or side-out, play is initiated from the right service court. Only one member of a doubles team serves on the first set of outs prior to the serve going to the opponents. After that, each partner serves consecutively when the team wins the serve.

Racquetball players initiate action, with the server serving a ball directly to the front wall. On the rebound, the ball must bounce from the front wall back beyond the short line with or without hitting one of the side walls. The server remains in the service zone until the served ball passes the short line. No part of the feet of the server may extend beyond the lines of the service zone. A server may step on but not beyond the lines. Stepping on a line is not an acceptable service technique in most other placement sports. Time also becomes a factor in racquetball as a deliberate delay may be called if more than two seconds is consumed by the server in getting ready to serve. In racquetball doubles play, the serving order is designated and only the first player serving the first turn at serve.

In table tennis doubles, the server must serve diagonally to a particular member of the receiving team, with the order of server and receiver changing at the beginning of each game. Whether a server initiates action in the left or right court is not important.

Serving is considered an offensive strategy. The server is in charge, the serve is an attacking element, and the server is attempting an ace or a score on the serve alone. A serve is a fault when any number of situations occur.

1. The server, in serving, misses the object entirely in racquetball and table tennis. It is not considered a fault in badminton, tennis, and volleyball.
2. The ball is tossed but no effort is made to strike the tossed object.
3. The badminton server hits the shuttle at a point lower than the server's waist while maintaining the racquet head below the shaft of the racquet at the moment of impact.
4. A contact is made between the implement and the serving object but it does not result in a serve.
5. A foot fault is called:
    a. in tennis or volleyball if the server steps on or over the service line in executing the serve.
    b. in racquetball or badminton if the server moves beyond the designated service zone in executing the serve. Standing on the lines of the boundary zone is also illegal in badminton, but it is not illegal to step on the boundary line in racquetball.
6. The serve is executed before the receiver is ready. Any attempt by the receiver to return the serve assumes the receiver is ready.

7. If the wrong person executes the serve and the error is identified before the point or side-out is awarded, most placement sports consider the serve a fault. If the error is not identified until after the point is complete and the play has continued, most placement sports allow the score to stand and rearrange the serving order at the next convenient interval.

8. Teammates fail to maintain their bodies in a designated area during the execution of the serve:
   a. in volleyball, in respective court positions.
   b. in the service box in racquetball. On each serve, the server's partner shall stand erect with the back to the side wall and feet on the floor within the service box until the served ball passes the short line.

9. The served object fails to go over the net in net sports, fails to bounce before and after it crosses the net in table tennis or fails to hit the wall above the designated line or between designated lines in wall sports. It is also a fault if the ball fails to hit the front wall in wall sports. Wall sports demand that the ball hit the front wall prior to hitting a side or rear wall. Objects going under the net in badminton and volleyball are faults.

10. Served objects landing outside the boundary lines are out:
    a. in volleyball and table tennis when the entire playing surface is the boundary
    b. when landing outside the designated diagonal service court in badminton and tennis
    c. when landing in front of the front line in racquetball or if after hitting the front wall and before bouncing behind the short line the object:
       (1) hits the side walls
       (2) hits the ceiling
       (3) hits the back wall

11. The object served hits a permanent fixture.

12. The object served hits the server's partner on its way to the net or to the wall, or on its rebound from the wall. Racquetball has an exception to this rule. A ball rebounding from the wall on the fly, hitting a partner of the server while the partner remains in the service box, is called a defective serve and is replayed.

13. The object served goes over the net but is outside the official designated net tapes.

14. A served object hitting the top of the net and going into the receiving team's court in the proper manner is called a let and is replayed. In badminton, a let is not called on this play and the shuttle remains in action with the game continuing.

15. Badminton reserves the title let to designate the repeat serve that is permitted when the shuttle gets caught in the net. As balls seldom become caught in a net, no such rule exists in the other sports.
16. In racquetball, a rebounding ball that passes so close to the server and the server's partner as to obstruct the view of the receiver is classified as a defective serve. Defective serves are replayed.
17. It is a fault in racquetball if the served ball hits the crotch in the front wall. Such a hit is treated the same as if it hit the floor before it hit the wall.

Receiving the Serve

Receiving the serve is considered a defensive maneuver because the server is in control and the receiver must wait to determine what the server will do. There are a number of rules specific to receipt of serve.

1. When receivers are designated, only the appropriate person may accept the serve.
2. In badminton, the receiver must stand within the limits of the receiving court; in racquetball, the receivers must stay behind the short line; and in tennis, the receiver may stand wherever he or she chooses. The receiver need not be at a complete stop but may not move forward until the server hits the ball.
3. The receiver returns the object:
    a. before it touches the ground in badminton and volleyball
    b. after it touches the court once but before it touches the court twice in tennis
    c. after it touches the front wall and rebounds beyond the short line either as a fly or after one bounce but before two bounces in racquetball
    d. after it hits the table once on the opponent's side but not twice in table tennis
4. The receiver may make as many attempts as possible at returning the object provided no contact has been made in earlier attempts.

Game Play

Once the object has been served and successfully returned by the receiver, play continues, alternating between each of the two teams in wall sports and driving the object back and forth across the net in net sports. Play continues until one team or player is successful in placing the object so that the opponent is unable to either reach the object or even if reaching it, is unable to keep it in play (thus the term *placement* is an indication of the method through which the performer succeeds in winning the score, game, or match). The objective is to place the object in a position or with such force and speed that the opponent will be unable to return the object.

Aspects of play may be analyzed as to the methods of putting and keeping an object in play, the role of the players, and the effect of the court and boundaries.

Putting and Keeping Object in Play.
1. Contact with the ball or shuttle is controlled.
   a. The ball must be hit by the racquet head in racquetball.
   b. The ball may be hit with either hand or with both hands in volleyball. Balls may be hit with a paddle or hand in table tennis; however, paddle must remain in the hand during play.
   c. The ball may not be held in volleyball or any of the racquet sports.
   d. Racquet contact, when required, also requires that the racquet be held in the hand and not thrown at the object.
2. A ball may be hit on the fly or after one bounce in tennis and table tennis. It must be hit before it takes a second bounce.
3. A ball is returned to the front wall in racquetball:
   a. directly
   b. after touching one or both side walls
   c. after touching the back wall or ceiling
   d. after hitting the front, back, and side wall a second time
   e. with any combination of these
4. A returned ball may not touch the floor before touching the front wall.
5. A returned object is hit only on the fly in volleyball and badminton. Once the object touches the floor within a court the point is awarded to the opponents.

Role of the Players.
1. The object may be touched only once by each player or team as they move from one side to the other in most placement sports. Volleyball is unique, permitting three players an opportunity to contact the ball on each side of the court. One volleyball player may contact the ball twice in succession if one of the contacts occurs in the following situations:
   a. simultaneous contact by teammates
   b. successive contacts by a blocker
   c. simultaneous contact by opponents
   A simultaneous hit by both teams (block) at the net is not considered as one of the three hits allocated to a side.
2. Contact between the object and a player that is not a hit is a point for the opponent(s) or a side-out.
3. In the closely confined wall sports, players may not contact or hinder one another in play. To police this rule, referees or a good honor system is necessary. A player's physical presence cannot hinder or prohibit the opponent from reaching the ball. Such hinders, when called on oneself, may result in a replay, a loss of point, or a side-out.

Court and Boundary Areas.

1. Objects that land outside of boundary lines result in points or side-outs for the opponents of the team causing the action.
2. Objects going under a net in badminton or volleyball are out.
3. Objects hitting court fixtures or other supports are out.
4. Objects struck by a player before they pass over the net into the player's court are out. A player may reach over the net in a follow-through but the player must have contacted the object on his or her own side of the playing court prior to the follow-through.
5. An object hitting the top of the net and going over the net remains in play. An object hitting the top of the net and falling back to the side from which it was hit is a point or side-out.
6. Badminton shuttles caught in the net are called lets and are replayed.
7. Balls hitting lines in tennis are good.
8. In net play, players cannot step over the center line under the net. They cannot hit the net or other supports but they may follow through over the net as described earlier, as long as no contact occurs.
9. In volleyball, if a ball is driven into the net and the net hits an opponent, it is not a foul. One has to make physical contact with the opponent before a foul is called.
10. Balls hitting the edge of the table are good in table tennis.
11. In doubles play, most placement sports require a designated receiver for the serve but permit either partner to play the object in game play. Table tennis does not accept this form. In table tennis, contact with the ball is rotated each time the ball comes to the respective side of the table. This means that one partner must move out of the area to permit the other person to play the ball and then immediately return to the original position for the next play.

▶ Convergence on a Goal

Convergence on a goal activities use the body, with or without the aid of an implement, to manipulate an object into a goal to score. These sports involve moving an object up and down a playing surface in an effort to score a goal at the opponent's end of the playing field or court.

All these sports have a goal at the end of the playing area. The size of the goal is influenced by the number of members on a team and the size of the playing area. Field hockey and soccer have fairly large goal cages; basketball and water polo have much smaller scoring areas.

The body, either arms and hands or legs and feet, is used for scoring in soccer, water polo, and basketball; field hockey uses a stick as an extension of the arms in scoring. Field size is influenced by the number of team members and the use of an extension of the body to manipulate the playing object.

Sports in this category include:

- Basketball
- Field hockey
- Soccer
- Water polo

Convergence on a goal organizations include discussion of:

1. Equipment
2. Playing environment
3. Strategy
   a. Players
   b. Team play
   c. Offense
   d. Defense
4. Rules
   a. Game and scoring
   b. Start of game
   c. Violations and penalties
   d. Fouls and penalties

Equipment

The ball is the standard piece of equipment in all convergence on a goal sports. It is projected by the body in all sports except field hockey. Field hockey requires a stick for use in dribbling and shooting. The stick is carried in a specific manner as described earlier and, by rules, must be swung in a controlled manner for safety.

Goals and baskets differ in these sports; sports played on large fields use goals attached to the ground at the end lines centered on the field. These goals encourage the performer to keep the ball on or close to the ground in scoring. Protective covering is provided for persons defending the goal in soccer and field hockey. Basketball and water polo have baskets above the head as their goals; the person scoring is encouraged to shoot the ball above the head, into the basket.

Playing Environment

The size of the playing area appears to influence the number of players on each team. Soccer and field hockey have teams of eleven players on a large field; water polo uses seven in a more confined area; and basketball has five people moving up and down the floor. Basketball is usually played on a court ninety-four feet long and fifty feet wide, or a minimum of seventy-four feet long and forty-two feet wide. Baskets are suspended ten feet

▼ **FIGURE 8-4**

Field hockey field.

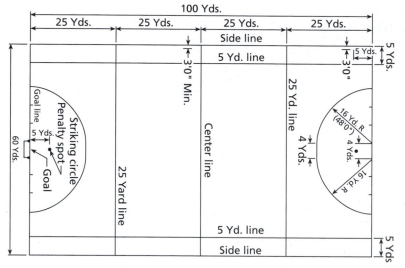

above the floor at the end of each court. The official ball is round with a circumference of 29 1/2 inches for men and 28 1/2 inches for women. The men's ball weighs twenty to twenty-two ounces; the women's ball weighs eighteen to twenty-two ounces.

Field hockey is ordinarily played on a grass field 100 yards long and 60 yards wide. Markings include sidelines, goal lines, center line, twenty-five-yard lines, five-yard hash marks parallel to the sidelines and sixteen-yard striking circles in front of each goal. The goal is four yards wide and seven feet high, with nets attached to form a box.

Sticks, shin guards, and a ball make up the equipment.

Soccer is played on a field of 100 or 120 yards in length and 65 or 75 feet wide. Field size may be reduced to accommodate the needs of young players.

The game of water polo is played in a thirty by twenty meter pool area with marks at two and four meters and at midcourt. Goals are made of plastic and painted white. The depth of the pool is a factor in putting up a water polo court. It is recommended that the current rule book be consulted for details on structuring a competitive environment.

Strategy

Players

Teams consist of different size groups, with five the smallest and twelve the largest. Basketball has five players and unlimited substitutes. Water polo has seven on a team—six players and a goalkeeper. Field hockey has eleven players on a team. Soccer also has eleven players.

Team Play

Overarm, underarm, and sidearm throws are the specialized skills used in basketball, water polo, and soccer goalkeeping and passing, and basketball and water polo shooting.

Passing.   Passes may be direct, quick, and for short distances, or they may be long to move the object a great distance. A variety of passes are used to confuse the opponent and to free the ball so that it can be caught in an effective manner. In water polo, only one hand can be used in picking up the ball. Passes are to be strong and direct. They may be wet, intending to land in the water, or dry, caught in the air. "Dry passes should be thrown in as flat a trajectory as possible without danger of interception, and they should be thrown so as to pass over the intended receiver forcing the receiver to reach up to catch the ball" (Cicciarella 1981, 11). Wet passes are used when the teammate is covered by opponents. The pass is made to a point in the water, usually about a foot away from the receiver.

Hook passes, hook shots, and lay-up shots are similar in water polo and basketball. They are used also when closely guarded and when the objective is to pass backwards.

To execute successful passes consider the following:

1. They should be thrown directly at a stationary partner or in front of or ahead of a moving partner.
2. Lobs may be used to move the object over a defense player who is in front of a teammate.
3. Passes should be quick and forceful.
4. A passing target should be identified before the pass is executed. A receiving player may meet the ball to avoid defensive players.

Field hockey passes, often called drives, make use of a swing rather than a throw. In a beginning pass or drive, the left foot takes the body weight and points toward the ball. The shoulders and hips turn toward the direction of the pass, enabling a swing. The performer places both hands as close to the top of the stick as possible to increase the length of the lever and thereby increase speed and range of motion. A performer may also use a flick, scoop, or short pass.

Passing is quicker than retaining the ball and dribbling it. Water polo passes are short and direct, with no lobs or crosscourt shots. The object is to keep the players spread out. Also, note that in swimming only one hand can be used to hold the ball. Again, as in other sports, a pass is directed to a space in front of the receiver.

Receiving.   Accuracy and speed are important aspects of passing. For a pass to be successful it must be caught, trapped, or fielded. As a result, accuracy is more important then speed in a pass.

The receiver of a pass:

1. maintains a position in open space to receive the pass
2. moves toward the ball in receiving the pass
3. is always on the move so that the defense becomes off guard
4. uses as much space as possible to keep the defense players spread out over the playing area
5. cuts or runs to get away from opponents to be free to receive the pass

Scoring.   Shooting, or passing the ball toward a basket, occurs in basketball and water polo; passing, or advancing a ball over or into a goal, is found in soccer and field hockey. Passing now becomes the method of scoring.

• *Basketball:* The following statements addressing basketball are important to performers in all convergence on a goal organizations: "Accuracy is dependent upon balance, concentration, confidence, and correct release. Balance can be achieved by keeping the center of gravity over the base. The head should be turned toward the basket and shoulders, hips, and feet should be squared to the basket. This brings the body in line with the target" (Barnes 1980, 29). Aiming at the stationary target is a must. Performers may aim at a selected spot on the backboard or at the rim of the basket. Aiming at the spot on the backboard means that the ball will hit the backboard and deflect into the hoop. Although selecting the spot may be difficult, estimating the correct force for the deflection is even more difficult. Most people use the rim as their first target and move to the backboard as their shots improve.

• *Field Hockey:* Shooting in field hockey is most efficient from in front of the goal; however, the front position is easily guarded by the goalkeeper. "As the shot is taken progressively closer to the sideline (with the distance into the field from the goal line held constant), the angle of the shot diminishes" (Barnes and Kentwell 1979, 81). Soccer and field hockey players shoot for goals while on the run. All shots and passes are followed by a rush toward the goal.

Feinting.   Feinting or faking is a technique used to deceive an opponent. Head, eyes, shoulders, arms, and feet often initiate the fakes. A feint may also be the start of a pass or shot. The objective is to make the opponent believe the performer is moving in one direction while the performer moves in the opposite direction. The feint may occur with or without the ball. Feints may be used to create open spaces, to pass, or to drive to the scoring territory. Feints without the ball serve to open up space, avoid contact with other players, close pathways available to opponents, and create possibilities for interceptions. Feints with the ball enable a performer to get around a teammate or to draw an opponent off guard and then shoot or pass.

Guarding.   Guarding is maintaining a close distance or shadowing another person. Anticipating the movements of the person is the most important element of guarding. A guard assumes a balanced or ready position in the direction that will best enable him or her to follow the movements of the person guarded. The guard watches the opponent's center of gravity to learn as early as possible when and how the opponent is going to move.

Covering.   Covering is the guarding of a space rather than a person. Players are assigned to guard all opponents who move into the space. It is often used in soccer and field hockey.

Rebounding.   Rebounding, used in basketball and water polo, is gaining possession of the ball following a missed shot. Position is the key to successful rebounding. In rebounding, a person makes the body as stable and takes up as much space as possible. Performers analyze where the ball will go and jump to meet the ball.

Dribbling.   Dribbling is the maintaining of contact with the ball and at the same time advancing it to accomplish one or more of these objectives:

1. Get the ball out of a congested area.
2. Start a fast break, run, or swim.
3. Drive for a goal.
4. Move the ball closer to a teammate before passing.
5. Create a better passing lane.

If the performer can pass, pass; if not, dribble. A high dribble is used in basketball when a performer is not closely guarded and wishes to make distances rapidly; a low dribble is used for quick changes of direction. A long dribble is used in field hockey and soccer when in the open; a series of short, fast dribbles are used when closely guarded. In water polo, the performer catches the ball and moves, by swimming, down the pool.

Goalkeeping

Water polo, field hockey, and soccer have goaltenders or persons responsible for keeping shots out of the goal; basketball does not have such a person. Goalkeeping is a designated role in soccer, field hockey, and water polo. The goalkeeper is expected to challenge a lone attacker by moving toward the shooter and the ball. The goalkeeper should maintain a ready position with the eyes on the ball and move toward the oncoming ball. The goalkeeper should stop the opponent's ball from making a score and clear all balls from the goal as rapidly as possible.

The soccer goalkeeper may touch the ball with the hands as well as the feet. Water polo players also use their arms and hands. Each may use two hands in playing the goalkeeping position. The field hockey goalkeeper is permitted to kick the ball, stop it with body parts, and allow it to rebound from the body or hand. It is a foul if any other player advances the ball with anything other than a stick.

Goaltenders should cut for the goal to increase the portion of the goal protected. They are cutting down the angle into the goal. The goalkeeper usually deflects the ball off to the side to get it away from the goal. It may also be pushed to a teammate.

Soccer.   The goalkeeper scoops up a low ball by aligning the body behind the path of the ball, bending down, extending the arms, and collecting the ball. He or she may fall on the ball by using the hands to stop it when there is insufficient time to get behind the ball. As the hands reach out to stop the ball, the performer throws the body to the side behind the ball, grabs the ball, rolls in a side roll, and gets ready to throw the ball away from the goal. All forms of catching are used to stop the ball and move it away from the goal.

The goalkeeper may use a punt. "A step with the nonkicking foot is taken in the direction of the punt. As the kicking leg, with knee bent, swings forward from the hip, the ball is dropped so as to contact the instep of the kicking foot as the knee extends. The closer to the ground that contact is made, the lower the flight of the ball, and conversely, the farther from the ground contact is made, the higher the trajectory of the ball" (Mushier 1983, 120–121).

Field Hockey.   As in soccer, the goalkeeper's body weight is forward and in a ready position. The goalkeeper may clear a ball on the fly and send it into the playing area to a teammate or the ball may be stopped and cleared to a teammate. Clears or passes are usually made with the inside of the foot near the toe.

In a two-foot stop, the goalkeeper gives with the body absorbing the force of the ball and allows the ball to fall into a position for a clear. The best position for clearing the ball is determined by the goalkeeper's size and speed.

When the goalkeeper does not have adequate time for the two-foot stop, a one step and a clear or a clear on a moving ball may be executed. Also, an aerial ball may be stopped, with the hands absorbing the force as the ball falls to the ground in an appropriate position for a clear. "Either catching the ball momentarily or letting it rebound from the palm of the hand is acceptable as long as the ball is controlled" (Barnes and Kentwell 1979, 149).

Team play is influenced by equipment and the type of goal in these ways:

1. Goals tend to be at either end of the playing area; however, some sports have a very small goal area, whereas others have a much larger area or the entire end line as the goal.
2. Soccer and field hockey have an end line or large goal area. The players either run or drive an object across the line.
3. Physical dimensions of the playing area appear to influence the size of teams. As the size of a team increases and as the players use equipment as extensions of the body, the area tends to increase in size.
4. Basketball and water polo require the shooting of a successful basket as a goal.
5. Field hockey uses equipment to increase the body's force in driving the object into the scoring area.
6. The designated use of equipment (e.g., dribble of the ball in basketball) and the value of increased strength as a result of the use of equipment (i.e., field hockey) influences the size of the playing field.

Offensive and Defensive Strategy

Convergence on a goal teams have players whose major responsibility is either offense or defense. The offensive players are responsible for maintaining possession of the object and for scoring; the defensive players are to gain possession of the object and stop opponents from scoring. These responsibilities change as the possession of the object moves from one team to the other.

Offense.
1. Offensive strategies are based on finding the shortest route to a score and using alternative plans to deceive the opponents.
2. Offensive players have predetermined positions.
3. The player who gets the ball starts the attack.
4. Balls are passed, thrown, kicked, or hit long distances coming downcourt; short, quick passes occur near the goal. Passing is quicker than maintaining the ball and dribbling it. This means the performers are aware of the opponents who have been selected to protect the goal and the role expected from them in intercepting passes as play moves closer to the goal. Field hockey and soccer players pass the ball to the outside lanes as they come down the field. The objective is to avoid the

players in the center of the field. Once inside the opponent's scoring territory, the ball is brought to the center for scoring, thus we use the term convergence on a goal.

5. Objects are to be thrown, kicked, or hit only when the performer is sure that the receiver is capable of catching or fielding the ball. In water polo, it may be necessary on occasion to establish eye contact prior to passing in order to avoid passing to a teammate who is under water.

6. The receiver must be capable of receiving the pass at the speed, distance, and angle at which it is projected.

Specific Plays.

• *Fast break:* The fast break is a quick movement down the playing area to the opponent's goal. One performer may break clear of opponents, two may break away with only one opponent, or three may break with only two opponents. There is always a greater number of offensive than defensive players on a fast break. Fast breaks start with possession, usually as a result of a steal, foul, interception, or rebound after a shot. As possession is gained, the players advance at full speed to the goal. Long, quick passes are essential to the fast break.

• *Hole person or pivot:* A hole person in water polo is similar to a pivot person in basketball. The player is stationed in front of the opponent's goal, waiting for a pass. Good defense people will usually force the hole person to have his or her back toward the goal.

• *Rotation offense:* The basic concept is that there is nearly continuous movement; no player remains stationary for any length of time.

Offensive strategy is the key to team strategy. When the team has the ball, they attack. One player has possession of the ball as the team moves down the field, floor, or pool. All other teammates continuously position themselves so that they are ready to receive a pass and support the performer. Players are spread over the field with at least one or more players behind and ready to assist the goalkeeper or defender should an interception occur; and one or more players are ahead of the performer in possession of an open space that the performer could use in passing. Specific rules may dictate the number of players (i.e., offside). This is a dynamic, not a static, method of play. All players know where the player with the ball is and where the player plans to move. The performer in possession of the ball is able to pass a number of different ways to a wide variety of locations.

Team members work to penetrate the opponent's territory or move positively toward the opponent's goal. They attempt to get the ball behind the opponents so that scoring is possible. Sometimes this advantage is gained by going straight down the field; at other times, moving to one side of the field may shorten the distance to the goal and eliminate a number of the defenders as the defenders fan out in protecting the goal. The best pass is nearly always the pass that brings the receiver closest to the goal or the one that moves the ball behind the defenders.

Another offensive tactic is to draw one or more defenders out of position and go in for the goal.

Defense.

1. Defensive players guard the goal closely as offensive opponents move toward the goal and the scoring area.
2. Defensive players learn goal protection strategy based on principles of specific offensive strategies and rules of a specific sport.
3. Where appropriate and according to rules, defensive players make every effort to avoid permitting an offensive player to move between them and their goal.
4. The movement of opponents dictates and influences decisions.
5. Constant pressure is kept on opponents by blocking passes and shots.
6. Defensive players anticipate opponent's moves as a result of knowing their assets and liabilities—what they can and cannot do effectively.
7. Guarding is employed as a defensive strategy. Man-to-man or close guarding tends to be employed close to the scoring area, and a zone or formation cover is utilized in areas far from scoring territory. In player-to-player defense, each player is assigned an opponent whom they "stay with" or guard throughout play. In zone defense, the position of the defenders shifts in relation to the ball rather than to the opponents. Zone defense is valuable in rebounding and in reducing close shots to the basket in basketball and water polo.
8. An opponent with the ball is guarded closely whereas one without the ball is given space.
9. When a player is attempting to score in basketball and water polo, team members and opponents immediately position themselves for a possible rebound or nonscore.
10. When the player in possession of the object is pressed, a pass is executed to free the object; when a player is not heavily guarded or pressed, all passes are planned to advance the offensive play of the game.
11. Defensive players anticipate passes and look for interceptions.
12. Defensive players guard the object; they keep their eyes on the ball.
13. Defensive players look for open space and move into it. The defense objective is to stop goals and to intercept or gain possession of the ball. The defense must limit offensive passing possibilities by covering all potential open space toward the goal. They constantly stress their opponents by blocking shots and passes. This pressure encourages mistakes by the offensive team.

Specific Plays.

- *Zone defenses:* Zone defenses include the fake 2–2–2, and 1–2–3. The fake defense is a shifting from a zone to a man-to-man in an effort to confuse the opponents. The other zone defenses are described as follows:
- *2–2–2 zone defense:* In this defense each player is occupying a portion of the defensive half of the area. The defensive persons farthest away from the goal may even cross the center line of the pool or playing field.
- *1–2–3 zone defense:* This defense is used when added pressure or double-teaming an opponent is needed.

Rules

Game and Scoring

Playing time for convergence on a goal sports is either in quarters or halves, with rest periods between each playing period. Field hockey has two 35-minute halves; basketball, soccer, and water polo are played in quarters. Soccer and basketball at the high school level use eight-minute quarters; water polo uses seven-minute quarters with two-minute rest periods.

Basketball has five one-minute time-outs. They are requested by the team in possession of the ball or while the ball is dead. Field hockey, soccer, and water polo have continuous play with no time-outs except for injury, suspension of play by officials (violations and fouls), scoring, and end of playing period.

A successful score in field hockey, soccer, and water polo is one point; a successful basket in most traditional basketball play is two points. Penalties for fouls in all convergence on a goal sports constitute an opportunity to score. In basketball, the person fouled may have one or two opportunities to shoot a goal unimpeded. The nature of the foul and/or the time in the game in which the foul occurred determines the number of free shots. Soccer, field hockey, and water polo have an opportunity to shoot or drive the ball to the goal, impeded only by the designated goalkeeper. Each of these foul shots is worth one point.

The winning of a game is determined by the final score at the completion of the designated time period. When ties exist at the end of the playing period in basketball, overtime periods continue until the tie is broken. One time-out is awarded for each overtime period. Water polo uses one or more periods of three minutes of overtime to break a tie. Field hockey and soccer games may finish as a tie.

Start of Game

The game is started in the center of the playing area in all convergence on a goal sports. Basketball players use a jump ball; field hockey, a bully; soccer, a midfield free kick; and water polo, a swim-off.

The basketball jump ball occurs when one player from each team jumps to tap the ball to their teammates after the official tosses the ball between them.

Field hockey is begun with a bully at the center of the field. Neither team has possession until the bully is over. The bully is taken by two players, each facing the sideline, with the goal to the right. They alternately hit their sticks on the ground on their side and on the flat side of the opponent's stick above the ball three times. After the third hit, the ball is in play and may be taken by either player.

Water polo is started with a swim-off. Each team lines up on its respective goal line while the official places the ball in the middle of the pool. When the official whistles, the players swim toward the center to gain possession of the ball.

All convergence on a goal organizations use violations and penalties as a means of controlling game play. Violations tend to be errors in the handling of the ball, whereas fouls occur when the safety of the players are involved. Violations result in loss of possession of the ball. Opponents are given an opportunity to enhance their score as a result of incurring a foul.

Violations and Penalties
Boundary lines account for violations in several situations.

Boundaries
1. The ball is considered out of bounds when it touches a player or object out of bounds or a player steps out of bounds while contacting the ball.
2. The last person touching the ball before it goes out of bounds is credited with the out of bounds.
3. The opponent is awarded the ball at the point where the ball went out of bounds following an out-of-bounds violation.
4. Stepping on a line determines that the performer is out of bounds, and the object goes to the opponent's team. The object is taken into bounds from the same spot that it left the court.
5. In all sports, the last person to make contact with the object with any part of the body or any implement held by a body part is responsible for the out-of-bounds violation.

Specific Violations
1. Basketball also has these violations: double dribble, traveling or running with the ball, striking the ball with a fist, consuming more than three seconds in throwing a ball in from out of bounds in a three-second lane, and taking more than a designated number of seconds before shooting.
2. Water polo violations occur when an offensive player consumes more than thirty-five seconds before shooting or enters the two-meter territory prior to the ball entering the area.

Penalties for Violations.   Violations result in an award of the ball to the opponent at the spot on the sidelines nearest to where the violation occurred.

Fouls and Penalties

Fouls.   Fouls usually occur when the play is thought to be sufficiently rough that a risk exists for the players' safety. Although most fouls are clearly defined in rule books, the officials are responsible for controlling play.

Personal fouls in basketball include pushing, blocking, charging, holding, and body contact. Technical fouls include unsportsmanlike conduct, delay of game, and excessive time-outs. Personal fouls are charged to individual players. Five fouls result in disqualification.

Field hockey fouls include: sticks (raising any part of the stick above shoulder level); dangerous hitting (causing the ball to go into the air); and advancing (permitting the ball to move forward while it is stopped). Using the wrong side of the stick, hitting the ball between one's own feet, slashing sticks, personal contact, and obstruction are also fouls. Personal fouls in soccer are kicking, dangerous charging from in front or behind, pushing or tripping, holding, striking, and jumping.

Two kinds of fouls are found in water polo: ordinary and major. Ordinary fouls are similar in nature to violations in the other sports; however, they are treated like other sports treat penalties. They include touching the ball with two hands (except for the goalkeeper), failure to shoot in the designated time, pushing off the bottom of the pool, and impeding an opponent. Major fouls in water polo are similar to fouls in other convergence on a goal sports; however, they are treated more severely in water polo. Major fouls include holding, sinking, and pulling back an opponent not holding the ball.

Penalties for Fouls.   The person or team fouled against is given a free opportunity or a limited opportunity to score. In basketball, an offended player gets one free throw if the foul occurs during a goal attempt and the basket was made; two free throws in the same situation if the basket was missed; no free throws before the fifth common foul; one free throw plus a second free throw following the success of the first free throw, after the five common fouls have occurred.

Personal fouls are penalized in soccer by the awarding of a direct free kick to the opposing team. If committed by the defending side in the penalty area, a penalty kick is awarded. The one technical foul, ball handling by a player other than the goalkeeper, is awarded a free kick outside the penalty box. In field hockey, a free hit is awarded the team fouled against. No one is to be closer than five yards during the free hit.

In water polo, once the foul is called, a flag is immediately displayed indicating by color the team awarded the free throw. As soon as the foul is called, the person awarded the free throw can take it without delay from the point of the foul. Failure to take the throw in reasonable time can cause the player to commit the foul of delay in taking a free throw. In water polo, the time between the foul whistle and the taking of the free throw is dead time. A foul committed during that time would result in a one-minute exclusion from the game.

Persons committing a major foul in water polo are ejected from the game for forty-five seconds or until a goal is scored. An ejection leaves the team short a player. If a person commits three major fouls, they are ejected from the game after the third foul. Their substitute may enter forty-five seconds later or after a goal is scored.

Following a goal or free throw, the ball is put in play from behind the end line at the end of the court where the basket was made by the opposing team. If such an award occurs after a missed free throw, it is awarded across from the free throw line. A person gaining possession of the ball has forty-five seconds before taking a shot.

▶ Target

Making contact with a target, stationary or moving, is the method of scoring in target sports. These sports include archery, bowling, fencing, golf, and softball. In archery and bowling, the target is established and consistent from one environment or game to another. Golf and softball use a combination of designated and identified targets. When the objective in golf is a flag or pin on the green, the target is established; on the course, the performer plans a series of targets according to personal skill or the ability to drive distances, and the terrain, weather, and condition of the course.

Targets used on golf courses are similar to targets used in softball. A softball player may bat a home run, or may drive the ball a shorter distance to a particular location on the field to put teammates in a better position to score.

Softball and fencing use tagging or touching to put a person out. Both involve the use of a moving or dynamic target. Performers in both sports attempt to stop a moving target or to score a touch or out.

Kinesthetic acuity and imagery play a prominent role in target sports. Archery, bowling, and home run batting in softball use a single sequence of movements: golf uses a number of modified versions of a single movement. These modifications are used in relation to the location of the ball on the golf course. Also, softball and fencing make use of predetermined patterns relative to the positions and actions of opponents. As a result of the limited number of movements in target sports, considerable emphasis is placed on perfecting the sequence. These sequences are rehearsed making use of imagery and kinesthetic acuity.

A commonality of all target sports is an emphasis on a single event. Effort is focused on the moment of release of the arrow in archery; the

▶ **FIGURE 8-5**
Archery target.

bowling ball's movement to the pins; the ball to the flag in golf; the tip of the blade on the opponent's target in fencing; and hitting the ball "out of the park" in softball. Target sports will be discussed in terms of playing environment, specific execution of skill, and rules.

Playing Environment

Archery

Only target, not field archery, is discussed. Concern for indoor or outdoor ranges are considered.

Archery usually has a thirty-six-inch-square round target with multicolored circles (see figure 8-5). The target is placed at a distance of twenty to sixty yards or less for beginners and indoor play, and 100 yards for skilled performers and outdoor events. Many indoor instructional facilities are twenty-two yards—twenty yards for the course and two yards for the archer's locale.

Archery equipment consists of a bow, arrows, arm guards, finger tabs, and a quiver or holder for the arrows. All equipment is to be properly fitted and used at all times. Detailed information on fitting equipment, including ascertaining eye dominance, is contained in Haywood and Lewis (1989, 11–25), and Pszczola and Mussett (1989, 6–19). Note should be made that Atkinson (1988) suggests that some methods for stringing bows may be unsafe.

Scoring in archery is determined by where the arrow lands on the target. Nine is the center of the target, and each ring of the target from the center to the outside circle is worth a smaller score, with the outside white ring valued at one.

Bowling

A bowling alley is a wood surface, forty-two inches wide and sixty-three feet long. Gutters are located on either side of the alley. An area behind the alley is used for the performer's approach. A foul line divides the approach area from the alley. Ten pins, located in a three-foot area at the end of the alley, constitute the target.

Bowling balls, often supplied by bowling concessionaires, are twenty-seven inches in circumference and weigh from nine to sixteen pounds. The weight and the position of the finger holes in the ball are two factors to consider in ball selection. Special shoes are worn to permit the performer to slide in the approach. The sole and toe of the shoe on the foot opposite the dominant bowling hand is rubber, thus permitting the slide.

The game of bowling is referred to as a line. Ten frames constitute a line. The purpose of the game is to knock down pins. Each performer has two balls, or chances, to knock down ten pins. This is called a frame. If all pins are knocked down on the first ball, a strike is called. If all or the remaining pins are knocked down on the second ball, a spare is called. Bonuses are awarded for strikes and spares. Strikes enable the performer to add the score from each of the next two balls to the current score, and a spare enables the performer to add the score from the next ball to the current frame. If less than ten are knocked down following the second ball, the total number knocked down is the score. A perfect game is 300 points.

Fencing

Fencing is a game that has grown from an activity whose goal was to kill to one in which the objective is to touch or make an official contact with the opponent. Protective clothing and flexible, blunted blade tips have made the activity safe. The objective is to outmaneuver the opponent and score a touch or point.

Foils are the form of fencing equipment used by beginners and are discussed in this chapter. The sabre and the épée are equipment used by advanced and competitive performers. Electrical foils, usually too expensive for instructional purposes, are often used by intermediate and advanced performers. The electrical foil records touches. The performer wears a metallic vest that covers the valid target area. If the tip of the opponent's foil touches the jacket, the touch is recorded.

Beginning fencing equipment consists of the foil, glove, jacket, and face mask. Jackets are fairly heavy and made of gabardine or canvas. Special pants are worn; however, beginners should only be conscious that the legs are covered. A padded glove is worn on the dominant or fencing hand to protect the hand from the opponent's weapon. The glove is leather and covers the performer's hand and wrist.

The foil consists of a blade, a guard, and a handle. Blades are often described according to their strength. Bower (1985, 12) states that the foil, a "steel, quadrangular blade, has three sections: the forte, or the strongest third of the blade; the middle third; and the feeble or weakest, most flexible third of the blade." The guard separates the performer's hand from the blade and serves as a protector from the opponent's blade. Handles come in many styles, with the French-style handle the most popular. The handle should be easy to grip and the weight of the foil comfortable. Foils are made for right- and left-handed performers. One should use the dominant hand in fencing.

A mask is a necessity. It should have a bib to protect the chin and neck and should provide clear vision for the performer. If rust appears on the mask, it is an indication that it could be pierced and should be discarded at once.

Fencing takes place on a strip six feet seven inches wide and forty-six feet long, and fencers ordinarily move back and forth on this strip. The event is conducted in bouts. Each touch is a point against the opponent. The body target is theoretically divided into four areas: high inside, high outside, low inside, and low outside. Upper lines are above the foil hand; lower lines are below the foil hand. Inside lines are toward the front of the body; outside lines are toward the back of the body. The hand moves from side to side to protect the body. When one fencer has been hit five times, the bout ends. In competitive events, time may be used to determine the length of the bout. When time is used, the person with the lowest score at the completion of time is the winner.

Golf

Golf to the television viewer and spectator is considered competitive. Performers, however, recognize that they are competing with themselves or against the course, as well as with one or more opponents.

Golf is a game of skill and decision making. It consists of the ability to hit the ball great distances and the capacity to assess the extent of the swing needed and the proper selection of club when the desired distance is less than one's maximum hitting range. The purpose of the game is to hit a small, hard, round ball into a four-and-one-quarter inch hole in as few strokes as possible. Nine or eighteen holes are considered a round. Scoring may be stroke play, the number of strokes each competitor uses in a round, or match play, the greatest number of holes.

Golf courses have holes varying in length and terrain; hills, trees, ponds, and sand traps are among the characteristics that challenge the performer. Although golf courses differ considerably, a few similarities exist: the teeing area, fairway, and green. Each hole has a teeing area or place for hitting or driving the first ball in play from the tee. The grassy area between the teeing area and the green is called a fairway. This is where the individual subtleties of the course affect the performer. The fairway may be long or short, straight or curved, and it will contain a number of individual characteristics.

The green is the area surrounding the cup or final target. The grass is usually very short and smooth. A putter or special club is used in this area and considerable attention is focused on the condition of the green and the speed and incline of the surface as the performer strokes the ball.

Golf is played with clubs. One may use as many as fourteen clubs; however, most people begin with as few as five or six. These clubs are ordinarily a putter, a nine, seven, and five iron, and a number two or three

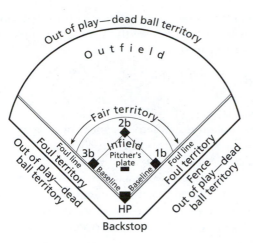

▶ **FIGURE 8-6**
Softball playing field.

wood. The number one wood is used on the tee; five, seven, and nine irons are selected for fairway play according to the distance desired from the stroke; the putter is used on the green.

Equipment is used in golf to alter the result of the swing. A person can acquire a drive, consistently use the drive, and vary results of the drive by using clubs that have different vertical angles to the surface (inclination of club face). The player chooses an implement that will alter the vertical angle of the shot. Golf club lengths also vary, thus the choice of club dictates the length of the swing.

Softball

Softball is a game of basic skills, rules, and strategy; it's a game for use early in the physical activity program. "The playing field is made up of fair territory, which is that part of the playing field between and including the first-and-third base foul lines and the outfield fence, including the air space above; and foul territory, that part of the playing field between the first and third-base foul lines and the out-of-play/dead ball territory. The playing field is further divided into the infield, that portion of fair territory that includes areas normally covered by infielders; and the outfield, that portion of fair territory that is outside the diamond formed by the baselines, or the area not normally covered by an infielder between first and third bases and the outfield fence" (Potter and Brockmeyer 1989, 1–2) (see figure 8-6).

Softball player positions include pitcher; catcher; first, second, and third base; shortstop; and left, center, right, and short fielders.

Softball equipment includes balls, a selection of bats comfortable for the players, gloves, mitts, pads, and mask for the catcher.

Games are played in innings. An inning consists of a time at bat in which each team is allowed three outs. Seven innings constitute an official game. Games are allowed to finish as ties or to enter into overtime innings to break a tie. The team at bat is on the offense; the team in the field is on the defense. Only the batting team can score.

Specific Execution of Skill

Archery

Archery's single action can be broken down into a stance, placing an arrow on the bow, draw, anchor, aim, and release. The single action is learned mechanically correct, internalized, and executed as a result of kinesthetic acuity. As each motion up to the release is executed in a slow, deliberate manner, the performer recalls the movement from memory and executes the action. The release is planned as an instant action to avoid any action or reaction of the arm, shoulder, and hand that might occur in a prerelease or slip.

Placing Arrow in Bow.   The bow is held in the nondominant hand. The dominant hand places the arrow on the arrow rest of the bow and puts the string into the groove of the arrow's nock with the index feather away from the side of the sight window. When complete, the arrow and string will form a ninety-degree angle.

The bow is gripped in a handshake position at the center by the non-dominant hand. In preparation for the draw, the middle three fingers of the dominant hand are placed on the string, with the index finger above and other fingers below the nock. The bow string is held in the pads of these three fingers.

Draw.   Archery uses a pulling technique in which potential energy is stored to be released as the arrow moves into flight. The muscles of the back, neck, and arm are employed to draw the bow back to the anchor position on the face. The dominant arm is kept straight or level, with the elbow bent and drawn directly back.

Anchor.   Ordinarily, the anchor is the position of the bow string at full extension on the center of the face (nose and mouth) of the performer. The fingers of the performer are on the string and located at the chin.

Aim.   Factors to be considered in the aim are string alignment, or setting the string, and target or picture sight. In aiming, the performer may choose to use the bow sight, a marker on the ground, or the target.

Release and Follow-Through.   In archery, the release is the most important skill. Quick or instant releases are good releases. The hand and fingers must release at exactly the same time.

Bowling

As in archery, there is only one specialized skill in bowling—the approach and sending the ball down the alley. It too involves building and releasing energy. In bowling, the energy is built up in the body, whereas in archery, the equipment as well as the body is used to build energy. The ready position, walk, and underarm throw are the fundamentals and patterns used in bowling.

Bowling incorporates a high level of kinesthetic acuity. Once the actions are acquired, the performer internalizes them and moves from memory. The feel of the most efficient movements is the key to success. The performer who knows whether the action was a success or failure will be able to either retain or repeat the successful movement or relearn the failed movement.

Mental practice and imagery are particularly important to archery and bowling.

Aiming. Accuracy is important to bowling. As a result of the length of the lane, a deviation of a couple of degrees at release results in significant change in the location of the ball at impact. The ball can be aimed at the pins a number of different ways. These include the straight, backup, curve, or hook balls. The straight ball is released with the thumb at twelve o'clock. It rolls in a straight line from the point of release to the pins. Spins are placed on the backup, curve, and hook. A backup ball has a reverse twist. The hand and wrist twist the ball clockwise at release so that the thumb comes out of the ball at the one o'clock position, thus causing a sidespin. The ball goes down the lane and when it is three-quarters of the way down, it breaks to the center of the lane. The curve ball has the opposite rotation. The thumb leaves the ball at the nine or ten o'clock position. The hook ball is rolled in the handshake position with a firm wrist and the thumb at ten o'clock.

Approach. The four-step approach is a series of steps taken in a straight line that allows the performer to gain momentum prior to delivery. Start by facing the pins squarely. Fix the eyes on the pins or a target on the alley. The distance required for the approach is paced off so that the performer can determine where to start the steps. Martin, Tandy, and Agne-Traub (1986, 16) note that "(1) speed is not the essential factor, (2) you are going to progress at a moderate pace rather than 'charge' toward the foul line, and (3) you will prepare to 'roll' the ball instead of 'throwing' it." The performer steps forward on the foot on the dominant hand side while at the same time pushing the ball forward and down to the dominant side of the body for the backswing of an underarm throw. Gravity assists the body in bringing the ball down, thus eliminating most of the push. The maximum use of gravity and the heavy ball increases the ball velocity. As the next step of the foot on the nondominant hand side of the body occurs, the ball is brought back and down in the backswing. On the third step, the back-swing is completed. The fourth step includes a slide on the nondominant foot as the dominant hand swings forward in an underarm throw and the ball is released. Follow-through occurs as the throwing hand moves near the head. The velocity acquired by the body in the approach is transferred to the ball in the swing and release.

Golf

Golf is another activity favoring the building of energy and kinesthetic acu-ity. The sport uses the fundamentals of walk, swing, and ready position. Unique to golf is the influence that the selected club has on the game. The player learns a particular stroke or drive and uses different clubs to alter the distance and trajectory of the drive. Cochran and Stobbs (1968, 8) state that a good golf swing has "speed, accuracy and the ability to repeat itself consistently."

Golf, a striking activity with a very long-shafted instrument (the club), produces a great deal of force. This force is directed from the clubhead through the center of gravity of the ball, moving the ball in a predetermined direction. The length of the club increases the momentum while at the same time decreasing the control of the club. Control, acquired through kinesthetic acuity and the acquisition of a consistent, efficient drive, is es-sential to the game.

Ball Position.   The ball is placed on a tee in the ground for driving. The distance that the performer stands from the ball determines his or her posi-tion—erect or bent over—at the time of the swing and ultimately the path of the swing.

Swing.   The need to develop an appreciation of one's capacity to deal with the potential for maximum force and to identify the force necessary to achieve a particular target in golf is similar to the dilemma mentioned ear-lier in tennis as one moves from the baseline to the net and as one finds that maximum force drives all balls out of the court. The internalization of the cognitive knowledge of distance must be organized with the kinesthetic sense of what the body can do to accomplish the desired goal or target.

Most kinesthetic acuity deals with memorizing a particular task such that muscle sense enables a consistent performance. Now kinesthetic sense is interfaced with visual perception of distance and cognitive understanding of what the body can accomplish (weight, height, skill, etc.), and a con-trolled sequence of actions is constructed that enables the performer to drive to meet the target.

Putting.   Putting, as in driving, includes a balanced body position square to the target, with eyes on the ball. The performer is usually positioned closer to the ball than in the drive because the putter is a much shorter club. Hands are positioned to work as a unit. The hands, arms, and shoulders are used in the backswing; the trunk and lower extremities are seldom called into action.

Fencing

Fencing is another sport in which kinesthetic acuity is primary. It is a sport that requires the learning of only one body position and an understanding of how to alter that position to be effective in attacking and retreating from an opponent. Force and the gaining of momentum is important to the sports of archery, bowling, and golf. Accuracy rather than force is the objective in fencing. Fencing is a game of speed and quick reaction time.

Fundamentals found most often in fencing are the walk, a very quick and short run (far less than a sprint), push, pull, and ready position. No traditional motor patterns are used in fencing. Adrian and Cooper (1989, 623) note fencing's unique characteristics: it "involves no ball, but does involve a long striking implement (foil, épée, or sabre). This implement is not swung but used as an extension of the arm. A sport of body propulsion, it involves neither running, jumping, or kicking, yet the body is propelled rapidly forward and backward during the course of the bout." Another unique feature of fencing is that a great deal of movement is required but that it is all forward or backward.

Softball

Softball players use three throwing patterns. Overarm throws are used for long distance throws from the outfield, from the shortstop, and from third to first base. Underarm throws are used while running; sidearm throws are used for pitching and quick throws following a catch.

Stopping is strategic in softball. Usually players are coached to run over the base to ensure they will reach the base. Game rules and strategy require the performer to be able to stop rapidly when necessary.

Base Runner.   As soon as the batter bats successfully, he or she becomes a base runner. Base runners are instructed to run as soon as they have completed the batting follow-through. Base runners are able to run quickly under control and are able to avoid other players by stopping, starting, and shifting directions. They should turn their bodies toward first base after the batting follow-through and run. The run is a sprint; they may run past first base and not be tagged out. If possible, they should continue to run to second, third, and, time permitting, to home plate. Each time they get to a base, they are to swing wide as they approach the base and then swing in and touch the corner of the base.

Runners often select a track start when running from one base to the next. Other starts are the rolling and leadoff starts.

Infield Position and Play.   Infield includes first, second, and third bases, shortstop, pitcher, and catcher. First base coverage is from midway between home plate and first base to midway between first and second base. The objective is to prevent persons from getting to first base. First base players are responsible for catching balls hit to first base and to other infielders, forcing out runners, throwing to second base to force out a runner, relaying throws from right field, and backing up second base.

The second base player covers an area from midway between first and second base to second base, and the infield behind the pitcher's area. This player is expected to field all balls sent into that area, throw to first or third for forced outs, tag players running between first and second base, and relay throws from the outfield.

The shortstop, positioned halfway between second and third bases, covers from second base to near third base. Shortstops are responsible for fielding all balls coming in their direction, for relaying balls from the outfield, and for backing up second base.

The third base player covers a short distance toward shortstop, from third to home, and the field in front. Because more balls are hit toward third base, third and shortstop often have a greater number of hits to field. A third base player backs up the shortstop, relays fielded balls, tags players out at third, and throws to first for forced outs.

In addition to pitching successfully and attempting to strike out as many players as possible, pitchers also back up plays and throws to home plate, cover first base when the first base player is fielding a ball, and back up second and third base players on throws from the outfield.

Catchers catch pitches, tag out runners attempting to score at home, throw to first, second, and third for tag outs, and field hits that remain near home plate.

Rules

1. Static sports require that the body be maintained behind a foul line. Archery has a foul line behind which the performer stands to make the distance equitable in target competition. Bowling has a foul line behind which one completes the approach prior to throwing the ball. Golf has a designated space in which one tees the ball and drives for the initial stroke in a regulation game.
2. In all target sports except softball, there is a specific target area in which the contact is made. The archery target, with its weighted value per circle, is one example. In fencing, the contact is between the collar and the bottom of the jacket.
3. The use of officials differs in these sports. Archery, bowling, and golf do not require officials. Players know the rules and attempt to monitor their behavior within the framework of the rules. Others are present while the performer is executing the skill and can remind the performer

should he or she violate a rule. Softball is played with the same honor system as archery, bowling, and golf with performers identifying violations as they commit them.

4. As softball players' skills improve, thus increasing the pace of the game, it becomes necessary to give the responsibility of officiating to an outside party. Fencing, in turn, is such a fast-moving activity that it is recommended that officials be introduced early in the learning process. Participants learn to officiate as they learn to participate. Fencing officials include a director and four judges. Judges determine touch and whether they have been made on a legal target. Four judges vote on each decision. Majority rules.

5. Offense and defense tactics are found only in softball and fencing in target sports. In fencing, one performer attacks, and the opponent either retreats or parries the attack. The retreat is often the favored tactic. The objective in fencing is to counter the attack and become the attacker.

6. Softball scores are obtained as a result of home runs, placement of hits, position of runners, and evasive tactics in response to opponents. Offensive tactics are based on place hitting, sacrifice play and stealing bases, and hit and run plays. Defensive tactics are catching batted balls and throwing to bases prior to the runner's arrival.

7. In dynamic or moving target play, the fencing and softball players are to make play difficult for opponents. Every effort is made to cause opponents to be off guard.

▶ Self-Dominated

Self-dominated activity organizations are person-centered sports. Often they represent movement for self or the joy of movement. Dance, gymnastics, skating, skiing, swimming, and track are self-dominated activity organizations. These activities can be participated in alone or as a member of a group; are enjoyed equally by novice and elite performers; and provide a framework for lifelong movement.

Self-dominated activities use the closed, not open, system of movement, or movement in an established sequence rather than reacting to the movements of others. Also, the closed system permits the performer to execute a movement alone or without other participants. The performers provide their own intrinsic or internal personal challenges to improve or to change movements; they do not rely on the performance of another for motivation.

Self-dominated organizations do not use as many specialized skills as placement and convergence on a goal organizations use. Their closed system is similar to a number of target sport organizations. Often the objective of self-dominated sports is the ultimate efficiency of the fundamental movement from a physiological and biomechanical perspective. This is true of track, swimming, speed skating, and skiing—sports in which speed is the objective. Style and creativity is the objective in dance, skating, and gymnastics. The ability to master movement under various conditions and terrains is the objective of downhill and cross-country skiing.

Balance is a primary element of all self-dominated activities. It is the performer's capacity to maintain an upright or inverted position. Balance and kinesthetic acuity are elements essential to the repetition of movement. Form is the word used to describe efficient movement repeated with consistency. Most discussions of balance focus on the inner ear and proprioceptor that tell the body how to maintain a stable position. In addition to the need for a high level of communication from these sense organs, the performer engaged in self-dominated physical skills must also possess sufficient strength to be able to carry out the message. Strength is necessary to maintain balance in the body, to assist the body in losing balance, and to enable the performer to regain balance. This emphasis on balance enables people to maintain regular lifetime movements. Everyday survival, particularly among the senior population, is often based on balance and the strength and confidence essential in retaining and maintaining daily living skills.

In addition to balance, nearly all basic skills are employed in self-dominated organizations. Two important differences in basic skills exist: objects are not projected or received, and equipment is used for performance in gymnastics and mobility in skating and skiing.

Self-dominated activities have movements that are either established, created by the performer, or a combination of established and performer-created. The traditional movements or form in each of these activities has evolved over time. Form is based on the principles of efficient movement and movements created to increase the difficulty of a performance. Track, swimming, skiing, and skating are activities in which the performer employs the principles of physics to obtain the most efficient movement. Winning in competition is based solely on the ability to cross a finish line faster than a competitor. Time is the objective against which the performer competes. These same activities, incidentally, are engaged in by most people in a non-competitive manner purely for the joy of movement or the sensation of maintaining fitness; they seldom engage in competition.

Another factor in self-dominated activity organizations, with the exception of skiing, is that the cost is low and within reach of most people.

Self-dominated organizations will be discussed in terms of playing environments and strategy expressed as performance, choreography, and speed. Playing environments are the spaces in which self-dominated organizations are performed. The strategy of performance includes those activities in which specialized skills are used in ways that are unique and or specified by the rules of competition for the sport. Choreography is the form used to present the sport or art form to the audience, whereas the element of speed becomes the strategy unique to those activities in which competition is a race.

Playing Environment

The play environment in self-dominated organizations is seldom specified until a competitive event is scheduled. Performers dance in the space available; ski on the hill that is convenient; swim in lakes, streams, and bodies of water; run and skate where they will not be disturbed; and engage in gymnastics wherever space is adequate.

Gymnastics, more than other self-dominated activities, requires a certain amount of space. The amount of space needed is influenced by the distance the performer plans to move to gain momentum prior to executing a stunt on equipment.

Performers engaged in synchronized swimming, skating, and free exercise in gymnastics or skiing are encouraged through choreography to use the space available. The use of floor space, and in swimming, the depth and surface of the water, is an element judged in rating the quality of a routine or performance. As a result of the universal acceptance of these elements, specific space dimensions have been assigned in free exercise in gymnastics and in some freestyle skiing events. Skating rinks and swimming pools are constructed for ice hockey and speed swimming, respectively, thus providing fairly stable environments for competition.

No effort, with the exception of gymnastics, is made to standardize the environments in which self-dominated activities are enjoyed for personal use. Again, gymnastics is monitored to assure that the performer has adequate space to execute stunts.

Although these activities are enjoyed while one performs alone, they present situations in which one needs to have another person available to ensure a safe environment. No one is to engage in any of these activities in an environment in which they would not receive immediate attention should they be injured. One is often cautioned not to ski, swim, or take part in gymnastics without a partner, lifeguard, spotter, or some other person available. Similar caution should be exercised in all self-dominated activities.

Strategy: Performance

Performance, or the ability to execute a movement as efficiently as the athlete's body will permit, is the objective of self-dominated activity organizations. Performance involves precision, timing, creation, and the ability to replicate the presentation of another. Precision, or the detailed form for each movement, is orchestrated in an array of time frames as dictated by the vision and illumination of the choreographer. The performance may be a verbatim replication of the work of another or a creation by a choreographer.

Ice skating, skiing, gymnastics, and dance are balance sports. Ice skates present a challenge to the performer's balance even before entering the ice. Performers must be able to control the body over a very narrow blade rather than the entire foot. Practice in placing the body weight equally over each blade is done prior to setting out on the ice. The performer is encouraged to find a barrier for balance and to practice weight transfers and two- and one-foot balances prior to moving on the ice.

Gymnastics, figure skating, and synchronized swimming are movement organizations in which competition is controlled by trained and certified judges who rate a person's performance by predetermined criteria. On occasion the criteria have been set to violate certain principles of efficiency in order to make success in competition more difficult. In synchronized swimming, for example, the performer in stunt competition must begin in a stationary position. Overcoming inertia and initiating the stunt is far more difficult than originating the stunt with a swimming stroke. The way in which a performer uses Newton's first law—a body at rest remains at rest; a body in motion remains in motion—causes the stunt to be either easy or difficult.

Style is a word often used in the category to describe how a performer puts a routine together or the way in which a certain skier or skater favors a position or moves the body. Creativity on the part of a performer is rewarded in dance, freestyle skiing, gymnastics, and synchronized swimming. As a result of these differences, choreography is discussed in strategy.

Examples of elements unique to performance in self-dominated activities are discussed in the next section.

Skating

Edge Control.   Once performers can maintain balance and propel themselves on the ice, they become concerned about the fine points of skating. Knowledge of body position and edge control becomes paramount. Each ice skate blade has an inside edge, or the edge nearest the center of the body, and an outside edge, or the edge to the outside of the body. When the weight is placed directly over the blade, the blade is skated flat or with weight equally placed over both edges. To use edges, the performer places the body weight over the edge used in performing the skill. Edges are practiced as half circles on the ice. A half circle is made using only the inside edge followed by a half circle using only the outside edge.

Skating routines consist of jumps, hops, and backward and forward stroking movements. With the exception of stroking or forward movements on the ice, skills used in skating are found in fundamentals, patterns, and the specialized skills used in other sports.

Skiing

Balance and rhythm are the basic elements of all forms of skiing. Kinesthetic acuity or Yacenda's (1987, 6) terms "ski feel" and "ski-snow sensitivity" describe skiing. Skiing may be cross-country or downhill. Considerable energy is needed, for example, in cross-country skiing when the body is to be moved uphill. The performer is aware of inertia and the forces essential to efficient acceleration and the maintaining or gaining of momentum. Downhill skiing, in turn, uses gravity to increase body speed as the person comes down the hill. Emphasis is placed on using force to control the body in a series of turns as the body comes down the hill, and to stop or slow the skis on command.

Dance

Square Dance. Square dance has its own structure and form. Four couples are in a square with each couple forming one side of the square. Home position exists when all couples face the center of the square with the males on the left. Many of the movements are circling to the right or left, with all members of the square holding hands, or sending two or more members of the square to the center of the circle. Promenade is a movement in which couples hold hands in a specific position and move forward in a circle. Couples are aligned one behind the next. A do-si-do is executed with partners facing each other and then passing around each other, right shoulders to right shoulders.

Allemande left and grand right and left are more advanced maneuvers. In an allemande left, the corner people link left arms, turn a complete turn, and return to their home position and partner. In a grand right and left, partners join right hands; one partner moves forward grasping the hand of a member of the next couple with the left hand and altering hands as the performer moves around the circle. Women move clockwise; men move counterclockwise (Harris, Pittman, and Walter 1988, 127).

Many steps similar to those explained constitute the content of square dance. Once these skills are acquired, the caller, or person in charge of the dance, may call out any step or combination of steps and the performer moves according to the command. Through the years, a number of sequences have been passed on from one generation to the next and have provided set routines for square dance.

Folk Dance. Folk dance, in contrast, consists of a sequence of dance steps that are performed in a specific manner to a certain piece of music. Most of these dances are traced to the unique customs of a country and were originated either to be used as exhibitions at festivals or to be the means of group interaction at large gatherings and social events. Some of these dances have costumes and highly stylized steps that speak of the country in which they originated. Ethnic dance is an important part of the culture of our country.

Gymnastics

The following are examples of activities that take on unique meaning in gymnastics. Traditional balance beam activities are recommended for all stunts as they use a wide range of skills. Note that the balance beam is not a competitive event in formal men's gymnastics.

Balance Beam.   Carpenter (1985, 156) recommends nine categories of balance beam movements: mounts, locomotor skills, turns, poses, jumps, leaps, tumbling, acrobatics, and dismounts. Mounts can be a V sit; a step-up, as a knee scale; or a variety of other poses, including jumping up onto the beam. Turns are another feature. A number of dance steps can be used effectively on the beam, as can jumps and leaps. Among the tumbling and acrobatics used on the beam are forward and backward rolls. The backward roll is modified to a shoulder roll so that the performer maintains close contact with the beam during the roll.

Dismounts or methods of leaving the beam range from merely jumping down to a somersault off the end.

Toe Stand—Dance Step in Gymnastics.   Body stands tall with the weight on the toes, and arms stretched out to the sides.

Arabesque.   This is a one-leg balance with the upper leg extended at a ninety-degree angle from the floor. The upper body is extended forward with the head held up slightly. A straight line is to exist from the extended fingers to the extended leg.

One-Leg Balance.   A one-leg balance has the body standing tall with the weight on one leg while the other leg is held straight up in the air.

Aquatic Skills

Swimming is using the water to support the body and using the arms and legs to propel the body through the water. Aquatic art or synchronized swimming is the use of the body to create unique shapes and figures, similar to those found in diving, gymnastics, and skating. These shapes, accompanied by swimming strokes, are often choreographed to music to create a routine. The aquatic environment is also used as an exercise spa for aqua aerobics. Here dance steps and free movements used in exercise are merely executed in the water.

Strategy: Creative Choreography

A quality piece of choreography, according to judges, is one that makes the viewer of the performance forget everything but the performance. The viewer is "literally stunned" immediately following the performance and can only think of what they have just seen. Minton (1986, 1) notes a "special quality about a piece of choreography that makes the observer want to get involved. In such a dance, the observer is lifted from his theatre seat and transported along during the performance." Hinkley (1980, 34) notes, "It is common knowledge that the combination of music and dance help create the artistic completeness which then arouses that reaction of aesthetic pleasure when we either watch a piece of work or dance in it ourselves." This statement is appropriate to all performances in which the freedom to create is part of the movement. Dance, gymnastics, skating, freestyle skiing, and synchronized swimming share this common bond.

All elements of choreography, down to the handling of the arms, is appropriate to each of these movement organizations. Adshead (1988) presents a framework for analyzing dance, a framework relevant to all self-dominated creative activities. Smith and Smith argue that aesthetic appreciation can be taught; they state that "appreciative encounters with aesthetic objects can be analyzed into something resembling a set of rules, steps and procedures." Compositions may be emotional or may involve a theme.

Themes

A composition in dance, skating, freestyle skiing, free exercise, or synchronized swimming has a theme. The theme conveys the purpose or idea of the presentation to the audience. The choreographer or the performer has an idea, and that idea is to be conveyed to the audience. The question is, what will the audience need to see in the movement in order to recognize and/or understand the theme? A choreographer is a broker of ideas. The choreographer takes an idea and recommends movements, music, and other art forms that will enable an audience to receive the idea. An understanding of who the audience is, what they will expect, and how they will react to a particular form or sequence of movements is important. Equal knowledge of the physical skill, repertoire of movements, and style of the performer(s) is essential. Themes can be controlled by the types of movements selected, the speed of movements, or the style and selection of accompaniments. The rules of competition in skating, free exercise, and synchronized swimming may restrict the creativity of the choreographer's work.

Minton (1986, 6), using ideas found in Blom and Chaptin's *The Intimate Act of Choreography* (1982), describes two traditional approaches to choreography: A, B and A, B, A. A, B consists of a composition with parts A and B. "While sections A and B fit together in terms of the common feeling of a composition, they each contain elements that are distinctly contrasting in tone." A and B may be alike or different. Transitions are used to enable the movements and ideas expressed in the movements to flow from A to B. Whether the transition is abrupt or continuous is up to the choreographer.

A, B, A is an approach taken from systems often employed in the creation of musical compositions. Again, two sections are created and executed in the typical A, B order. However, the performer returns to the A theme as a finish. Often the performer approaches the final A theme in a new and different manner; however, the basic theme remains the same.

Rondo, another common approach, makes use of multiple sections or many miniselections, with the repetition of one section from time to time. Section A may be repeated following every other section, or after two or three other sections. A dominant section exists and is used often.

Other forms of choreography focus on either movement or music. When the movement is the focus, a series of movements are put together as a theme. This series may be executed in a number of different ways involving levels, pathways, etc., while maintaining the timing and sequence, or they may be executed in the same style many times altering timing and sequence.

Aerobic dance choreography faces a different set of problems. The dance itself is expected to be aerobically efficient, or able to raise the heart rate to a certain level and sustain that rate for a designated period of time. Enjoyable music with a routine that maintains aerobic fitness while increasing flexibility, strength, and muscular endurance without injury is the goal of the composition or activity.

Composition

The preparation of a composition can be compared to writing a short story. It has a beginning, a middle, and an ending. Each paragraph or part of the composition is essential to the whole. All parts of the composition are to have meaning and be part of the theme. Movements that do not contribute to the theme are to be avoided even if they are some of the finest skills the performer executes. The beginning introduces the composition, the middle provides the story of the composition, and the ending serves as a summary or an end to the thematic presentation.

Unity, continuity, transition, variety, and repetition are essential. All segments of the composition are attached to the theme in a meaningful way. One movement is to flow to the next and to be an integral part of the composition. Continuity is best sensed when the beginning, middle, and ending follow logically. The audience senses the theme or that a theme exists. "Such a dance provides a natural and organized progression of phases so that one movement phase flows naturally into the next!" (Minton 1986, 4).

Transitions are movements selected for their capacity to make the movement flow. Synchronized swimmers use floating formations, rolls, or regular swim strokes such as the breaststroke as transitions. Skaters employ stroking forward or backward as transition movements.

Variety and repetition are to be examined in the context of every theme. Variety is used to carry out the theme while at the same time maintaining the attention of the audience. Repetition, in contrast, is used to impress upon the audience the importance of the theme. Variety is necessary to maintain audience attention; repetition is essential to enable the audience to recognize and feel the theme. Each must be used to balance the presentation.

If possible, movements involving more than one performer are to be executed so that each performer's role is integral to the movement. In other words, the movement could not be executed or the theme could not be carried out if one of the performers was not present. Each is needed for the part he or she plays in the whole. Identical movements executed by more than one performer are to be closely associated with the theme, be making a needed statement, or be avoided. Identical movements of the type described are often found in synchronized swimming; they are seldom found in skating and dance.

Accompaniment.   The choreographer, after selecting the theme, decides whether to create the composition and select music to accompany it, or to select music or art and create a composition to accompany the music or art. Creative dance, gymnastics, skating, and synchronized swimming compositions may be works in their own right or choreographed merely to accompany some other art form, usually a musical selection.

Creation of a composition to music is often easier than locating music to accompany a finished product. As a result, the beginner will often use the musical accompaniment approach in those first efforts with choreography. For detailed information on music and gymnastics routines, consult Gula (1990).

When the composition is choreographed to music, the composer analyzes the music and decides whether the music is an A, B; A, B, A; rondo; or another form. If the form of music is a suite, the beginning is usually moderate, followed by "a slow second part, and a fast, lively third section" (Minton 1986, 8). Some music changes form rapidly after a few bars, while other music is typical A, B or A, B, A form.

Creating the Composition.   Experimentation with a variety of movements enables the choreographer to identify those movements that best portray the ideas to be conveyed. The performer explores all the moves that accompany emotions relating to the theme. If a musical selection is the focus, the performer moves freely to the music, allowing the music to suggest timing, emphasis, and movement sequences. Movements that are best for the performer and that will be understood by the audience are selected.

On occasion, the amount of space and the length of the presentation are factors in designing the composition.

Strategy: Speed

Swimming, skating, skiing, and track have competitive events in which speed is the objective. Starting, pacing within the event, and finishing are the commonalities of these events. Starts require a vast burst of energy or thrust onto the race course. The ability to respond instantly to a gun or other method of starting is important. Once on the course, the performer needs to acquire a system for self-pacing for the length of the event. Pacing, or the capacity to obtain the fastest speed for the total event, is an individual matter. For some, the early part of a race may be at 80 or 90 percent capacity with energy reserved for all-out movement near the finish line.

▶ References

Adrian, Marlene, and Cooper, John. (1989). *Biomechanics of Human Movement.* Indianapolis, Indiana: Benchmark Press.

Adshead, Janet (Ed.). (1988). *Dance Analysis, Theory and Practice.* Cecil Court, London: Dance Books.

Atkinson, Jim. (1988). *Archery, A Sport for All Seasons.* Bessemer, Alabama: Colonial Press.

Barnes, Mildred J. (1980). *Women's Basketball.* Boston: Allyn and Bacon.

Barnes, Mildred J., and Kentwell, Richard G. R. (1979). *Field Hockey, the Coach and the Player.* Boston: Allyn and Bacon.

Bower, Muriel. (1985). *Foil Fencing.* Dubuque, Iowa: Wm. C. Brown.

Carpenter, Linda Jean. (1985). *Gymnastics for Girls and Women.* West Nyack, New York: Parker.

Cicciarella, Charles F. (1981). *The Sport of Water Polo.* Boston, Massachusetts: American Press.

Cochran, Alastair, and Stobbs, John. (1968). *The Search for the Perfect Swing.* Philadelphia: J. B. Lippincott.

Fabian, Lou. (1986). *Racquetball: Strategies for Winning.* Dubuque, Iowa: Eddie Bowers.

Gula, Denise A. (1990). *Dance Choreography for Competitive Gymnastics.* Champaign, Illinois: Leisure Press.

Harris, Jane A., Pittman, Anne M., and Waller, Marlys S. (1988). *Dance a While.* New York: Macmillan.

Haywood, Kathleen, and Lewis, Catherine F. (1989). *Teaching Archery, Steps to Success.* Champaign, Illinois: Leisure Press.

Hinkley, Carolie. (1980). *Creativity in Dance.* Chippendale, Sydney: Alternative Publishing Co-operative Limited.

Martin, Joan L., Tandy, Ruth E., and Agne-Traub, Charlene E. (1986). *Bowling.* Dubuque, Iowa: Wm. C. Brown.

Minton, Sandra Cerny. (1986). *Choreography, A Basic Approach Using Improvisation.* Champaign, Illinois: Human Kinetics.

Mushier, Carole L. (1983). *Team Sports for Girls and Women.* Princeton, New Jersey: Princeton Book.

Potter, Diane L., and Brockmeyer, Gretchen A. (1989). *Softball.* Champaign, Illinois: Human Kinetics.

Pszczola, Lorraine, and Mussett, Lois J. (1989). *Archery.* Dubuque, Iowa: Wm. C. Brown.

Yacenda, John. (1987). *High Performance Skiing.* Champaign, Illinois: Leisure Press.

Foundations of Physical Activity

Part II contains the foundations upon which the hierarchy of movement was constructed. Chapters 9 through 13 are summaries of the content of human movement. Nutrition, physiology, biomechanics, psychology, and sociology are included. Each chapter gives an overview of the area and a comprehensive list of references. The instructor should seek out those sources that will provide greater detail in the areas that they wish to obtain further assistance.

NUTRITION

Nutrition is the study of foods and how food affects the body. What one eats affects how one feels, how one's body grows and develops, how one looks, and how one performs in physical activity. Williams (1988, 4) defines nutrition as "the sum total of the processes involved in the intake and utilization of food substances by living organisms, including ingestion, digestion, absorption and metabolism of food." Understanding nutrition enables a person to:

- maintain optimum body weight and body composition
- know what to eat, when, and why
- become an informed consumer

Nutrition plays an important role in physical activity because the participant's success or ability to move at an optimum level is directly related to the nutritional status of the body. Essential to success is that the performer maintain a balanced diet. A second and equally important nutritional consideration is that exercise plays a vital role in weight maintenance and reduction. The person interested in reducing body weight or in maintaining an attractive appearance must exercise and eat the suggested amount of each recommended food. An understanding of nutrition is essential to all persons engaging in physical activity. It is particularly important to teenage athletes and dancers because research (Douglas and Douglas 1984; Benson 1985) suggests that neither male nor female performers are eating a balanced diet.

▶ Nutrients

Nutrients are the basic substances within food for which the body has use. They

- provide energy for metabolism
- build and repair body tissue
- regulate body processes

The six major categories of nutrients are

1. Carbohydrates
2. Fats
3. Proteins
4. Vitamins
5. Minerals
6. Water

Energy for metabolism is provided by carbohydrates and fats; proteins assist in this function. Proteins build and repair body tissue, primarily muscles and soft tissue. Minerals, particularly calcium and phosphorus, build the skeleton. Vitamins, minerals, and proteins work together to regulate body processes.

Carbohydrates

Carbohydrates are compounds composed of carbon, hydrogen, and oxygen. They are the major sources of energy for the body, serve as fuel for the central nervous system, and play an important role in the metabolism of fats. The basic carbohydrate unit used in the body is glucose, also referred to as dextrose or blood sugar.

Carbohydrates are converted by the body to glucose and then transported through the bloodstream to the body parts. Glucose is (1) used by the cells for energy, (2) stored as glycogen in the muscles, and (3) converted to fat and stored. When glucose is needed as an energy source by exercising muscles, the glycogen stored in the muscles is used and the glycogen in the liver is reconverted to glucose and transported by the blood to the working muscles. This process is called glycogenolysis. Adequate carbohydrates must be included in a diet for an active person to be able to maintain energy.

The primary function of carbohydrates is to provide an energy supply to the body cells. When the amount of glucose is insufficient to power the cells, the glucose stored as glycogen in the muscles is recruited into action. Blood sugar levels are higher following a meal, thus providing glucose to the cells for energy. Excess glucose is converted to glycogen and stored in the muscles for later use. When the muscle's capacity for storage has been exhausted, the excess glucose may be converted to fat and stored beneath the skin.

Carbohydrates have traditionally been categorized into simple and complex. The simple carbohydrates are referred to as sugars and the complex carbohydrates as starches and fibers. Note should be made that some of the sugars come from fruits, which also contain vitamins, minerals, and fibers, in contrast to the concentrated sugar found in cookies and cakes.

It is thought that American people fail to use the amount of carbohydrates necessary for proper nutrition. Figure 9-1 describes the recommended diet changes in carbohydrate consumption.

For most athletes, carbohydrates are recommended in the same percentages as for the general population. Higher carbohydrate levels, up to seventy percent, have been recommended for heavy endurance training athletes only.

▼ **FIGURE 9-1**

Actual and recommended carbohydrate intakes for Americans. Reproduced by permission from Hockey, Robert V.: *Physical Fitness: The Pathway to Healthful Living,* ed. 6, St. Louis, Times Mirror/Mosby College Publishing.

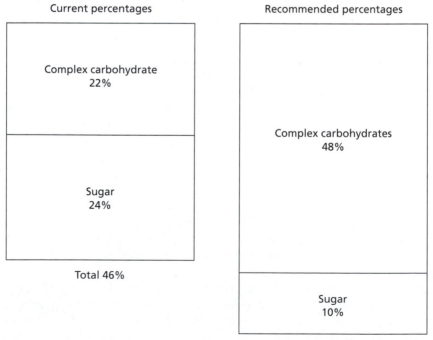

Carbohydrate Loading

Carbohydrate loading is a system in which endurance athletes regulate the intake of carbohydrates over a period of time prior to an event, in an effort to maximize the value of carbohydrates on the day of the event. Carbohydrate loading may be recommended for endurance athletes participating in cycling, running, and swimming events or athletes required to participate for long periods of time in stop and start activities such as tennis. Further details on carbohydrates and carbohydrate loading can be found in Katch and McArdle (1988, 47–48), Williams (1988, 69), and Blom, Costill, and Vollestad (1987).

Fats

Fat is an essential dietary component. It has both positive and negative effects on the body (excess fat is the negative effect). Among the positive effects are that fat slows the digestive process, making people feel full for a longer period of time. It serves as support and protection for vital organs such as the heart, liver, kidneys, spleen, brain, and spinal cord. Fat is an insulator against cold environments, particularly cold water environments. It transports vitamins A, D, E, and K to the cells of the body. A certain quantity of fat in the body can be an advantage as a heat regulator. The disadvantages of excessive fat, particularly in warm environments, far outweigh the advantages.

There are two types of fat, saturated and unsaturated. Saturated fats are fats such as butter that are animal in origin and remain in solid form at room temperature. Unsaturated fats such as peanut oil that are plant in origin remain liquid at room temperature. Common sources of fat are listed in table 9-1.

All fats, saturated and unsaturated, have the same number of calories.

In light and moderate exercise, energy comes from the body's stores of carbohydrates and fats in equal amounts. In endurance or prolonged exercise exceeding an hour, the body's fat supplies provide a significant amount of the energy. Very long exercise periods may cause the percentage of energy from fat to be as high as ninety percent.

▼ TABLE 9-1

Common sources of fat

	SATURATED	UNSATURATED
	Beef	Avocadoes
	Butter	Olives
	Cheese	Peanuts
	Chocolate	Peanut butter
	Ice cream	Corn oil
	Lamb	Mayonnaise
	Milk	Soybeans
	Veal	Vegetable oil

Fat provides the greatest amount of energy and the most efficient storage in the body. Although carbohydrate metabolism is the preferred source of energy in exercise of high intensity, fats play a major role in mild to moderate exercise intensity and in exercise of prolonged exertion (more than an hour or two of activity). In mild exercise (fifty percent of VO_2 max) about fifty percent of the energy is from carbohydrates and fifty percent from fat. Fat has nine calories per gram, more than twice that of carbohydrates and proteins. Little water is stored with fat, whereas three to four grams of water are stored with each gram of protein or carbohydrate.

Women possess a greater percentage of body fat than men. Various authors have speculated that this should enable women to be superior in events of prolonged exertion (Dyer 1982, 26). Many attribute women's success in the Iditarod Trail Race, a dogsled competition held in Anchorage, Alaska, to this factor. Williams (1988, 91) states that under well-controlled studies in which men and women have been matched for aerobic capacity, there has been no difference between the sexes in the utilization of fats.

Studies of trained athletes show that they use more fat as energy than untrained athletes. Training helps one learn to use fat. Costill's (1979) research notes that highly trained runners derive as much as seventy-five percent of their energy from fat.

Fat, a source of energy, is secondary to carbohydrates in providing fuel for the body's work. Fat, however, is the nutrient of greatest interest to the American public because excessive consumption of fat is believed to be associated with heart disease and cancer. Hockey (1989, 213) lists several reasons for reducing one's fat content:

1. Each gram of fat provides you with more than twice as many calories as each gram of carbohydrate or protein.
2. Fat energy is easily stored, whereas excess proteins and carbohydrates must be converted to fat to be stored. For this reason excess calories from protein and carbohydrates will affect metabolism differently from excess calories obtained from fat. It has been shown that the 'metabolic cost' associated with 100 excess calories of fat is only 3%; thus 97% of these calories will be stored as fat. With 100 excess calories of carbohydrates the 'metabolic cost' is 23%, and only 77% of these calories will be stored as fat.
3. Dietary fat is thought to be a contributing factor in the development of certain diseases, including cardiovascular disease, diabetes, and certain forms of cancer. Reproduced by permission from Hockey, Robert V.: *Physical Fitness: The Pathway to Healthful Living,* ed. 6, St. Louis, Times Mirror/Mosby College Publishing.

Cholesterol, a fat-like substance found in animal tissue, has been receiving a great deal of attention recently. It is consumed while eating animal products. Cholesterol may also be synthesized within the body processes. Although cholesterol's association with heart disease gives it a negative image, the performer in physical activity should note that a certain amount of cholesterol is essential for the manufacture of bile in the digestive system and of the hormones estrogen, androgen, and progesterone. These hormones are responsible for the development of male and female sex characteristics.

Research (Katch and McArdle 1988, 10) indicates that lowering blood cholesterol has a significant effect on the reduction of the incidence of heart attacks and the chances for survival among those sustaining such attacks. Studies show that the improvement in heart disease risk is related to a reduction in cholesterol by a factor of one to two. A one percent reduction in cholesterol causes a two percent reduction in risk.

Protein

Protein is the nutrient used to build, repair, and replace cells in the body. It forms the structural base of muscle tissue, is a component of muscle enzymes, and serves as an energy source in muscle contraction. It is important in the regulation of metabolism. Protein is used in the formation of hemoglobin, hormones, and antibodies. It is used in the transportation of fats and the regulation of fluids in the bloodstream. Hair, fingernails, and the protective layer of skin are also composed of protein. Protein plays a major role in the formation of new bone and in blood clotting. Hemoglobin, the oxygen and carbon dioxide in the red blood cell, consists of an iron-containing compound and a protein. The body does not maintain protein reserves. Once the body has consumed the protein it needs, the remainder is used for energy or stored as fat.

Protein is usually associated with animal products such as meat, fish, poultry, milk, or eggs. But, plants such as dry beans, lentils, and peas are also good sources of protein.

The body uses protein by breaking down the food substances in digestion to amino acids. Enzymes in the stomach and small intestine break the food protein into polypeptides and then into amino acids.

Amino acids are absorbed through the intestinal wall and are taken by the blood through the bloodstream to the body cells. There are twenty-two amino acids—thirteen that can be made by the body and nine that have to be taken in with foods. A food containing all nine amino acids is called a complete protein; those containing less than the nine are called incomplete proteins. Animal products, such as meat, fish, poultry, cheese, and eggs usually contain all nine amino acids; vegetable products, such as rice, beans, seeds, and nuts are low in one or more amino acids. Eggs are considered the best source of protein. Among the plant sources, peas and beans have the greatest protein.

The recommended daily allowance for protein (RDA) is set at eight to ten grams per kilogram of body weight. Determine your recommended intake by completing this calculation:

1. Record your body weight in pounds (_____ lbs.)
2. Convert your body weight to kilograms by dividing by 2.2

$$\text{body weight (kg.)} = \text{body weight (lbs.)}/2.2$$
$$= \underline{\hspace{2cm}} /2.2$$
$$= \underline{\hspace{2cm}} \text{ kg.}$$

3. Multiply your body weight in kg. by .8

$$\text{RDA for protein} = \text{Body weight (kg.)} \times .8$$
$$= \underline{\hspace{2cm}} \times .8$$
$$= \underline{\hspace{2cm}} \text{ grams}$$

Proteins are not considered as important to the exercising body at the time of activity as are carbohydrates and fats. They are, however, needed to maintain healthy muscles and body structures. Recently, researchers have shown that protein may be a significant source of energy when exercise is of a prolonged endurance. Research supports the concept that aerobic endurance training enhances the muscle cell's ability to use carbohydrates and fats as energy during exercise. Aerobic endurance training may also enhance the muscle cell's ability to absorb proteins; however, research is inadequate to permit such a conclusion.

Vitamins

Vitamins are organic substances used by the body to perform metabolic functions within the cells. Although they are essential in the regulation of body functions, they do not contain calories and are, therefore, not a source of energy. Their major role is in growth and development of the nerves and muscles. Vitamins work with other chemicals in the body to create enzymes. Enzymes digest food, make muscles contract, release stored energy, transport gases, assist in growth and development, and play a role in blood clotting.

Vitamins are not manufactured by the body; they must be provided by the foods ingested. There are thirteen vitamins that must be consumed. Nine are water soluble; four are fat soluble. Water soluble vitamins cannot be stored and must be used each day. Fat soluble vitamins are stored in the fat deposits in the body and are used at a later date. The fat soluble vitamins are A, D, E, and K (see table 9-2 for more information).

▼ **TABLE 9-2**
Essential vitamins

VITAMIN NAME (other terms)	U.S. RDA OR ESADDI for adults and children under four	MAJOR SOURCE
FAT SOLUBLE VITAMINS		
Vitamin A (retinol; provitamin carotenoids)	5.000 IU or 1,000 RE	Retinol in animal foods: liver, whole milk, fortified milk, cheese. Carotenoids in plant foods: carrots, green leafy vegetables, sweet potatoes, fortified margarine from vegetable oils.
Vitamin D (calciferol)	400 IU	Vitamin D fortified foods like dairy products and margarine, fish oils. Action of sunlight on the skin.
Vitamin E (tocopherol)	30 IU	Vegetable oils, margarine, green leafy vegetables, wheat germ, whole grain products, egg yolk.
WATER SOLUBLE VITAMINS		
Thiamin (vitamin B_1)	1.5 mg	Ham, pork, lean meat, liver, whole grain products, fortified breads and cereals, legumes.
Riboflavin (vitamin B_2)	1.7 mg	Milk and dairy products, meat, fortified grain products, green leafy vegetables, beans.
Niacin (nicotinamide, nicotinic acid)	20 mg	Lean meats, fish, poultry, whole grain products, beans. May be formed in the body from tryptophan, an essential amino acid.
Vitamin B_6 (pyridoxal, pyridoxine, pyridoxamine)	2 mg	Protein foods, liver, lean meats, fish, poultry, legumes, green leafy vegetables.
Vitamin B_{12} (cobalamin; cyanocobalamin)	6 micrograms	Animal foods only, meat, fish, poultry, milk, eggs.
Folic acid (folacin)	400 micrograms	Liver, green leafy vegetables, legumes, nuts.
Biotin	300 micrograms	Meats, legumes, milk, egg yolk, whole grain products, most vegetables.
Pantothenic acid	10 mg	Beef and pork liver, lean meats, milk, eggs, legumes, whole grain products, most vegetables.
Vitamin C (ascorbic acid)	60 mg	Citrus fruits, green leafy vegetables, broccoli, peppers, strawberries, potatoes.

From Melvin H. Williams, NUTRITION FOR FITNESS AND SPORT, 2d ed. Copyright © 1988 Wm C. Brown Communication, Inc., Dubuque, Iowa. All Rights Reserved. Reprinted by permission.

Vitamin B_{12} is the only vitamin synthesized in animals; the rest are manufactured in the leaves and roots of plants in a process called photosynthesis.

Vitamin supplements are popular among athletes and physically active people. Medical authorities support the view that a well-balanced diet will provide the vitamins essential for the body. It should be noted that foods may lose their vitamin value through refining processes, improper storage, or overcooking. Purchase naturally vitamin-rich food, store according to directions, and eat it as soon as possible.

Minerals

Minerals are inorganic substances that maintain the acid base and water balances within the body. They play a role in blood clotting, absorption of nutrients, oxygen transportation, nerve conductivity, and formation of bones and teeth.

Minerals function in the conversion of food to energy; they are also used in the synthesis of glycogen from glucose and protein from amino acids. Calcium, the greatest mineral, combines with phosphorus to form bones and teeth. Calcium is also used by the muscles for blood clotting and transporting fluids across cell membranes. Phosphorus, a component of the high energy compounds, is essential to all-out exercise (adenosine triphosphate [ATP] and creatine phosphate [CP]).

Adequate minerals should be obtained from a well-balanced diet. Mineral supplements are recommended only in unusual cases. Natural iodine is a mineral unavailable in some geographic regions of the country. Iodine is stored in the thyroid gland. A diet deficient in iodine may result in overenlargement of the thyroid gland. The use of iodized salt is a solution to the problem.

Iron is a mineral often found to be insufficient among women and women athletes (Risser et al. 1988). This condition in women is directly related to the menstrual cycle. Endurance performers must have adequate iron because it is critical to the oxygen energy transport system in the body. Iron-deficient anemia will reduce a person's chances of performing endurance activities at a maximum level.

Haymes (1987) describes iron deficiency as taking place in several well-defined stages. Iron depletion is stage one. As a result of insufficient iron in the diet, the body will use up its stores in the bone marrow and liver. Stage two is iron-deficient erythropoiesis. Stage three is being anemic and four is having iron deficiency anemia. She notes that studies show iron depletion in adolescent girls at 24.5 percent, women, 21.1 percent, and children, 17.7 percent (Haymes 1987, 246). Foods rich in iron include:

- liver and organ meats
- meat, fish, and poultry
- shellfish
- dried apricots, dates, figs, raisins

- dried peas and beans
- whole grain products, breads, cereals
- broccoli, asparagus, and green leafy vegetables

Although growing children need a high level of calcium daily, adults should also consume 800 milligrams of calcium, or about that contained in three eight-ounce glasses of milk. Katch and McArdle (1988, 27) stated that "25% of all females in the United States consume less than 300 mg of calcium on any given day." This imbalance causes the body to draw upon its reserves in the bones. When the imbalance is prolonged, osteoporosis occurs.

Osteoporosis causes the bones of the body to become porous and brittle. Bones may break under the strain of regular movement. The comment that the "bone broke before the fall" is often the description of osteoporosis. Osteoporosis affects nearly twenty million people in the United States and accounts for 1.3 million fractures per year and more than eighty percent of all hip fractures among females (Shangold 1988). Nearly twenty percent of all hip fractures among the elderly result in death. Of those who survive, more than half go to nursing homes. The medical cost of osteoporosis in the United States exceeds $6.1 billion annually.

A prime defense against osteoporosis is calcium. Some believe that the 800 milligram RDA standard of calcium is too low and should be raised to 1200 to 1500 milligrams for women after menopause (Heaney, Recker, and Saville 1978). In addition to adequate calcium, regular exercise may help to slow the rate of aging of the skeleton (Smith, Reddan, and Smith 1981).

Water

Water is the most important nutrient needed by the body; in fact, it represents about sixty percent of the body weight. Nearly two-thirds of the water in the body is located in the cells; one-third of the remaining water is extracellular and contributes to the plasma volume. Plasma transports oxygen and removes waste during activity. It is needed in digestion, absorption, circulation, excretion, nutrient transport, tissue building, and maintenance of body temperature. The body must maintain its water balance. Failure to do so results in dehydration and if severe enough, will result in death. Water comes from the breakdown of many foods in digestion and from that taken in directly. The amount of water one needs depends on the body weight of the individual and the stresses, including body temperature changes, placed on the body. The amount needed is often perceived to be two quarts per day.

▶ Energy

Energy is the ability or capacity of the body to do work. Energy may be chemical, mechanical, or electrical. Energy, by definition, is the capacity to work. Energy expenditure within the body differs considerably from resting to strenuous exercise. Fatigue or lack of energy may be due to inadequate carbohydrate ingestion, thus reducing the supply of muscle glycogen or blood glucose. It may also be due to a deficiency in vitamins and minerals.

Energy is usually measured by the amount of oxygen a person consumes. It is measured in kilocalories, commonly known as calories. One calorie is the amount of heat required to increase the temperature of one gram of water one degree Celsius. Energy is obtained from carbohydrates, proteins, and fats:

- Carbohydrates: 4 calories/gram
- Proteins: 4 calories/gram
- Fats: 9 calories/gram

Vitamins, minerals, and water do not contain calories.

The first law of thermodynamics states that energy can neither be created nor destroyed. Human energy comes from the food we eat. Nutrients are broken down to carbon dioxide (CO_2) and water (H_2O) by a metabolic process called respiration. This metabolic process supplies energy for body growth and development and for muscle contraction.

Carbohydrates, fats, and proteins ingested into the body are converted to chemical properties and stored as high energy phosphates. Adenosine triphosphate (ATP) is the fuel used for all energy processes in the cell. ATP is one molecule of adenine and ribose, called adenosine, combined with three phosphates, each consisting of phosphorus and oxygen. Energy is released when ATP breaks down as a result of the action of enzymes and is transferred to the cells (figure 9-2). This breakdown results in an immediate source of energy for action. For example, when ATP is transferred to the cells that are part of the contractile elements in muscle tissue, the cells cause the muscle to contract.

ATP breakdown is essential for muscular contraction. The muscle cells are able to retain only a limited supply or storage; therefore, there must be a continuous regeneration of ATP. This requires energy. Fox, Bowers, and Foss (1988) describe this energy-yielding system as three distinctly different processes: (1) the phosphagen system (in this system the energy comes from phosphocreatine {PC}), (2) the anaerobic glycolysis or the lactic acid system, or (3) the "oxygen system," which includes the oxidation of carbohydrates or the oxidation of fats. Both parts of the oxidation system result in something referred to as the Krebs cycle.

Energy-releasing reactions that depend on oxygen are aerobic. Energy-releasing reactions that can occur in the absence of oxygen are anaerobic. The ability to release energy without oxygen means that the body can attain a great amount of energy on a moment's notice. This permits a person to

▼ **FIGURE 9-2**

Energy release from ATP by the activation of the enzyme ATP-ase. From Jack H. Wilmore and David L. Costill, *Training for Sport and Activity*, 3d ed. Copyright © 1988 Wm. C. Brown Communications, Inc. Dubuque, Iowa. All rights reserved.

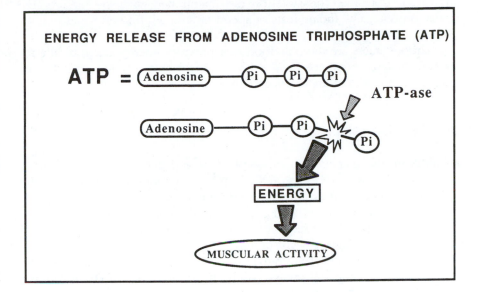

run very fast for a few seconds or lift a heavy weight. The phosphagen system and the anaerobic glycolysis system are anaerobic or without oxygen whereas the oxygen system is aerobic.

Phosphocratic System

The phosphocreatine system makes use of the creatine phosphate (CP) that is stored in the muscle cells. When CP breaks into creatine and phosphate, it releases energy at once without the aid of oxygen. The energy is immediately available and becomes part of the resynthesis of ATP.

Anaerobic Glycolysis

A second anaerobic system or metabolism in which ATP is resynthesized within the muscle is in the breakdown of carbohydrates to lactic acid. This breakdown is incomplete and the system is inefficient. As a result, lactic acid is created, causing muscle lactic acid levels to rise. High acid content in the muscle fiber can alter the muscle's ability to contract. Without oxygen, the cell can realize less than ten percent of the ATP that it would receive in an oxygenated environment.

During short, all-out bursts of activity or in the early moments of longer activities, the body is not capable of providing oxygen sufficient to regenerate ATP. During this time, the phosphocratic and anaerobic glycolysis systems can generate enough energy with oxygen to maintain the athlete for a short period of time. This system is also mentioned when people are able to demonstrate outstanding feats of speed or strength for very short periods of time.

Carbohydrates are the only food that provides energy anaerobically for ATP. In heavy, endurance exercise, when anaerobic reaction must supply energy, carbohydrates are the main contributor.

▶ Metabolism

Metabolism, the combination of all physical and chemical changes in the body, involves two processes: anabolism and catabolism. Anabolism is the building-up process or synthesis of basic nutrients; catabolism is the breaking down or disintegration of the body compounds. For example, the energy released from the breaking down of muscle glycogen, to be discussed later, supports the energy needs of anabolism.

The metabolic rate of an individual represents the speed at which the body is using its stores of energy. Body functions of heart beat, breathing, and the activity of the nervous system consume energy. Basic metabolic rate (BMR) is the energy required to maintain physiological activities at rest. Exercise such as walking, lifting, or climbing increases the metabolic rate. For example, walking at three miles per hour results in an expenditure of 4.2 calories per minute; running at five miles per hour results in an expenditure of 9.4 calories per minute (Williams 1988, 35).

The intensity of the exercise determines the number of calories expended. Skill level of the athlete may also be a factor in calorie expenditure, with beginners who engage in considerable nonproductive movement consuming more calories per minute than those whose high level of skill permits a streamlined performance.

Intensity and duration are the key elements in exercise for energy expenditure. Gross motor movement or large muscle exercises use the greatest number of calories. Activities such as running, walking, swimming, and cycling provide intense activity for long periods of time.

Exercise will not only increase the metabolic rate during the activity but will keep the rate elevated during recovery from the activity. An increase in body temperature and in amounts of circulating hormones, particularly adrenalin, and elevated circulation and respiration will remain for a limited time following exercise. These metabolic aftereffects of exercise will expend calories, thus having implications for weight control. The greater the intensity of the exercise, the greater the effect of the recovery.

Exercise intensity determines the nutrients to be ingested. Persons engaged in mild to moderate exercise should consume about fifty percent carbohydrates and fifty percent fat. Muscle glycogen, glucose from the liver, and fat deposits from the tissue are used. As the exercise increases in intensity, the performer's body relies increasingly on carbohydrates as the energy source. When intense exercise is sustained for an hour or more, carbohydrates may become depleted and fats will take over as the primary source of energy.

▶ Oxygen System

For persons to be able to engage in all-out activity, they must have a continuous supply of energy. Aerobic metabolism, or the breaking down of carbohydrates, fats, and proteins in the presence of oxygen, creates a supply of energy. Metabolism of these nutrients in the absence of oxygen is inefficient and unavailable for exercise lasting more than a short period of time. Endurance events place a heavy role on the supply of energy.

Fox, Bowers, and Foss (1988, 20) further break the oxygen system into aerobic glycolysis, Krebs cycle, and electron transport systems. The aerobic glycolysis system is similar to the anaerobic glycolysis system discussed earlier, except that lactic acid does not accumulate in the presence of oxygen. "Oxygen does this by diverting the majority of the lactic acid precursor pyruvic acid into the aerobic system after the ATP is resynthesized."

The Krebs cycle takes the pyruvic acid formed during aerobic glycolysis and oxidizes it, producing CO_2.

The electron transport system or the respiratory chain is the reaction in which water (H_2O) is formed as the end product of the glycogen. "H_2O is formed from the hydrogen ions and electrons that are removed in the Krebs cycle and the oxygen we breathe" (Fox, Bowers, and Foss, 1988, 21).

Fats and proteins can also be aerobically broken down to carbon dioxide and water, thus releasing energy for the resynthesis of ATP. As mentioned earlier, fats are stored as fatty acids beneath the subcutaneous tissue and at other protective sites in the body, whereas proteins are stored in the liver.

Different demand for energy and for the nutrients supplying energy is required for rest, short-term duration exercise, and endurance or long-term events. The resting state metabolism is supplied by oxygen or aerobic. Approximately two-thirds of the fuel used is fat and one-third is carbohydrate.

Exercise of two or three minutes, such as sprinting events of 100 and 200 yards, fast-moving, long tennis rallies, and fencing points are termed short duration. In short duration events, the major fuel is carbohydrates with fats playing a minor role. The metabolic system is anaerobic. Energy is supplied by the phosphagen and the anaerobic glycolysis systems. It takes the body two or three minutes for oxygen consumption to increase to a higher level, thus resulting in the anaerobic metabolism. The period of time in which the oxygen consumption is below that necessary to supply the ATP required is called oxygen debt. As the body metabolism increases, the anaerobic glycolysis, an increase in lactic acid, will also occur. Due to the effect of lactic acid on the muscles, the body, using an anaerobic metabolism, must either reduce activity considerably or move to an aerobic state at the end of two to three minutes.

Prolonged exercise is defined by Fox, Bowers, and Foss (1988, 32) as ten minutes or longer. Carbohydrates and fats make up the nutrients, with carbohydrates playing an important role in exercise of ten to twenty minutes' duration. As the exercise period extends beyond twenty minutes, glycogen stores begin to deplete and fat becomes a more important source of energy for the resynthesis of ATP.

In intense exercise of duration, such as maximal isometric contractions, the glycogen stores of a given muscle can be exhausted in ten to twenty contractions of thirty seconds or less. That means that activity beyond the twelve repetitions would require use of fat stored in the body. Fat will also be metabolized as athletes required to use the fast shuttle movements of soccer, tennis, and football exceed an hour to an hour-and-one-half of play.

Glycogen stores require one to two days for replacement. If the performer exercises before the stores are replenished, fat will be used by the body to create energy.

The point at which the glycogen reserves deplete and fat begins to be utilized is influenced by the proportion of fast-twitch–slow-twitch muscle fibers, the state of training, and initial glycogen stores.

This information is important to teachers concerned with the pacing of performers. It is considered unwise to start an endurance event in an all-out pace, creating an oxygen debt and the resulting accumulation of lactic acid. Pacing needs to be such that the athlete will not experience a lactic acid or oxygen deficit until the final sprint. Performers, when possible, should maintain a steady state throughout a performance and finish with an all-out effort. Tennis advisors should be particularly sensitive to the potential length of a match and to the need for sprint activity within the match. If the performer is challenged to all-out activity early in a match, there will be a need to replace carbohydrate stores during the rest periods.

Another factor in athletic performance is related to muscle fibers. Two types of muscle fibers, slow-twitch and fast-twitch, are found in the body. Fast-twitch fibers have a high capacity for anaerobic metabolism in the production of ATP. Fast-twitch fibers also have a high contraction speed. They are activated in short-term sprint activities. Slow-twitch muscle fibers favor aerobic metabolism. They have the capacity to generate ATP aerobically much faster than fast-twitch. Slow-twitch muscles are used in endurance activities where sustained energy is important. Swimming, running, and cycling require aerobic and anaerobic capacities (Katch and McArdle 1988, 69).

It should be noted that the percentage of fast-twitch and slow-twitch muscles differs from person to person. Although metabolic capacity is improved by training, distribution appears to be genetically determined. This is the basis on which scientists have stated that certain people are genetically predisposed to success in certain sports.

▶ Oxygen and Recovery Rate from Exercise

Breathing, pulse rate, and body processes do not recover immediately after exercise. Light to moderate exercise results in a rapid recovery while exhaustive exercise will require a much longer time for recovery. A deficit in oxygen occurs in the first two or three minutes of all exercise and continues to increase in exhaustive exercise. In light exercise, the body recovers rapidly upon stopping the exercise. In prolonged endurance exercise, a steady state is not reached and anaerobic reaction provides energy. This is accompanied by an accumulation of lactic acid.

In light exercise, recovery of oxygen rate returns to resting levels in one to two minutes. In strenuous exercise, there is a lactic acid accumulation usually accompanied by an increase in body temperature, and it may take one to two days to return to the preexercise condition. The amount of time required for the replacement of muscle glycogen is dependent on the type of exercise that caused the depletion and the amount of carbohydrates consumed during the recovery period. Hermansen and Vaage (1977) and MacDougall and associates (1977) have examined glycogen replenishment in intermittent, short duration exercise and found that much of it is resynthesized in less than two hours without food intake. They also found that thirty-nine percent recovery was in the first two hours and fifty-three percent recovery was in five hours. Twenty-four hours on a normal diet seemed to complete the process.

In continuous exercise, about twice as much glycogen is depleted and extra carbohydrates in the diet increase the speed of resynthesis. Fifty percent of the lactic acid caused by anaerobic metabolism of carbohydrates is removed in twenty-five minutes (Hermansen 1975). All of it will disappear in about an hour.

▶ Weight Maintenance and Reduction

Maintenance of body functions is essential to the control of optimum body weight. Maintenance of body functions is even more important to the athlete reaching optimum or elite physical skill status. Physical performance is known to decrease when nutrition is poor. Adequate nutrition in general and for serious athletes can be maintained through a balanced diet. The addition of over-the-counter nutrients to the diets of persons in nutritional balance does not appear to enhance physical performance.

▶ Diet and Exercise

An optimal diet is one with enough nutrients to enable tissue maintenance, repair, and growth. Exercise does not require a change in diet; it merely requires the same balanced diet expected of all people. Strenuous and prolonged exercise often requires a greater intake of calories than the intake required of a sedentary person.

Physically active people should obtain sixty percent of their calories from carbohydrates, usually unrefined starches. Katch and McArdle (1988) recommend a four-food-group plan to provide the essentials of nutrition (see table 9-3).

▶ Diet and Body Fat

Most people want an ideal body weight. Numerous systems exist for determining ideal body weight. The charts from these systems do not agree and as a result are subject to criticism. They do, however, give people a general idea of what an individual's weight should be.

There are a number of ways to measure body fat. A common research technique is underwater weighing. This is an expensive technique and one that will seldom be used with large groups of people. The skin fold technique and the more recent sensor technique are preferred.

The following facts about weight loss must be considered: One pound of fat is thought to be approximately 3,500 calories. Calories are expended in daily movement and in all-out exercise. To maintain current weight, one must ingest the same number of calories as that used. If more are ingested than used, weight will increase; if fewer are ingested than used, weight will decrease.

▼ TABLE 9-3

The four-food-group plan

FOOD CATEGORY	EXAMPLES	RECOMMENDED DAILY SERVINGS
1. Milk and milk products	Milk, cheese, ice cream, sour cream, yogurt	2
2. Meat and high-protein	Meat, fish, poultry, eggs—with dried beans, peas, nuts, or peanut butter as alternatives	2
3. Vegetables and fruits	Dark green or yellow vegetables; citrus fruits or tomatoes	4
4. Cereal and grain food	Enriched breads, cereals, flour, baked goods, or whole-grain products	4

From F. Katch and W. McArdle: *Nutrition, Weight Control, and Exercise,* 3d edition. Philadelphia, Lea and Febiger, 1988. Reprinted with permission.

▶ Diet and Endurance

Continuous moderate exercise requires body fat and carbohydrates for energy. If exercise continues and glycogen stores in the liver and muscles are used up, the breakdown of fat becomes the chief source of energy. Strenuous endurance training such as running, cycling, or swimming can bring on staleness as a result of training. This occurs when the body's carbohydrate reserves are depleted. This can occur even though the person maintains a normal diet. It may take from two to five days to restore muscle glycogen after such strenuous, long-term bouts of exercise. Rest of two days and high carbohydrate intake will restore optimal muscle glycogen levels (Katch and McArdle 1988, 46). Katch and McArdle (1988, 46) report research that found that "endurance capacity varied considerably depending on the diet each consumed in the days prior to the endurance test. The endurance capacity of the subjects fed the high carbohydrate diet was more than three times greater than the endurance capacity of the same subjects on the high fat diet. Clearly, these findings emphasize the important role of nutrition in establishing the appropriate energy reserve." A high carbohydrate diet is used by athletes whose activities exceed seventy-five minutes in duration.

Excess weight or overfat can lead to numerous diseases and a general condition of poor health. Obesity can also make it difficult for a person to perform certain physical skills. Further, excess weight contributes to a negative self-image and other personality problems. Excess weight occurs when the body consumes more calories than it needs to function effectively. The overfat person can either reduce the number of calories taken in each day or increase the amount of physical activity or calories expended. A sound weight maintenance program includes a combination of decreased caloric ingestion and increased exercise.

Katch and McArdle (1988) recommend a desirable body fat content of twenty-five percent for women and fifteen percent for men. They suggest that approximately thirty percent of today's females and twenty percent of today's males are overfat.

▶ Summary

1. Good nutrition or a balanced diet is essential for optimum physical performance.
2. A balanced diet is important to weight maintenance and reduction.
3. The addition of over-the-counter nutrients to the diets of persons in nutritional balance does not appear to enhance physical performance.
4. Nutrients are the basic substances within food for which the body has use. Six major categories of nutrients are carbohydrates, fats, proteins, vitamins, minerals, and water.

5. Carbohydrates are the major source of energy for the body; they serve as fuel for the central nervous system and metabolize fats.

6. Fatigue or lack of energy may be due to inadequate carbohydrate ingestion. It may also be due to vitamin or mineral deficiency.

7. Mild to moderate exercise requires the ingestion of fifty percent carbohydrates and fifty percent fat. As the exercise increases in intensity, a greater amount—up to seventy percent—of carbohydrates are used. When the exercise is sustained for an hour or more, carbohydrates are depleted and fats take over as the primary source of energy. Very long exercise periods may cause the percentage of energy from fat to be as high as ninety percent.

8. Fat has negative and positive effects on the body. It is easily stored by the body and it is thought to be a contributing factor in heart disease, diabetes, and certain forms of cancer. The positive effects include slowing the digestive process, insulating against cold, protecting body organs, and transporting vitamins to the cells.

9. Trained athletes learn to use fat effectively; untrained athletes do not use fat as effectively.

10. Proteins are used to build, repair, and replace body cells, including muscle tissue. They are also important to metabolism regulation.

11. Vitamins are organic substances that work with other chemicals in the body to create enzymes for regulation of growth and development, for the release of stored energy, and for blood clotting.

12. Minerals maintain acid-base water balances, blood clotting, nutrient absorption, oxygen transport, nerve conductivity, and the formation of bones and teeth. Endurance performers must have adequate iron to facilitate oxygen transport in the body.

13. Calcium intake is particularly important to ward off osteoporosis among the elderly. What one consumes as a young person and in midlife determines one's sensitivity to osteoporosis as an older person.

14. Water, the most important nutrient, represents sixty percent of the body weight. Failure to maintain an appropriate water balance based on the person's body weight and temperature can result in dehydration and, ultimately, in death.

15. The intensity of the exercise determines the number of calories expended. The skill level of the performer may also affect the caloric expenditure, with beginners using more energy than elite performers.

16. To maintain current body weight, one must ingest the same number of calories as one burns in exercise. To increase body weight, one must ingest more calories than are burned; to decrease body weight, one must ingest fewer calories than are burned or used.

17. Regular exercise may help to slow the aging rate of the skeleton.

▶ References

Benson, Joan, Gillien, Donna, Bourdet, Kathy, and Loosli, Alvin R. (1985). Inadequate nutrition and chronic calorie restriction in adolescent ballerinas. *Physician and Sportsmedicine, 13*(10), 79–90.

Blom, P., Costill, D., and Vollestad, N. (1987). Exhaustive running: inappropriate as a stimulus of muscle glycogen supercompensation. *Medicine and Science in Sports and Exercise, 19,* 398–403.

Costill, D. L., Fink, W. J., Getchell, L. H., Ivy, J. L., and Witzmann, F. A. (1979). Lipid metabolism in skeletal muscle of endurance trained males and females. *Journal of Applied Physiology, 47,* 787–791.

Douglas, P. D., and Douglas, J. C. (1984). Nutrition knowledge and food practices of high school athletes. *Journal of the American Dietetic Association, 84,* 1198–1202.

Dyer, K. F. (1982). *Challenging the Men: Women in Sport.* New York: University of Queensland Press.

Fox, Edward L., Bowers, Richard W., & Foss, Merle L. (1988). *The Physiological Basis of Physical Education and Athletics.* Dubuque, Iowa: Wm. C. Brown.

Haymes, Emily M. (1986). Nutrition and ergogenic aids. In Vern Seefeldt (Ed.), *Physical Activity and Well-Being.* Reston, VA: AAHPERD.

Haymes, Emily M. (1987). Nutritional concerns; need for iron. *Medicine and Science in Sport and Exercise, 19*(5), 5197–5200.

Heaney, R. P., Recker, Robert R., and Saville, Paul D. (1978). Menopausal change in calcium balance performance. *Journal of Laboratory Clinical Medicine, 92,* 953–963.

Hermansen, L. (1975). Lactic removal at rest and during exercise. In H. Howald and J. R. Poortmans (Eds.), *Metabolic Adaptation to Prolonged Physical Exercise.* Basel, Switzerland: Karger.

Hermansen, L., and Vaage, O. (1977). Lactate disappearance and glycogen synthesis in human muscle after maximal exercise. *American Journal of Physiology, 233*(5), E422–E429.

Hockey, Robert V. (1989). *Physical Fitness: The Pathway to Healthful Living.* St. Louis: C. V. Mosby.

Katch, Frank I., and McArdle, William D. (1988). *Nutrition, Weight Control and Exercise.* Philadelphia: Lea and Febiger.

MacDougall, J. D., Ward, G. R., Sale, D. G., and Sutton, J. R. (1977). Muscle glycogen repletion after high-intensity intermittent exercise. *Journal of Applied Physiology, 42,* 129–132.

Risser, William L., Lee, Eva J., Poindexter, Holly B. W., West, M. Stewart, Pivarnik, James M., Risser, Jan M. H., and Hickson, James F. (1988). Iron deficiency in female athletes; its prevalence and impact on performance. *Medicine and Science in Sport and Exercise, 20*(2), 116–121.

Shangold, Mona M., and Mirkin, Gabe. (1988). *Women and Exercise: Physiology and Sports Medicine.* Philadelphia: F. A. Davis.

Smith, Everett L., Reddan, William, and Smith, Patricia E. (1981). Physical activity and calcium modalities for bone mineral increase in aged women. *Medicine and Science in Sport and Exercise, 13,* 60–64.

Williams, Melvin H. (1988). *Nutrition for Fitness and Sport.* Dubuque, Iowa: Wm. C. Brown.

Wilmore, Jack H., and Costill, David L. (1988). *Training for Sport and Activity.* Dubuque, Iowa: Wm. C. Brown.

Physiology

Physiology is the study of the structure and function of the body. Exercise physiology is the "study of how the body, from a functional standpoint, responds, adjusts, and adapts to exercise" (Fox, Bowers, and Foss 1988, 1). An understanding of how the body functions will aid the professional in designing exercise, fitness, and conditioning programs for active people. Also, it will enable the professional to understand and recognize the ability and potential capacity of each individual. Muscular and cardiorespiratory systems are discussed. Theories, taken from research and practice, are incorporated into training programs.

▶ Muscles

Muscles give form and shape to body contours; functionally they produce movement. The muscles possess tissue that connects with the dense connective tissue of the tendons. Tendons connect to the bony framework of the body. Muscles work through the tendons to move the bones of the body. An adequate supply of arteries and veins provide blood to the muscles, tendons, and connective tissue. Motor and sensory nerves supply the body with information from the central nervous system and the muscle sense organs.

Muscles constitute about forty percent of the body mass. When a muscle acts, it produces tension and attempts to work. Work does not necessarily mean shortening of the muscle, although muscles often shorten as they work. Thus, a contracting muscle may shorten, lengthen, or stay the same.

Muscles can be categorized as prime movers, antagonists, and stabilizers. Prime movers are muscles principally responsible for the movement at a given joint. Muscles that produce joint actions equal and opposite that of prime movers are antagonistic muscles. Antagonistic muscles relax and lengthen during a movement. They often change roles and become prime movers as the body action is reversed. Stabilizers are muscles responsible for stabilizing a joint to allow the range of movement desired by the prime mover. Shoulders, hips, and back muscles make use of many stabilizers.

Muscles contract when force is developed within the muscle. The force occurs at the time the energy of the ATP, discussed in chapter 9, is released. This contraction is regulated by a motor unit. Motor units are motor neurons and muscle fibers that receive stimulation from the nerves. The strength of a muscle contraction is controlled by the frequency of nerve impulses and the number of motor units activated. Adjustments are made by changing the nerve impulses and the number of working motor units. Muscle strength increases as the frequency of nerve impulses increases; muscle strength decreases as the frequency of nerve impulses decreases.

Even though the central nervous system plays a major role in the strength of a contraction, slow-twitch and fast-twitch muscle fibers are also a factor. Fast-twitch muscle fibers favor maximum force, whereas slow-twitch muscle fibers favor submaximal force production. Fast-twitch fibers produce a high force concentration for short periods of time whereas slow-twitch fibers provide low force contractions for long periods of time. Genetic background, predetermined muscle composition, and type of exercise contribute to the amount of slow- and fast-twitch muscles in a given individual. (See Fox, Bowers, and Foss 1988 and Wilmore and Costill 1988 for more information.)

The arrangement of muscle fibers also contributes to their capacity to work. Muscles with long fibers that run parallel to the line of pull produce little force but allow a wide range of movements. Muscles with short fibers that run diagonally to the line of pull produce greater force and have a small range of motion. Long-fibered muscles favor range of motion whereas short-fibered muscles favor force.

Muscular Strength

Muscular strength is the maximal force or effort a muscle or a muscle group exerts against a resistance in one trial or execution. The ability to exert tension and produce force is specific to the muscle group. Strength is essential to the development of physical skills, efficient athletic performance, good posture, elimination of low back pain, avoidance of injury, and the ability to react positively in emergency situations. Muscles generate force; some amount of force is requisite to all movement. To improve strength, the muscle works at maximum contraction with few repetitions.

Research (McDonagh and Davies 1984) suggests that gains in strength may occur when participants are able to recruit additional motor units and to synchronize the firing of the motor units to facilitate contraction. Strength is also related to the size of the muscle. The larger the muscle, the stronger it is.

In training for muscular strength, the overload principle is applied. Either the load or the resistance is increased. To develop strength and endurance, the muscle performs at its maximum against workloads that are above that normally encountered. Eccentric, concentric, and isometric contractions are used for strength training. No research has concluded that muscular overload significantly stimulates the development of new muscle fibers. Existing muscle fibers become larger; new muscle fibers are not created.

As muscle strength increases, muscles become larger. Historically, women were hesitant to develop strength for fear of acquiring bulging muscles. Although exercise increases the size of the muscle mass, hypertrophy does not occur among women, even when they are lifting the same amount of weight as the men are lifting. Researchers have hypothesized that the male hormone testosterone is responsible for hypertrophy. Dyer (1982, 83), in discussing the results of a compilation of studies, noted that "strength in these women increased by up to 50 percent with virtually no increase in muscular size. . . . Women, in other words, will not inevitably end up as muscle bound he-men (or she-women)."

Power is the product of strength and speed. Increase in power results from increase in strength or speed, or both. Training will increase muscular strength and speed of movement. Strength is acquired through few repetitions at maximum resistance. Strength training increases the amount of work that can be accomplished in a short period of time. Costill (1986, 119) states "that it appears that strength is one of the major determinants of muscle endurance in explosive sprint events."

Muscle soreness, occurring in the later stages of activity or immediately following activity, is usually due to the accumulation of end products of exercise or the damage caused by the pressures that force fluids to shift the blood plasma to the tissue. This pain or soreness usually lasts for only a brief time.

The muscle soreness that occurs twenty-four to forty-eight hours following activity has a number of theories. Wilmore and Costill (1988) state that the phenomenon is still not clearly understood. Theories include structural damage to muscle membranes or muscle tissue breakdown, inflammatory reactions within muscles noted by an increased white blood cell count, or a deficiency of blood.

Muscular Endurance

Muscular endurance is the ability of a muscle or muscles to sustain a contraction over a long period of time or to perform repeated contractions against a load without fatigue. Muscular endurance is dependent on strength. Dynamic endurance is the repeated lifting of a fixed weight at a set cadence until fatigue or until the pace can no longer be maintained. Corbin and Lindsey (1988, 73) define dynamic muscular endurance as the "muscle's ability to contract and relax repeatedly. This is usually measured by the number of times (repetitions) you can perform a body movement in a given period of time." Static endurance, in contrast, is a "muscle's ability to remain contracted for a long period of time. This is usually measured by the length of time you can hold a body position."

Muscular endurance, like muscular strength, is acquired through the use of the overload principle. Overload means that strength and endurance will increase only when the muscles perform for a given period of time at their maximal capacity against a workload in excess of that routinely encountered. The resistance must be continuously increased throughout the program for strength and endurance to be gained. Today, overload is often used in progressive resistance exercises—including using devices that stretch or compress muscles, progressive calisthenics, and weight training.

Flexibility

Flexibility is the range of motion around a joint. The extent of the range of motion is influenced by the joint structure and the extensibility of tendons, ligaments, and attached muscles. Each joint has a maximum range of motion through which the person can move the limbs uninhibited by soft tissue or structural design. It is influenced by temperature, with heat increasing the range and cold restricting it. A person can be flexible in one joint and not in another. To increase flexibility, muscles are usually stretched.

Flexibility is particularly important to athletes engaged in gymnastics, synchronized swimming, and dance. These activities require a high level or range of flexibility. Flexibility or the maintenance of a complete range of motion decreases the chance for injury in nearly all sport and physical activity. Flexibility plays an equally important role in the capacity of seniors to remain mobile. It will ensure less chance of injury. Poor flexibility can hinder performance, influence posture negatively, and increase the chance of injury.

Cardiorespiratory Endurance

Cardiorespiratory endurance is the capacity of the body to take in and effectively transport oxygen to the tissues. It is the major factor limiting performance. The cardiorespiratory system delivers nutrients to the cells, removes waste from the cells, provides a cooling system, controls acidity and alkalinity, and promotes resistance to disease. Cardiovascular endurance is the ability to perform intense or heavy physical activity using large muscle groups for extended periods of time. It is the maximum amount of work one can perform in one bout. The twelve-minute run test is often used to measure cardiovascular endurance. It is the distance one can run all-out for twelve minutes.

The movement of air into and out of the lungs is called ventilation. Minute ventilation is the amount of air one inspires or expires (not both) in one minute. There are two major changes in ventilation during exercise: (1) a rapid increase within only a few seconds after the start of exercise stimulated by the joint receptors, and (2) a rapid rise replaced by a slower rise that levels off in submaximal exercise. In maximal exercise, leveling off does not occur; ventilation continues to increase until the exercise is terminated (Fox, Bowers, and Foss 1988, 207). When exercise stops, ventilation decreases. It continues to slowly decrease until it returns to the resting value.

Second wind, an unexplained physiological phenomenon, is experienced by the participant when the participant moves from a feeling of respiratory distress or fatigue early in a workout to a feeling of comfort.

▶ Heart

The heart is a muscular pump that circulates blood throughout the body. At rest, the heart beats 60 to 80 beats per minute. In sedentary, poorly conditioned people, the heart may have as many as 100 beats per minute; in highly conditioned people, the rate may be 40 or below. The lowest heart rate for a subject is found while the subject is lying down. Sitting increases the heart rate. Heart rate decreases with age and increases with extremes in body temperature.

Heart rate will increase with the intensity of exercise until exhaustion is reached. The maximal heart rate is the rate achieved just before exhaustion. Steady-state heart rate is of concern to all persons engaging in physical activity and all persons wishing to have a healthy heart. When the level of exercise is submaximal, about seventy percent of maximum, and the rate of energy expended or work is held constant, the heart will increase rapidly until it reaches a plateau. The plateau is the steady state. The heart should reach this steady state in one to two minutes. The greater the intensity of the exercise, the longer it will take the heart to reach the steady state. Physically fit persons, as measured by cardiorespiratory capacity, will have lower heart rates for the same level of work or energy output than those persons who are not physically fit.

▶ Vascular System

The vascular system consists of vessels that transport blood from the heart to the muscles, organs, and tissues. Blood is then transported back to the heart. The heart muscle has its own vascular system to supply nutrients and return waste from the heart muscle.

Arteries, arterioles, capillaries, and veins control changes in blood pressure. The arteries move blood from the heart to the muscles and organs of the body; the veins carry the blood back to the heart. As the blood moves to the muscles and organs, the arteries decrease in size, becoming arterioles or the smallest vessels in the transport system to the organs and tissues. Capillaries are the smallest vessels used for transport from the organs and tissues to the veins.

Blood pressure is the force exerted by the blood against the walls of the heart and blood vessels. It is measured by an instrument that gives readings for systolic and diastolic pressure. Systolic blood pressure is a reading of blood flow as it moves into the arteries; diastolic blood pressure is a reading of blood flow as the blood leaves the arteries. Systolic pressure increases in direct proportion to the increase in intensity of exercise with changes of from "120 mm Hg at rest to 200 mm Hg or greater at the point of exhaustion" (Wilmore and Costill 1988, 77). The increase in systolic pressure signifies the increase of effort required by the heart and circulatory system in intense exercise. Diastolic pressure will change little in the intense exercise situation.

Hypertension is a condition that results from a constriction of the blood vessels or an increase in pressure within the system. When blood pressure is consistently higher than normal, the person is said to have hypertension.

Lymph and blood are the vehicles of transportation in the circulatory system. Lymph plays an important role in maintaining good health and warding off disease and infection. Blood plays a major role in physical activity because it transports nutrients to the muscles and removes waste, regulates temperature, and maintains an acid-base balance. This transportation system carries oxygen and nutrients to the cells. Metabolic wastes, carbon dioxide, and lactate acid are removed from the muscles and taken to the lungs, liver, and kidneys. Also, blood is vital in the regulation of temperature because it delivers heat from the core of the body to and from areas of increased metabolic activity and to the rest of the body under normal conditions. It delivers heat to the skin when the body becomes overheated. The blood neutralizes the acids produced in anaerobic metabolism to maintain the acid-base balance.

Blood flow patterns change with exercise. In the resting state fifteen to twenty percent of the blood flows to the muscles; in exhaustive exercise, as much as eighty to eighty-five percent of the blood may go to the muscles. This increase in flow to the muscles is a result of a decrease in flow to the body organs. If the body becomes overheated in heavy exercise, the blood will flow to the skin to dissipate the heat. This redirection of blood flow to the skin will result in a decrease of blood flow to the muscles. Often athletes find it more difficult or impossible to perform at optimum levels in very hot weather.

Sweating in warm to hot weather will result in a reduction of blood volume because of the loss of water. The loss of volume, accompanied by the redirection of blood to the skin to dissipate heat, results in a decreased return of blood to the heart. As a result of the decreased volume, a reduction in stroke volume will occur. The heart will compensate by increasing the heart rate to maintain the stroke volume. If the exercise is light to moderate, the body will accommodate the changes in blood flow and the person can continue the activity. When the exercise is of high intensity, the maximum heart rate will be attained at a much lower level, thus reducing the body's capacity to engage in all-out activity.

▶ Body Temperature Regulation

Normal body temperature is 98.6 degrees Fahrenheit (37 degrees Celsius); 97 to 104 is the range for humans. As warm-blooded animals, humans will adjust to varying body temperatures. Humans produce heat through the oxidation of carbohydrates, fats, and proteins. Increased metabolic rate, disease, shivering, and exercise may increase heat production.

Heat is lost by water and oil flow over the body, dissipation of energy, and sweat or evaporation. Body heat is regulated by the hypothalamus or body thermostat. Information from skin receptors and blood temperature will be used by the hypothalamus to either lose or gain heat. To lose heat, the hypothalamus will channel the blood closer to the skin so that it can be radiated away, or sweating will occur so heat will evaporate. When the skin

▼ TABLE 10-1

Heat injuries: causes, clinical findings, and treatment

HEAT INJURIES	CAUSES
Heat syncope	Excessive vasodilation; pooling of blood in the skin
Heat cramps	Excessive loss of electrolytes in sweat; inadequate salt intake
Salt-depletion heat exhaustion	Excessive loss of electrolytes in sweat; inadequate salt intake
Water-depletion heat exhaustion	Excessive loss of sweat; inadequate fluid intake
Anhidrotic heat exhaustion	Same as water-depletion heat exhaustion
Heat stroke	Excessive body temperature

receptors and the blood temperature identifies cold, the body will conserve heat by shunting the blood from the surface to the central core of the body and by causing shivering, which will produce extra heat through muscle contraction.

Two health conditions are produced by heat or lack of heat. Hypothermia, or a rapid loss of heat, may be triggered by falling into cold water or placing the body where heat loss will exceed the energy created by exercise. Hyperthermia, the reverse, occurs in high temperature situations. Caution is advised to those exercising in temperatures exceeding eighty degrees Fahrenheit, in relative humidity exceeding fifty to sixty percent, in air stagnation, and under direct heat from the sun. One or a combination of these may cause hyperthermia. For a list of heat injuries, see table 10-1.

The following guidelines have been created by the authors using Williams (1988) and the *American College of Sports Medicine Position Stand: The Prevention of Thermal Injuries During Distance Running.*

1. Check the temperature and humidity conditions daily. Warm, humid conditions will cause fatigue sooner, so slow the pace or decrease the amount of time spent exercising. Even if the dry temperature is only sixty-five to seventy degrees Fahrenheit, a high humidity will increase the heat stress.

CLINICAL FINDINGS	TREATMENT
Fainting, weakness, fatigue	Place on back in cool environment, give cool fluids
Cramps	Rest in cool environment; oral ingestion of salt drinks; salt foods daily; medical treatment in severe cases
Nausea Fatigue Fainting Cramps	Rest in cool environment; replace fluids and salt by mouth; medical treatment in severe cases
Fatigue Nausea Cool pale skin Active sweating Rectal temp. lower than 104° F	Rest in cool environment; drink cool fluids; cool body with water; medical treatment if serious
Nausea; sweating stopped; dry skin; rectal temperature lower than 104° F	Same as water-depletion heat exhaustion
Headache Disorientation Unconsciousness Rectal temperature greater than 105.8° F	Cool body immediately to 102° F (38.9° C) with ice packs, cold water; give cool drinks with glucose if conscious; get medical help immediately

2. If freedom exists in scheduling activities, plan events and workouts in the early morning or evening to avoid the heat of the day.
3. Locate exercise sessions in the shade, if possible, to avoid radiation from the sun.
4. Wear as little clothing as possible. That which is worn should be loose to allow air circulation, white to reflect radiant heat, and porous to permit evaporation.
5. Provide cold fluids for participants. Take frequent water breaks, consuming about six to eight ounces of water every fifteen minutes. During exercise, thirst is not an adequate stimulus to replace water losses; participants should be encouraged to drink before they get thirsty.
6. Participants are to keep a daily record of their body weight. For each pound lost, they should be encouraged to drink one pint (sixteen ounces) of fluid. Body weight should be back to normal before their next exercise workout.
7. Electrolytes (salt) lost through sweating should be replaced. A little extra salt on one's meals coupled with eating food high in potassium, such as bananas and citrus fruits, will replenish electrolytes.
8. Excessive intake of protein is to be avoided prior to all-out exercise. Protein metabolism will produce extra heat in the body. Excess protein may contribute to heat stress.
9. Beverages with caffeine are to be avoided several hours prior to exercising. Caffeine may increase stress in two ways. First, it is a diuretic and may increase body-water losses. Second, caffeine will increase metabolic heat production at rest, which will raise the body temperature prior to exercise.

Metabolic rates increase in cold climates; this should be considered when the temperature decreases or people compete out of doors.

▶ Oxygen Systems

Exercise may be aerobic (in the presence of oxygen) or anaerobic (in the absence of oxygen). The details of the metabolic functions that affect oxygen consumption in exercise are described in chapter 11. Most people think that all exercise is performed in an aerobic environment or in the presence of oxygen. This is not true, because people have limits or ceilings for their aerobic power, or the maximum rate at which they can consume oxygen. It usually takes two or three minutes of all-out activity for oxygen consumption to increase to a higher level. The period of time in which the body makes the adjustment to the new demand is called oxygen deficit or anaerobic. While diet plays an important role in this adjustment, training programs can be designed to facilitate the adjustment from anaerobic to aerobic.

▶ Exercise and Health

Exercise is essential to ward off heart disease and osteoporosis. Hypertension (high blood pressure), atherosclerosis, arteriosclerosis, coronary occlusion, angina pectoris, and congestive heart failure are among the more common forms of heart disease. Studies (Blair 1989, 2395) show a direct relationship between cardiovascular disease and physical activity. Blair provides evidence that physical fitness is associated with lower rates of all causes of mortality as well as cardiovascular disease. A second and equally important result of the study was that moderate exercise such as walking was found to be sufficient to increase longevity.

Heart disease is the leading cause of death in males thirty-five to forty-five years of age. In the United States, the ratio of male to female deaths from coronary heart disease up to ages forty-five to fifty is five to one. Interestingly, Wells (1985, 162) reported that the difference is "2:1 in Italy and 1:1 in Japan." Following fifty years of age, women gradually increase their risk of coronary heart disease. It is thought that the sex differences are directly related to the fact that estrogen protects the female from heart disease. The critical differences from one country to another places that fact in question; however, differences in diet from one country to another may be a factor.

Extreme muscular inactivity results in bone demineralization. Bone is tissue that responds to stress. Wells (1985, 177) takes from Smith in citing the following as contributing factors to the increase in mineralization with exercise: "Increased stress on the bone as a result of increased weight bearing; increased stress applied to bone by increased muscular contraction; increased bone growth as a result of physical activity; and increased blood flow to the bone as a result of cardiovascular stimulation."

Bone demineralization or differences in bone mineralization have been found in dominant versus nondominant arms of tennis players. Results of research suggest that all parts of the body should be stressed equally. Effort should be made to increase the amount of physical activity and the desire for physical activity, particularly among females, to ward off bone demineralization.

▶ Training

Training is taking on a new definition as society becomes aware that everyone should be involved in physical activity. The middle-aged person who wishes to remain fit and to maintain an attractive waistline will need to establish a training program. The overweight or obese person should be interested in a program that will enable him or her to lose weight while getting into shape. Those interested in achieving an elite level in competitive events have long recognized the need to establish and implement a training program. Today, people engage in competition at levels other than that of an elite athlete and often stress themselves in recreational pursuits. If they want to avoid injury and be able to keep up with others, they will recognize the need for a training program.

The term fitness is used in many different ways. Some people refer to fitness as the avoidance of disease; others as the ability to execute routine life activities. Fitness for some is reaching an optimal quality of life physically, psychologically, etc. To some, fitness is everyday efficiency and freedom from disease. Others believe that physical fitness is used in so many ways that it is a term to be avoided by professionals.

All training, conditioning, or fitness programs have a number of elements in common.

1. Programs are adhered to so that a person's body functions at the optimum level. Some people may have an objective (i.e., to be able to play tennis); others may wish to enjoy day-to-day activities at a comfortable level. Some programs stress physical fitness; others enable participants to function as elite athletes.
2. Programs are planned with knowledge of which major energy system, aerobic or anaerobic, is to be developed.
3. An overload system is used to design programs unique to each person's needs.
4. Training programs are specific to each person's needs and to an energy system that will be essential to success in sport.
5. Strength, endurance, and flexibility are developed to the body's optimum capacity.
6. Endurance is an outgrowth of the activity.
7. Programs are planned.
8. Initial baseline information is obtained as a result of the administration of a battery of fitness tests and a medical evaluation. If the acquisition of physical skills is a goal of the program, motor ability, motor capacity, and sports tests are to be included (see chapter 15).
9. Programs are tailored to the demands of the activity, the person, and the appropriate energy system.

Muscular strength, endurance, and flexibility are the major objectives of training. A wide array of principles and concepts are involved in achieving each of those major objectives. The first step is for the individual to reach an optimum level of personal fitness so that energy and capacity for all life needs and emergencies are available. Then the specific personal needs of training to reach excellence in identified sports are pursued. Training programs are far more important for adults than for young, prepubescent, or pubescent children. In fact, Oded Bar-Or (1989) noted that aerobic power, muscular strength, and anaerobic muscle power are trainable in prepubescent children. In comparing children to adults, he found aerobic power lower for children. He also cautioned against permitting children to lift maximal weight or engage in general strength training unless the program was designed for rehabilitation or the development of well-defined skills.

There are two basic types of muscle training: static and dynamic. Dynamic training can be broken down into the areas of isotonic, isokinetic, and variable resistance. All training will increase strength and power; only dynamic training will increase muscular endurance. Training programs are also based on specific types of contributions:

- **Concentric, isotonic, or dynamic contraction**—the muscle exerts force, shortens, and overcomes resistance.
- **Eccentric contraction**—the muscle exerts force, lengthens, and overcomes resistance.
- **Isometric or static contraction**—the muscle exerts force but does not change in length. The force exerted by the muscle is equal to the force exerted by the resistance. No movement occurs. Isometric contractions are used in stabilizing joints and movements.
- **Isokinetic contraction**—the muscle exerts force while shortening at a constant speed over the full range of motion.

Static Training

Static, or isometric, exercise is based on the training theory that strength can be efficiently gained by moving the muscle or muscle group against a fixed resistance. Isometric means constant length. An isometric contraction is one in which tension occurs but there is no change in the muscle length. The contraction is always performed at 100 percent strength. The resistance is constant throughout the full range of the movement. Strength is highly specific and usually only gained by the muscles around the specific joint involved.

Isometric exercises require little or very inexpensive equipment and can be done anyplace. The negative side of isometric exercise is that it can be harmful to individuals who have or tend toward cardiovascular disease (heart disease, hypertension, or stroke). This harm occurs when the performer creates high pressure in the chest cavity by closing the glottis or holding the breath. The high pressure in the chest cavity makes it difficult for blood to return to the lower extremities. The blood pressure increases, and there is less blood for the heart and brain.

Dynamic Training

Dynamic exercise may be isotonic, isokinetic, or variable resistance. Isotonic training usually includes barbells, dumbbells, or pulleys. Two concepts essential to an isotonic exercise program are overload and progressive resistance. Overload means that to gain strength in the muscle, it is necessary to load the muscle beyond that point to which it is normally loaded. Once one adjusts to a particular load, the muscular strength levels off to accommodate that load. Loads must continue to increase in order to strengthen the muscle or muscle group.

Progressive resistance is the systematic application of the overload theory. Exercise is done according to sets of a specific number of repetitions against resistance that will cause maximum strength gains. The application of the theory has evolved and changed since the 1940s. Wilmore and Costill (1988) state that isotonic training should be performed at five to seven repetitions per minute with three sets per training session. It should occur in three to five sessions each week.

A new form of isotonic exercise called plyometrics became popular in the 1970s and 1980s. Plyometrics are bouncing exercises that use the stretch reflex to facilitate the employment of additional motor units. It is often described as a prestretch of muscle tendons followed by an isotonic contraction.

Isotonic exercise requires that the resistance be constant throughout the full range of movement. The velocity at which the exercises have been performed are low—six to ten sets.

In isokinetic exercise, the resistance varies and is matched to the exact force applied by the muscle. In this environment, the resistance has been set to move at a preset speed or cadence—no faster, no slower. The fact that most sport activity requires very quick movements suggests that this may be the approach of the future. Equipment such as Cybex, Hydra-Fitness, and minigyms facilitate this movement. Little research exists at this time.

Variable resistance training matches the force-producing capabilities of the muscles with a resistance. They include Nautilus, Cam, Universal, Hydra-Fitness, power exercises, and others. For detailed discussions and research on the various strength development training systems, see Westcott (1987, 43).

Circuit Training

Circuit training is an all-purpose training for the development of strength, power, muscular endurance, speed, agility, flexibility, and cardiovascular endurance. Circuits are set up with the exercise needs of the participants in mind. Circuit training uses a number of exercise stations for building flexibility, strength, and aerobic fitness. Although there may be short bursts of all-out activity, circuit training is not considered an activity for improving cardiorespiratory endurance because most participants consume too much time moving from station to station. A participant can usually move through the circuit in thirty minutes.

Strength Programs

Westcott (1987, 101) uses these factors in designing a strength training exercise program:

- selection
- frequency
- duration
- intensity
- speed
- progression
- continuity

Selection

Exercise training is specific. To improve strength, the muscle and muscle groups involved in the activity must be used. If they are not, strength will not be acquired. Equally important to the training is the development of muscle groups in opposition to those expected to produce energy for a specific activity; this is to retain balance in the body. Those muscles serving as stabilizers for the particular joint involved and for the body in general are trained so that the joint can handle the added strength of the primary muscle group. General strength is as important as specific strength.

Frequency

It is possible to train too much. Muscles need to rest. The higher the intensity level of the exercise or training schedule, the longer the rest period. The results of research suggest that in all-out strength training, three days per week is the best method. People will react differently. Performers must be called on to acquire a high level of body sense and to be able to recognize the feeling when the weight load is a little easier to handle. When that happens the rest period is adequate. If there is no feeling of difference in the weight load after a two-day rest, the participant may wait three days. In turn, those who recognize a change in the weight load on the second day would be wise to use a four-or five-day-a-week program. Three days a week is the recommended program.

Duration

Duration, or length of the exercise program, is determined by the optimum training load and the number of repetitions. For strength to develop, a person must be at or above sixty-five percent of maximum weight load. To stress the anaerobic energy system, a person should complete the exercise in 90 to 120 seconds, or two minutes. If the exercise lasts longer than two minutes, aerobic energy systems are stressed. If one repetition of an exercise takes 7 seconds, it will take 105 seconds to complete fifteen repetitions. Therefore, fifteen repetitions at sixty-five percent or greater workload are recommended as a safe program.

Intensity

To work for maximum strength, a person will employ a high-intensity training, completing eight to twelve repetitions before muscle failure occurs as a result of fatigue. The activity is to be conducted in a biomechanically sound form.

Speed

Slow strength training, which produces a longer period of muscle tension, is recommended because more muscle fibers are recruited and both fast-twitch and slow-twitch muscles are involved. Heavy weight loads should be used with slow contractions. If heavy weights are moved rapidly, injury may occur. It is better to use light weights when moving the object rapidly.

Progression

Strength is increased through progressive increases in resistance. Too much stress or too many abrupt movements can cause injury. Weight load increase occurs when one is no longer fatigued after twelve repetitions of the exercise. Five percent increases are recommended.

All exercises are to be through the full range of movement of the joint. The muscle should be stretched to full extension. As one muscle is fully contracted, the opposite muscle will be fully extended. Exercise is to be performed slowly and smoothly through a full range of motion.

Continuity

Exercise must challenge the entire body as well as the specific groups of muscles singled out for attention. Increased total body strength is the goal.

Endurance

Endurance is the ability to perform long bouts of work without fatigue or exhaustion. Endurance conditioning and fitness programs are designed to stress one or more of three energy systems: speed/strength, aerobic, or anaerobic. The energy system most often employed in the activity is identified. Then a program to challenge that energy system is created (see table 10-2). Sports and predominant energy systems will assist the professional in identifying the energy system in use in a particular activity. What is the amount of time the performer is engaged in strength, all-out bursts of activity, and sustained continuous performance? All three energy systems are challenged but emphasis is placed on the system that will be called on for

▼ **TABLE 10-2**
Sport and predominant energy systems

SPORT OR ACTIVITY	PERCENT EMPHASIS ACCORDING TO ENERGY SYSTEMS		
	ATP-PC & LA	LA-O2	O2
Baseball	80	20	—
Basketball	85	15	—
Fencing	90	10	—
Field hockey	60	20	20
Gymnastics	90	10	—
Lacrosse			
goalie, defense, attack	80	20	—
midfielders	60	20	20
Soccer			
goalie, wings, strikers	80	20	—
halfback	60	20	20
Swimming			
50 yard	98	2	—
100 yard	80	15	5
500 yard	20	40	40
Tennis	70	20	10
Track			
100 yard	98	2	—
440 yard	80	15	5
1 mile	20	55	25
3 mile	10	20	70
marathon	—	5	95
Volleyball	90	10	—

Taken in part from Mathews (1974) *Interval Training: Conditioning for Sports and Physical Fitness.* Reprinted by permission of Dr. Donald Mathews.

ultimate performance in a given activity. Time of performance is a key in constructing training programs. For example, a certain percentage of time is dedicated to speed, another to aerobics, and a third to anaerobics.

Again, the overload principle comes into action. You will recall that in acquiring muscular endurance, a person should gradually increase endurance as the resistive muscle increases in size. Intensity, frequency, and duration are the three factors in the overload system. Intensity seems to be the factor most closely related to improvement in conditioning and, therefore, the factor to be most closely monitored. Intensity is usually determined by monitoring the heart rate. The higher the heart rate, the greater the intensity of the exercise; the lower the heart rate, the lower the intensity of the exercise. Heart rate monitoring is an indirect way of estimating the body's oxygen utilization. As a result, it becomes necessary to determine a target heart rate. There are a number of methods for arriving at the target heart rate. The next section presents one that will be useful in group instruction.

Target Heart Rate

To obtain the target rate, the participant must know the resting and maximal heart rates. The resting heart rate is obtained by palpating the radial artery at the wrist or the carotid artery in the neck. Obtain resting heart rate by taking it in the morning before getting out of bed. Count the beats for one full minute. An alternate method is to count the beats for fifteen seconds and multiply by four. Repeat the process for several days and obtain the average of the days. This is the resting heart rate.

Maximal heart rate is obtained by subtracting the age from 220:

$$Maximal\ heart\ rate = 220 - age$$

Endurance exercise should cause the heart to function at approximately eighty-five percent of the maximal heart rate. Twenty minutes is often recommended.

The frequency and duration of the training tends to increase the fitness level and is good for the subject.

Flexibility

Flexibility is measured with a goniometer, a protractor-like device that measures the angle of the joint at both extremes in its range of motion. Flexibility is a capacity that needs to be trained at all times throughout life because failure to use the joint to its maximum range tends to decrease joint flexibility or capacity to function.

Flexibility is maintained through the use of stretching exercises. These exercises may be of three types: (1) static, (2) ballistic, or (3) proprioceptive neuromuscular facilitation (PNF). Static is a slow, sustained stretch held for a given amount of time. Ballistic stretching involves bouncing or active movements. PNF involves a static stretch to the limit of motion against opposition. The stretch is held for a couple of seconds. The static method is best.

Types of Training

Training may be interval, continuous running, jogging, fartlek, or sprint. These programs either favor aerobic (endurance) or anaerobic (sprint) fitness.

Interval

Interval training is a series of repeated exercise periods with rest or mild exercise between each workout. The rest periods between bouts enable performers to increase bouts before fatigue sets in. At the completion of the intermittent exercise, less lactic acid will have accumulated in the muscle and thus less fatigue. Interval training "allows the stores of ATP and PC to

▼ **TABLE 10-3**
Recommended interval training workouts

LEVEL	INTENSITY DURING TRAINING PERIOD	INTENSITY DURING TRAINING PERIOD	DURATION
Beginner	70–75% of maximal heart rate	30–35% of maximal heart rate	20 min.
Intermediate	75–85% of maximal heart rate	35–40% of maximal heart rate	30–40 min.
Advanced	85–95% of maximal heart rate	40–45% of maximal heart rate	40–60 min.

Reproduced by permission from Prentice, William E., and Bucher, Charles A.: *Fitness for College and Life,* ed. 2, St. Louis, 1988, Times Mirror/Mosby College Publishing.

be used over and over . . . provides an adequate stimulus for promoting an increase in the energy capacity . . . and aids in delaying the onset of fatigue" (Fox, Bowers, and Foss 1988, 303).

Interval training may allow for work at up to eighty-five percent for a short period of time, followed by a recovery period of thirty to forty-five percent maximal heart rate (Prentice and Bucher 1988, 82) (see table 10-3). Sports such as tennis, soccer, fencing, and basketball involve short bursts of intense activity or are anaerobic. Interval training allows one to be more sport-specific in training.

Continuous Running

Continuous running for long distances can be separated into continuous fast running, continuous slow running, and jogging. The oxygen aerobic system is stressed in all three instances. Slow continuous running brings the runner's heart rate to seventy to seventy-five percent. Continuous fast running brings on fatigue at an earlier stage and results in less distance achieved.

Jogging

Jogging is a term used to describe all types of running and in some cases, walking. In most cases, jogging refers to slow, continuous running that involves the placement of the heels on the ground during each stride. Programs vary considerably in distance and speed. Most people jog three days per week for two miles each session.

Fartlek

Fartlek, a Swedish word for "speed play," involves alternating fast and slow paces. Runners select the combination of fast and slow paces somewhat at will or according to how they feel. A person may run as fast as possible for a given distance, walk five minutes, do easy running, run at full speed again, and then run at a certain predetermined pace. Each person sets his or her own plan for intensity and path for running. Hills and obstacles such as rocks or trees are often part of the course.

Sprint

Sprint training is running short distances at top speed. It is used to develop speed and strength. The person accelerates as rapidly as possible and runs for fifty or sixty yards. The training may be incorporated into an interval sprint by following the short-distance, high-speed sprint with a jog for a specific distance.

Dance Aerobics

Aerobic dance is not unlike many activities (Slimnastics, Jazzercize) that have been part of physical education and physical activity for many years. Aerobic dance consists of preplanned fundamental movement and basic dance steps choreographed to music. Appropriate choreography will assure that the routine attains certain predetermined aerobic fitness levels. Warm-ups for aerobic dance consist of stretching exercises for the total body.

Accompanying the popularity of aerobic dance has been an increase in injuries. Aerobics, as currently choreographed, forces all performers to execute the same step the same number of times in the same manner. People are different and need different messages or activity routines. To maintain the same delivery, aerobics has taken on an easy or less strenuous style by offering "low impact" aerobics. In this form of dance, one foot is kept in contact with the floor at all times, thus reducing the chance of injury. Note should be made that Williford and associates (1987, 95–109) suggest that low impact aerobics may not be sufficiently strenuous to meet minimum cardiorespiratory standards or be able to assist in weight reduction.

Walking, running, hopping, jumping, and leaping constitute the fundamentals of movement used in aerobic dance. Combinations such as the grapevine, the step-over-step, the hop kick, or the flea hop (step, hop) are used. Typical dance steps include the polka, mazurka, and others.

Aqua Aerobics

Aqua aerobics takes fundamentals into the swimming pool and uses the pool as if it were a gymnasium. The water level and traditional swim strokes do not seem to influence the activity.

Elements of Warm-Up, Workout, and Cool-Down

Proper training involves warm-ups, workouts, and cool-downs. Warm-ups and cool-downs are events often overlooked in establishing a training program.

Warm-Up

Warm-up exercises increase muscles, body temperature, metabolic systems, blood flow, and oxygen utilization; they stretch ligaments and muscles, and decrease contraction and reflex time. Stretching exercises are often used to increase flexibility or the range of motion around a joint, to avoid tearing muscles, and to lower body tension. Warm-ups are generalized total body activity. They advance from very low-key movements to a more intense set of exercises, and just before formal activity, the body is engaged in warm-ups that mimic the sport or event in which the participant intends to engage. Initial exercises are of a stretching nature; the second generation exercises move to muscular contractions and then to actual sport movements or specialized sport skills. Warm-ups are to last five to ten minutes. Popular warm-ups often include slow jogging. Activity is to commence immediately following the warm-up.

Cool-Down

Following the activity, the participant performs a mild to light exercise, or cool-down. This activity will speed up the lactic acid or fatigue recovery. Light to moderate exercise will also keep the muscles pumping blood and thus ward off the pooling of blood in the lower extremities. These exercises include stretching activities. A five-to-ten minute cool-down should permit the body to return to its resting state.

▶ Summary

1. Muscles give form and shape to the body. They also produce movement.
2. Muscles are categorized as prime movers, or those that do the work; antagonists, those that relax and lengthen, permitting the prime movers to function; and stabilizers, those that permit a full range of movement in the joint.
3. Muscular strength is the maximal force a muscle or muscle groups can exert against a resistance in one execution. The larger the muscle, the stronger the muscle.
4. Overload means that the performer is asked to work against a resistance or workload in excess of that routinely encountered.
5. Flexibility is the range of motion around a joint. A maximum range of motion is essential to success in a number of physical activities; a satisfactory range is important to the maintenance of movement functions in the elderly.
6. Cardiorespiratory endurance is the capacity of the body to take in and effectively transport oxygen to the tissues. It is often measured by the distance the performer is able to run in twelve minutes.
7. Normal resting heart rate varies between 60 and 85 beats per minute. Highly conditioned performers may have a rate as low as 40, while poorly conditioned people may have a rate of 100 or more.
8. Heart rate will increase with the intensity of the exercise until exhaustion is reached.
9. The lymph system plays an important role in maintaining good health and warding off disease and infection.
10. Humans will adjust to various external temperatures through the hypothalamus or body thermostat. To lose heat, the hypothalamus will channel the blood close to the skin so that sweating will occur; to conserve

heat the body will shunt the blood from the surface to the central core of the body and cause shivering, thus producing extra heat through muscle contraction.

11. Exercise is important as a deterrent to heart disease and osteoporosis.
12. Every member of society should structure his or her own conditioning and fitness training program.
13. Muscular training programs are static or dynamic. Static involves moving the muscle or muscle group against a fixed resistance; dynamic training involves moving the body through space.
14. Strength training is specific to the muscle or muscle group involved.
15. Endurance is acquired by stressing the various energy systems.
16. Warm-ups, workouts, and cool-downs are the essentials of a training program.

▶ **References**

Blair, Steven N., Kohl, Harold W., Paffenbarger, Ralph S., Clark, Debra G., Cooper, Kenneth H., and Gibbons, Larry W. (1989). Physical fitness and all-cause mortality. *Journal of the American Medical Association, 262*(17), 2395–2401.

Corbin, Charles B., and Lindsey, Ruth. (1988). *Concepts of Physical Fitness with Laboratories*. Dubuque, Iowa: Wm. C. Brown.

Costill, David L. (1986). *Inside Running: Basics of Sports Physiology*. Indianapolis, Indiana: Benchmark Press.

Dyer, K. F. (1982). *Challenging the Men: Women in Sport*. New York: University of Queensland Press.

Fox, Edward L., Bowers, Richard W., and Foss, Merle L. (1988). *The Physiological Basis of Physical Education and Athletics*. Dubuque, Iowa: Wm. C. Brown.

McDonagh, M. J. N., and Davies, C. T. M. (1984). Adaptive response of mammalian skeletal muscle to exercise with high loads. *European Journal of Applied Physiology, 52,* 139–155.

Oded Bar-Or. (1989). Trainability of the prepubescent child. *Physician and Sports Medicine, 17*(5), 64.

Prentice, William E., and Bucher, Charles. (1988). *Fitness for College and Life*. St. Louis: C. V. Mosby.

Wells, Christine L. (1985). *Women, Sport and Performance: A Physiological Perspective*. Champaign, Illinois: Human Kinetics.

Westcott, Wayne L. (1987). *Strength Fitness: Physiological Principles and Training Techniques*. Boston: Allyn and Bacon.

Williams, Melvin H. (1988). *Nutrition for Fitness and Sport*. Dubuque, Iowa: Wm. C. Brown.

Williford, Henry N., Blessing, Daniel L., Olson, Michele S., Smith, Furman H. (1987). Is low-impact aerobic dance an effective cardiovascular workout? *Physician and Sportsmedicine, 17*(3), 95–109.

Wilmore, Jack H., and Costill, David L. (1988). *Training for Sport and Physical Activity: The Physiological Basis of the Conditioning Process*. Dubuque, Iowa: Wm. C. Brown.

Biomechanics

Biomechanics is the application of physics to the study of movement of the human body. It is used primarily to improve performance and prevent injury. The human body, a system of weights and levers, moves according to the principles or laws of physics. Impetus for muscle contraction, which causes the levers of the body to move, is provided by the nervous system. Physical skills are most easily acquired when instruction is based on the laws of physics and knowledge of the performer's body build, strength, and motor ability. Models of human movement based on biomechanics were described in chapters 4, 5, 6, and 7.

A problem often faced by the instructor of physical skills is whether to present a skill to the learner according to the observed performance of outstanding athletes or to instruct using a theoretical model of most efficient movement derived from physics. Three typical approaches to instruction are: (1) copy the form used by elite or outstanding athletes, (2) create a mechanically correct movement model using elements of physics, or (3) provide the learner the freedom to explore a range of movements, analyze the performer's choice in light of physics, and correct inefficient movements.

Knowledge of the mechanical principles, taken from the discipline of physics, are also used to assess performance that is effective but is contrary to the typical teaching model. A movement appearing inefficient and subjected to a detailed examination may be found to meet most of the elements of efficient movement. The movement may contain certain idiosyncrasies that would prohibit its use as a teaching model but would not suggest that it be corrected or changed. In this case, the performance should not be copied but it should not be changed.

Learners often wish to emulate elite athletes, not recognizing that in some cases such athletes do not possess mechanically correct form or form that would be successful for people in general. Learners are also unaware that beginning and advanced performers may possess different form in movement. Students and clients tend to assume that there is only one way to execute a skill. When the instructor relies on mechanical principles in teaching, there are, on occasion, multiple ways of achieving successful performance.

▶ Muscular System

Movement occurs when muscle groups work with the joints to make the bones move. Muscles contract to cause the levers (bones) to move, to stabilize body parts, or to neutralize the action of the moving levers. Muscles are classified as movers or stabilizers. Movers may be agonists or antagonists. Agonists are the principal movers of the levers of the body. Antagonists are muscles that produce movement opposite that of the movers, or agonists. While an agonist sustains a maximum contraction, an antagonist relaxes the opposing muscles to permit the movement. The same muscle may be an agonist in one movement and an antagonist in another movement. Stabilizers are the muscles that support or stabilize the joint. They are used to combat the pull of gravity and to prevent unwanted or potentially injurious movement.

Muscles have four generally known characteristics: irritability, contractility, distensibility, and elasticity. Irritability is the muscle's response to stimulation. Ability to pull or contract is contractility. Relaxation is the capacity of the muscle to become passive, which is the opposite of contractility. Distensibility is the lengthening or stretching of the muscle by forces outside the body. When the muscle is stretched beyond its physiological limits, injury will occur. Elasticity is the speed in which a muscle is able to return to its original shape after it is hit. When persons collide or an object collides with a person, the muscle will change in shape. The speed in which the muscle returns to its original shape is important. Muscles obtain a rich blood supply from the circulatory system. Nerves enter the muscles near the arterial branches.

▶ Joints

A joint is the location in the body at which various bones come in contact with one another. This contact, according to the design of the human body, determines the quality of the movement. For example, the overarm throw involves movements in a number of joints, with the shoulder joint being of greatest importance. The ball and socket movement of the bones of the upper arm are free to rotate in the box-like area structured by the bones of the shoulder and back. The box-like area is created by the muscles that serve as stabilizers. The action of the throw is caused by the agonist or moving muscles.

Rotation or action around a joint is determined by the muscles and the location of the bones. The location and strength of the attachments of the muscles to the bones play an important role in range of movement and strength.

▶ Effects of the Nervous System on Biomechanics

The brain and the spinal cord make up the central nervous system. The peripheral nervous system consists of the spinal nerves and the autonomous nervous system. Within the brain are the bases of voluntary muscular control and reflex behavior. The cerebrum, a large mass of gray matter, provides the basis for consciousness and thought. At the rear of the brain is a section of gray matter, important to movement, called the cerebellum. Schmidt (1978, 198) states that the "cerebellum is chiefly concerned in 1) programming rapid movements, 2) correcting the course of each movement and 3) correlation of posture and movement."

Nerve fibers and cell bodies work with the spinal cord. Nerve fibers that conduct impulses away from the cell bodies are axons; those that conduct impulses toward the cell bodies are dendrites. Impulses pass from the axons of one cell to the dendrites of another at the synapses. These connections are found at each level of entry to the spinal cord and brain.

The spinal cord enables the brain to interact with the peripheral muscles so that movement can occur. Enoka (1988, 183) describes the muscle as an "effector organ because it translates neural commands into force." The muscle is activated by the neurons and sensory receptors of the nervous system (see figure 11-1).

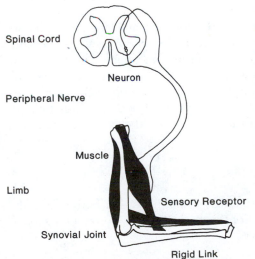

Spinal Cord

Neuron

Peripheral Nerve

Muscle

Limb

Sensory Receptor

Synovial Joint

Rigid Link

▶ **Figure 11-1**

Neuromechanical bases of the simple joint system. From *Neuromechanical Basis of Kinesiology* (p. 97) by R. M. Enoka, 1988, Champaign, IL: Human Kinetics. Copyright 1988 by Roger M. Enoka. Reprinted by permission.

The peripheral nervous system includes parts of the autonomous nervous system and the cranial and spinal nerves. The autonomous system serves the heart, blood vessels, glands, viscera, and smooth muscles. Cranial nerves connect the muscles of the face and head with the central nervous system. They carry impulses from the olfactory, visual, and auditory senses to the central nervous system. Spinal nerves are involved in the movement of the trunk and limbs.

A motor unit consists of a muscle fiber innervated by a neuron. Most muscles have many muscle fibers. A muscle can develop as much strength as it wants in a contraction by calling into play the appropriate number of motor units to accomplish the desired task.

Nerve impulses stimulate motor units into action. Specific receptors called interoceptors, exteroceptors, and proprioceptors accomplish the work. Interoceptors are sense organs located in the visceral organs. Exteroceptors are stimuli coming from sight, smell, sound, and pressure. Proprioceptors are sense organs located in the muscles, tendons, and joints.

Proprioceptors include muscle spindles, Golgi tendon organs, Pacinian corpuscles, and skin receptors. Together they are referred to as kinesthetic acuity. Proprioceptors are responsible for reflex actions, adjustments in performance, repetition of performance, and learned skills. They permit reflex movement as well as fully thought-out skills. They are among the sense organs that are trained in imagery and mental rehearsal.

Muscle spindles are small groups of fibers found between and parallel to muscle fibers. Although they are located throughout the muscle, they are concentrated in the center of the muscle. Muscle spindles are sensitive to lengthening of muscles and to changes in posture. According to a survey of recent studies (Hutton 1987, 2), muscle spindles contribute to the perception of movement. They receive and transmit impulses and are activated by the stretching of the muscle. As a proprioceptor, they play a major role in movement.

Golgi tendon organs are found in the tendons and connective tissue. When the tendons and connective tissue are stretched, they conduct impulses to the central nervous system. Golgi tendon organs are particularly valuable in identifying overstretching of muscles, which can result in tearing a muscle. Pacinian corpuscles are found in the joints and in the skin. They provide a source of information about the change of body position. Skin receptors respond to touch and pressure. They alert the body to change in muscles and in body position.

Kinesthesis

A person must acquire the sense to know where his or her body is and the position of his or her body in relation to space. Further, he or she needs to be able to quickly find and adjust for proper position, if momentarily lost. Kinesthesis is the ability to sense the positions of the body and to sense changes in movement of the body. The senses permit one to know the:

- position of the body segments
- rate, extent, and direction of movement
- position of the entire body
- characteristics of total motion (Scott 1963, 325)

Movement of the muscles or the joints causes the kinesthetic receptors to signal change in the body position. The performer depends on these messages while a sense of specific body movements develops. The potential for the kinesthetic receptors to signal change exists at all times; thus, the performer is continuously aware of such signals in movement. Although muscle sense is extremely important and should be emphasized in all activities, it is most often stressed in gymnastics, diving, and dance.

Stretching for Flexibility and Proprioception

One of the many systems for stretching is called proprioceptive neuromuscular facilitation (PNF). The hold-relax stretch begins with an isometric contraction of the muscle to be stretched, then a relaxation of the muscle, and finally a stretch. A second method referred to as against-contraction uses a submaximal contraction of an agonist while the antagonist is stretched. The rationale for this technique is that the "agonist activity will produce reciprocal inhibition, and hence relaxation, in the antagonist during the stretch" (Enoka 1988, 142).

▶ Principles of Biomechanics

The principles of biomechanics will be discussed as supportive tasks, suspension tasks, tasks involving motion, tasks involving the application of force, and tasks involving receiving force. This system was originated by Marion Broer (1960) in her first edition of *Efficiency of Human Movement*. Application of the principles requires that the instructor know the specific plane or set of planes in which the body can move. Planes of the body are sagittal, frontal, and transverse. The sagittal plane is an imaginary line passing through the body from front to back, dividing the body into right and left halves. The frontal plane is an imaginary line passing through the body from side to side, dividing the body into anterior and posterior halves. The transverse plane is a horizontal imaginary line passing through the body and dividing the body into upper and lower halves.

Supportive Tasks

A supportive movement is designed to support the body in general or involves supporting an object or objects. Support for the body may be on a solid surface or on a surface that gives, such as sand or water.

Balance

Balance is the process of maintaining control of the body or the adjustment of all body parts in relation to each other. Equilibrium is the state of balance or of maintaining all parts of an object in balance. Stability is the bringing of an object into balance. These definitions are so closely related that the terms are often used interchangeably.

Balance may be static or dynamic. Static balance describes the body holding a position. If a pose such as an arabesque is held against gravity or an outside force, equilibrium is maintained by active muscle tension. Dynamic equilibrium is the balance maintained by a person involved in motion and locomotion. It includes the adjustment involved in adding an external object to the body and the compensating change with relationship to body parts that will occur as a result of such an addition. An object's ability to maintain or gain balance is referred to as stability.

1. Stability is related to the area or size of the base of support of the object.
- The larger the base of support within the body framework, the greater the stability. The term base of support includes the area created by the body parts touching the base. It can be one foot, two feet, one foot and one hand, or the head.
- For the purpose of establishing stability within the human body, the "ready position," or placing the feet shoulder or hip distance apart, is recommended. The position enables the force applied by the feet against the floor or ground to be at a ninety-degree angle in relation to the body. This position is effective in initiating movement.
- When the feet are placed in the ready position but more than shoulder or hip width apart, the force of the feet against the surface is applied at an angle other than ninety degrees, thus creating an outside force that can easily move the body off balance. The position also requires greater effort to move the body.
- When the feet are placed close together, thus decreasing the size of the base (feet) beneath the body frame, stability is sacrificed.
- All body components—head, shoulders, hips, and knees—are aligned one beneath the other for maximum up-down stability.
- The body is intentionally placed in a position of overbalance in the swimming racing start.
2. Stability is related to the distance of the center of gravity within the body above the base of support. The greater the distance, the less stable the object; the lesser the distance, the more stable the object.

- A dancer standing on toes is not as stable as in walking across a room.
- A person standing tall in a stationary position is not as stable as in a position with the knees relaxed and the body lowered slightly.
- A person is more stable in a crouched position, provided the body is aligned with one major body segment directly above the other. The ready position involves lowering the center of gravity over the base of support while keeping the body segments aligned. This is accomplished by lowering the body and relaxing the knees.

3. Stability is related to the weight of the object. The heavier the object, the more stable it is; the lighter the object, the less stable it is.

4. Stability is directional.

- A performer is to be stable in the direction he or she expects to give or to receive force. The forward-backward stride position in throwing and catching provides such stability.
- A side-to-side stride position is taken when the performer expects to receive force from either the right or left side. It is also used when one expects to be knocked off balance by the weight of another person.

5. For equilibrium to exist, the center of gravity must fall within the base of support.

- In a headstand, the hips must be aligned directly above the shoulders or balance will be lost.
- "In an arabesque penché, for instance, in which the mass of the body shifts forward as the leg rises and the torso leans forward, there must be a conscious effort to allow the body as a whole to shift to the rear so that its center remains over the supporting foot" (Laws 1984, 22).

6. When a performer adds a heavy object to the total body weight, that object must be balanced over the base of support as part of the body.

- In the bowling approach, for example, the participant shifts body weight to the nondominant side to accommodate the weight of the bowling ball and to evenly distribute the total weight of the ball and body over the feet.
- A dancer standing on one foot distributes body weight so that he or she will be balanced over the single contact with the floor.

7. Loss of stability is essential to certain kinds of movement. For example, one must work to become unstable in activities such as walking, running, or diving.

- Running is a series of steps in which one is balanced, loses balance, and regains balance. To lose balance, one places the upper body outside the base of support while applying force against the ground to drive the body forward. The driving foot that moves ahead brings the body back into balance. (See descriptions of walking and running in chapters 4 and 6.)
- To execute a racing dive from blocks or the edge of a pool, the performer must lose stability by placing the upper body forward of the base of support or feet.

8. Balance is regained by shifting body parts to enable the body to become aligned over the base of support. The feet will be returned to the ready position, the arms brought in close to the body, and the body brought into a crouched position. The lower body is responsible for the massive shifts to regain balance, whereas it is believed that a relaxed upper body "can contribute to a sensitivity to slight displacements from balance, and make the small subtle adjustments smoother" (Laws 1984, 22).

9. Balance is affected by visual stimulation. If one does not focus on a specific spot while turning in dancing or skating, one tends to lose balance. Failure to focus usually results in the performer becoming dizzy.

Gravity

Gravity, the pull of an object toward the center of the earth, is a major force in human movement. It facilitates movement downward and inhibits movement upward. Every object, including the human body, has a center of gravity or a point about which the weight in all directions is balanced.

Gravity, the noncontact force, is the attraction between an object and the earth. It affects the flight of an object. Weight is the word used to express the amount of gravity. Weight varies in proportion to the mass of the object. The greater the mass, the greater the attraction. Magnitude depends on both the mass and the distance.

- Gravity decreases as altitude increases.
- If the object is dropped directly down with no force, gravity will pull it down with a uniform acceleration of thirty-two feet per second, per second.
- If the object is thrown straight up in the air, it will go up until the force applied equals the force of gravity. It will decrease in speed as it reaches the point at which the two forces are equal, stop for a moment, and begin its flight down as a result of the pull of gravity.
- If the object is pushed down, the amount of force exerted in the push is added to the pull of gravity.
- The center of gravity of an object is a center or balance point around which the object is distributed. For a human being, the center may be within the body, as occurs in a somersault, or outside of the body, as found in the high jump.
- If the object is given a forward force, gravity will cause it to curve downward as it moves forward. The height and angle of the projectile's release, the weight of the object, and the amount of force applied to the object will determine the period of time the object will travel before gravity brings it to the ground.

Buoyancy

Buoyancy is the state of a body in water buoyed up or lifted by a force equal to the weight of the displaced fluid. If the weight of the body is equal to the weight of the water it displaces, the body will remain suspended. If the weight of the body is more than the weight of the water it displaces, the body will sink. If the weight of the body is less than the weight of the water it displaces, the body will float.

Heavy bones and solid muscles make people heavy in the water and, therefore, tend to make them sink. Fat people find it easy to float. This results from the facts that adipose tissue or fat is less dense than water and that the fat will provide a person with a greater amount of surface in contact with the water. Muscle tissue is far more dense than adipose or fat tissue. Women, with a higher percentage of body fat than men, often find it easier to float than men. Although no research has been conducted in the area, the observed success of females over males in synchronized swimming might be attributed, in part, to their superior potential for floating. Weight as well as the amount of surface in contact with the water are factors in achieving a successful floating position. Buoyancy can also be improved by filling the lungs with air.

Suspension Tasks

An object or a person is suspended when the center of gravity is below its point of support. Examples are found in gymnastics, in the parallel bars, and in ropes. In suspension, gravity pulls the body straight down and assists in controlling the body.

Broer and Zernicke (1979, 98) note a problem in suspension as "that of applying sufficient force to stabilize the body segment that is above the supporting surface." An example is the problem encountered by the learner on the still rings who is hanging by the hands, or by the knees and the hands, or by the knees alone, and who must be stabilized (all motion stopped) before a movement can be successfully executed.

When a force is exerted against an object that is already in motion, the resulting movement may not be in control. Performers suspended in air may also encounter problems in obtaining adequate force to change position or to bring the body into an upright position against the pull of gravity. (See the section titled Motion in this chapter for a further discussion of this problem.)

Tasks Involving Motion

Tasks that involve motion include those that move the entire body or a segment of the body on the ground, through the air, or in water. The impetus for the movement may be external or internal. External force may be of long or short duration.

Leverage

A lever is a machine. Often defined as a rigid bar that revolves around an axis, it enables the body to move. Leverage is a mechanical advantage for

▼ **FIGURE 11-2**

Types of lever systems: (a) first class—axis (A) lies between effort (E) and resistance (R); (b) second class—resistance lies between axis and effort; (c) third class—effort lies between axis and resistance. EA, effort arm; RA, resistance arm. From Marlene J. Adrian and John M. Cooper, *Biomechanics of Human Movement.* Copyright © 1989, by Benchmark Press, Inc. Reprinted by permission of Wm. C. Brown Communications, Inc., Dubuque, Iowa. All Rights Reserved.

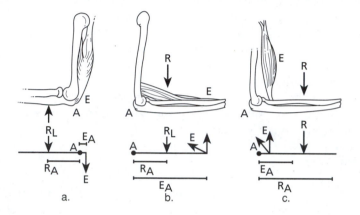

modifying force and motion. In order to gain force through leverage, the force arm is lengthened and the resistance arm is shortened. In order to gain speed and range of movement, the resistance arm is lengthened and the force arm is shortened. There are three types of lever systems: first, second, and third class (see figure 11-2).

First Class Lever.   The first class lever is used to gain speed if the fulcrum is nearer the point of applied effort or to gain force if the fulcrum is closer to the resistance. A playground teeter-totter is an example of a first class lever.

Second Class Lever.   In the second class lever, the resistance lies between the axis and the effort so that the length of the effort arm is greater than the length of the resistance arm. A person pushing a wheelbarrow is an example of the second class lever.

Third Class Lever.   The third class lever is the type most frequently found in the human body. The majority of muscles have their distal attachment near the joint, thus creating a third class lever. In a third class lever, the muscular effort always exceeds the resistance to be overcome. If the load is heavy, the system does not result in a mechanical advantage.

The third class lever favors speed and range of motion. "Given the same amount of shortening of a muscle and the same amount of time to produce the shortening, muscles that have the shortest effort arms will produce the greatest distance of travel of the distal end of the lever" (Adrian and Cooper 1989, 116). The use of an extension of the arm, as with a bat or a tennis racket, increases the speed and range of motion of the third class lever.

In analyzing the arm as a third class lever in a tennis drive, note that the bones of the arm and the tennis racket constitute the resistance, while the muscles of the upper arm and back provide the force. As the arm is lengthened or straightened in the forehand drive, resistance increases, and the speed and range of movement is improved.

Sequential use of levers increases power.

- When several levers are working at once, the resultant force is the sum of the forces of each lever. When forces are added successively, each force is added as the previous one reaches its maximum potential.
- Flow, referred to in dance and movement education, occurs when the sequential addition of levers creates momentum within the body. A more complex example of the sequential addition of levers is found in the combination of the catch and throw when the throw is executed immediately following the catch.

Motion

Motion is the process of movement. A force is required to start, stop, or alter motion. The occurrence of the force and the results of its occurrence are related to the amount of force exerted.

Newton's First Law.   Newton's first law, often referred to as the law of inertia, states that a body at rest tends to remain at rest, whereas a body in motion tends to remain in motion.

- To initiate movement, force must be applied to overcome inertia. A person, for example, will remain floating on the surface of the water but will not move forward until such time as force is exerted with either the arms or the legs. Another performer, on the starting blocks for a dash, will not move until force is applied with the balls of the feet against the blocks.
- A body in motion remains in motion and in a straight line unless acted on by a force that causes a change in direction.
- This principle is more easily observed in aerial movements because the body has a period of time in which a new force is not allowed to influence its direction. Once the body leaves the surface, movements can be changed only by body rotation or the use of arms or legs to influence the direction. Direction can be influenced more easily when the body maintains contact with the floor or with some other object so that it can be pushed in a specific direction.

- The law of inertia is sometimes called the law of the automobile whiplash. As the car is hit, the head is in motion and remains in motion.
- In running, every time the foot makes contact with the ground, a new movement or a new force has been initiated to overcome resistance and inertia.

Newton's Second Law.   When a body is acted upon by a force, its resulting acceleration is directly proportional to the force applied and inversely proportional to the mass. The rate of change of movement is in relation to the amount of force applied.

- The law of acceleration notes that the force acts in the direction it was applied.
- When two performers of different size are given an equal amount of force, the smaller person will create a greater acceleration than the larger person. Acceleration is change in velocity during motion. These changes may be an increase in velocity, a decrease in velocity, or a change in direction.
- Within human capacity, the greater the force, the faster the acceleration:

$$\text{Acceleration} = \frac{\text{velocity}}{\text{time}}$$

Newton's Third Law.   Newton's third law, or the law of action/reaction, states that for every action there is an equal and opposite reaction. The body moves in a direction opposite to the direction of the applied force.

- In walking on a hard surface, the foot presses against the floor and the floor presses against the foot. The forces are near equal.
- In walking on a soft surface, like a beach, the surface allows the foot to be absorbed by the surface before the foot can react, thus requiring considerably more force from the foot to accomplish the same movement that was obtained on the hard surface.

Translatory and Rotatory Motion

Motion may be translatory or rotatory. Translatory motion is the movement of the body from one place to another, with each body part moving an equal distance. Rotatory movement occurs when the body or a body segment rotates around an axis. An example of a rotatory movement of the entire body is a person performing a giant swing on a high bar; a rotatory movement of a body segment is a somersault in synchronized swimming.

Circular Motion

Circular motion is a combination of centripetal and centrifugal force. Centripetal force is the force pulling toward the axis of the motion. Centrifugal force, in contrast, is the force pulling away from the axis of motion.

- "A sprinter running around a curve experiences an inward centripetal force against his feet which allows him to change direction (to follow the curve) while an equal and opposite centrifugal force is applied outward by the feet" (Ecker 1985, 62).
- These forces are equal and opposite. If one of the forces is released, the other force is released.

Momentum

Momentum describes the quantity of motion, or mass times velocity. It is the product of mass and velocity. Mass is the weight of an object; velocity is the speed at which it will move.

In angular motion, the greater the distance from the center of rotation to the center of gravity of the body, the slower the angular velocity. All factors being equal, a somersault in tuck position moves faster than one in pike position. This principle is often used in diving. The diver will tuck the legs and arms as close to the body as possible to reduce the moment of inertia of the body around its axis. Angular velocity will increase while the body maintains angular momentum, thus allowing the diver to rotate in a short period of time. The same concept is applied in the front tuck somersault in synchronized swimming and the tuck somersault on the trampoline.

Tasks Involving Application of Force

Force is an action that produces a change in the state of an object. The change is influenced by whether the object is in motion or at rest. Kinetics, a component of mechanics, is the study of force. Brancazio (1984) has identified forces as contact and noncontact. Contact forces include pushes, pulls, friction, reaction of the ground, air resistance, and muscle force.

- The most important noncontact force is gravity.
- Force has both magnitude and direction.
- Force is movement applied to overcome inertia, resistance, or friction.
- Force applied over a longer period of time will develop more momentum than force applied for a short period of time.
- Transfer of momentum occurs as a result of the addition of levers. In movement, the momentum of the first lever is transferred to the next acting lever. The momentum gained as a result of each move in the overarm throw is transferred to the next lever as the person throws.

- When two objects hit, the total momentum after impact equals the total momentum before impact (Law of Conservation of Momentum), and the resultant motion is in the direction of the greater of the two forces.
- A tennis player receiving a serve applies force to the ball to send it back to the opponent. The speed of the returned ball is a combination of the force placed on the ball by the server and the force placed on the ball by the receiver.
- The concept of elasticity or restitution is built into landing surfaces in springboard diving, pole vaulting, and the trampoline. The deformed materials store energy that is imparted to the athlete, causing the athlete to have greater spring.

Torque

When force produces a rotatory rather than a linear movement, it is called torque. Torque is equal to the magnitude of force times the perpendicular distance from the line of action of the force to the axis of rotation. The direction of the force causes an object to move in a specific direction.

Friction

Friction is resistance that opposes the force of objects. Condition or composition of surface, velocity of objects, and amount of load are elements considered in analyzing friction.

- Greater energy is needed to overcome friction at the start of a movement than to maintain the same movement.
- Friction is used in slowing or stopping an object.
- Some sport skills favor friction whereas others attempt to reduce friction. As a result, friction is always discussed as optimal for the event that is under consideration.
- Well-lubricated surfaces reduce friction; smooth and hard surfaces also reduce friction. Rough and soft surfaces increase friction.
- When friction is low and the chance of slipping is great, individuals— including athletes—walking on wet or icy surfaces need to lower the center of gravity of their bodies and maintain it over their feet or the base of support.

These principles apply:

1. The greater the friction, the greater the muscle effort to oppose it.
2. The greater the friction, the greater the reduction of speed in human movement or object.
3. Friction in one movement can be utilized in a successive counter movement (Adrian and Cooper 1989, 135).

Fluid Resistance

Objects moving through gaseous or liquid fluids transfer their energy to the fluid, thus influencing their movements. This is called fluid resistance. Thrust, drag, and lift are the terms used to describe movement through water.

- Thrust is the force in the direction of velocity, the force that maintains the motion.
- Drag is the component of motion in opposition to velocity or motion. Drag is parallel to the direction of the flow of the fluid. It opposes the motion between the body and the water. Drag is also the resistance caused by the shape of the object. It exists in the air or water. The more streamlined the body, the less drag is created.
- Lift is a force exerted perpendicular to the flow of the fluid or perpendicular to velocity. Lift is generally thought of as an up-down movement disturbing the object.
- In swimming, the lift caused by the hands, arms, and legs contribute to the forward motion. Lift and drag are used to enhance the quality and the speed of a swimmer's performance.
- Frictional drag occurs in swimming between the body moving through the water and the water. Because the body is not as streamlined as it could be, eddies are formed and disturb the flow. To minimize the drag, the swimmer is instructed to pull the hand down under the water on the long axis of the body.
- Thrust is the force exerted by the body in the swimming strokes. The amount of surface and the direction of the stroke serve to enhance thrust.
- Linear force is the force that occurs when all forces act in a straight line.
- Torque occurs when two forces of equal magnitude are applied in opposite directions at a distance from one another. It causes the object to rotate.

Applying Force to Objects

The point of application of force determines the type of motion.

- A force applied directly behind the center of the object will cause linear motion; the object will move straight ahead.
- A force applied either above or below the center of the object will cause rotatory motion. The object will rotate end over end.

The direction of force causes an object to move in a specific direction.

- A basketball aimed in a specific direction will go in that direction. The direction of the arm or leg at the time of impact will determine the direction the object will move.

▼ **FIGURE 11-3**

Flow patterns produced by spinning balls as viewed sagittally to path of travel.
T = topspin: turbulent, high-pressure flow pattern at top of ball causing topspinning
balls to fall more rapidly than normal. B = backspin: turbulent, high-pressure flow
pattern at bottom of ball causing backspinning balls to rise more than normal.
Rotations of right- and left-spinning balls can be visualized with the figure as an
overhead view. From Marlene J. Adrian and John M. Cooper, *Biomechanics of Human
Movement.* Copyright © 1989, by Benchmark Press, Inc. Reprinted by permission of Wm.
C. Brown Communications, Inc., Dubuque, Iowa. All Rights Reserved.

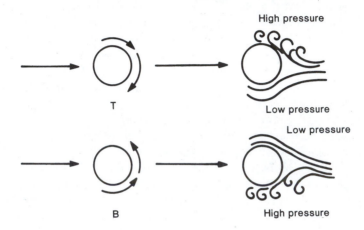

- Effort is made to eliminate movements that do not contribute to the desired direction of force. Swinging the arms past the front of the body or
  rotating the shoulders backward and forward in running are examples
  of unnecessary movement.

Spins.   Spins occur when force is applied to an object at a point other than
the center of the object.

- If the force is applied above the center of the object, the object will
  have topspin (see figure 11-3).
- A topspin will cause a ball to bounce low and move forward in a low,
  long arc. "The air pressure on the top of a ball hit with top spin forces
  that ball to fly forward in a low arc" (Die 1981, 19).

A backspin or underspin will cause the ball to move directly into the air
from the bounce.

- If the force is applied below the center of the object, the object will
  have backspin or underspin. "When under spin is applied, the lower
  half of the ball is deterred by the air, making the ball spin backward
  and producing a higher arc. After the ball lands, it bounces higher and
  shorter than a ball hit with top spin" (Die 1981, 20).

- Spins on a tennis ball, table tennis ball, basketball, or volleyball are created by the point of application of force and the length and direction of the contact.
- If the force is applied directly behind the object, it will move straight ahead.
- Drag may also be a factor in spins. For example, the backspin to the tennis ball by a tennis racquet may create high and low pressure areas, thus causing drag (Adrian and Cooper, 1989, 146).

Angle of Rebound.   An object hitting a surface will rebound from the surface. The angle at which it meets the surface (angle of incidence) and the properties of the surface will influence the angle of rebound.

- Angles are equal. By definition, an object (without spin) hitting a surface will rebound from that surface at exactly the same angle.
- Theoretically, if a ball is hit toward a solid wall at a ninety-degree angle, it will rebound from the wall at a ninety-degree angle. An object hitting the floor at a forty-five-degree angle will rebound at a forty-five-degree angle.
- Research (Dowell 1984, 1) has determined that when compressible balls without spin contact a smooth surface, the angle of rebound is greater than the angle of incidence.
- Factors that may alter the angles of rebound of an object include properties of the object projected, placement of spin, and the surface hit.
- The composition of the wall or of the ball may alter the angle of the return.
- Placement of the forearm, wrist, and hand in the volleyball pass (bump) will alter the angle of rebound.
- In golf, the club face rather than a wall or the ground becomes the surface. The angle desired is determined by the selection of a specific implement. Use of a three iron instead of a seven iron alters the angle that the ball will leave the ground.
- The type of spin affects the angle of rebound.

Projectiles
A body or an object may be projected into the air. Horizontal and vertical motions influence the path and the potential for flight of an object or person.

- The optimum theoretical angle for flight of a projectile is forty-five degrees; however, research (Dowell 1984, 2) has demonstrated that it is impossible to prescribe an optimal angle for all persons or objects.
- Factors affecting the decision include the purpose, shape, and size of the projectile, and the height and optimal angle of release.

- Ball distance is related to the angle at which the ball is released.
- The fast pitch in softball is most effective when the point of release permits a low, fast flight.
- Gravity and air resistance affect the flight of a projectile.

The relationship between position, velocity, and acceleration serve to explain the trajectory of a thrown or kicked object. Enoka (1988, 21) cites the following facts that aid in exploring the motion of a projectile.

- The path that the object travels while it is in the air is parabolic.
- The time that the object spends in the air depends on the magnitude of its velocity at release.
- The only force that the projectile experiences will be that due to gravity, and this will cause a vertical acceleration.
- Because there is no force acting in the horizontal direction, the horizontal acceleration of the object will be zero, which means its horizontal velocity will be constant.
- At the peak of its trajectory, the object changes its vertical direction of motion, which means that its vertical velocity will be zero at this point.

Tasks Involving Receiving Force

Although most movement involves giving or imparting force, receiving force is a skill used in numerous sports. Receiving force is catching an object, landing from a jump, or coming to a stop. The body learns to receive and to dissipate, or absorb, the force.

Absorption of Force

Absorption of force is related to the size of the surface: The greater the surface area, the more easily force is absorbed.

- Increase the size of the surface, such as in catching a ball by using two hands.
- Absorption of force is related to the texture and qualities of the surfaces. Surfaces are classified as resistive and nonresistive. Resistive surfaces are surfaces that push against the object or person and cannot be penetrated.
- The greater the time, distance, and area over which the force is dissipated, the less force is received by the body upon impact (see figure 11-4).
- In a fall, the body completes the fall with a forward or a sideward roll, increasing the time and distance over which the force of the body at the time of the fall is dissipated.

▼ **FIGURE 11-4**

Giving with the ball at the elbows and shoulder joints increases the distance over which the force is absorbed. Reprinted with permission from *Kinesiology, Basic Stuff Series I, Vol. II,* 1987, American Alliance for Health, Physical Education, Recreation, and Dance, 1900 Association Dr., Reston, VA 22091.

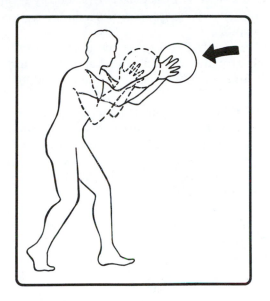

- Nonresistive surfaces can be penetrated by an object or a person. With a nonresistive surface, the objective is to hit the surface with as little area of contact as possible.
- Aerobic dance participants have sustained stress fractures and shin splints as a result of performing jumps, leaps, and bounces on nonresistive surfaces. The solution to these problems is to decrease the acceleration by using shoes with good absorption properties, gymnastics mats, or resilient floors. By reducing the force of impact, injuries should decrease.
- Follow-through, often described by sport skill specialists, is really an explanation of dissipation or absorption of energy. The longer the time over which the negative acceleration occurs, the less chance there is for joint injuries resulting from abrupt stops. This is important in batting and in golf.

▶ **Summary**

1. Movement is best acquired when the principles of mechanics, taken from physics, are used.

2. Muscles play one of three roles in movement. They move the limbs, relax muscles so that other muscles can move the limbs, and stabilize the joints. One muscle may perform each of the three roles at different times.

3. Muscles are activated by the neurons and sensory receptors of the nervous system. Sensory receptors include interoceptors, exteroceptors, and proprioceptors.

4. Kinesthesis is the ability to sense the position of the body in space. The potential for the kinesthetic receptors to signal change exists at all times, thus enabling the performer to be aware of change in performance.

5. Balance is the process of maintaining all body parts in control, one segment above the next. Balance may be static or dynamic. Static balance is holding a position; dynamic balance involves motion and locomotion.

6. Stability is related to the area or size of the base of support.

7. The ready position or placing the feet shoulder or hip distance apart is recommended for stability.

8. Loss of stability is important in movements like diving.

9. Fat people will find it easier to float in water than thin people. Women have a higher percentage of body fat than men. As a result, women have been observed to achieve greater success in synchronized swimming.

10. Leverage is using the muscles and bones as machines. Most human movement is of a third class lever.

11. Motion is the process of movement.

12. Newton's laws:
- A body in motion remains in motion; a body at rest remains at rest.
- When a body is acted upon, its resulting acceleration is proportional to the force applied and inversely proportional to the mass.
- For every action, there is an equal and opposite reaction.

13. Newton's third law, action/reaction, occurs when one walks across a hard surface and the feet press against the surface and the surface presses back.

▶ References

Adrian, Marlene, and Cooper, John M. (1989). *The Biomechanics of Human Movement*. Indianapolis, Indiana: Benchmark Press.

Brancazio, P. J. (1984). *Sport Science: Physical Laws and Optimum Performance*. New York: Simon and Schuster.

Broer, Marion R. (1960). *Efficiency of Human Movement*. Philadelphia: W. B. Saunders.

Broer, Marion R., and Zernicke, Ronald F. (1979). *Efficiency of Human Movement* (4th ed.). Philadelphia: W. B. Saunders.

Die, Ding Shu, Fang, Wang Lian, Zuo, Zhu Ding, and Lu, Yuan Hai. (1981). *The Chinese Book of Table Tennis*. New York: Atheneum.

Dowell, Linus J. (1984). Contributions of research conducted in the kinemechanics laboratory at Texas A & M University (unpublished materials).

Ecker, Tom (1985). *Basic Track and Field Biomechanics.* Los Altos, California: Tafnaws Press.

Enoka, Roger M. (1988). *Neuromechanical Basis of Kinesiology.* Champaign, Illinois: Human Kinetics.

Hutton, Robert S. (1987). Status of research in the perception of movement: Kinesthesis/proprioception. *Research Consortium Newsletter, 10*(1), 2.

Laws, Kenneth (1984). *The Physics of Dance.* New York: Schirmer Books.

Schmidt, R. F. (1978). Motor systems. In R. F. Schmidt (Ed.), *Fundamentals of Neurophysiology.* New York: Springer-Verlag.

Scott, M. Gladys. (1963). *Analysis of Human Motion.* New York: Appleton-Century-Crofts.

Ulibarri, Dianne V. (1987). *Kinesiology, Basic Stuff Series I, Vol. II.* Reston, Virginia: American Alliance for Health, Physical Education, Recreation and Dance.

Psychology

The use of psychology in sport is varied because psychological concepts encompass a wide range of scientific facts and theories. Gill (1986, 6) defines sport psychology as the "scientific study of human behavior in sport." Within the sport psychology community there are further subdivisions. The North American Society for the Psychology of Sport and Physical Activity (NASPSPA) has three interest groups: (1) sport psychology, (2) motor learning/control, and (3) motor development. Sport psychology draws from the personality and social elements of psychology. Motor learning and control involves the learning process: cognition, perception, and kinesthetic acuity. They draw from experimental psychology. Motor development deals with the physical growth and development of the person.

This chapter focuses on all three aspects of psychology, addressing each in the context of the learner of physical skills. Sport psychology is addressed first in the discussion of personality and the social influences of psychology. Motor learning and control, discussed second, features an understanding of the learning process and the elements of cognition. (Perception and kinesthetic acuity were addressed in chapter 11.) The discussion of motor development includes a brief overview of anatomic and physical development from youth to old age.

▶ Sport Psychology

Personality

People are different. Each person is an individual. Some people enjoy every moment of competition and cannot wait for the opportunity; other people are in fear right up to the start of an event but choose to compete in spite of their feelings. Others will not compete because of the stress associated with the activity and with competition. When the activity involves risk, such as gymnastics or skiing, many people will believe they possess the skills and are ready to perform effectively. Others who possess comparable skills avoid participation because they believe they will not succeed. Some people enjoy scrambling and engaging in other forms of body contact while other people avoid body contact at all cost.

Personality is usually described as the relatively consistent behavior of an individual. Butt (1987, 95) states that personality is "the unique expression and character of the individual." Some people are consistently shy and timid; other people may be consistently aggressive. Personality is usually thought to be a description of the individual's social skill. Personality also includes the individual's ability to concentrate and the desire to excel.

Personality is influenced by inherited biological characteristics, by unique life experiences, and by environmental influences. Through the years psychologists have evolved a number of theories. Many early theories focused on abnormal behavior while today's theories are often dedicated to understanding healthy, normal human beings. Personality testing has evolved from the theories and has been used in research that will be provided to substantiate certain points in this chapter. Coaches and persons working with adult activity programs may decide to use personality tests with their clients or athletes. Personality tests may be useful when followed up with personal counseling and guidance; if such support is not available, administering personality tests is not recommended.

Research on sport participants has been extensive. Do certain kinds of people participate in certain sports? Results of research suggest that a sound mental health has a positive relationship with athletic success. Browne and Mahoney (1984, 609) note that "extroverts are more socially inclined, more adventurous, take higher risks, and in general are more involved in sports . . . at least in those where there is a high level of incoming stimulation."

Some evidence also suggests that drive and determination can be measured by pencil and paper tests. The use of personality tests to screen participants for the opportunity for instruction that will permit them to become elite athletes is not recommended. The potential for eliminating outstanding performers is great. Another factor to be considered is that nearly all the research has been conducted on elite athletes or those with aspirations of becoming elite athletes. Little research has been conducted on the general public.

Smith and Theberge (1987, 86–88), in examining personality research with people in general, were able to identify only three studies. Although they clearly state that the research techniques were shaky at best, they concluded that among the general public, physical activity or sport participation tends to be higher "for persons with greater extroversion, especially in team rather than individual sport, . . . greater ego strength and adjustment . . . greater emotional stability . . . greater emotional detachment and less emotional closeness . . . greater assertiveness . . . greater sense of efficacy and need for achievement . . . greater need for prominence or prestige . . . greater morality and altruism . . . greater flexibility . . . greater energy level . . . greater deliberateness . . . greater stimulation need . . . and greater self actualization and creativity." *Note:* From *Why People Recreate: An Overview of Research* (pp. 86–88) by D. H. Smith and N. Theberge, 1987, Champaign, IL: Human Kinetics. Life Enhancement Publications. Copyright 1987 by David H. Smith and Nancy Theberge. Adapted by permission.

Butt (1987, 97–98) expresses the concerns that professionals have addressed in examining the research literature on personality and sport.

1. The type of individual who is attracted to a specific sport may not be the one most naturally suited to it once the selection process of the sport takes place by coaches, sport organizations, and the social and cultural values which surround the sport. Thus, on the one hand those best suited to a sport may not be encouraged to remain in it. On the other hand those encouraged to remain in a sport by external or extraneous factors (i.e., work well with a specific coach, have socioeconomic support from family) may not be the most naturally suited for it.
2. Personality changes may occur over time as the individual is socialized by and adapts to the intensive subculture of sport. . . .
3. The sex and sex roles of athletes complicate the comparability of results due to the extreme types of both male and female found in many, if not most, sports. . . .
4. Individual versus group sport differences further increase error variance in studies of sport. The socialization process and demands on athletes are clearly different across many types of sport. The individual versus group sport division is one of the more obvious.
5. Position played skews the results in studies of personality by sport. There are different demands upon athletes fulfilling specialized roles in a sport. . . .
6. Finally, studying sport at different performance levels yields noncomparable results. There are many changes in role demands and personal adjustment as the athlete, regardless of age, climbs the sport ladder from local, to national, to international competition and from there to the professional level. From Dorcas Susan Butt, 1987, *The Psychology of Sport,* Van Nostrand Reinhold. Reprinted by permission.

Social Influences of Psychology

Social elements of psychology include aggression, competence, competition, cooperation, and complementation.

Aggressive Behavior

Butt (1987, 15) defines aggression as "the energetic assault on animate or inanimate objects for a purpose . . . the purpose of aggression is to inflict pain, to dominate, to obtain, to outperform, to prevent." Sports such as football, basketball, and hockey that are visible on television and well-known to the public appear to reward aggressive behavior. The National Collegiate Athletic Association's (NCAA) revenue-producing sports also appear to reward aggressive behavior. Some people are aggressive by nature; most sport participants are taught to be aggressive. Many people have been either turned off or frightened out of physical activity as a result of the aggressive behavior of others who were learning to acquire skills in the same environment. At times, certain sport situations require aggressive behavior (e.g., football) and successful strategies within sports use aggression as a means of control.

Researchers, in dealing with aggression, have observed that animals of common species often fight but they seldom kill one another. They have also observed that among animals there appears to be ritual and possibly rules in their fighting. They liken this ritual among animals to contemporary societies' use of sport as a ritual for acceptance of fighting or sanctioned aggressive behavior among humans.

The physical skills teacher is placed in a dilemma when it comes to the acceptable use of aggression in activity. Fostering aggressive feelings may be helpful to the person who is fearful of risk activities or to the individual who is not able to obtain a right to equipment and other resources. Fostering aggression may be harmful in situations when one's aggressive behavior is already high.

The use of sport to channel aggressive behavior is often recommended in prisons and in working with "acting out youth." Some classroom teachers and school authorities would like to see the major objective of the physical education program be the positive channeling of aggressive behavior. Many pick-up basketball, football, and soccer games are engaged in to channel aggressive behavior.

If the reason for physical activity for the entire group is to channel aggressive behavior, the channeling is a worthwhile goal. Problems in the physical activity environment occur when the group is mixed. When the group consists of people who are there to acquire physical skills and others whose needs are to channel aggressive behavior, an impossible learning environment has been created. Many people avoid physical activity because their early experiences consisted of being hit, pushed, or beaten up. Whether an organized physical activity or sport learning environment should include the channeling of aggressive behavior needs to be evaluated. Whether an instructor can effectively channel aggression for some members of the class while developing sequential competencies for others in a single environment needs to be studied. Unfortunately, teachers are often asked to conduct activities in ways and among divergent groups that theorists and researchers have neglected to study. This is one such area.

Competence

Competence is how the individual interacts in the environment. Butt (1987, 39–41) identifies five categories of competence: physical, intellectual, emotional, social, and spiritual. Physical competence includes strength, endurance, flexibility, speed, coordination, visual and auditory acuity, and skill. "Intellectual competence is the ability to use the mind to reach desired solutions or decisions" (Butt 1987, 39). Can the learner size up the situation and create an effective plan of action in game play? Can one plan a smart game of tennis? Emotional competence is when people can manage their emotions such that their skill in play is enhanced. Positive emotions of confidence, stability, and feelings of success will be used rather than negative emotions of frustration, failure, blame, and fear. Social competence is the ability to work with others. Loyalty and morale are important factors. Relations with others are positive. Spiritual or existential competence refers "to the individual experiencing intrinsic satisfaction from the appreciation of morality, contentment, and the ability to be philosophical about victory and defeat" (Butt 1987, 40).

The objective in competence is to prepare self-sufficient performers. They know their strengths and weaknesses. They also appreciate the strengths and weaknesses of others, including teammates and opponents.

Competition and Cooperation

Competition is the capacity to outplay another person or group; cooperation is the capacity to join one or more persons in directing energy toward a common goal. Competition and cooperation can be examined from the standpoint of the desire of the performer or from the context that advanced forms of physical activity demand certain types of behaviors. Some people enjoy competition and appear to be able to maintain a higher level of skill when confronted with competition. Placing a person whose skills are not fully learned in a competitive or distractive situation may cause the skills to deteriorate. Research (Butt 1987, 59) confirms this theory.

Deutsch (1982), who has conducted research on cooperation and competition for nearly forty years, states that the notion of competition in our society must be placed in an appropriate perspective and reduced. Today's classroom literature contains a plea for teaching cooperation and avoiding competition.

Cooperation is easily included in the physical skill learning environment as the professional implements the practice progression explained in Part III.

Competition, or the stressing of an individual or a group of individuals to outperform another group, is introduced to advanced or skilled physical activity performers. At this point, the performer is challenged either to reach a particular standard of skill or to, for example, produce the best balance beam routine in an instructional environment, local competition, or the Olympic Games. Competition is the objective in many activity

▼ **FIGURE 12-1**
Information process system

Input		Output
Vision		
Smell		
Taste	HUMAN PROCESSING	Performance
Tactile		
Auditory		
Kinesthetic		

organizations. Nearly all games, and all sports involving teams, draw upon the competitive elements for achievement and bringing the game to a completion. The nature of the activity organization is to provide competitive challenges to performers.

▶ Motor Learning and Control

Information Processing

Information is available in the environment and is received by the body through one or more of the sense organs. Information is taken into the memory and processed. Output occurs as an observable motor performance (see figure 12-1).

Schmidt (1982, 94–113) discusses three possible stages of processing the input: (1) stimulus-identification, (2) response selection, and (3) response program stage. In stage one, the person becomes aware of the stimulus, hears the sound of the audience, and sees the opponent move in front of him or her. Becoming aware means that the stimuli are acknowledged and identified. Details of the stimuli, which may be simple or complex movements, are also recognized. After recognition, the information is coded by the brain. Experience is a factor that assists the person in abstracting or identifying those elements that will be most helpful in determining how the person will choose to move later on. In the second or response selection stage, the person analyzes each stimulus, selects a number of potential alternative responses, evaluates each one, and executes the one that appears to be most appropriate. The third stage, the response program, involves carrying out the movement. If the movement works, the process is correct. If the movement does not work, the person returns to stage two and examines the alternatives, using information acquired from the most recent act as well as previous information.

Schmidt (1982, 438) defines motor learning as a "set of processes associated with practice or experience leading to relatively permanent changes in skilled behavior." "First, learning is a process of acquiring the capability for producing skilled actions. That is, learning is the set of underlying events, occurrences, or changes that happen when people practice allowing them to become skilled at some task. Second, learning is a direct result of practice or experience. Third, learning cannot . . . be measured directly, as the processes leading to change in behavior are internal and are usually not available for direct examination; rather, one must infer that learning (the processes) occurred on the basis of the changes in behavior that can be observed. Fourth, learning is assumed to produce relatively permanent changes in skilled behavior; changes in behavior caused by easily reversible alterations in mood, motivation, or internal states . . . will not be thought of as due to learning." *Note:* From *Motor Control and Learning: A Behavioral Emphasis* (pp. 437–438) by R. A. Schmidt, 1982, Champaign, IL: Human Kinetics. Copyright 1982 by Richard A. Schmidt. Adapted by permission.

Cognition

Cognitive psychological elements include concentration and attentional focus, and imagery or mental rehearsal. Aspects of arousal and self-confidence will be addressed under concentration. The idea of what to concentrate on and when to concentrate, what to imagine and when to imagine, are all part of the area of cognitive psychology.

Concentration and Attention

In the early 1970s, Green and Green (1977, 244–275) concluded that persons or performers could learn to control the autonomic functions of the body. They could influence muscular and hormonal changes. In their study of Yogis from India, Green and Green found that Yogis could alter their brain waves, heart rate, breathing, blood pressure, body temperature, and other processes. Green and Green further concluded that these changes could be controlled by a person and that individuals could be taught to exercise such control. Unestahl (1983, 15) describes concentration as "a more intense attentiveness to a narrow attention area (concentration) . . . accompanied by a general inattentiveness (dissociation) to everything outside this area." In essence, a human body can learn to do what it is told to do if we understand how to tell it to behave.

Nideffer (1986a, 10) can best be described as the father of the study of concentration or attention in athletics. He points out in the *Athletes Guide to Mental Training* that "for integration of mind and body, all mental and physical energy must flow in the same direction." Basically, that is the ability to shut out from the mind everything but the movement to be executed and the environment in which it is to be executed. The ability to focus attention on the task to be performed and to eliminate all irrelevant internal and external stimuli is concentration (Schmid and Peper 1986).

To be successful in concentration, it is also essential that the performer know all biomechanical and motor aspects of the skill and that skill components be correct and efficient. Execution of each skill must be so perfect that it is an automatic execution. Nideffer (1986a, 15) states that "a prerequisite to optimal performance is your having developed a skill to the point where it is possible to execute it automatically." The performer learns the skill through imagery and visual analysis. When it is learned and has become automatic the performer is free to turn to concentration.

Many teachers tell performers to concentrate but few tell them what they mean by concentrating. Nideffer (1986b, 258–259) provides eight principles that underlie his program of attention control:

1. Athletes need to be able to engage in at least four different types of attention.
2. Different sport situations will make different attentional demands on an athlete. Accordingly, it is incumbent upon the athlete to be able to shift to different types of concentration to match changing attentional demands.
3. Under optimal conditions, the average person can meet the attentional demands of most sport situations.
4. There are individual differences in attentional abilities. Some of the differences are learned, some are biological, and some are genetic. Thus different athletes have different attentional strengths and weaknesses.
5. As physiological arousal begins to increase beyond an athlete's own optimal level, there is an initial tendency for the athlete to rely too heavily on the most highly developed attentional ability.
6. The phenomenon of `choking,' of having performance progressively deteriorate, occurs as physiological arousal continues to increase to the point of causing an involuntary narrowing of an athlete's concentration and to the point of causing attention to become more internally focused.
7. Alterations in physiological arousal affect concentration. Thus, the systematic manipulation of physiological arousal is one way of gaining some control over concentration.
8. Alterations in the focus of attention will affect physiological arousal. Thus, the systematic manipulation of concentration is one way to gain some control over arousal (e.g., muscle tension levels, heart rate, respiration rate). Reprinted from "Concentration and Attention Control Training" by Robert M. Nideffer in *Applied Sport Psychology: Personal Growth to Peak Performance,* Jean Williams, ed., by permission of Mayfield Publishing Company. Copyright © 1986 Mayfield Publishing Co.

The performer learns to concentrate. It is not an innate skill that a good performer will acquire without a plan. The activity or skill itself and the environment in which it is executed dictates the type of concentration.

Concentration, according to Nideffer (1986a), may be internal or external and broad or narrow (see table 12-1). Although it is never mentioned, these contrasting characteristics seem to relate to the open-closed theories developed by Robb (1972) based on Knapp and Poulton's theories and classification system. Knapp (1963) and Poulton (1957) believed that the key to success was knowledge of the environment in which the skill was to be executed. If the environment was a predictable, relatively stable setting, it was a closed environment. If the skill was to be executed in an unpredictable and constantly changing environment, it was called an open environment (Robb 1972, 121). In a closed environment theory, a performer knows exactly what the activity will be and executes the skill according to a carefully rehearsed pattern. A gymnastics routine, a serve in tennis or volleyball, or a figure skating or synchronized swimming routine represents the closed theory. Closed theory resembles the narrow internal or external categories found in table 12-1. Open theory of sport requires that the performer respond to clues in the game and move accordingly. Basketball shooting, soccer movements, and fencing rallies use an open theory of sport. Open theory is the broad internal and external type of attentional focus.

Whether performers use a broad or a narrow focus in the execution of skills, they will process considerable information prior to executing the skill. If the skill is closed, the information is gathered, sifted for relevant items, and the skill is executed. Fully rehearsed closed skills may have a narrow internal focus. The performer makes sure that the body is not too relaxed or too tight. Then the concentration usually goes to the object to be hit or the skill to be executed. When the activity is open, the performer will be forced to gather information, sift the information, and construct a plan of action in a very short period of time. The focus will be broad and external for most of the time.

Persons performing in open environments are often rewarded by the number of alternatives they can envision in a short period of time. The greater the number, the better the chance of finding one that will succeed. (See Schmidt, 1982, pp. 89–127, for a detailed discussion of these theories.)

▼ **TABLE 12-1**

Types of attention

	EXTERNAL (OPEN)	**INTERNAL (CLOSED)**
Broad	Used to size up a situation and react, as in a return of a tennis serve or a soccer play	The plan of a gymnastics or a synchronized swimming routine
Narrow	Focus on the ball in basketball	Rehearsal of a skip in dancing

Idea taken, in part, from "Concentration and Attention Control Training" by Robert M. Nideffer in *Applied Sport Psychology: Personal Growth to Peak Performance,* Jean Williams, ed. by permission of Mayfield Publishing Company. Copyright © 1986 Mayfield Publishing Co.

Athletes successful in an open environment often possess a high level of awareness or the intuitive capacity to anticipate how others will move and will perform in a given situation. Some of this ability is cognitive knowledge read from the current performance of both the opponent and teammates. Some is knowledge acquired in viewing films and watching opponents, and some is intuition. Cognitive knowledge will be studied in depth under visual analysis.

Arousal.   To be successful in concentration, the performer is in touch with his or her personal level of arousal. Arousal is not only a state of alertness of an individual but an opportunity for the person to organize the body's resources for intense and vigorous activity. Landers and Boutcher (1986, 164) use Martin's comparison of a car engine speed to human arousal. "The engine may run very fast, or just idle slowly. . . . The ideal intensity should match the requirements for the desired task outcome (e.g., quick acceleration) in order to produce the greatest performance efficiency." The arousal level cannot be too high or too low. Maximum arousal is usually characterized by a fast-pumping heart. Too high an arousal or tenseness may cause the body to tighten up and not be able to perform. High arousal can result in muscle cramps, a loss of flow in movement, choppy execution of the skill, and early fatigue. Too-low arousal can cause a performer to get bored and lose interest in the performance. Amount or level of arousal may also be dictated by the event: high arousal is appropriate, on occasion, for very short all-out activities; low arousal is appropriate for long endurance events.

Nideffer (1986a, 19) notes that the "greater your level of self-confidence, the higher the level of arousal that you can tolerate, and the more likely you are to make mistakes because you were not aroused enough." Choking is the slang term often used to describe a high level of arousal at the wrong time. The athlete chokes and is not able to execute the skill in the manner that he or she was able to on previous occasions. This often occurs when the performer is subjected to stresses such as knowing the performance will be particularly important, that relatives and friends are attending the event, or that the event is a national or regional championship. Persons scheduled to leap from airplanes or to swim their first length of the pool have also been known to choke.

Performers who choke when asked to execute skills in stressful situations may not have the skill performance requisite to the stressful situation. Performers cannot be expected to concentrate until the skill is automatic. This theory will serve as the basis for advice to the teacher (discussed in Part III) that the skill must be learned before the stress of game play is introduced. It will also serve as the basis for the learning levels of play alone and side-by-side play.

Learning to Concentrate.   Concentration means focusing totally on what is happening at present. One cannot be thinking of the past or the future and still be concentrating. Schmid and Peper (1986, 274) provide the single best advice to teachers working in physical activity who wish to develop concentration or a focused attitude among their performers: "Athletes need to experience simulated competition training in which they practice their physical skills while being exposed to all possible external stimuli that can occur during a real competition." Examine the drowning victim rescues taught in many activity settings, including school programs, to identify a simulated learning environment or an example of rehearsal. Simulation and rehearsal are important aspects of the learning continuum and are visited a number of times in this text.

In closed events such as gymnastics, synchronized swimming, diving, figure skating, riflery, or target sports, rehearsal can be of the actual event. External factors, such as an audience and judges, will be the only difference. Sometimes the changes in a room or in pool depth in synchronized swimming become a serious external factor. These changes must be anticipated and rehearsed. In open skill rehearsal, all possible situations are identified and solutions prepared for each situation. Then the various solutions are rehearsed. Situations in which quick decisions are to be made and executed are also rehearsed.

These rehearsals are not just for the elite athlete. As soon as the performer has acquired the fundamentals, he or she begins to rehearse the skills in a closed environment. During this time, only internal and predictable external stimuli are allowed to influence the performance. The same opportunities are provided for learners at the combination, motor pattern, and specialized skill levels. When the learner has acquired the specialized skills for activities in which the play environment demands an open environment, the instructor begins to prepare the learner for the use of the skills in this environment.

Imagery

Sheikh (1983, xi), in *Imagery,* points out that imagery, a very popular psychological theory, was banished from scientific psychology by John B. Watson, one of the great psychologists, and has returned to favor only in the 1970s and 1980s (p. xi). Athletes and coaches have used imagery, often titled mental practice, for many years. As a result, the topic of mental practice has been researched (Richardson 1967a and 1967b) by physical educators. Most elite athletes have used imagery or mental practice at one time or another. Some outstanding athletes have attributed their success in sport specifically to imagery. Imagery employs the senses of vision, sound, smell, taste, touch, and kinesthetic acuity or "feel of the body in space."

When people engage in physical activity, the brain constantly transmits impulses to the muscles. Similar impulses can be transmitted to the muscles when the performer imagines the movement. Movement is not necessary for the impulses to be transmitted. Through imagery, it is thought that the neural pathways for certain movements are enhanced (Hale 1982, 379).

▼ **TABLE 12-2**
Sequence in the use of imagery

TYPE OF IMAGERY	WHEN USED
Third person	To learn skill
First person	To enhance performance of the learned skill

The terms imagery and mental practice appear to be defined in a number of ways. One is that the image may be first person or third person (Mahoney and Avener 1977, and Hale 1982). A first person image is one in which the person imagines full participation and muscle stimulation is achieved (see table 12-2). The third person image is the capacity to imagine a performance of a skill or an event that may or may not include the participant (see table 12-2). In third person imagery, the person is a spectator; in first person imagery, the person is a participant, without physical movement. Third person is the first type of imagery to be learned by a performer. Successful achievement of third person imagery enables a performer to learn first person imagery. As a result of this sequence, third person imagery is reviewed first.

Third Person Imagery.   Prior to engaging in third person imagery, these prerequisites are to be met.

1. The instructor and the performer are to have a prototype of the sequential series of movements fixed in their heads. That prototype is to be of the skill executed in an efficient or biomechanically correct manner. If the prototype is faulty, the outcome will be faulty. It is believed that many inexperienced performers lose considerable performance time or never reach their optimum skill level as a result of the memorization of faulty or poor performance. If one is good at imagery, one will be able to memorize the prototype. If one's biomechanics are faulty, one may have memorized a fault that will require days and even years of retraining in order to rid the body of the wrong message. For examples, one needs only to look at a skilled player whose game falls apart under extreme pressure, or a sound adult intermediate performer who falls into an old habit when faced with the stress of performance under other than ideal conditions. How many intermediate skiers lose their parallel form when faced with a black diamond pitched slope? These people have, in fact, reverted to an old pattern once memorized.

   The visualization of the prototype is learned while the performer is learning the skill. In fact, the memorization of how the skill is to be executed, the watching of an efficient performer, or the film of an efficient performer will enhance the process of learning the prototype.

2. The instructor and the performer are able to view others performing the movement and to determine the efficiency of their movement. In other words, they are able to see efficient or mechanically sound technique in the performance of others.

When these prerequisites have been met, the performer uses imagery as well as physical practice in acquiring the skill. The use of video equipment to guide the learner in removing errors and as a means of reinforcing efficient movement is recommended. The writers are well aware that in certain chartered school environments, neither time—due to large classes—nor finances for such equipment exist.

Once the performer has acquired the skill and can consistently perform it or can differentiate between a good and a faulty performance, the performer is ready to move to first person imagery.

First Person Imagery. First person imagery is initiated when the performer's technique somewhat consistently meets the standard that he or she wishes to maintain. Individual differences will occur and will be appropriate. When individual differences are programmed into first person imagery, the teacher and learner should be aware of the difference, and be willing to accept the outcome of the performance.

Kinesthetic acuity, described in chapter 11, is called into play to enable the athlete to feel each and every movement of the performance such that each muscle group within the body will be stimulated. This phase of rehearsal is not to be executed until the performer is capable of executing the skill at a proficient level. The feel of a faulty movement or the feel of an undetected error will result in the memorization of an error. In addition to kinesthetic acuity, touch and other senses are called into play to further enhance the performance.

Use in the Learning Environment. With the prerequisites in mind, the instructor is ready to fashion a program of imagery and mental rehearsal for performers. The progression will include the vivid picture, first of an abstract performer and then of the learner performing the skill. These sessions will encourage the performer to remain a spectator, thus engaging in third person imagery. Once the performer can visualize him- or herself in movement, the next step is to neurologically stimulate the muscles as the movement is perceived (first person imagery). The performer goes through the entire sequence of movements, stimulating each and every muscle of the body that is involved in the actual movement.

Timing, or the speed of the rehearsed performance, becomes an important factor. Early visualization is often in slow motion. As the picture becomes vivid, the performer speeds up the performance to that expected in its formal execution. This change in speed is to be emphasized.

In addition to the rehearsal of the skill itself, performers need to be encouraged to imagine the correct execution of the skill. Rehearsing failure is much like rehearsing a faulty movement—failure will occur.

Imagery will be influenced by whether the environment in which the skill is to be executed is an open or closed environment. A closed environment will require the elements discussed above. An open environment will require all of the above and the imaging of all the possible alternatives with which one might be confronted in an actual play situation. Potential solutions to each alternative situation must be worked out using cognitive skills. Movement associated with each solution is then memorized. The performer visualizes all players on the floor or field, rehearses each player's possible actions, and imagines, while sending the stimulus to the muscles, his or her role in the solution. The ability to imagine other players involved in each play requires a high level of knowledge of strategy and game play as well as a sense of the number of performers that are really a part of a particular play.

Persons working at the activity organization level will find that recommended situational play permits the focus mentioned above. Players discuss the possible ways of moving an object. They may rehearse beginning plays by walking through the floor pattern merely to understand their positions with respect to other performers. At this stage, learners should be encouraged to diagram the play, to memorize it, and to rehearse, seeing themselves as part of the play. It will, for example, enable children learning sport or game for the first time to internalize basic strategies.

The point should be made that visual analysis, imagery, and rehearsal are methods of skill practice. This form of practice is to be terminated at some point prior to a presentation or performance. One should be analytical only when there is time to stop and repeat a movement. When such time no longer exists, the time for analysis is gone. Mental rehearsal or imagery of an analysis nature is not to be engaged in prior to competition.

Motivation

Motivation is why people do what they do. Probably the most important motivation that the professional in physical activity hopes to achieve is to inspire the learner to want to continue to pursue physical activity. If the professional is a school physical educator, the aspiration is that the learner will be a physically active person throughout life. The tennis professional or the aerobics instructor may wish to channel the learner's motivation toward the particular activity represented. Motivation, like arousal, is a form of human energy. It differs from arousal in that the energy has direction. A performer's motivation is influenced by intrinsic and extrinsic factors (see table 12-3). Extrinsic or external motivation is influenced by feedback from others and from the environment in which one performs. Intrinsic or internal motivation comes from within the performer.

▼ **TABLE 12-3**
Learning incentives

	POSITIVE	NEGATIVE
Internal (or intrinsic)	Joy of movement	Failure
	Excitement	Forecasting an accident
	Thrill	Inability to learn complex skills
External (or extrinsic)	Attention	Criticized by teacher or colleagues
	Respect from others	Failing proficiency tests for risk
	Awards	activities

Intrinsic Motivation

Little is known about intrinsic motivation; however, it may, on occasion, be the factor that keeps a poor performer returning to practice or a good performer challenged, such as a skilled skier being out on the hill 100 days each year. Intrinsic motivation involves the excitement, challenge, and sense of accomplishment that often accompanies participation in physical activity. The fact that a person can get lost in the physical activity is possibly one of the most important intrinsic values of a person under stress. Even though some members of society believe that the extrinsic threat of a heart attack or osteoporosis will keep people moving, some believe that those who will exercise seriously will participate because of the joy of movement (Clement 1988).

Extrinsic Motivation

Extrinsic motivation is the motivation inspired by external forces. Many people exercise to ward off the chance of a heart attack or osteoporosis. Others allow the mirror to suggest that their weight needs to be decreased or merely shifted around. Threats of increased health care costs serve to motivate certain people. Among young people, attention and respect accorded elite athletes has been found to be a high motivator.

Feedback serves to influence motivation. All forms of feedback, from brainwashing to the absence of reinforcement, affect the learner. Motivation may be influenced by others or may be controlled by the performer.

Reinforcement

Considerable writing and research has been conducted on behavior and behavior modification. Reinforcement or feedback may be negative or positive. The object is to strengthen certain behaviors whether the behaviors are positive or negative. Punishment differs from reinforcement in that its purpose is to terminate certain behaviors. Reinforcement is used extensively in teaching. It is the continuous feedback provided to the performer about his or her achievement. At the beginning level, all performers need to be successful. Simplistic skills are mastered and reinforced. Difficult skills are introduced only after the elementary skills can be repeated consistently in a stressful situation.

Characteristics of a good reinforcement program are that it is:

- consistent
- immediate
- administered in small increments
- a combination of positive criticisms given first, followed by negative criticisms

Feedback in the learning environment is most successful when the instructor first points out and reinforces the good parts in the performance. This is followed by the negative criticism of one or two of the most serious faults or the faults the instructor knows the learner will be most likely to change. Gill (1986, 137) uses the word *shaping* to discuss the instructor's guidance of an athlete toward a particular performance. The teacher makes the sequence known to the performer and then slowly guides the performer toward a successful acquisition of the sequence.

Many physical activity environments use various extrinsic awards, such as medals, T-shirts, etc., to encourage participation and improve performance. The Canadian and Norwegian Sport Federations have created an entire system of medals that are used to encourage participation. Research results have provided mixed messages about the value of these extrinsic awards. Speculation also exists as to whether some people, particularly young children, become more interested in the award than in the participation.

Social reinforcement includes comments like "good job" and "nice work." They tell the performer he or she is doing well but they are not specific in describing what is considered good.

Learners are influenced by the expectations of instructors, by other members of the group, and by their own expectations. A number of studies confirm the fact that teachers tend to spend more time, provide more sophisticated advice, and ask questions that will elicit detailed responses from the learners they expect will succeed. Students that are ignored in the learning environment may not receive the instruction essential to success or the feedback that they, in fact, could be successful. If the teacher expects the learner to succeed or believes the learner has superior capabilities—whether this fact is valid or not—the teacher will find the learner succeeding. Teachers' expectations are, in fact, a self-fulfilling prophecy.

▶ Motor Development

Motor development may be defined as "changes in motor behavior that are related to age" (Williams 1989) or a "continuous, age related process whereby an individual progresses from simple, unorganized, and unskilled movement to the achievement of highly organized, complex motor skills and finally to the adjustment of skills that accompanies aging" (Haywood 1986, 7). Individuals' lives and bodies are shaped by a combination of genetic background and the environment in which they live. The extent to which inherited and environmental factors affect the potential for success in physical skills has been debated extensively without resolution. Some aspects of body size as well as whether one possesses many or few fast- and slow-twitch muscles are thought to be genetically determined. Economic factors and basic needs such as standard of nutrition and amount of rest also influence the performer's success in physical skill.

Members of society associate the acquisition of many of the fundamentals described in Part I of this text as within the natural development of the child from two to six years of age. It is true that children, if left to their own devices, will acquire some of the fundamentals described. The normal, healthy child will learn to crawl, to walk, and to run. When crawling becomes comfortable, they will begin to climb, with stairways and high, out-of-reach furniture serving to add risk to their learning. Hopping and jumping will be acquired, but in some cases direction from others will be necessary to facilitate learning these activities. Static and dynamic balance are skills acquired by children in the natural environment.

Children grow at a relatively slow pace from six to twelve years of age. As a result of this period of slow incremental growth, opportunity exists for all children to acquire the fundamentals, combinations, and motor patterns (see table 12-4).

Sex differences in childhood are consistent but minor. "The sitting height/stature is identical for boys and girls until about 10 or 11 years of age, when it becomes slightly higher in girls and remains so through adolescence and into adulthood" (Malina 1986, 13). This means that boys and girls have approximately the same leg length until eleven years of age; leg length for boys increases following the age of eleven. Some boys will be slightly taller and heavier than girls; however, this will be reversed for a brief time, with girls taller and heavier, at the onset of adolescence (Malina 1986, 9). These minor general differences in body size are not considered adequate by program development specialists to warrant planning activities according to body size.

Childhood is followed by a rapid growth spurt at pubescence. Growth and development researchers report that this rapid growth to full adult status, or when bodily functions become structurally and functionally mature, occurs in the age range of eight to nineteen for females and ten to twenty-two for males (Malina 1986, 7) (see table 12-5). Biologically, the most important development at this stage is the reproductive system. This is accompanied by major changes in size, with boys exceeding girls in height and weight.

▼ **TABLE 12-4**

Summary of general developmental characteristics during late childhood

CHARACTERISTICS

1. Relative stability in growth
2. Limbs continue to grow more rapidly in proportion to the rest of the body
3. Some preadolescent changes in the shoulder/hip ratio for the sexes
4. Preadolescent fat spurt for some individuals, particularly males
5. Differential growth rates become more marked at end of period as early maturers begin adolescent growth spurt
6. Balance becomes well developed
7. Basic motor patterns are more refined and adapted to structural differences
8. Better coordination and body control
9. Continued increase in strength and endurance
10. Eye-hand coordination improved; increased proficiency in manipulative skills
11. Increased attention span
12. Sees need to practice skills for improvement, to gain social status and to develop endurance
13. Spirit of adventure high
14. More socially mature; interested in group welfare
15. Intellectually curious
16. Greater interest in proficiency and competitive spirit—hero worship of athletes
17. Some sex differences in performance and some antagonism towards opposite sex

Reproduced from Eckert, Helen M. (1987). *Motor Development*. Indianapolis, IN: Benchmark. p. 277. By permission of author.

Until twelve, the differences in size between males and females are individual in nature. Following the pubescent growth spurt, the majority of boys will be larger than the majority of girls. These size differences will be noted later in program planning.

Specific Sex Differences

Eckert (1987) classifies adolescent sex differences into anatomical and physiological differences and provides these specific points to be used in program planning and identifying potential interests of adolescents.

Differences resulting from anatomical changes
1. Height and weight: males taller and heavier
2. Shoulder width: males wider, more rotation torque
3. Forearm length: males longer, more lever torque
4. Hip shape: insertion of femur more oblique in females
5. Elbow and knee joints: males parallel; females) (shaped
6. Leg length: relatively longer in males
7. Chest girth: males greater thoracic cavity

▼ **TABLE 12-5**
Summary of developmental characteristics during adolescence

CHARACTERISTICS

1. Development of secondary sex characteristics and biological maturity due to increased hormone secretion; estrogen for females and androgen for males
2. Rapid growth spurt resulting in marked gains in height and weight
3. Differential growth rates of body parts during growth spurt
4. Greater shoulder width gain for males raises center of gravity; greater hip width gain for females lowers center of gravity
5. Proportionately longer limb length growth for males
6. Changes in physiological systems (e.g., cardiovascular and respiratory) result in higher levels of physical activity tolerance for males than females
7. Increased sex differences in body tissue composition: males more muscle and females more fat
8. Increased limb length increases leverage for speed
9. Rapid and very marked gain in strength for males
10. May be some plateauing in balance, coordination, eye-hand coordination, and/or endurance activities during growth spurt
11. Attention span high
12. Very peer oriented
13. Great interest in proficiency
14. Competitive spirit high, especially in males
15. Interest in opposite sex increases
16. Increase in social maturity
17. Greater between individual variability due to differences in maturation rates, that is, early and late maturers

Reproduced from Eckert, Helen M. (1987). *Motor Development.* Indianapolis, IN: Benchmark. p. 326. By permission of author.

8. Center of gravity: males higher, females lower
9. Fat free weight: males more muscle, bigger bones

Differences resulting from physiological functioning

1. Resting heart rate: slightly higher in females
2. Maximal heart rate: slightly higher in females
3. Heart volume: higher in males
4. Red blood cells: greater number in males
5. Hemoglobin (total body): greater in males
6. Vital capacity: greater in males
7. Ventilation volume: greater in males
8. Maximal oxygen uptake: greater in males
9. Oxygen content in blood: greater in males
   Reproduced from Eckert, Helen M. (1987). *Motor Development.* Indianapolis, IN: Benchmark. p. 325. By permission of author.

The period from adolescence to sixty-five is characterized by a gradual increase in growth to the maximum for the individual. Eckert (1987, 347), using the work of Montoye and Lamphiear and A. M. Master, concluded that "it appears that the peak in maximal strength is achieved by both sexes from 25 to 29 years of age . . . and that the peak work performance also occurs within this age grouping."

Today the population of persons over sixty-five has increased significantly. Accompanying this increase is a growing interest in the group. Age reflects a progressive loss in muscle mass, bone, and fat in addition to a loss of body tissue from the organs and nervous system. This loss is influenced by the activity level of the person. Greater loss occurs when activity is low; decreased loss occurs when activity is high.

Strength, endurance, and balance are essential to enable the older person to remain active and self-sufficient. It should be noted that balance rather than strength or endurance is important to the senior. Due to the female's superior longevity, a capacity for efficient balance is essential for all women. Therefore, all physical activity programs from childhood to adulthood are to include activities that will foster balance and balance skill. (For a comprehensive discussion of the physical and developmental characteristics and research on seniors, see Eckert 1987, 365.)

▶ Summary

1. Each person is an individual. Physical and psychological differences exist such that no two people are exactly alike.
2. Personality is a combination of inherited biological characteristics, unique life experiences, and environmental influences.
3. As a result of personality differences, some people will crave risk activities, competition, and aggressive demands while others will avoid these experiences.
4. Research suggests that sound mental health has a positive relationship with sport success.
5. Aggressive behavior is both positive and negative. Physical activity can meet both needs; therefore, aggression is a consideration in the selection of sports. Some sports provide an outlet for pent-up aggression and other sports encourage aggressive behavior as part of the activity.
6. A competent performer knows his or her strengths and weaknesses, and recognizes and appreciates the strengths and weaknesses of others.
7. Concentration in sport may be external or internal; it may be broad or narrow.
8. Arousal, the state of alertness of an individual, must be under control. Too high a state of arousal or choking may cause muscular tension such that the person cannot perform efficiently. Too low a level of arousal results in inattention or boredom.

9. Imagery is the ability of the body to visualize and feel the movements of the activity. It is described as third person spectator imagery or first person participative imagery. First person imagery involves the stimulation of the muscles within the body as the action is visualized.
10. Successful imagery requires an understanding of biomechanics, including the coordination of movement.
11. Motivation is the why or the reason the performer engages in physical activity. Motivation may be extrinsic or intrinsic. Extrinsic is the external motivation influenced by feedback from others and from the environment in which one performs. Intrinsic is internal motivation coming from within the performer.
12. Motor development, or the rate at which the body grows and develops, influences the physical activity program.
13. Males and females experience fairly similar growth patterns from ages six to twelve. After twelve years of age, growth patterns change such that strength activities favor males and balance activities favor females.

▶ References

Browne, M. A., and Mahoney, M. J. (1984). Sport psychology. *Annual Review of Psychology, 35,* 605–625.

Butt, Dorcas Susan. (1987). *The Psychology of Sport.* New York: Van Nostrand Reinhold.

Clement, Annie. (Fall, 1988). The joy of movement for its own sake. *NASPE News.* Reston, Virginia: AAHPERD, p. 2.

Deutsch, M. (1982). Interdependence and psychological orientation. In V. J. Derlega and J. Grzelak (Eds.), *Cooperation and Helping Behavior, Theories and Research.* New York: Academic.

Eckert, Helen M. (1987). *Motor Development* (3rd ed.). Indianapolis, Indiana: Benchmark Press.

Gill, Diane. (1986). *Psychological Dynamics of Sport.* Champaign, Illinois: Human Kinetics.

Green, E., and Green, A. (1977). *Beyond Biofeedback.* New York: Dell.

Hale, B. D. (1982). The effects of internal and external imagery on muscular and ocular concomitants. *Journal of Sport Psychology 4,* 379–387.

Haywood, K. M. (1986). *Life Span Motor Development.* Champaign, Illinois: Human Kinetics.

Knapp, B. (1963). *Skill in Sport, the Attainment of Proficiency.* London: Routledge and Kegan Paul Ltd.

Landers, Daniel M., and Boutcher, Stephen H. (1986). Arousal-performance relationship. In Jean Williams (Ed.), *Applied Sport Psychology.* Mountain View, California: Mayfield.

Mahoney, M. J., and Avener, M. (1977). Psychology of the elite athlete: an exploratory study. *Cognitive Therapy and Research 1,* 135–141.

Malina, Robert M. (1986). Physical growth and maturation. In Vern Seefeldt, *Physical Activity and Well-Being.* Reston, Virginia: AAHPERD, 3–40.

Malina, Robert M. (1988). *Young Athletes, Biological, Psychological and Educational Perspectives.* Champaign, Illinois: Human Kinetics.

Nideffer, Robert M. (1986a). *Athletes Guide to Mental Training.* Champaign, Illinois: Human Kinetics.

Nideffer, Robert M. (1986b). Concentration and attention control training. In Jean M. Williams (Ed.). *Applied Sport Psychology, Personal Growth to Peak Performance.* Mountain View, California: Mayfield.

Poulton, E. C. (1957). On prediction of skilled movements. *Psychological Bulletin, 54,* 467–478.

Richardson, A. (1967a). Mental practice: A review and discussion, Part I. *Research Quarterly, 38,* 95–107.

Richardson, A. (1967b). Mental practice: A review and discussion, Part II. *Research Quarterly, 38,* 263–273.

Robb, Margaret D. (1972). *The Dynamics of Motor-Skill Acquisition.* Englewood Cliffs, New Jersey: Prentice-Hall.

Schmid, Andrea, and Peper, Erik. (1986). Technique for training concentration. In Jean M. Williams, (Ed.). *Applied Sport Psychology, Personal Growth to Peak Performance.* Mountain View, California: Mayfield.

Schmidt, Richard A. (1982). *Motor Control and Learning: A Behavioral Emphasis.* Champaign, Illinois: Human Kinetics.

Sheikh, Anees A. (1983). *Imagery.* New York: John Wiley and Sons.

Smith, David H., and Theberge, Nancy. (1987). *Why People Recreate: An Overview of Research.* Champaign, Illinois: Human Kinetics.

Unestahl, Lars-Eric (Ed.). (1983). *The Mental Aspects of Gymnastics.* Orebro, Sweden: Veje Public.

Williams, Jean M. (Ed.). (1986). *Applied Sport Psychology, Personal Growth to Peak Performance.* Mountain View, California: Mayfield.

Williams, Kathleen. (1989). What is motor development? *Quest, 41,* 179–182.

Sociology

The social system's structure and composition, its functions and changes related to human behavior, are the foci for sociological inquiry. Social systems are composed of individuals whose interests and expectations are similar in beliefs and standards. Sport is an example of a social system and the analysis, research, and study of this system has resulted in the formulation of the subdiscipline of sport sociology.

In this chapter, sport is examined from the standpoint of a social institution or system. The use of pattern mechanisms by persons in the system is fundamental to the system's integrity and to the solution of functional problems. Examples of pattern mechanisms germane to physical activity are cooperation, competition, and complementation.

Personality development and the relationship of individuals in the sport system involves the behaviors of aggression and violence. Within the instructional setting these behaviors have a particular impact on the functional problems of sport social interaction and socialization.

Skill appreciation and social development in and through the sport (physical activity) system are fundamental to the system's integrity and function. A focus on these cultural elements is necessary for regulation, change, and instruction in movement.

Social systems are large and small, simple and complex. One system is sport. This sociocultural dimension involves a form of human movement called play. Understanding this cultural expression sets the stage for understanding sport as a social institution.

Sociology, or the social aspects, of sport and physical activity are varied. A person's reasons for acquiring and using physical activity skills may be solely for socialization. Some professionals provide an environment in which physical activity is used principally for socialization. An approach to physical activity is to enable the participants to acquire the skills essential to shared activity and then to join others or socialize in game or sport. Another approach is to create the game, sport, or social environment and then to attempt to develop skill even though the group's effort is social.

▶ Play

Play as a form of movement is an important cultural expression. It can be:

* recreative or instinctive
* self-expressive
* a directed release of surplus energy

Singer (1976, 40) defines play as "an enjoyable experience deriving from behavior which is self-initiated in accordance with personal goals or expressive impulses; it tolerates all ranges of movement abilities; its rules are spontaneous; it has a temporal sequence but no predetermined ending; it results in no tangible outcome, victory, or reward." Play often refers to intrinsic motivation on the part of the performer. Performers are usually motivated to participate and receive satisfaction from participation in the event itself. Huizinga (1950, 1–27), in *Homo Ludens,* a classic writing on play, noted that play was free and voluntary, usually nonserious, and unrelated to material interests or the concerns of daily life. Sport, in turn, is highly organized with many rules and traditional rituals. Winning and losing, the primary aspects of sport, are based on rules and rituals. Sport is like work; play is spontaneous. Sport is extrinsically motivated; play is intrinsically motivated.

Today's participant is often physically active because of health reasons such as weight loss or the maintenance of a healthy heart—extrinsic motivators. Intrinsic motivation for movement may be for the enjoyment of doing an activity or for the personal challenge. Csikszentmihalyi (1975, 36) uses the term *flow* to describe the "holistic sensation that people feel when they act with total involvement . . . in the flow state, action follows upon action according to an internal logic that seems to need no conscious intervention by the actor. He experiences it as a unified flowing from one moment to the next, in which he is in control of his actions, and in which there is little distinction between self and environment, between stimulus and response, or between past, present, and future." Some people engage in human movement merely for the "flow" described by Csikszentmihalyi or the "joy of movement for its own sake" (Clement, 1988).

Recreative or Instinctive

Play is spontaneous, instinctive, and brings out the creative nature in a person. Play can be an attitude rather than a place or an event. One can be playful, spontaneous, and creative at one's place of employment or vocation as well as in one's avocation. Play is how one looks at something. When physical activity becomes routine and requires extrinsic motivators, it becomes work.

Play is used by participants to allow themselves to get in touch with the real person, their likes, desires, and dreams. Play can be imaginary; it can be real. People often refer to the feeling of freedom that comes with the joy of movement. The runner's high and the total involvement experienced by a tennis player or swimmer are examples of play.

Self-Expressive

Physical skills, particularly dance and synchronized swimming, allow for personal expression and creativity. A piece of music, a poem, or a reading can be interpreted in movement on the gym floor or in the swimming pool. Persons can also be self-expressive in the types of physical activities they choose to pursue. Those engaged in risk-type activities are expressing different feelings from those engaged in safe, quiet activities. Selection as well as the nature of the activity will contribute to one's opportunity for personal self-expression.

Release of Surplus Energy

A theory exists that following a long period of sedentary behavior, one should engage in an all-out physical activity in order to release energy pent up in the body. It is probably a crude form of tension release or stress reduction. This theory assumes that the activity is one in which tension will not be created. Release of surplus energy also relates to the performer's ability to become so involved in the activity that all other thoughts and distractions are eliminated.

Some people find this high level of concentration, explained in psychology, easy to attain; others find such concentration nearly impossible. Some events, particularly dangerous and/or fast-moving, demand such attention. Assuming the performer is capable of attaining a high level of concentration or the event is one that demands a high level of concentration for success, the performer must analyze whether tension and worry preceding the event counteracts the release of energy in the event. The skier, gymnast, or swimmer who worries all night before the event as to whether he or she will succeed receives little or no assistance from the tension relief provided by participation the next day.

Tension release and fatigue, another factor of surplus energy, will be reduced by activities requiring all-out physical effort and risk-taking activities. The performer's ability to concentrate will be a factor in one's success. The form that play, game, and sport take may be spontaneous, informal, or organized.

▶ Competition

The dictionary refers to competition as a contest for a prize or advantage. How well one person performs in comparison to the performance of others is competition. The evaluation or reward system may be a highly structured event—a formal competition at a local, regional, or national level. At times the evaluation system is one's personal system; this can occur when a performer determines his or her skill and ability within a specific group of people. Other times it is the judgment of members of the group that determines who is the best performer. Coakley (1982, 63), in discussing competitive reward structures, noted that in "competition not everyone can be a winner. The success of one participant or team automatically 'causes' the failure of others." This is the typical situation in most team and individual sports and games in the United States.

Choreographed dance and swimming presentations are forms of physical activity that allow for mastery rather than competition. When one sets out to participate in a production, one has a prototype of what an outstanding performer looks like and thus one spends practice time attempting to achieve that predetermined model. The authors note that the learning of most skills needs to be placed on a mastery level rather than a competitive level. In many countries in which physical activity participation is fostered, mastery level acquisition is also encouraged.

Two recent phenomena in the United States need to be mentioned. One is the number of people who enter marathons with the hope of finishing, not winning, as the objective and the number that run only to achieve a predetermined personal best time. These people, although competing in an event in which only one person is a winner, have carved out a new form of accomplishment that does not involve competition as society traditionally views it. Another phenomenon is the effort of sport organizations to place judgment standards on aquatic art, gymnastics, free exercise, and figure skating routines so that a single winner can be selected. In aquatic art, for example, a performer is striving for a Class I, II, or III award. Theoretically, all performers in a competition could receive a Class I or none could receive a Class I. Success, if achieved, is obtained by the reaching of a certain, very difficult level. That level is available and within the theoretical reach of all who aspire to the goal.

True competition occurs when only one individual or group can win. Accepting this type of contest, winning or winning at all costs, becomes the goal. The notion of ultimate in competition, or becoming number one, is paramount. A participant must eventually realize that as one continues to compete, one will eventually lose even if the first loss is in international competition. Eventually only one person can be a winner in a particular event in any one year. All others are losers.

Sherif (1976, 19) takes a different tack in defining competition and in attempting to bring it into reality or everyday life. She states that "competition consists of activities directed more or less consistently toward meeting a standard or achieving goals in which performance by a person or by his group is compared and evaluated relative to that of selected other persons or groups." Here competition is identified as a process of equating one's skill or talent with others. It is not defined as a product or a win at all costs. Competition is positive when goals are realistic and within reach.

▶ Appreciation of Skill

The performer has to become aware of his or her skill capacity; what the novice, intermediate, and elite performer can do, and the sequence involved in moving from novice to elite. Once this information is within a person's reach, one can begin to acquire an understanding of the skill level of another. With that understanding will be an appreciation of the other's skill. Only when an appreciation for one's own skill and that of others is acquired can one effectively cooperate in group play.

▶ Cooperation

A cooperative setting involves two or more people working together toward a common goal. The reward structure must foster cooperation. Derlega and Grzelak (1982, xvi) note that "cooperative behavior leads to maximum joint profit for all involved parties (i.e., individuals, groups, or organizations) in a situation in which all of the parties are interdependent (the actions of each influence others' gains or losses)." Neither cooperation nor competition is inherent; both are learned behaviors.

Cooperation within a group leads to sharing of ideas, full contribution by each member, coordination of effort, and concern for and appreciation of members and friendliness. It usually occurs in a higher level of accomplishment. Orlick (1978, 34) dispelled the myth that children need to compete to succeed in school. He noted "that children perform at least as well in cooperative as in competitive classroom settings."

Cooperation is essential for people to build trust, self-confidence, and self-acceptance. It also plays a role in friendship, appreciation of others, and ultimately in guiding people of a country and of a nation to work effectively with people of other nations.

Game play includes competition and cooperation in the same setting. To be successful within a team, one cooperates or works effectively with other members of the team so that the best environment for obtaining maximum skill performance is achieved by all members. Each person strives to bring out the best in every other team member. Cooperation is playing in such a way that the performer's execution has the optimum positive impact on every other person's performance. This positive impact is influenced not only by how the performer executes the skills but the body's messages, speech, and attitudes toward fellow players. A cooperative player:

1. identifies the assets and liabilities of each teammate.
2. figures out the best contribution that can be made to maximize a teammate's talent. Is it a medium speed throw of the ball or a hard throw accompanied by a positive comment that will cause success for a teammate?
3. experiments with this knowledge in each and every practice.
4. attempts to build trust in competence and in verbal support with every player. Merely being liked and respected is not enough; there must be a faith that one's throw or kick will be of the pace and position essential to the teammate's success.

▶ Complementation

Complementation, an aspect of cooperation sometimes referred to as helping behavior, is significant in the learning environment. Although it is important, it is seldom used in a competitive event. Complementation is the individual coaching of a fellow team member. It is the hitting of hundreds of tennis balls to the location where the teammate or friend needs practice. In the instructional environment, it is assisting another performer in acquiring the skill the performer wants or needs. It is playing "minicoach." Complementation involves the day-to-day refinement of the skills of another. Before one can strive to bring out the best in another through cooperation, one has to become acquainted with the needs of every learner.

Complementation in the learning environment often involves the rehearsal of strategies, and collective thinking and decision making about how to handle certain strategies. Learners are encouraged to interact in a complementing mode prior to competition. Given the stresses that accompany competition, a complementing approach to the learning of skills will, for most performers, relieve or lessen that stress.

▶ Violence/Aggression

Violence in physical activity and sport is usually the result of a complete abandonment of rules and a decision by the group to do anything that will cause them to win. Often violence becomes a means of acting out one's emotions when one feels hurt or believes that as a result of success or achievement one is now allowed to do anything one wishes in celebration.

Aggression usually refers to a forceful and determined desire to achieve one's objective. Aggression is the attitude; violence is one result of such an attitude. Butt (1987) identified six types of aggression: (1) trait, (2) socialized, (3) game, (4) strategic, (5) situational, and (6) postgame. Many sports and physical activities attract persons who are aggressive by nature. These people possess the traits that will cause them to want to climb mountains, run marathons, etc. Socialized aggression is that aggression that results from training and practice. Various strategies develop specific aggressive tactics. Knowledge of one's skill and ability may also enhance one's aggressive feelings.

Certain games require aggressive behavior. All body contact sports automatically contain aggressive strategies. Basketball, for one, requires that the performer be aggressive. Even if the sport itself does not dictate aggressive behavior, many situations occur in play in which the aggressor is rewarded by the rules. Aggressive play, used as strategy in certain situations, may serve to make opponents aggressive in return or cause them to let the aggressor win. Aggressive behavior may also occur following an event. This is seen on nationwide television and in the junior high school locker room.

Aggressive behavior may be good or bad. People must stand up for their rights and for what they believe. Commitment and enthusiasm may be seen as aggressive behavior in the self-confident individual. Speed of decision making, a must in many physical endeavors, is influenced by positive aggression. Aggressive behavior is bad when it results in destruction or when it inspires violence in others.

For some, sport is seen as a vehicle for venting pent-up aggression. These people look at humans as animals in nature. They believe that individuals carry numerous frustrations from everyday life. Thus they see a need for people to work out their physical aggression in a structured environment, hopefully arranged so that no one will get hurt. This release of stress and frustration is a popular notion held by the public in general.

Sport provides bench marks for people to use in differentiating positive and negative aggressive behavior. This theory assumes that considerable opportunity exists within sport for the venting of aggression. It also suggests that aggression will exist in sport as each player strives to maintain and achieve personal self-esteem and status.

Sport has been known to cause the frustrations and anxieties often thought to result in aggressive behavior. Anger occurs when the golf ball goes into the woods, the tennis ball goes over the fence, or the learner cannot make the racquet contact the shuttlecock.

▶ Social Development

Social development refers to the social characteristics and skills acquired by a person. The influences of genetic background and environment have been debated for years and will not be mentioned further in this source. Mention will be made of the fact that many experts believe the first eight to ten years of life play a major role in establishing one's social characteristics. Play and physical activity are known to provide an opportunity in which many of these social characteristics are thought to be acquired. Coakley (1982, 348), in summarizing the works of a number of social scientists, notes that they "suggest that the social context in which sport activity takes place determines its social outcome. They have contrasted the peer-organized, spontaneous, free play of youngsters on playgrounds with the sport activity found in adult-organized youth sport programs."

Attention needs to be focused on the fact that peer-organized, spontaneous play has become the participatory choice of today's adult. Although some people play organized games and matches in tennis, golf, and handball and racquetball clubs, many are engaged in noncompetitive free play. The popularity of aerobic dance, running, cycling, skiing, skating, and hiking attests to the desire of people for free play or free forms of movement. The objective of beating one's neighbor or classmate at some event exists and is popular but it is often not the reason for participation.

Chalip and associates (1984), using the flow model created by Csikszentmihalyi in an earlier study, compared informal play settings, organized sport, and physical education classes. The flow model, designed to assess the quality of the activity experience, includes subjective measurements of self-consciousness, mood, motivation, sense of control, ability to concentrate, and perception of how much is at stake in activity. Sports were found to be more positive for the subjects than the rest of their everyday lives. The results of the study were that "sense of control was highest in gym class and lowest in informal sport; sense of skill was highest in informal sport and lowest in gym class; and significantly more was perceived to be at stake in organized sport than in informal sport or gym class" (Chalip 1984, 109).

Physical activity is unique. It is essential to one's social development.

▶ Summary

1. Play may be recreative or instinctive, self-expressive or a direct release of surplus energy.
2. Play may be an attitude rather than a place or an event.
3. Sport is highly organized with rules and rituals, and extrinsically motivated.
4. When physical activity becomes routine and requires extrinsic motivators, it becomes work.
5. All-out activity may or may not release pent-up tensions or stress. The performer's ability to concentrate and fear of the results of the event are important in the successful release of stress.

6. Competition may be described as attempting to be number one or mastering a skill.
7. Cooperation is the sharing of ideas, full contribution by each member, coordination of effort, concern for and appreciation of members, and friendliness.
8. Cooperation builds trust, self-confidence, and self-acceptance.
9. Game play uses cooperation and competition.
10. Complementation is playing "minicoach."
11. Appreciation of one's own skill and that of others is essential to competition and cooperation.
12. Violence is often the result of abandonment of rules.
13. Today participation in physical activity is peer-organized, spontaneous play.

▶ **References**

Butt, Dorcas Susan. (1987). *The Psychology of Sport*. New York: Van Nostrand Reinhold.

Chalip, Laurence, Csikszentmihalyi, Mihaly, Kleiber, Douglas, and Larson, Reed. (1984). Variations of experience in formal and informal sport. *Research Quarterly for Exercise and Sport, 55* (2), 109–116.

Clement, Annie. (Fall, 1988). The joy of movement for its own sake. *NASPE News*. Reston, Virginia: AAHPERD, p. 2.

Coakley, Jay J. (1982). Play, games and sport: developmental implications for young people. In Janet C. Harris and Roberta J. Park, *Play, Games and Sports in Cultural Contexts*. Champaign, Illinois: Human Kinetics.

Csikszentmihalyi, Mihaly. (1975). *Beyond Boredom and Anxiety: The Experience of Play in Work and Games*. San Francisco: Jossey Bass.

Derlega, Valerian J., and Grzelak, Janusz. (1982). *Cooperation and Helping Behavior: Theories and Research*. New York: Academic Press.

Huizinga, J. (1950). *Homo Ludens: A Study of the Play Element in Culture*. Boston: Beacon Press.

Orlick, Terry. (1978). *Winning Through Cooperation*. Washington, D.C.: Acropolis Books.

Sherif, Carolyn W. (1976). The social context of competition. In D. M. Landers (Ed.), *Social Problems in Athletics*. Urbana, Illinois: University of Illinois Press.

Singer, Robert N. (1976). *Physical Education: Foundations*. New York: Holt, Rinehart and Winston.

Preparing the Learning Environment

Part III is designed to guide the professional in using Parts I and II in planning. Chapter 14 identifies a system for planning. The system includes goals, objectives, program design, program implementation, evaluation, and program revision. Chapter 15 provides a comprehensive discussion of individual and program evaluation. Observation, a diagnostic and evaluative tool popular in physical activity, is the subject of chapter 16. Instructional strategies and planning the learning environment is addressed in chapter 17. Liability concerns found in the learning environment and recommendations for the retention of documents is the focus of chapter 18.

Planning

Physical activity content has been defined; rationale for the content has been identified. This chapter will guide the professional in selecting physical activity content for specific learning experiences. Planning and implementing programs, units, and lessons for a wide range of clients are addressed.

Considerable instruction in physical activity occurs without a plan. Some instruction is guided only by the selection of a structured sport. For example, basketball is selected as the sport. Participants immediately enter into game play using traditional skills of basketball. Little time for skill acquisition is provided novice players. Some correction of individual skills may occur in play.

The most important concept in planning is that a plan should exist. The plan is to be comprehensive and in writing. Schools usually use the term curriculum or curricular plan to describe the plan and the planning process. This term comes from the fact that the physical activity program is one aspect of the curriculum and is expected to be an intricate part of the entire school curriculum. Businesses tend to use the word planning when describing the same processes that schools identify as the curricular plan. Many clubs, spas, and sport organizations require all employees to use a syllabus or detailed list of content in teaching. The American Red Cross, for example, provides a detailed plan for its certified instructors to use in presenting a particular course. Agencies teaching aerobic dance often require instructors to use specific music and dance routines. Agencies using the syllabus or detailed sequence approach to instruction tend to be agencies that cater to a specific population of learners and are owned by people who believe it is necessary to dictate a program for safety concerns or for some other reason. Other agencies expect the professional to design programs with the needs of each learner in mind.

This chapter will guide professionals in responding to clients' needs. It is designed to assist teachers in planning in a corporate setting, in their own business, or as members of a school district team.

The planning process is to be continuous, not merely in response to an accreditation or other request. It provides information needed when budget changes are necessary and when programs are to be expanded or eliminated. Such a planning process may be particularly valuable in the event of a legal complaint.

Steps in the planning process are:

1. Goals
2. Objectives
   a. Product/Outcome
   b. Process
3. Program design
   a. Content
   b. Instruction
4. Program implementation
5. Evaluation
6. Revise and recycle

▶ Goals

The goal is the target or major purpose of the instructional program, series of lessons, coaching season, or individual skill or fitness program. Usually there is only one major purpose or reason for conducting a particular program. The type of agency sponsoring the program and the control of the client or the control of the professional will determine who establishes the goal. When an agency advertises instruction in specific activities such as fitness, tennis, aerobic dance, ballet, golf, or skiing, the agency controls the major goal, that is, the acquisition of skill in a specific activity organization.

The goal may be client-controlled, teacher-controlled, or at some point on a continuum between the two. The party that pays the instructor often plays a major role in this decision. Required, in contrast to elective, offerings also dictate the person responsible for decision making.

A tennis professional, for example, is often considered to be in a client-controlled instructional environment. The professional structures the program to strive for the client's goal and at the same time attempts to improve the client's tennis skills. A client's goal to play a social game competently is different than a client's goal to be the number one player in the city. The difference between achieving an elite or a social level of competence will alter the immediate and long-term objectives and the evaluation system. Professionals need to be sensitive to the changing goals of clients; today's social player may become tomorrow's elite athlete.

A client who returns for instruction year after year or who publicly praises the professional as a skilled teacher is a client who has achieved his or her goal and, in turn, the professional's goal. This is a client-controlled environment.

Swimming instructors are professionals who establish a goal with a paying client, a situation similar to the example in tennis. However, the importance of safety and the acquiring of the capacity to be able to save oneself if thrown into deep water gives the swimming instructor an opportunity to persuade the client to accept a goal that may be classified as instructor-dominated. Even though the client may desire to learn to swim only for its social value or only to compete in district meets, the instructor will persuade the client of the value of safety.

School programs are usually based on an instructor-determined goal. Often this goal is to enable each student to attain optimum performance in a wide range of physical skills and fitness performances. This means that the entire program is structured to challenge all students to achieve their maximum capacity.

Physical skill instructors in specific sports often tailor their business around an established goal. Some gymnastics and ice skating schools cater only to clients aspiring to national teams; ski camps are focused toward citizen racing. Other businesses attempt to meet the goal of any client wanting instruction. Some dance studios cater to any client interested in learning to improve dance skills.

The goal is established within the context of the activity by the instructor or the client or by mutual agreement between instructor and client. Whether the program is elective or required and whether the client pays for the instruction may determine who assumes the decision-making role in choosing goals. Only when the business establishes a goal prior to obtaining clients does the business control the goal.

▶ Objectives

Objectives delineate the goal(s), what the program includes, how the program will be conducted, and what is to be accomplished. Objectives are statements of intent. The needs, desired expectations of the clients, and content of the activity or discipline influence the establishment of objectives. Objectives dictate the content selected, sequencing of activities, and the delivery of program, and they include evaluation. The relationship between objectives and elements of evaluation is close because information gathered with evaluative instruments determines success or failure of the objectives and ultimately the program in general. Objectives and the means to evaluate them are to be planned for each individual.

For planning to be effective, a teacher should have accurate diagnostic assessment information for each learner. The teacher should be able to establish the level of the student's learning at the beginning of the experience. Until this baseline information can be established, no lesson can be successfully prepared nor can success or failure be recorded.

▶ Product and Process

There are two types of objectives: product and process. Product objectives are the outcomes of the learner's performance; process objectives are what the instructor does to assist the learner in performing.

Product

The product or behavioral objective or outcome statement describes what the student or client will be able to do at the completion of a lesson, a series of lessons, or the entire program. Product objectives are statements of behaviors and how the behaviors will be executed. They identify the skills, levels within each skill, and conditions under which the behaviors will be executed. Clients' desired outcomes or objectives will be influenced by the requirements of the discipline or activity, previous experience, and desired achievement. The role of the individual and the instructor or agency in determining the objective or outcome is critical.

School teachers will find the definition of the physically educated person in the 1992 report of the National Association for Sport and Physical Education Outcomes Committee helpful in establishing behavioral objectives.

A PHYSICALLY EDUCATED PERSON:

1. HAS learned skills necessary to perform a variety of physical activities. This person
   . . . moves using concepts of body awareness, space awareness, effort and relationships.
   . . . demonstrates competence in a variety of manipulative, locomotor and non-locomotor skills.
   . . . demonstrates competence in combinations of manipulative, locomotor and non-locomotor skills performed individually and with others.
   . . . demonstrates competence in many different forms of physical activity.
   . . . demonstrates proficiency in a few forms of physical activity.
   . . . has learned how to learn new skills.
2. DOES participate regularly in physical activity. This person
   . . . participates in health enhancing physical activity at least three times a week.
   . . . selects and regularly participates in lifetime physical activities.
3. IS physically fit. This person
   . . . assesses, achieves and maintains physical fitness.
   . . . designs safe, personal fitness programs in accordance with principles of training and conditioning.

4. KNOWS the implications of and the benefits from involvement in physical activities. This person

. . . identified the benefits, costs and obligations associated with regular participation in physical activity.

. . . recognizes the risk and safety factors associated with regular participation in physical activity.

. . . applies concepts and principles to the development of motor skills.

. . . understands that wellness involves more than being physically fit.

. . . knows the rules, strategies and appropriate behaviors for selected physical activities.

. . . recognizes that participation in physical activity can lead to multicultural and international understanding.

. . . understands that physical activity provides the opportunity for enjoyment, self-expression and communication.

5. VALUES physical activity and its contributions to a healthful lifestyle. This person

. . . appreciates the relationships with others that result from participation in physical activity.

. . . respects the role that regular physical activity plays in the pursuit of life-long health and well-being.

. . . cherishes the feelings that result from regular participation in physical activity. Reprinted with permission from Outcomes of Quality Physical Education Programs, 1992. National Association for Sport and Physical Education. Retail cost $5.95 plus postage (call 1–800–321–0789).

Process

Process or instructional objectives describe the materials the teacher will use and how the teacher will interact with students. They describe how the instructor will guide individual client learning and how the results of diagnostic assessment will be used to enable the instructor to focus on the client's most appropriate "next element" in the learning sequence and the basis for the selection of a particular teaching style. Further, process objectives will guide the teacher's selection of instructional aids and the selection and use of evaluative strategies and measurements. Process or instructional objectives guide the instructor in creating the entire learning environment.

When appropriate, instructors who work with groups need to consider teaching strategies that will enhance group performance. Consideration must also be given to behavioral changes that will occur as group performance progresses.

The difference in the instructor's role in the selection of behavioral objectives was explained in the discussion on goals. They are instructor- or student-dominated or a combination of both. Teachers may be in a position to dictate, persuade, or accept the client's goals. When dictation or persuasion are used, the instructor's personal values and prejudices may influence the objectives selected. Teachers may use the results of diagnostic instruments as a means of persuasion.

▶ Program Design

The program is designed with the content of physical activity and the most appropriate methods of instruction in mind. The experiences that will best meet the goals and objectives (content) of the learner and the most efficient method of presentation (instruction) are the major components of program design.

Content

The content is structured according to the hierarchy of movement discussed in Part I previously.

Diagnostic tests are used to ascertain where on the skill continuum the client should be placed. These assessments are conducted in all learning environments. When the program goals and objectives result in a series of lessons in figure skating, for example, only fundamentals, combinations, patterns, specialized skills, and the activity organization related to figure skating are used. When the program is a fourth-grade physical education class, the performer's skill placement in all skills in the hierarchy of movement are identified. In addition to identifying the skills in each of these situations, the participant's physical fitness level is assessed.

Fitness levels are to be identified prior to establishing goals or objectives because the performer's fitness and conditioning level will influence the skill level. This is particularly true of intermediate and advanced or elite athletes. Poor fitness levels will often contribute to an assessment of low skill. When the fitness level is improved, the person may demonstrate intermediate or advanced skill form.

Content is sequenced. Learners are made aware of the sequencing or progression of the content, the progressions that are imperative from a safety standpoint, and the progressions that can be disregarded. Once a teacher has an opportunity to work with a client, the teacher becomes aware of the client's speed of learning, another factor to consider in selecting and planning content. When learners constitute a group, it is important that the instructor be aware of the location in the learning sequence of each member of the group.

Instruction

Instruction, like content, is linked to objectives. The first concern of the teacher is to determine whom the program is for. Why are the performers participating? Will the activity make a difference? Is this the best activity for achieving the stated objectives?

Equipment and facilities influence content delivery. The number of clients performing in a facility will determine the level and amount of equipment that can be used. The number of people involved will determine the safety precautions to be put in place. Access to video equipment may, for example, have a significant impact on the speed in which students learn to correct personal errors and the errors of others. Free wall space will enable a learner to rapidly acquire throwing and kicking skills.

Instructors are to convey the goals and objectives to the students. Clients need to know the objectives and know what is expected of them. Further, they should know if they are succeeding or failing and they should be rewarded accordingly.

When presenting content, teachers are to capture the attention of the learner and communicate precisely what is to be learned. Instruction is clear, is to the point, and considers individual differences. Accurate feedback to the learner is probably the single most important role of the teacher. Various techniques for acquiring information to be used in feedback are discussed in chapter 15. Instructional strategies and organizational methods to be incorporated in program design are found in chapter 8 and chapter 17.

▶ Program Implementation

Whether the program is for an eighth-grade physical education class, an adult aerobic group, or an individual striving for an elite tennis status, the program implementation will be determined by the goal, objectives, content of the discipline or specialty, and the preferred learning style of the participant(s).

Program implementation is influenced by the appropriateness, quality, and quantity of facilities and equipment. Class size and preferred learning styles play a role. Effort is made to ensure that each performer has appropriate equipment. The equipment should be of adequate size and quality. Space is to be sufficient enough to enable all performers to execute skills at their maximum capacity without interfering with the safety of others. There are no lines or waiting to use equipment or to execute skills.

Specifics related to all physical activity instruction are that all intense physical activity is to be preceded by a comprehensive warm-up that includes stretching of all areas of the body and, most importantly, those areas to be used in the activity. The main body of the lesson content needs to be practiced, under supervision, until retention occurs. All lessons terminate in a cool-down routine, enabling the performer to slowly return to normal cardiovascular and respiratory functions.

▶ Evaluation

Evaluation is described in detail in chapter 15. A specific form of evaluation, observation, is described in chapter 16.

▶ Revise and Recycle

Evaluation is both individual and programmatic. Analyzing the information gained enables the professional to know whether the goals and objectives have been attained or whether the program in general or isolated components have failed.

At the completion of a specific period of time or an exact date, the information is analyzed to determine success or failure of each objective. When the objective has been met and that portion of the program has been determined to be successful, the professional or business owner again reviews the importance of the objective and whether it should be continued for a future program. When the objective has not been met and that portion of the program has been determined to be a failure, the choices are to recycle the objective into the next program and make changes that will cause the objective to be met and the program to succeed; to change the objective in such a way that it will better meet the needs and desires of clients; or to discard the objective.

▶ Sample Goals, Objectives, and Program Designs

In this section, three physical activity programs are used for sample goals, objectives, and program designs: an eighth-grade school physical education class, an aerobic dance course, and a youth tennis camp. These programs were selected to show the wide range of programs possible and to demonstrate that the contents of the book can be used in any setting in which the teaching of physical activity occurs.

Eighth-Grade Physical Education Class

Goals and Objectives

Goal. To develop within each student the ability to move at maximum physical capacity.

Objectives:
- Is physically fit (cardiovascular endurance, muscular strength and endurance, and flexibility) (Frank 1990, 9, 10)
- Possesses a variety of skills for use in leisure activities (Frank 1990, 2, 3)
- Is able to move efficiently in a number of sports (Frank 1990, 4)
- Knows limits of fitness and skill capacity, particularly as they relate to risk activities (Frank 1990, 12)

Goal.   To learn how to maintain a healthy lifestyle and to learn sport skills.

Objectives:
- Understands and is able to use the concepts of nutrition, physiology, biomechanics, psychology, and sociology in the movement environment (Frank 1990, 6, 13)
- Benefits from the use of mental practice
- Appreciates quality movement in self and others
- Knows a wide range of games and strategies that enhance one's ability to be an informed spectator
- Promotes the joy of effort or movement for its own sake (Frank 1990, 20)
- Is an informed consumer of the level of expertise of professionals who program, teach, and guard, and the nature of equipment in sport and physical activity
- Is able to play at least three sports at an intermediate level (Frank 1990, 5, 15)
- Knows how to select a sport professional and to evaluate the quality of the professional's instruction

Program Design

Baseline Information.   Use these guidelines for preassessment or gathering of baseline information.

1. Select one of the tests of physical fitness referenced in chapter 15. Contrast student results with national norms and determine each student's level of physical fitness.
2. Various evaluative devices, including observation, are used to identify each student's skill level in fundamentals, combinations, and patterns. An effective way to gather a great deal of information in a short period of time is to plan a lesson that uses as many fundamentals and patterns as possible and video the class in action. The tape is analyzed to identify the level of performance of each learner. The tape is to be kept for a number of months and examined in the midyear and year-end assessment. If possible, the same or a similar lesson is videotaped and the results of students' performances compared. Diagnostic evaluative tests are used to provide additional information.

3. Eighth-grade students have usually acquired an array of specialized skills. These should be assessed using the tests found in measurement books mentioned in chapter 15 and the observation techniques found in chapter 16.
4. Sport organization knowledge and skill can be identified through the use of pencil and paper tests on rules, strategies, and game films.
5. Attitude tests and sources mentioned in chapter 15 influence the selection and use of an attitude toward physical activity inventory.

The information is gathered, individual profiles are created, and the instructor is ready to select content appropriate for each class member.

Content Selection

The baseline information has identified the placement of each learner in the learning sequence for fundamentals, combinations, patterns, and specialized skills. When working with a large group of students, the teacher is forced to identify, for practice, those skills in which the majority of the class is deficient. When the level of accomplishment within a particular skill is vast, the teacher determines if direct presentation (method) of the skill at a level beyond what the lowest skilled performer can accommodate would be dangerous and present a risk of physical injury. When a risk of physical injury is possible, the teacher is forced to juggle the method of instruction to decrease the risk involved. These concepts will be discussed in detail in chapter 17.

Content for an entire year is selected and organized into logical units or time periods of instruction and into lessons. All activity sequences are identified. The teacher should note that this approach to content selection may result in more than one program for two different sections of eighth-grade physical education.

Instruction

Results of the attitude survey, range of skill within the group, level of skill, techniques used in other areas of the educational program, and level of risk found in activities influence the instructional method selected. Activity progressions described in chapter 17 are used in the learning environment when the population consists of beginners. These progressions can be used effectively without accommodating for age.

Attitude surveys may reveal students' choices of learning styles—verbal or auditory, visual, kinesthetic, or some combination of these. Visual and verbal tutorials may be prepared and used in the learning environment.

Large groups with a wide range of skills will be challenged and teachers will avoid some risk of liability if nondirective methods are employed. Nondirective methods force the learner to determine his or her capacity to carry out the activity he or she chooses to perform.

Much of the teaching in physical skills is individual and in response to continuous evaluation of the performer. The teacher needs to be able to recognize error, to know how to confirm the error, and to use verbal, visual, and kinesthetic feedback to correct the error. The teacher should be sure the error exists before an intervention or correction is recommended. A teacher's failure to detect error or to provide effective feedback once the error has been determined is faulty instruction.

Aerobic Dance

Goals and Objectives

Goal.   To challenge students to optimum performance in one or more dance forms.

Objectives:
* Enables students to acquire basic dance steps
* Provides students with a knowledge of and the capacity to use recommended sequences in aerobic dance
* Enables students to learn to be physically fit
* Enables students to be able to monitor cardiovascular efficiency at a personally selected target rate
* Encourages learners to practice outside of the class environment

Goal.   To meet the student's personal goal in taking an aerobic dance class.

Objectives:
* Provides opportunities for socialization before, during, and following instruction
* Provides a broad range of easy-to-execute skills early in the learning experience, thus enabling the performer to enjoy practice

Goal.   To entice the client to return for more instruction and to share a positive feeling about the learning experience with others.

Objectives:
* Knows the client's objectives and whether these objectives are being achieved
* Monitors client's absence record
* Knows what client is thinking
* Monitors client's skill accomplishment level
* Enables client to assess the speed and quality of learning
* Provides measuring techniques and the knowledge of results to enable the client to measure personal objectives

Program Design

Baseline Information.   Use an attitude inventory, a fitness test, and an array of tests of fundamentals to ascertain level of skill and fitness. The participant's ability to move to various musical rhythms and beat, drum cadences, and verbal cues is a must. The testing environment is often structured as a lesson, with videotaping as well as pencil and paper used to gather information.

Results of the tests will be used to determine the position of the participant and recommended percentage of all-out activity. Is jumping appropriate for this group? What is the recommended speed of music? Will hand weights, stepping boxes, or other equipment be used in the activity?

Content Selection

Fundamentals, excluding the projection of objects, and specialized dance techniques, particularly traditional dance forms and fitness components choreographed to music, constitute the content of the physical activity organization called aerobic dance.

Instruction

Aerobic dance uses music, specific sequences of fundamentals, and dance steps in a directed teaching environment. This approach is valuable in encouraging all performers to operate at a fairly high level of cardiovascular efficiency; however, the failure to monitor individual heart rates may mean that such an objective is not being met. Enthusiasm and energy are the vehicles of persuasion used in presenting the materials. Instructors—or videos of instructors teaching—usually lead the class in the exercises; class members are expected to copy the performance viewed. Performance is to be efficient and correct. The use of additional instructors to correct individual performance is recommended. Also, mirrors can assist students in identifying correct performance.

Youth Tennis Camp

Goals and Objectives

Goal.   To enable students to perform effectively in regional, state, and national youth competition.

Objectives:
- Is able to use mental practice effectively
- Understands how to achieve physical fitness
- Is able to analyze and correct errors in personal skill
- Recognizes strategy errors in films

Goal. To enable performers to understand their talent level and potential for growth.

Objectives:
* Acquaints the learner, through film and play, with as many potential competitors as possible
* Analyzes top contenders' strengths and weaknesses in comparison to learner's strengths and weaknesses
* Assesses the appropriate level of strength, flexibility, and endurance considering the performer's body build and desired approach to play
* Provides opportunities for competition

Goal. To enable the performer to recognize the range of values of engaging in tennis.

Objectives:
* Learns social values
* Learns appreciation and enjoyment of singles and doubles play
* Is able to officiate the sport
* Learns to coach and guide others in play
* Recognizes the many careers that might be available to a person with tennis knowledge

Program Design

Baseline Information. The results of tennis skill and strategy performance, knowledge tests, and attitude inventories are examined in an effort to determine where to start tennis instruction.

Content Selection
The professional usually uses the elementary skills of tennis identified in chapter 7. Then the professional moves to the fundamentals, combinations, and patterns that contribute to those specialized skills. When a performer is identified as weak in a specialized skill, the professional determines whether the performer can execute the fundamentals and patterns that relate to that skill. If the performer is not able to execute those skills, the tennis professional creates challenging practice routines that incorporate the skills in tennis-like activities. This is a classic example of the use of the hierarchy of movement in reverse order.

Instruction
Most tennis instruction, even in fairly large classes, is individualized, with group methods used only in the presentation of new content or the review of previously learned content. New content presentations may be verbal or

visual in demonstration or on videotape. When videotapes are used, they should be available for students to refer to throughout instruction and practice.

▶ References

Frank, Marian (Ed.). (1990). *Definition of the Physically Educated Person, Outcomes of Quality Physical Education Programs.* Reston, Virginia: National Association for Sport and Physical Education.

Outcomes of Quality Physical Education Programs. (1992). Reston, Virginia: National Association for Sport and Physical Education.

▶ Recommended Readings

Gibbons, Sandra L., and Bressan, Elizabeth S. (1991). The affective domain in physical education: a conceptual clarification and curricular commitment. *Quest, 43* (1), 78–97.

Jewett, Ann E., and Bain, Linda L. (1985). *The Curriculum Process in Physical Education.* Dubuque, Iowa: Wm C. Brown.

Lawson, Hal A., and Placek, Judith H. (1981). *Physical Education in the Secondary Schools, Curricular Alternatives.* Boston: Allyn and Bacon.

Logsdon, B. J., Barrett, K. R., Ammons, M., Broer, M. R., Halverson, L. E., McGee, R., and Roberton, M. A. (1984). *Physical Education for Children: A Focus on the Teaching Process.* Philadelphia: Lea and Febiger.

Morris, G. S. Don, and Stiehl, Jim. (1989). *Changing Kids' Games.* Champaign, Illinois: Human Kinetics.

Elementary School Physical Education. (1978). Columbus, Ohio: Ohio Department of Education.

Tyler, Ralph W. (1949). *Basic Principles of Curriculum and Instruction.* Chicago, Illinois: University of Chicago Press.

Vickers, Joan N. (1990). *Instructional Design for Teaching Physical Activities.* Champaign, Illinois: Human Kinetics.

Accountability

▶ The System

Accountability, evaluation, assessment, and measurement are the ingredients in the formula that eventually tells the learner, instructor, and agency whether they were successful in what they set out to do. "Accountability is the provision of evidence that predetermined goals and objectives have been met" (Wood and Safrit 1990, 29). It is used to determine the success or failure of a single participant and/or the program in general. An accountability system includes all elements of the planning process but focuses specifically on the objectives and the measurement of the objectives.

In teaching physical skills in fitness clubs, corporate environments, schools, and professional sports, the accountability system provides information about the magnitude, or amount and speed of learning, and acquisition of skill by the participants. Often health club members quit when their skill and fitness levels fail to improve. The golfer who continues to slice or the tennis player who never makes a first serve will drop out of instruction after a period of time. Win/loss records are highly significant to the career of coaches, athletic trainers, and the personal fitness advisors of elite athletes.

Accountability uses the results of assessment tools. When, where, and how each is used differs. For example, the teacher usually provides the client as much feedback as possible following the first lesson. In turn, the client becomes aware of his or her present level of skill and fitness, and potential achievement to be anticipated. The teacher recommends a sequence of skills in a particular sport or activity and the amount of time and effort it will take to acquire those skills. The time to be spent in fitness training and skill practice, under the guidance of the professional, is outlined as is the reasonable expectations of the learner.

Accountability to a school district may include an explanation of the baseline skills of each class of students according to the hierarchy of movement described earlier. Based on a general-to-specific schema, a written statement expressing the skill and fitness level of the students representing the weakest, the strongest, and the quartiles in between is given to the school district at the beginning of the year. Objectives for the year are based on this information.

Accountability includes the entire program plan: stating objectives, identifying content and process, planning a program to achieve the objectives, carrying out the program, and using various measurement instruments to determine whether the objectives are met. Accountability uses investigative techniques to determine if an agency is accomplishing what it set out to achieve. Statements of goals and objectives become the basis on which programs are evaluated and decisions are made. The next section contains discussions of evaluation, measurements, and assessment.

Evaluation

Barrow, McGee, and Tritschler (1989, 4) define evaluation as the "process of interpreting the results of measurement." It is the feedback system provided for the instructor, performer, manager, and others involved in the learning environment. Evaluation is essential in all physical skill learning environments. It identifies change in the performer's skill. The change is identified in terms of direction (increase or loss of skill); rate or speed in which the learner improves (slow or fast); and significance of the accomplishment (moving toward a finished skill or lost in a segment of a movement). The real test of the value or the need for an expert, coach, professional, teacher, or other specialist is directly related to that professional's skill in analyzing the learner's characteristics and translating the information into cues that will improve the learner's performance. Every learner is someplace on a continuum from beginning to elite, or the execution of fundamentals to Olympic performance, in every skill they execute.

Evaluation may be of an individual or of the entire program; when the entire program is evaluated, it is called program evaluation. The methods for establishing baseline data, creating goals, and determining success or failure within these parameters are included.

Evaluation is often discussed in terms of the point in time in which it is used; the following categories are identified in the literature:

- formative
- diagnostic
- summative

Formative evaluation is the evaluation that takes place throughout a unit of work; summative evaluation is the evaluation at the end of a unit.

Formative evaluation provides data upon which teachers can make daily instructional decisions within the framework of established goals and instructional sequences, whereas summative evaluation provides a rationale for arriving at grades, team selection, or competency attainment. Also, formative evaluation is used for initial placement and includes basic aptitudes and prerequisite behaviors. The results of such evaluation are often referred to within this text as baseline information or initial learner placement data.

Diagnostic evaluation is the continuous assessment of a student's learning. Each time an instructor provides a clue to a learner while teaching a skill, the selection of that specific clue is based on a diagnostic evaluation of the learner's most recent performance. Diagnostic evaluation is the set of decisions an instructor arrives at based on knowledge of content in action. Diagnostic and formative evaluation may, on occasion, resemble one another. In general, diagnostic evaluation occurs from sequence to sequence, whereas formative evaluation occurs at the completion of a task or a series of tasks. Summative evaluation is the evaluation used at the completion of a unit, series of lessons, or a number of years of instruction. Grades and written evaluations are most often based upon summative evaluation.

Measurement

Measurement is an individual or a set of tests, instruments, or tools usually involving the assignment of a score. Safrit (1990, 4) defines measurement as "the process of assigning a number to an attribute of a person or object." Measurement is the device or devices used to gather data or information.

Norm- and Criterion-Referenced Tests

Measurement instruments are either norm referenced or criterion referenced. Norm-referenced tests are used to compare the scores of one person to the scores of a large group of other similarly situated persons, all of whom have taken the same test. Many of the physical fitness tests are norm-referenced. Criterion-referenced tests are tests in which the scores are based on an established criterion of what constitutes the successful accomplishment of a certain skill. Success on the test is achieving a designated satisfactory level of performance. A checklist for use in an overarm throw skill test is a criterion-referenced test. Criterion-referenced instruments are the tests used in mastery learning.

Validity and Reliability

Tests are to be valid and reliable. A valid test measures what it says it measures; a reliable test consistently measures skill, knowledge, and attributes.

" 'Test' generally is used to describe instruments, procedures or techniques that result in responses that can be evaluated in terms of their correctness" (Barrow, McGee, and Tritschler 1989, 4). Tests measure the attributes of one person. They include performance experiences, anecdotal records, and interviews. They are to be selected with care. Tests are used in the physical activity setting for team selection, achievement, improvement, diagnosis, prescription, grading, motivation, and sport reporters' predictions.

Results of tests identify the achievement of an individual, usually in the context of a much larger group. Results may signal previous learning or how much a person has achieved as a result of a specific series of lessons. Testing motivates the learner in many ways. The mere taking of a test causes some people to practice longer and with a higher level of intention; results of tests might motivate others, for example, to lose weight or to strive for excellence. Comparing physical best times or scores is motivating to many.

Tests are used to diagnose error or fitness levels. Once errors have been identified, a prescription or list of objectives for attaining the desired skill are given to the learner. Grading, a system required by schools, serves to identify attained achievement. Another form of achievement is recognized by sports reporters and those who select athletes for high-level competition. These tests are usually referred to as game and individual statistics.

Assessment

Assessments are decisions and explanations of results based on the use of tests and measuring tools. Assessment refers to the instruments, strategies, and tests used to identify the performance level. Visual analysis, or observation, one of the most frequently used assessment tools in physical activity, is described in chapter 16.

Assessment System
1. Pretest to gather baseline data.
2. Analyze results.
3. Design learning experiences with test results in mind.
4. Conduct program.
5. Use formative or continuous assessment throughout program.
6. Alter day-to-day experiences with attention to the results of continuous assessment.
7. Use summative evaluation to determine where the performer is at the completion of the experience.

In using the assessment system, the instructor determines the students' current abilities. The remainder of the plan is created after the learners are observed and the instructor is aware of each learner's needs.

▶ Accountability in Practice

This section discusses individual and program evaluation and reviews assessment tools and methods of accounting to various persons and agencies. Given an instructor that

- knows content and the sequencing of learning within physical activity,
- executes the processes involved in organizing and transmitting information effectively, and
- communicates so that others comprehend and use information,

the instructor is ready to monitor levels of skill and performance as well as the learner's understanding and attitude. Learner entry-level capacities are identified and documented. Day-to-day means of assessing progress and diagnosing error are also essential to the learning process. And finally, a means must exist to enable the instructor to discuss and provide written reports of competency acquired by clients; to certify performers for athletic competition; to account for the results of physical skills and fitness to corporate management; and to satisfy the needs for grades in school systems.

The entire sequence, from the identification of the learner's needs to the interpretation of the data gathered at the completion of instruction, constitutes the accountability system.

Individual Evaluation

Initial Assessment

All instructors are faced at the first meeting with the need to ascertain the client's level of skill, fitness, and knowledge. Whether the learning environment includes one or thirty participants, information about each performer needs to be gathered. The instructor assesses the movement patterns, specific sport skills, and game awareness of each learner. Also, the instructor determines the knowledge level of sport possessed by the student.

Some may ask why it is important to raise these concerns. For many years teachers made a series of value judgments about what learners were going to be like, what physical skills and knowledge they would possess, and the areas they would be most interested in pursuing. Texts written for schoolteachers contained rather precise teaching formulas based upon accepted growth and development standards of what children should be able to execute at certain grade levels. Armed with this information, instructors planned activities for the entire school year. Seldom did the teacher observe the students in action before they established objectives. If throwing skills were deemed important to third-grade students, they were taught in the third grade. Sometimes the skills were taught in situations where every child could throw successfully and at other times when only two or three learners were ready for the skill.

Previous learning experiences and current student capacity were ignored; the only sequence was in the planned events for each grade. A need for each student to progress according to personal learning stages was ignored. Many students were forced to relearn activities that they had already mastered while others were forced to execute skills beyond their ability and without adequate progression.

With the advent of movement education in the 1970s, and the increasing demand by society for instruction in physical skills, attention was directed to the individual accomplishments of learners. The existing skill level of participants began to dictate the appropriate content for the next level of instruction. Coaches immediately recognized the merit of continuous evaluation in planning team practice and in preparing athletes for competition. The fitness movement, with its one-to-one learning environment, accepted the idea of knowing the skill, and the ability and efficiency of the performer, before progressing to new materials. Today, nearly all instruction in all environments—spa, club, and school—is based on a comprehensive analysis of the current skill level of the learner.

Continuous Evaluation

Continuous evaluation is used throughout the learning process to assist the instructor in diagnosing error, identifying the speed of learning, and motivating the learner. This information provides objective evidence upon which the instructor can determine what has been learned and can create the next step in the learning sequence for a particular performer. Also, information obtained through continuous evaluation provides immediate feedback to the learner. Often the learner becomes cognizant of the various forms of evaluation available in the learning process and how to use them as feedback.

Terminal Assessment

Learners appreciate information about the quantity and quality of their learning as they complete a series of lessons in a particular activity. Schools require grades; other agencies provide anecdotal records of the accomplishments of performers. Fitness tests are often used as either an initial or a terminal means of assessment.

Instrument Selection

Instructors of physical activity have available to them checklists, anecdotal records, skill tests, motor ability tests, motor capacity tests, fitness tests, physiological and psychological inventories, and a wide range of pencil and paper tests. Although certain of these instruments are applicable only in specific situations, all can be used in one or more forms of evaluation. Observation, a technique used for years by persons committed to the application of biomechanics or the analysis of human motion in teaching and stressed in the writings of McGee (1977), Barrett (1977, 1979), and Cartwright and Cartwright (1974), takes on new meaning in today's evaluation. The technique of observation, including specific strategies for receiving, coding, and recording data, is discussed in chapter 16.

The components of evaluation significant to accountability have been defined in situations in which they could be used. The task is to identify the evaluation instruments that can be employed in a physical activity setting. In order to identify the most appropriate evaluation instrument or strategy, a number of educational environmental influences are to be considered:

- content of activity
- learning process selected
- management of learning environment

Content of Activity

Evaluation is conducted in terms of the objectives of the individual and the content of the activity. Goals and objectives determine what is to be measured. They are the reasons for measuring (Kirkendall, Gruber, and Johnson 1987). The content of the discipline and its inherent sequential progressions have been described in chapters 4, 6, 7, and 8. The hierarchy of movement is the model influencing curricular decisions. Various measuring devices and strategies for charting the progress of human movement skills are designed in line with each level on the hierarchy and in line with the specific statements of movement content outlined in the earlier chapters.

Learning Process

An important aspect of the learning environment is the process or methodology the professional selects for interaction with clients. Educational leaders have, in recent years, suggested that learning should be individual, humanistic, personal, and, in most cases, sequential. To design an evaluation, the professional decides whether students will be permitted to progress as fast as they can or will progress as a group. Will students wait for a majority of the class to master a skill before they go to new material or will they go to new material when it has been determined by measurement instruments that the content has been learned? The use of the results of measurement instruments becomes the means through which clients and professionals certify a person's ability and permit the person to move to a more difficult activity or skill.

The responsibilities for learning allocated to the teacher and to the learner determine whether the client learns to use the measuring instruments or relies upon the instructor to administer and analyze the tests. **As greater freedom is accorded the learner, increased opportunity must exist for the learner to acquire the conceptual design of what and how a particular skill is learned.** For example, when the student is expected to exercise advanced decision-making capacity, the provision of a personal performance tape for review and analysis is an assessment tool that is far superior to a student or teacher checklist. On the other hand, if the teacher is charged with the assessment decision, the instructor's visual analysis may be adequate.

Management of Learning Environment

When the learning environment is a one-to-one organization, the teacher and the student use evaluative devices continuously to determine when to move to a more difficult sequence of skills. The teacher will prepare task sheets, interact with students about progress, diagnose problems through the use of observation and skill tests, and certify accomplishment permitting the learner to move to a more difficult skill. Also, results of assessment techniques enable the instructor to create future lessons.

The problem-solving approach to learning is discussed elsewhere; however, it is imperative that the reader recognize the impact of problem solving in class management, evaluation, and decision making following data gathering. If the students select or design their personal learning sequences, they will be expected to play a principal role in selecting the means through which they will be judged as successful or failing. If, in individualized learning, the teacher has established a progression and has essentially freed the learner only from the standpoint of time in learning the sequence, the instructor, in turn, will probably devise the evaluation.

Specific Tests and Inventories

Tests, inventories, and other ways of communicating with the learner can be created by the professional or can be taken from the works of experts in the field. The next section contains a discussion of popular tests of physical fitness and examples of skill tests and inventories.

Physical Fitness Tests

A minimum level of physical fitness is essential for an individual to carry out the tasks of daily living; a higher level is needed before one can successfully engage in the improvement of physical skill. Today's society is eager to attain a high level of physical fitness to ward off disease, to improve skill, and to enjoy physical and risk activities. Schools may rely upon physical fitness tests as a means of selecting and rewarding students. If they are used in this manner, professionals are encouraged to examine the issues related to criterion-referenced standards (Cureton and Warren 1990, 7–19).

The following pages explore five different tests of physical fitness available at nominal fees. Packets for each test provide detailed explanation of the administration of the test, recommended warm-up for the test, and suggestions for incorporating fitness concepts in physical activity. Programs for handicapped persons are available for nearly all the tests. All tests have standards for children and youth; most tests have standards for adults.

Awards are available to successful achievers in each of the fitness tests. An additional award for sport and physical activity participation is available from the President's Council on Physical Fitness.

Major components of physical fitness—cardiorespiratory endurance, muscular strength, muscular endurance, and flexibility—were described in chapter 10. These components, along with agility, speed, and body composition, are measured by one or more of the tests. Body composition is the percent of body that is fat. To retain health and a positive self-image, body fat should be within a specified limit.

Table 15–1 compares the five fitness tests. Note should be made that components of the tests are similar. As a result of extensive study, the Canadian Physical Fitness Committee made two changes in their test in 1984. Pull-ups were changed to push-ups as a result of the popularity of push-ups, and sit-ups were replaced by curl-ups for safety reasons.

▼ **TABLE 15-1**

Comparison of tests of physical fitness

	PRESIDENT'S COUNCIL	AAHPERD	CANADIAN	CHRYSLER AAU	PRUDENTIAL FITNESSGRAM
Strength & endurance tests					
Abdominal	Curl-up	Bent knee sit-up	Curl-up	Bent knee sit-up	Bent knee sit-up
Upper body	Pull-up flexed arm	Pull-up flexed arm	Push-up	Pull-up flexed arm	Pull-up flexed arm
Lower body			Standing long jump		
Aerobic tests	1-mile walk/run	1-mile walk/run	Endurance run	1/4- to 1-mile run	1-mile walk/run
Body composition tests		Triceps and calf skin fold test			Skin fold test or body mass index
Flexibility	Sit and reach	Sit and reach		Sit and reach	Sit and reach
Agility tests	Shuttle run		Shuttle run		
Speed tests			50-meter run		

Examples of skill tests are presented here using the hierarchy of movement structure. These selected tests cover fundamentals, patterns, specialized sport skills, and activity organizations.

Fundamentals

Hopping.

- Task: Hopping (one leg) to and over foam blocks, maintaining balance.

- Equipment: 12 foam rubber blocks, masking tape, tape measure.

- Practice Trials: Experimenter demonstrates task by hopping on one leg to a foam rubber block, hopping over it on the same leg and proceeding for at least two more hops (about ten feet total). Demonstrate that the blocks are soft. Two practice trials are allowed for each leg (5 hops). A five-year-old child is given practice trials one and two without a block. If he or she succeeds, one block is added for test trials one. This rule applies separately for each leg. Children six years of age and older do two practice trials per leg using one block. However, if the child fails practice trial one, the block is removed. If the child succeeds, he or she starts the test trial on the level started for the age.

- Test Trials: A child starts the test trial at a block height determined by age and success on practice trials.

Starting levels:
- 5 years—0 blocks
- 6 years—1 block
- 7 & 8 years—3 blocks
- 9 & 10 years—5 blocks
- 11 & 14 years—7 blocks

- If a child (7 years or older) does not succeed at the height determined, the first trial is started using one block. A child is given three chances to perform the task.

- Instructions: "Start hopping on one leg, hop over the blocks, and hop at least two more times on the same leg. Do not touch the floor with your other leg."

- Scoring: Three points are awarded for each level 0–12 (13 levels) if the child succeeds on the first trial. Two points are awarded for success on the second trial. One point for success on the third trial. Failure occurs when (a) the opposite leg touches the floor, (b) the blocks are kicked over, and

(c) after hopping over the pile, less than two hops are taken. The test is terminated when the child fails to accumulate five points on two preceding trials. A maximum of 39 points may be awarded per leg for a total score of 78. (From *Measurement & Evaluation in Contemporary Physical Education* by Douglas N. Hastad and Alan C. Lacy. Copyright © 1989 by Gorsuch Scarisbrick, Publishers [Scottsdale, AZ]. Used with permission.)

Rockport Fitness Walking Test. The Rockport Fitness Walking Test has been developed for both younger and older adults. The test can be self-administered. Before taking the test, the examinee goes through a pretest warm-up. After walking in place for 30 seconds, the resting pulse is determined.

The test requires walking a mile as fast as possible. Record time to the nearest second. Record heart rate immediately at the end of the mile. The examinee should stretch for 5–10 minutes before beginning the test.

Refer to the Rockport Fitness Walking Test chart (The Rockport Company, 1986) for the examinee's age and sex-relative fitness level. Use the chart to evaluate test performance. One strong point of this test is that, after the self-test has taken place, an exercise program is recommended for the examinee's age and sex. A 20-week walking program is recommended, followed by a repetition of the Rockport Fitness Walking Test. (Reproduced by permission from Safrit, Margaret J.: *Introduction to Measurement in Physical Education and Exercise Science,* ed. 2, 1990, Times Mirror/Mosby College Publishing.)

Patterns

Modified Underhand Pitching or Throwing.

- Instructions: The student pitches the ball underhand at a rectangular target from a 40′ restraining line. Fifteen trials are allowed.

- Equipment needed: Marking tape, measuring tape, softballs, and a rectangular target(s) constructed according to the following dimensions: The outer borders measure 42″ long × 29″ wide and enclose an inner rectangle measuring 30″ × 17″.

- Scoring Procedures: Balls hitting the center area of the target count two points, balls hitting the outer area count one point. The sum of the points made on 15 pitches is recorded as the student's score.

- Organizational Hints: One practice trial is allowed before the 15 pitches. The student must keep one foot on the restraining line while stepping forward to throw the ball toward the target. (Modified from *Measurement & Evaluation in Contemporary Physical Education* by Douglas N. Hastad and

Alan C. Lacy. Copyright © 1989 by Gorsuch Scarisbrick, Publishers [Scotts-dale, AZ]. Used with permission.)

Specialized Sports Skills

Control Dribble.

• Instructions: On the signal to start, the student begins dribbling with the nondominant hand from the nondominant side of starting cone A to the nondominant side of the center cone B and proceeds through the course as depicted in figure 15-1, using either hand for dribbling. A practice trial is followed by two officially timed trials.

▼ **FIGURE 15-1**
Layout for control dribble for right-handed students (a) and left-handed students (b) Reprinted with permission from "Basketball Skills Test Manual," American Alliance for Health, Physical Education, Recreation and Dance, 1900 Association Drive, Reston VA 22091.

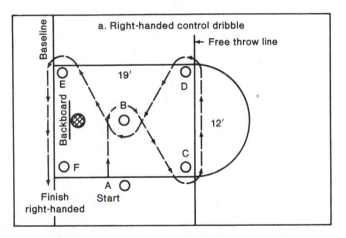

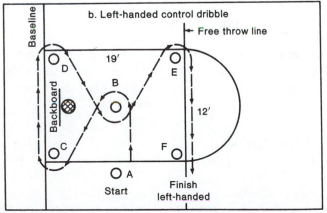

•   Equipment Needed: A basketball, stopwatch, and six fluorescent boundary cones.

•   Scoring Procedures: The score for each trial will be the elapsed time required to correctly complete the course. Scores should be recorded to the nearest tenth of a second for each trial. The final score is the sum of the two trials.

•   Organizational Hints: The stopwatch is stopped as soon as the student passes both feet past the finishing line. Any ball handling violation (i.e., traveling or double dribbling) results in a retake of that particular trial. Inappropriate movement around the cone also results in a retake of the trial. (Reprinted with permission from "Basketball Skills Test Manual," American Alliance for Health, Physical Education, Recreation and Dance, 1900 Association Drive, Reston, VA 22091.)

Activity Organization

Jeffreys Rhythmic Aerobics Rating Scale.

•   Purpose: To measure knowledge and ability in rhythmic aerobics, especially in grading large classes (30 or more).

•   Development: No reliability or validity is given. The agreement between the two judges performing the rating was reported to be high. The components to be measured are (1) the quality of movement and body alignment area, (2) the effectiveness of warm-up and stretching exercises, (3) the cardiovascular conditioning phase, and (4) the cool-down phase.

•   Level and Gender: Beginning rhythmic aerobics classes at the college level.

•   Uses: This scale can be used to measure the knowledge and ability of students in beginning rhythmic aerobics classes or to serve as a content guide for a rhythmic aerobics routine.

•   Directions: This scale is a group measure. Groups of from 3 to 5 students design a routine that they feel will combine all the elements of the rating scale. They perform this routine before two instructors or judges.

• Scoring: Group members will receive one grade based on the combined averaged ratings of the two judges. The scale has 14 elements. Each has the same value and is rated from 1 to 3. There are a possible 42 points.

1—poor   Group shows lack of organization and preference for this activity. Group is not at ease.

2—average   Group is at ease, working together, and sharing the experience by contributing and communicating. All members contribute to the performance.

3—good   Group is very enthusiastic. Bouts are unique, innovative, and creative.

I. Movement and Body Alignment Cues
_____   1. Move with the music, proper tempo and rhythm.
_____   2. Correct body positions to reduce compromising positions and injuries.
_____   3. Transitions and progressions noted by adding/combining several arm works to the same leg movement. Bending of movements smooth, permitting participants to follow with little difficulty.
_____   4. Eye contact along with verbal, body, and directional cues, singly or in combination.

II. Warm-up and/or Stretches
_____   5. Static stretches held 10 to 30 seconds. Stretching several muscle groups without compromising body alignment.
_____   6. Standing and floor stretches appropriate (correct sequencing).
_____   7. Duration adequate, includes most major muscle groups.

III. Cardiovascular Phase
_____   8. Interval training combining low, nonimpact aerobics with recovery periods.
_____   9. Duration and intensity sufficient to reach medium and submaximinal rates, gradually increasing, intensifying, and decreasing. Follows the aerobic curve.
_____   10. Heart rate monitored 2 to 3 times with the last count being after a recovery period of 3 minutes.
_____   11. Bout dense enough to allow most to reach and sustain their targeted heart rate for 15 to 20 minutes without overtaxing and causing strain.
_____   12. Static stretching of the legs and achilles tendons sufficient.
_____   13. Relaxation, stretching, walking movements included. Supportive, encouraging, and informative.
_____   14. Time for questions and answers, sharing before departure.

• Comments: This scale can be used with smaller groups. It can be used for either men or women, and although it was developed for college classes, it can be used for any age group for whom rhythmic aerobics is appropriate. In many situations using two judges would not be practical, so considering the objectivity reported, it would seem adequate to have the instructor rate the groups. As this scale is set up, each element is of equal value. The user may want to adapt the elements or their values to fit the situation in which it is to be used or the philosophy of the instructor. For some situations it may be appropriate to use the results of this scale along with the results of a routine constructed by the instructor. (From Jeffreys, A.: A rating scale for rhythmic aerobics. Unpublished Paper, University of North Carolina at Greensboro, 1987. Used by permission of the author.)

Softball Distance Throw.

• Purpose: To measure the distance a softball can be thrown with accuracy.

• Field Markings: A throwing zone is marked off at one end of the field, 6 1/2 feet wide and deep, from which the throw is made (Figure 15-2). A 50-foot tape measure is laid out from A to B, and a longer tape, 100 to 200 feet, is laid out from B to C. The first tape marks the 50-foot line from which right angle measures must be made. Two markers are placed 60 feet apart on either side of the throwing zone, and two more are placed 60 feet apart approximately 150 feet from the throwing zone.

• Directions: The player takes a position in the throwing zone with a softball in hand and throws as far as possible within the 60-foot width. The player may throw with either hand. Players must stretch their arms prior to throwing. The player makes three throws.

• Scoring: A testing assistant stands where the first throw hits. If the second or third throw is longer, the assistant moves to the new point. The best of the three throws is the score, so only the longest throw is measured. The score is the distance of the farthest throw, measured, to the nearest foot, at a right angle from the throwing line. If the student is outside the throwing zone when the ball is released or the throw hits outside the 60-foot wide area, the throw counts as one of the three trials, but is not scored. (From H. M. Barrow, R. McGee, and K. A. Tritschler: *Practical Measurement in Physical Education and Sport,* 4th edition. Philadelphia, Lea & Febiger, 1989. Reprinted with permission.)

Hamer "Mini-Match" of Tennis Ability.

• Purpose: To measure playing ability of beginning . . . tennis players with a test that simulates actual game play.

▼ **FIGURE 15-2**
Field markings for the softball distance throw. From H. M. Barrow, R. McGee, and K. A.
Tritschler: *Practical Measurement in Physical Education and Sport,* 4th edition.
Philadelphia, Lea & Febiger, 1989. Reprinted with permission.

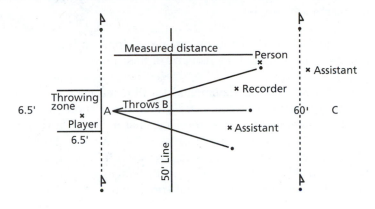

• Development: Hamer used four beginning tennis classes to investigate the appropriateness of a "mini-match" tournament as an indication of tennis playing ability. The official rules of the USLTA 7-out-of-12 tie break were used for the mini-match round robin tournament in each class. The rules for this particular tie break were used because the service rotation and open-ended scoring were believed to allow the fairest opportunity for each player. . . . At the same time, two judges rated each student once each week. Each student was assigned a rank within [his or] her class according to the number of wins and losses recorded. Each student also received a rank from the average of the four subjective ratings by the two judges. . . .

• Directions: A class plays a round robin tournament using the mini-match format. Player A serves Points 1 and 2, right court and left court. Player B serves Points 3 and 4. A serves Points 5 and 6. The players then change sides. B serves Points 7 and 8. A serves Points 9 and 10. B serves Points 11 and 12. If a player wins 7 points, and is at least 2 points ahead, the player wins the match. If the score reaches 6 points all, the players change sides and play continues with serve alternating on every point until one player establishes a margin of 2 points, as follows:

• A serves Point 13 (right court). B serves Point 14 (right). A serves Point 15 (left). B serves Point 16 (left). If the score is still tied, the players change sides every 4 points and repeat this procedure. (From Hamer, D. R.: The "Mini-Match" as a Measurement of the Ability of Beginning Tennis Players, PED Dissertation, Indiana University, 1974. Used by permission of the author.)

Sport Orientation Questionnaire—Form B.

• Purpose: To measure competitiveness and achievement behavior in sport and exercise settings . . . [it] was developed using high school and college age men and women. . . .

• Use: Coaches will find this questionnaire helpful as they explore the competitiveness, win, and goal orientations of their players.

• Directions: The following statements describe reactions to sport situations. We want to know how you *usually* feel about sports and competition. Read each statement and circle the letter that indicates how much you agree or disagree with each statement on the scale: A, B, C, D or E. There are no right or wrong answers; simply answer as you honestly feel. Do not spend too much time on any one statement. Remember, choose the letter that describes how you *usually* feel about sports and competition.

A. Strongly agree
B. Slightly agree
C. Neither agree nor disagree
D. Slightly disagree
E. Strongly disagree

1. I am a determined competitor.	**A. B. C. D. E.**
2. Winning is important.	**A. B. C. D. E.**
3. I am a competitive person.	**A. B. C. D. E.**
4. I set goals for myself when I compete.	**A. B. C. D. E.**
5. I try my hardest to win.	**A. B. C. D. E.**
6. Scoring more points than my opponent is very important to me.	**A. B. C. D. E.**
7. I look forward to competing.	**A. B. C. D. E.**
8. I am most competitive when I try to achieve personal goals.	**A. B. C. D. E.**
9. I enjoy competing against others.	**A. B. C. D. E.**
10. I hate to lose.	**A. B. C. D. E.**
11. I thrive on competition.	**A. B. C. D. E.**
12. I try hardest when I have a specific goal.	**A. B. C. D. E.**
13. My goal is to be the best athlete possible.	**A. B. C. D. E.**
14. The only time I am satisfied is when I win.	**A. B. C. D. E.**

15. I want to be successful in sports.   A.   B.   C.   D.   E.

16. Performing to the best of my ability is   A.   B.   C.   D.   E.
    very important to me.

17. I work hard to be successful in sports.   A.   B.   C.   D.   E.

18. Losing upsets me.   A.   B.   C.   D.   E.

19. The best test of my ability is competing   A.   B.   C.   D.   E.
    against others.

20. Reaching personal performance goals   A.   B.   C.   D.   E.
    is very important to me.

21. I look forward to the opportunity to   A.   B.   C.   D.   E.
    test my skills in competition.

22. I have the most fun when I win.   A.   B.   C.   D.   E.

23. I perform my best when I am   A.   B.   C.   D.   E.
    competing against an opponent.

24. The best way to determine my ability   A.   B.   C.   D.   E.
    is to set a goal and try to reach it.

25. I want to be the best every time I compete.   A.   B.   C.   D.   E.

• Scoring: The Sport Orientation Questionnaire yields three scores: Competitiveness, Win orientation, and Goal orientation. Each item is scored from 1 to 5 (A = 5, B = 4, C = 3, D = 2, E = 1). To obtain the three scores total the responses as follows:

• Competitiveness—Total items 1, 3, 5, 7, 9, 11, 13, 15, 17, 19, 21, 23, 25.
• Win Orientation—Total items 2, 6, 10, 14, 18, 22.
• Goal Orientation—Total items 4, 8, 12, 16, 20, 24.

• It would be inappropriate to total the three separate scores. The Competitiveness factor is the strongest and includes the 13 odd-numbered items on the SOQ. If a single score is needed, probably this one would be the most useful. (From Gill, D. L., and Deeter, T. E., "Development of the sport orientation questionnaire.") This article is reprinted with permission from the *Research Quarterly for Exercise and Sport,* vol. *59,* no. *3* (September, 1988). The *Research Quarterly for Exercise and Sport* is a publication of the American Alliance for Health, Physical Education, Recreation and Dance, 1900 Association Drive, Reston, VA 22091.)

A number of books on the evaluation of fitness and physical skills provide tests of physical and sport skills. They should be consulted by professionals selecting instruments for diagnostic and evaluative purposes.

Program Evaluation

Program evaluation is the examination of the entire program at the end of a specified period of time. Again, program objectives have been specified; they become the guide in creating instruments to assess the success or failure of the program.

Program evaluation may be used to indicate the status and progress of the program, to compare programs, and to identify strengths and weaknesses for budget consideration and external review or accreditation. For example:

- Did students enjoy the program?
- Were skill goals accomplished?
- Was the pacing of activities appropriate?
- What was the injury rate?
- What was the absentee rate?

In program evaluation, product and process are measured. Process evaluation examines techniques used in the program. It may be a measure of the quality of program delivery, the instructor evaluation, or the environment in which it is presented. Product evaluation is an assessment of what the participant is able to do or has accomplished at certain key points in the learning process and at the completion of the program. When standardized tests are available, they are often used to measure the quality of the program.

Most program evaluation includes a cost benefit and cost effectiveness analysis. Cost involves the resources essential in providing a service. Often, alternative ways of conducting the program are available and a manager must decide which costs to incur. Benefits from each of the alternatives is assessed. Cost effectiveness deals with balancing the cost among programs when benefits appear to be the same.

Program evaluation is the single best tool in determining the discontinuation of a program. Comparison of various approaches to a particular objective and their accompanying expenses enables the program director to decide what direction to take.

Instructor Evaluation

The process goal and objectives set the stage for teacher evaluation. Did the teacher do what he or she set out to do and were those objectives effective in meeting the client's needs? Usually an instructor's objectives are in concert with the client's objectives. An instructor wants the client or learner to return for further instruction, and to be pleased with the instruction given. Most teachers pride themselves in knowing that the learner has achieved a higher level of skill and knowledge as a result of the instruction. Usually the latter is also the client's objective. To meet the client's and the instructor's objectives, measurement of these teacher skills is essential:

1. Knows content and demonstrates this knowledge
   a. in the initial teaching and presentation of a skill or strategy.
   b. in the selection of an appropriate sequence for the learner.
   c. in the identification of error and use of correction in coaching the learner. Are errors identified early and is identification accurate? Are corrections accurate, to the point, and easy to assimilate?
2. Provides needed supervised practice time and information about how clients are to practice on their own.
   a. Client knows which skills are sufficiently learned so that practice can be free, and which skills need to be executed under supervision. A free movement approach to teaching eliminates this area as clients are always free to execute movement.
   b. Client is aware of accepted form and can identify such form in a film or the play of another.
3. Inspires clients to maximize participation.
4. Senses how to interact with each client.
5. Enables clients to feel a sense of accomplishment.

Many clients are not sufficiently sophisticated to be able to assess the above but they do know if they are learning and if they like the teacher.

When someone other than the client or learner evaluates the instructor, questions are raised about the qualifications of the individual selected to carry out the evaluation. In evaluating instructors, important questions include who should evaluate, how should information be gathered, and how should the results of the evaluation be used?

Evaluations are often conducted by supervisors, peers, and clients. In these cases it is important to remember that the process goals and objectives are the basis for the evaluation. Instruments are created to gather information about the goals and objectives. Frequency of evaluation and content of the instrument is influenced by the use of the results of the instrument. Portable cassette recorders and VCRs permit documentation of events and allow for self-evaluation. If the results of the data gathering include a reprimand or termination and if a challenge occurs, a videotape could serve as documentation.

Systematic observation instruments permit valid and reliable evaluations. Hastad and Lacy (1989, 440) classify the data collection recording procedures as "event, interval, duration, group-time sampling." Also, they note that these procedures may be simple or complex; often the complex instruments may be the most valid.

Event Recording

Recording and analyzing specific events in the physical activity environment—for example, teaching ball passing and dribbling—serves as a viable instructor and client evaluation tool. The event may be recorded for its entire length or duration, at selected intervals, every fifteen minutes, or only during specific activities; group sampling is observing the students.

In event recording, each behavior exhibited by a teacher or a student in a particular situation or for a specific time frame is recorded and analyzed. All events are totalled to assist in identifying behaviors. "By gathering information on the frequency of a specific behavior, an observer using event recording provides a cumulative record of 'discrete events' occurring during the observation" (Hastad and Lacy 1989, 442).

What is observed and measured is important. The teacher's use of biomechanics and physiology in skill description and analysis is probably the single most important factor to measure. Are skills presented correctly? Is the speed in which the teacher detects error efficient? How long does it take for the teacher to detect an error in a student's performance? Once detected, how is the error corrected? Characteristics such as praise, criticism, and quantity of attention to a single student are also recorded.

Video recordings, with a microphone attached to the teacher, are used to gather information. This comprehensive record will assist parties in analyzing the quality of the teaching, speed of error detection, and appropriateness of error corrections. When videotaping is not available, paper and pencil records are used.

Certifying, Reporting, Accounting, and Grading Achievement

The professional uses a number of different methods to certify, report, account, and grade achievement. Anecdotal records, standardized tests, and skill and fitness improvement scores and grades are used to accomplish these objectives. Anecdotal records are given to clients, physicians, coaches, and others. They describe skill and fitness improvement from first performance to present, with reference to the average person in society, on the basis of a standardized test, or as a result of the professional's observation. Health spas tend to use computer programs that record the client's current fitness sequence or capacity and recommend the next lesson.

Grades are hypothetical marks, based on previously devised criteria, that compare one performer with others in the class and/or in society in general. Grades are usually identified as A to F with A the highest and F the lowest.

- A—Excellent
- B—Good
- C—Acceptable
- D—Poor
- F—Failing

Other forms of grading are percentages, standard scores, or actual test scores.

Mastery learning is the use of a contract by a student and teacher that encourages the student to strive for a specific level of mastery of a topic before moving onto a new topic. The student and teacher also agree on a grade and the criteria essential to obtaining the grade. Attainment of mastery is available to all students and usually constitutes a grade of A. Sometimes people do not wish to attain mastery; other times the period of time available is inadequate for some to achieve mastery.

▶ References

Barrett, Kate R. (January, 1977). We see so much but perceive so little: Why? Proceedings of the NAPECW/NCPEAM National Conference: The National Association for Physical Education for Colleges.

Barrett, Kate R. (1979). Observation for teaching and coaching. *Journal of Physical Education, Recreation and Dance, 50* (1), 23–25.

Barrow, Harold M., McGee, Rosemary, and Tritschler, Kathleen. (1989). *Practical Measurement in Physical Education and Sport.* Philadelphia: Lea and Febiger.

Basketball Skills Test Manual. (1984). Reston, Virginia: American Alliance for Health, Physical Education, Recreation and Dance.

Cartwright, Carol A., and Cartwright, G. Phillip. (1974). *Developing Observation Skills.* New York: McGraw Hill.

Cureton, Kirk J., and Warren, Gordon L. (1990). Criterion-referenced standards for youth health-related fitness tests: A tutorial. *Research Quarterly for Exercise and Sport, 61*(1), 7–19.

Gill, D. L., and Keeter, T. E. (1988). Development of the sport orientation questionnaire. *Research Quarterly for Exercise and Sport, 59* (3) 191–202.

Hamer, D. R. (1974). The "mini-match" as a measurement of the ability of beginning tennis players. PED Dissertation, Indiana University.

Hastad, Douglas N., and Lacy, Alan C. (1989). *Measurement and Evaluation in Contemporary Physical Education.* Scottsdale, Arizona: Gorsuch Scarisbrick.

Jeffreys, A. (1987). A rating scale for rhythmic aerobics. Unpublished Paper, University of North Carolina at Greensboro.

Kirkendall, Don R., Gruber, Joseph J., and Johnson, Robert E. (1987). *Measurement and Evaluation for Physical Educators.* Champaign, Illinois: Human Kinetics.

McGee, Rosemary. (1977). Evaluation of processes and products. In Bette Logsdon et al., *Physical Education for Children: A Focus on the Teaching Process.* Philadelphia: Lea and Febiger.

Safrit, Margaret J. (1990). *Introduction to Measurement in Physical Education and Exercise Science.* (2nd ed.). St. Louis: Times Mirror/Mosby College Publishing.

Wood, Terry M., and Safrit, Margaret J. (eds.). (March, 1990). Measurement and evaluation, theory to practice, a bridge to the future. *Journal of Physical Education, Recreation and Dance, 61*(3), 29–44.

▶ Books Containing Tests

Barrow, Harold M., McGee, Rosemary, and Tritschler, Kathleen. (1989). *Practical Measurement in Physical Education and Sport*. Philadelphia: Lea and Febiger.
Hastad, Douglas N., and Lacy, Alan C. (1989). *Measurement and Evaluation in Contemporary Physical Education*. Scottsdale, Arizona: Gorsuch Scarisbrick.
Johnson, Barry L., and Nelson, Jack K. (1986). *Practical Measurement for Evaluation in Physical Education*. (4th ed.). New York: Macmillan.
Kirkendall, Don R., Gruber, Joseph J., and Johnson, Robert E. (1987). *Measurement and Evaluation for Physical Educators*. Champaign, Illinois: Human Kinetics.
Safrit, Margaret J. (1990). *Introduction to Measurement in Physical Education and Exercise Science*. St. Louis: Times Mirror/Mosby College Publishing.

▶ Physical Fitness Test Sources

The Prudential Fitnessgram
Institute for Aerobic Research
12330 Preston Road
Dallas, Texas 75230

President's Council on Physical Fitness and Sport
450 5th Street, N. W., Suite 7103
Washington, D.C. 20540

Fitness Canada
Fitness and Amateur Sport
365 Laurier Avenue West
Ottawa, Ontario
KlA OX6

Physical Best
American Alliance for Health, Physical Education, Recreation and Dance
1900 Association Drive
Reston, Virginia 22091

Chrysler Fund/AAU Physical Fitness Program
Poplars Building
Bloomington, Indiana 47405

Observation: The Critical Eye

In *The Enlightened Eye,* Elliot Eisner (1991, 1) noted that "to imagine is to generate images; to see is to experience qualities." "Observation is the process of systematically looking at and recording behavior for the purpose of making instructional decisions" (Cartwright and Cartwright 1974, 3).

Medicine provides us with a long-neglected model for use in the observation of physical skills. When a physician examines a patient, he or she systematically gathers as much information as possible by observing the person's appearance, skin color, hair, eyes, capacity to move joints, pep in step, etc. Then judgments are made based on those observations, and, finally, the doctor employs a battery of assessment techniques to test or validate those judgments. The same thing occurs in the learning of physical skills: the teacher continuously forms impressions that consciously or unconsciously influence decisions. These impressions are refined and used as a meaningful information system.

Clinical reasoning is the word used by professionals in the medical field to describe the "critical eye." Cohn (1989, 241) notes that "clinical reasoning has been interpreted as having a reason for connecting a particular treatment decision to a particular frame of reference." Clinical reasoning calls into play theory and practical experience. It asks us how we behave under various circumstances. Even more important, it encourages the instructor to reflect upon previous knowledge and background before taking action in a situation where theory and practice have failed to provide a model (Schon, 1987).

Teachers of physical skills have used observation extensively in coaching and teaching; however, they have been hesitant to accept observation as a primary form of evaluation. Coaches often look on the critical eye approach in recruiting and coaching as one of the closely guarded secrets of their success. Most competent coaches recognize early in their careers that the speed with which they visually monitor total and key components of performance determines how successful they will be in recruiting top performers and in leading good performers to the ultimate performance. Their level of knowledge and ability to see the physics of the human body in action positively influences their decisions.

Elliott and Kilderry in the *Art and Science of Tennis* note that "a large proportion of any coach's time should be concerned with the analysis of stroke production. The first step in this analysis requires that the coach assess performance visually" (Elliott and Kilderry 1983, 99). Weismeyer (1984) supports Elliott and Kilderry in her plea for an emphasis on sports skills analysis in the preparation of physical activity specialists.

In the late 1970s, Barrett (1979) called for a new look at observation as an essential component of the teaching process and for definitive techniques in the use of observation. This resulted in the examination of the teacher as the observer and in the use of the observed information in formative evaluation, or immediate feedback, and summative evaluation, or assessment of the status of the performer in the learning environment.

Also, learners may be taught to observe. They may acquire the understanding of the ideal model and the ability to examine a videotape of their performance. A learner's ability to reference these models and detect error and elements for improvement enables the learner to engage in self-criticism and self-teaching.

For the purpose of this chapter, seeing is observing. Observation is one of the most important evaluative skills available to the instructor of human movement. The professional is challenged to understand what *is* taking place as opposed to what one *thinks* should be occurring in the performance of the client or athlete. The objectives are based on the instructor knowing the content and the instructor developing the capacity to identify, through observation, whether the student is acquiring the content. Systematic observation involves creating a plan based on instructional objectives and recording observations.

Training the critical eye for viewing human movement is a combination of the following factors: understanding the physics of human movement and, thus, the most efficient form for each movement; creating an image or a model of an efficient movement (seeing the details of movement); training the eye to observe images and to break them down into components of the movement (encoding); and comparing the "captured image" of the learner's performance with the model of an efficient movement.

▶ Understanding the Physics of Human Movement

The instructor knows the physics of the human body as a result of viewing films, studying texts, and watching efficient performers execute skills. The ability to process skills visually differs among professionals and clients. Some people spend considerable time observing films of efficient movement; others are able to sense efficiency in action with far less practice.

Part I and chapter 11 will guide the professional in the acquisition of knowledge of the physics of human movement. In addition, the works of Scott (1963), Broer (1961), Broer and Zernicke (1979), Hay (1973/1985), and Hoffman (1977), all of whom have formally analyzed the relationship between kinesiology/biomechanics and pedagogy in the physical activity and sports environments, will assist the professional.

Mechanical and anatomic principles guide the viewing of the individual in simple movement. Physiology and motor learning play an important role in understanding complex skills. Physiology or fitness in action is fairly easy to assess. Performers are flexible (able to move the entire range of motion of the joints); strong (able to lift a fairly heavy object a few times); have muscular endurance (able to sustain muscular activity for a long period of time); and have cardiorespiratory endurance (able to move the whole body rapidly for a sustained period of time in running, swimming, or cycling).

Complex skills often require that the action phase be further divided into three or four subphases. The number of phases within a particular specialized skill influences the need to break the movement down for ease of understanding. The system selected for subdividing a skill is influenced by the instructor's ability to observe complex movement and the intricacies of the skill under observation.

Subcomponents of the skill are memorized and reviewed mentally for error. Then they are joined. It is important to move toward the whole and not dwell too long on any one subcomponent. Even in difficult-to-analyze skills such as dives, the analysis of twists and somersaults are viewed in segments; viewing the entire sequence rapidly enables the instructor to see the origins of force and other movements. Instructors are able to view these movements in slow motion in their heads. Whenever the memorization of a skill is difficult to acquire, instructors return to films or videotapes to guide them in viewing human movement.

A series of phases are identified to enable the viewer to code movement. These phases are influenced by changes in body parts, speed, and planes of the body. For example, the reviewer of a gymnastics skill may practice viewing individual components of the sequence; combination of sequences; timing within and between sequences; initiation, control, and decline of force; and finally, the entire movement.

Next, the human body is coded. Different movement patterns dictate an emphasis on viewing specific body parts; however, general concepts of balance and body alignment suggest that certain areas of the body be observed in all movement and movement sequences.

▶ Training the Critical Eye

Attention is now focused on the performer. To enhance concentration and avoid distracting stimuli, the observer creates a plan of action for observation and adheres to the plan in data gathering. This plan is created with this information in mind:

- complexity of the movement
- speed of the movement
- accuracy
- distracting visual displays
- image retention
- visual discrimination

Human movement in sport, dance, and physical activity is often a series of rapid moves. The individual observing movement "must make accurate perceptual judgments quickly" (Morris 1977, 15). Attention and concentration is essential to accurately see the movements. Although a sophisticated skill, dynamic visual acuity can be measured, taught, and improved with continuous use (Morris 1977; Morris and Kreighbaum 1977). An opportunity for the instructor to acquire static and dynamic visual acuity must exist as part of the teaching and learning process. The use of baseline information on the client's dynamic visual acuity is information to be acquired prior to expecting the performer to receive or make contact with an incoming object or to view films of personal performance in evaluating and detecting errors.

Visual search patterns have been explored among expert and novice gymnastics coaches (Bard et al. 1980). Expert coaches were found to have fewer fixations per minute than novice coaches had. Also, experts were found to have fixations on different body parts than novices had. Expert coaches were "more apt in making fine discriminations and more capable of ignoring trivial information" (Bard et al. 1980, 273).

A systematic approach to the training of the critical eye includes the observation of the correct form in static movement, followed by an observation of the same form in dynamic movement.

Instructors organize the movement as a cognitive model. They know what the form should be. Ultimately they will be able to close their eyes and see the movement in its correct form. Fundamentals, patterns, and specialized skills provide assistance in gaining a comprehensive knowledge of appropriate form. The skill is memorized so that the instructor can play an imaginary film of the skill. The cognitive picture is such that the skill can be rehearsed in memory and can be felt by the muscles of the body.

Coding Specialized Skills

Specialized skills are broken down into phases. Professionals are provided with few fully researched systems of visualization; therefore, instructors should examine the movement and the best thinking among professionals of how the movement is to be broken down, and then create their own model. The one accepted approach to this form of analysis is a four-phase model often used in teaching sport skills. It includes (1) the position assumed prior to action, (2) preparation or backswing, (3) action, and (4) follow-through. Tennis, golf, volleyball, and basketball make use of this sequence in organizing the teaching of skills.

The head and center of the body is examined first. Movement of limbs, particularly as they relate to the generation of force, is analyzed next. Analysis is from the cephalic to the caudal, and from the center of the body outward. Many of the underlying principles of anatomic growth and motor development play a role in this approach to the study of human movement.

The viewer begins by observing a single image. Skills are examined as though they are closed or prerehearsed movements. Such examination reduces the barrage of stimuli created by the movements of others—teammates and opponents—in the learning environment. Different body positions of the performer in action are examined. The performer is observed from the anterior and posterior and from the side.

The observer places his or her body in a position that will enable the learner to be viewed with a direct or ninety-degree angle view of the movement. Every effort should be made to obtain as precise and accurate a picture as possible; observing the body at an angle other than ninety degrees can create a faulty image.

The professional begins by freezing a static picture of one movement for analysis. The body within the picture is isolated into three areas—trunk, head, and limbs—while viewing the movement as a whole. The trunk position is identified in relation to the perceived motion. What is the alignment? Does stability exist in movements that are forward-backward, side to side, and up and down? Are twists, pivots, and turns involved? If they are part of the movement, how are they initiated and stopped? What is the head position and what impact does it have upon the movement? The impact that it should have is identified. That impact is then compared with what is actually taking place. In running, for example, what role do the arms play? Do they contribute to the force? Note that it will be necessary to view the body at an angle in order to see rather than imagine the body initiating force.

What is the effect of the use of equipment upon the body and the effect of the body upon the equipment? Is the most efficient use of equipment made? What is the purpose of the equipment? Has the purpose been met?

▶ Referencing the Captured Image

When the instructor is confident in his or her ability to see movement in a rehearsed, accurate form, he or she is ready to view learners in action. Now the instructor is ready to ascertain success or failure in the movement. When confidence with the static picture analysis exists, an instructor is ready to look at the static actions of learners; when confidence with film or videotape exists, an instructor is ready to analyze dynamic movements. It is important that the instructor observing the movement be willing to watch the performer execute the movement a number of times before analyzing it for errors. Often movements of players are inconsistent, and it may take a number of viewings for the professional to be able to acquire a picture of how the learner performs in general.

The total group is scanned before isolating one person for observation. Scan rapidly, moving eyes over the entire group. Look for outstanding and very weak performers first or movement that can be described as different. Complex movements such as the extent and direction of motion at key times and the moment of rotation are viewed next.

Key elements involved in the movement are identified and rehearsed. Changes in limbs and the relationships of body parts are monitored. When the movement is deemed inefficient, the instructor returns to the conceptual model for identification of faults in the trunk, head, or limbs. What is the problem? What are the head, body, and limbs doing? Where does the movement force start?

Each fundamental, pattern, and specialized skill is a series of prerehearsed movement actions first observed as closed movements. Characteristics to observe are body alignment, head position, and use of limbs. As the body actions become easy to view, the observer concentrates on the flow of the movement and asks these questions:

Does the performer move from one body action to the next in a continuous flowing sequence, or do noticeable jerky motions characterize the movement of the performer's body from, for example, the catch to the throw? Do the movements appear as one series of actions, or can the actions be described as isolated movements not well-connected? Is the application of force continuous from one movement to the next, or is the force or speed gained in the first movement and then lost prior to the second action?

▶ Observation, Imagery, and the Performer

An even greater challenge to the instructor is to prepare the learner or client to process images so that the learner or client can understand and correct his or her own movements. The latter involves the concept of imagery discussed in chapter 12. Visual analysis is a skill that can be taught to the learner as part of the acquisition of physical skills. Carroll and Bandura (1982, 153), in their research with undergraduate college students, "tested the hypothesis that concurrent visual feedback enhances observational learning of a novel action pattern that normally would be unobservable."

The conceptual representation is constructed "by transforming observed sequences of behavior into symbolic codes which are cognitively rehearsed to increase the probability of their retention. During the course of rehearsal, these codes may be further modified by meaningful elaboration and/or conversion into more concise codes which, in turn, further reduce memory load and maximize retrievability" (Carroll and Bandura 1982, 154).

Once learners are able to code and retain the ideal model in their minds, they are ready for work in the area of imagery. Imagery requires more than visualization; sound, touch, smell, taste, and proprioception become part of the learning experience. Imagery, based on a model of efficient movement, is the preferred approach to learning physical skills by athletes at all levels, particularly the elite performer.

Imagery is one of two types: external or internal. "External imagery is to view oneself from the perspective of an external observer, much like seeing oneself on film. Internal imagery, on the other hand, requires the person to imagine actually being inside their body and experiencing those sensations that might be expected in the actual situation" (Fishburne and Hall 1987, 108). It is known that during mental practice or imagery, minimal or low-gain neuromuscular efferent patterns identical to those found in overt movement have been noted on electromyographic records (Feltz and Landers 1983, 48). The instructor can actually feel him- or herself executing the skill. This technique is acquired by the learner later in imagery.

The instructor will check personal perception of success, improvement, or feeling of the skill. The instructor will think through movements, be able to picture himself or herself in action (external imagery), or feel himself or herself doing the skill (internal imagery). As internal imagery is gained, the instructor will concentrate on the feel of the effort or force, absorption of force, and various components of timing. Kinesthetic acuity is sharpened in order to be a successful teacher.

▶ Observation of Groups

Movement in relation to the movement of others, or open movements, is the next step in observation. Now the instructor observes the movement from an open concept or how the learner moves in relation to the movement of others. The instructor looks for body position, alignment, and stance; knowledge of the movement of others; and efficiency in executing skills. The instructor monitors two observations at once: the individual performer and the performer interacting with another performer. Mere segments of movement are viewed at first; later the instructor views the first performer's response to the play of one or more players and to the environment in general.

Movement as it relates to others includes viewing body position, alignment, and stance. Knowledge of the movements of others (empathy) and efficiency in executing skills are important.

Movement of individuals is monitored in relation to many others:

1. Observe the sense of location in relation to task.
2. Observe body alignment with capacity to be stable or unstable, depending upon the need.
3. Observe such factors as aggression, capacity to take over, etc.

Monitor larger groups, observing these characteristics:

1. Physiological readiness
2. Mechanical efficiency
3. Movement game sense (i.e., where to be on certain plays)
4. Ability to get into position rapidly

Observe two teams. Do they possess these characteristics?

1. Capacity to reference key indicators for potential problems
   a. Physiological and mechanical
   b. Play reaction
   c. Motivation, sportspersonship
2. Capacity to replay events
3. Ability to identify the central issue most significant to problem solution

Observe the effects of individuals not directly related to the learning environment:

1. Officials
2. Spectators

Observe the influence of coaches, teachers, etc., on the learning environment.

This system focuses on an individual's movement while providing a sequence through which the teacher can enhance skills in observation. In addition to tracking a single student, the teacher develops the ability to track a number of students at any one time. Teachers memorize a sequence of events in play and systematically reinforce students regarding their performance at any one of the breaks.

▶ Methods of Communication

Given running, jumping, reaching, throwing and catching, how does the teacher identify each student's level of performance within the skill? Currently, few checklists or inventories for assessing these characteristics exist; however, most professionals in the field possess the knowledge essential to create one. Using the information contained in Parts I and II, answer these questions:

1. How do you describe a perfect run?
2. How do you describe an immature or a faulty run?
3. Why is this run immature?
4. Why is this run faulty?
5. In describing the run in questions 3 and 4, did you consider:
   a. lack of practice
   b. faulty mechanics
   c. physiological factors
6. Given a group of students beyond the age when growth and development should influence a running pattern, how do you describe runs at various points on the continuum?

When the instructor has successfully identified a client's skill level, the instructor can predict the amount of time it will take the learner to reach a level considered outstanding. After the learner's level of skill has been identified, the verbal cues that will be most valuable to the learner to reach success will be identified and used in instruction.

Although pencil and paper will be essential in the development of observational skills, the teacher should strive for the capacity to make these judgments without the need of notation. An experienced instructor will develop these skills so that observations are valid and without bias. On occasion, an instructor can test personal observation validity by using a checklist. An effective instructor, hoping to maintain contact with and individualize for a large group of students, will find it essential to carry out these observations in his or her head.

Skill errors are to be divided into categories according to their level of severity. Not all errors can be corrected at once; this is a concept that is often difficult for the new instructor. It is wise to concentrate on one error at a time. The error having the most profound impact on the skill should be handled first.

Instructors' and learners' observations and imagery are vital to the full skill development of human movement. Research (Meacci and Price 1985, 178) has found that this approach is "particularly valuable in crowded classes, classes with short time periods, and limited equipment situation."

▶ Transferring Skills of Observation to Performers

As the learner reaches the level where he or she is comfortable and consistent with the skill, the instructor makes the mechanics of the movement an increasingly conscious part of the instruction. The learner not only knows what he or she is doing but why. Effort is then focused on feeling the muscles in action. Incidentally, many teachers ask their clients to focus on body actions from the first time they execute a movement.

Performers are asked to identify their own movement as correct or faulty and to identify what caused their movement to be either correct or faulty. This constant examination of what constitutes an efficient movement is internalized until the performer can sit quietly and cause his or her body to feel all the movements of an efficient skill.

The athletes' ability to send signals to all muscle groups with timing appropriate to an efficient movement is the secret behind mental practice and imagery. Even more important to imagery is whether the performer can differentiate between error and correct messages in imagery. Spending time rehearsing a faulty movement will sabotage one's success. Performers are to be discouraged from using imagery until the proper form is acquired and is the subject of their mental rehearsal. Imagery of a closed skill is to be acquired and is used prior to using imagery in an open environment. This is in line with the suggestion that all skills are to be learned in a closed environment prior to using them in an open environment.

▶ References

Bard, Chantal, Fleury, Michelle, Carriere, Lise, and Halle, Madeleine. (1980). Analysis of gymnastics judges' visual search. *Research Quarterly for Exercise and Sport, 51*(2), 267–273.

Barrett, Kate R. (1979). Observation for teaching and coaching. *Journal of Physical Education, Recreation and Dance, 50*(1), 23–25.

Broer, Marion R. (1961). *Efficiency of Human Movement*. Philadelphia: W. B. Saunders.

Broer, Marion R., and Zernicke, Ronald F. (1979). *Efficiency of Human Movement*. Philadelphia: W. B. Saunders.

Carroll, Wayne R., and Bandura, Albert (1982). The role of visual monitoring in observational learning of action patterns: Making the unobservable observable. *Journal of Motor Behavior, 14*(2), 153–167.

Cartwright, Carol A., and Cartwright, G. Phillip. (1974). *Developing Observational Skills*. New York: McGraw Hill.

Cohn, Ellen S. (1989). Field work education: shaping a foundation for clinical reasoning. *The American Journal of Occupational Therapy, 43*(4), 240–244.

Eisner, Elliott W. (1991). *The Enlightened Eye*. New York: Macmillan.

Elliott, Bruce, and Kilderry, Rob. (1983). *The Art and Science of Tennis*. New York: Saunders College Publishing.

Feltz, Deborah L., and Landers, Daniel M. (1983). The effects of mental practice on motor skill learning and performance: a meta-analysis. *Journal of Sport Psychology, 5,* 25–57.

Fishburne, Graham J., and Hall, Craig R. (1987). Visual and kinesthetic imagery ability in children: Implications for teaching motor skills. In Gary T. Barrette, *Myths, Models and Methods in Sport Pedagogy* (pp. 107–112). Champaign, Illinois: Human Kinetics.

Hay, James G. (1985). *The Biomechanics of Sports Techniques.* (3rd ed.). Englewood Cliffs, New Jersey: Prentice Hall. (Original work published 1973)

Hoffman, Shirl J. (1977). Toward a pedagogical kinesiology. *Quest, 28,* 38–48.

Meacci, William G., and Price, Eldon E. (1985). Acquisition and retention of golf putting skill through the relaxation, visualization and body rehearsal intervention. *Research Quarterly for Exercise and Sport, 56*(2), 176–179.

Morris, G. S. Don. (1977). Dynamic visual acuity: Implications for the physical educator and coach. *Motor Skills: Theory into Practice, 2*(1), 15–20.

Morris, G. S. Don, and Kreighbaum, Ellen. (1977). Dynamic visual acuity of varsity women volleyball and basketball players. *Research Quarterly for Exercise and Sport, 48*(2), 480–483.

Schon, D. (1987). *Educating the Reflective Practitioner: How Professionals Think in Action.* New York: Basic Books.

Scott, M. Gladys. (1963). *Analysis of Human Motion.* New York: Appleton-Century-Crofts.

Weismeyer, Helen. (1984). Picture analysis. *Journal of Physical Education, Recreation and Dance, 55* (8), 72–73.

The Learning Environment

The learning environment is the locus where the client receives information about the execution of skills and strategies; where the skill is executed in its initial stages; and where the skill is practiced. Facility size, quantity and quality of equipment, and the interaction of the teacher and student are among the many components that influence the learning environment.

People learn in many different ways. The best method of learning for a particular client is influenced by the learner's personality, previous learning, skill capacity, and motivation. Motivation as generated by the teacher and the nature of the skill are two additional important factors.

▶ Visual, Verbal, and Kinesthetic Learning

The three most popular theories of how physical learning occurs and how the learner processes information are visual, verbal, and kinesthetic. Visual learning is further analyzed as visualizing content and pictures on a printed page or viewing a demonstration of the actual performance.

Most physical activity movements have been depicted at some time in a book. Many books show pictures of a movement in action, some provide detailed sequences, and others show only an isolated picture of one point in the total sequence. Today videotape is the technique most often used as a visual aid in teaching physical skills. Nearly all of the texts and many videos present problems for the learner who finds it difficult to assimilate information from a picture or a film. The ability to transpose information from right to left and from forward to back is a quality essential to success in visualizing texts and videos. Live demonstrations are more acceptable to the person who favors visual learning techniques because the learner can move around the performer, viewing the demonstration from the most acceptable angle.

Whether the performance used in teaching should be at the regular movement speed or in slow motion has long been debated, without conclusive acceptance of either approach. Some learners favor the slow-paced presentation, while others find that a reduction in pace confuses the learner's understanding of timing in the movement.

Strategy and game rules are often learned effectively through the use of books, pictures, and videos. As strategies and rules become complex, the viewing of a particular strategy or the rule in action may be valuable. The learner's understanding of the skills, strategies, and rules enhances his or her ability to profit from the use of texts and videos.

Videotaping the learner's performance is recommended. When learners see their performance—how they move in relation to others in strategy and what constitutes the violation of a rule—they are eager to correct the errors and believe that instruction has been tailored to their individual needs.

Verbal learning is readily accepted in the physical skill environment, particularly when the learner possesses the cognitive skills to envision a word picture of the verbal statement. Verbal learning can be used only after the learner possesses a framework for use in understanding the verbal comments. The framework is based on knowledge of the foundation content of the skill that is being executed. When the client possesses such a framework, he or she usually prefers the verbal presentation.

Teachers providing instruction for left-handed performers and others whose movements may not be mainstream may use verbal instruction as the preferred method. The verbal instruction enables the learner to participate in the transfer of the word picture to accommodate the learner's needs. When nonmainstream performers favor visual instruction over other forms of instruction, the teacher is forced to prepare pictures or tailor films to their individual needs (i.e., films of athletes performing with the equipment in their left hands).

The kinesthetic approach to learning is the development within the learner of a feeling for the actions and changes in body position that are part of a movement. The learner is encouraged to focus on how the body feels as the learner moves from one action to the next. A capacity to differentiate the feel of efficient form and timing from inefficient form and timing is one of the learner's objectives.

Strategy instruction may involve the placement of each team member in a certain location on the floor and an emphasis on the relation of each player to every other player. The ability to sense the location of each player is another facet of the kinesthetic approach.

A higher order kinesthetic approach to learning is the one described earlier as kinesthetic acuity and is used in mental practice. Here the learner, as a result of either a visual or verbal cue, transfers the information obtained in the verbal or visual cue to the muscles. The learner is able to execute the entire movement through "muscle messages" before moving.

Even though the learner may demonstrate a preference for one of the other approaches to learning, the teacher of physical skills must emphasize the learner's need to visualize the performance of others in game play and to acquire kinesthetic acuity. The faster a performer learns to monitor the movement of others in game play, the sooner the performer will be able to use that information to score and execute successful strategies. Kinesthetic acuity will be the vehicle through which the skilled learner will monitor current levels of performance, error, and/or improvement. Only when this stage is reached is a learner free to create a personal learning environment.

▶ Information Processing Approach

Performers, from the first time they execute a skill to the high-level performance they give before an Olympic audience, are required to process a great deal of cognitive information. Beginners concentrate on the mechanics of the performance and how to make their bodies as efficient as possible in movement. Attention to the efficiency of movement continues as the learner strives for higher levels of performance. When the activity is a closed activity or a prerehearsed set of movements, the attention to efficiency remains foremost as the performer approaches an elite level. The only other element to which the performer must attend is safety or what to do and how to move in the event that the performance or some part of the performance goes wrong.

Many physical skills, once learned, are executed in settings in which the performer is bombarded with stimuli; for example, the actions of other players, teammates, and opponents. In addition to maintaining top form in the execution of skills, they monitor, for example, the behavior of all others in the playing environment of a soccer or basketball game or the condition of the snow and steepness of the hill in skiing.

This information is organized in a manner to be used effectively in making decisions. The performer adopts a plan of concentration that recognizes the amount of information that he or she can assimilate, identify, and classify. The person retains only pertinent stimuli, filtering out the unwanted. Knowledge of the amount of information one can handle in decision making is vital. The ability to select valued information from extraneous information is one sign of a skilled athlete.

▶ Novice to Skilled: An Interpersonal Structure for Acquiring and Using Physical Skills

The novice-to-skilled progression for learning is a logical sequence through which a person can progressively increase skill: It takes into consideration the performer's need to acquire a level of competence in a skill before using the skill in a formal setting. The progression provides the teacher and the learner with a guide, based on learning theory, for organizing learning environments in which various levels of skill acquisition will be fostered. Playing alone is the earliest form of activity and used by beginners. They progress through a number of structured learning experiences while acquiring physical activity skills until they are able to be a member of a large group, competitive environment. The progression for learning continuum includes the following:

- Play Alone
- Side by Side
- Paired Play—Complement
- Paired Play—Competitive
- Small Group Play—Cooperative
- Small Group Play—Competitive
- Large Group Play—Cooperative
- Large Group Play—Competitive

Although there is a sequential hierarchy in the continuum, the learner is not required to succeed within each area before progressing to another. Rather, the learner is encouraged to select the interaction most attractive to the learner's skill and social needs. The first area suggests play alone or isolation; the rest of the system provides a road map to play as a means of cooperative behavior. Learners are encouraged to play with someone else as soon as they are able to execute a skill reasonably well. Then they proceed through a series of steps in which they intentionally throw or kick an object such that another person can easily receive it. They also drill their partner on skills in which the partner's performance is weak.

Performers progressively increase the difficulty of their execution to meaningfully challenge the partner. Meaningfully challenging a teammate is to cause them to work knowing they have a fair chance of success. It is not meaningful when the player believes the situation is hopeless. Only after skills have been acquired in this manner is competition introduced.

When the performer wishes to practice or to increase a particular skill, he or she returns to the point on the progression for learning continuum that will best allow for improvement in the selected skill.

In activities such as dance, yoga, or aquatic art, contemporary societies' use of the content precludes certain potential means of interacting. For example, group competition in aquatic art, yoga, or dance in a common environment has not occurred.

Play Alone

Play alone enables the learner to structure the environment exclusively for personal skill development and to ignore distractions created by having to interact with others. This is important to success in the initial learning phase. Thirty learners may share a common gymnasium or field, but each is successfully learning the skill as an individual. An example of this is found in tennis, where beginners hit balls at a backboard or hit balls delivered by a machine before attempting to play across a net with someone else.

Components essential to success in skill development in play alone are:

1. motivation to learn the skill
2. ability to comprehend the skill through
   a. visual demonstrations
   b. verbal demonstrations
   c. synthesis of previously learned concepts
3. knowledge of how the skill will be used to score or win in a competitive situation
4. development within the learner of the kinesthetic feel or visual pattern of the skill
5. development of the skill
6. use of the skill in an imaginary game situation
7. development of body awareness in executing the skill

Side by Side

Side by side provides a certain form of socialization in the learning environment without interfering with the singular acquisition of the physical skill. Although the learner is encouraged to play according to the tenets of play alone, the learner is also encouraged to interact with others. The learner is encouraged to become aware of how the other person executes the skill.

Paired Play—Complement

This is where two players play together with a primary objective of helping one another improve their skills. Throwing and catching skills, for example, are enhanced when the thrower throws to the location where the catcher will be challenged. A great deal of empathy is essential at this level of play, and no effort is made to compete with the other individual. Examples of this type of play are:

- volleyball—two people volleying back and forth across the net
- softball—playing catch
- basketball—throwing and catching
- tennis or badminton—hitting an object back and forth

Within the process, the learner becomes concerned with the capacity and potential of the other player to move, and gains insight into possible methods of helping the second player achieve his or her objective. Performers often return to this phase of learning as they attempt to further develop skill. It appears that the emphasis on complementation in team practice accounts for much of the success observed in competition. Complementation is the level at which most recreational play occurs and is a prime form of socialization.

Although complementation is used in nearly every instruction and team practice situation, little is found in the literature regarding this form of practice and the values emanating from it. Complementation appears to have been subliminated to the point where few recognize its useful role.

Paired Play—Competitive

When performers have learned to successfully complement one another's play, aspects of competition are introduced. Rules are introduced as performers move into paired competition. This is formal game play in tennis and badminton singles. Competitive paired play in field hockey occurs in practice when one individual assumes the role of goalie while others attempt to play through the goalie to score.

The primary objective of the competitive paired play process is to provide an opportunity for the learner to

- acquire the capacity to alter body position in a designated game in relation to the objective or goal as a result of interaction with another person
- to develop an appreciation of one's personal skill and the skill of another

Small Group Play—Cooperative

Many of the characteristics of complemented paired play exist in cooperative small group play. The group is increased to three or four players. Incidentally, this is the typical learning setting that one sees when competitive or professional teams practice. The skill patterns and specialized skills have been learned; each player can use them in a competitive situation with one other person. Now the object is to be able to use the skills to complement three or more players. The learning situation is now evolving toward a specific sport or game, and rules are being introduced as they become important to play. Examples are:

- a volleyball group of three practicing set-ups and volleying across or setting up smashes
- a basketball group practicing passes and shooting
- hockey players moving down the field in small groups, passing the ball back and forth.

Small Group Play—Competitive

The players, who have learned to control their bodies in relation to other players and have developed the capacity to sense the movements of others, are now ready to compete with other groups. The concept of winning and losing in the context of a particular set of rules and strategies becomes important.

- Winning in terms of the sport is defined.
- Makeshift rules still control the space as the number of people dictate the space needed until the requirements of a regulation game are enforced.
- Appreciation of skilled form is developed in self and in others.

A client will gain

- knowledge with regard to the use of his or her body in relation to the performance of team members and opponents
- insight as to how one can bring out the best and the worst in a group of players
- an appreciation for the product of the total group

Large Group Play—Cooperative

The entire team is assembled, all rules of play are shared, and strategies essential to total group play take precedence over the ministrategy that has been used in the small group play. Practice involves simulating real situations; however, the removal of the distraction of the opponent allows each player to become aware of what team members anticipate doing in certain situations. Adequate time is permitted in this phase or process of learning to enable team members to become aware of their capacity to play within the total team structure, and to understand the theory upon which strategies and plays are based.

Large Group Play—Competitive

It is the scholastic, collegiate, intramural, or professional game that uses competition, or stressing that an individual or a group of individuals outperform another group. At this point, the performer is challenged to reach a particular standard of skill; to, for example, produce the best balance beam routine in an instructional environment, local competition, or the Olympic Games. Competition is the objective in many activity organizations. Nearly all games, and all sports involving teams, draw on the competitive elements for achievement and for game completion. The nature of the activity organization is to provide competitive challenges to performers.

Games are controlled by established sets of rules: referees are used to enforce the rules. The performer's primary objective is to win or to succeed within the context of the rules. Performers make every effort to play as effectively as possible and to stop the progress of the opponents as quickly as possible. Team members' placement in various positions is done with the success of the team as a unit in mind.

▶ Management of the Learning Environment

Space, equipment, and attitudes toward activity influence the organization of the learning environment. The size of the facility and the number of people participating in an activity are important to the management of the environment. Size of the facility may be adequate or inadequate for recommended equipment. Teacher/student interaction may be one to one, small groups, or a large group of thirty or more. The number of participants may change significantly or remain stable. The role accorded to the instructor by the industry and the teaching style selected by the instructor determine the freedom given the learner in decision making.

The instructor is an important element. Traditionally, the coach or physical activity specialist was the key element and directed all movement. With the exception of roles dictated by game play, learners were executing the same skill at the same time. The range of performance appearing in the setting would be attributed to a student's previous learning and innate capacity; for all practical purposes, the instructor's command resulted in identical movement for each performer. This type of instruction has nearly disappeared from physical activity and has been replaced by a wide range of learning styles.

Individualized instruction sees the instructor as a facilitator; one who organizes the learning environment prior to instruction; one who prepares task sheets; and one who interacts with individual students throughout the class period, diagnosing problems, recommending ways of performing, and gathering data essential to the creation of a meaningful structure for the next lesson. Seldom will this instructor direct the entire group. As the instructor moves from one student to the next or on occasion to a small group, the instructor may use an array of methodologies. The methods selected are influenced by the personality and capacity of the learner and by the nature of the activity.

▶ Responsibility for Learning

The responsibility for learning or acquiring skills involves a partnership between the instructor and the client. Instructor and client personality and age, and environment, content of activity, facility, and equipment influence leadership and responsibility awarded the teacher and the learner. The learning environment is to be planned so students acquire optimum skills and are able to design future personal learning experiences.

Teacher's Role in Learning Environment

The teacher may select either a direct or a nondirect approach. In a classic direct environment, the teacher controls learning using verbal, visual, or kinesthetic cues, organizing the students to move at the same time executing identical skills. A nondirective approach enables the teacher to provide a single learning cue that challenges each student to execute a skill at his or her appropriate level of learning, or encourages students to design their learning experiences. Most teachers use an approach somewhere between the strict direct and totally free nondirect.

Direct

The teacher-directed learning environment is generally known for its high level of organization. Students are given verbatim instruction on skills; performance is by the entire group on a specific skill. A new skill is introduced when the majority of students have acquired the current skill. The approach is often used when the group possesses a common level of skill and simulation is known to produce improved performance in a skill. Also, it can be an important approach when used in a one-to-one setting in guiding students' timing in complex skills.

Nondirect

In a nondirective learning environment the teacher asks a series of questions to guide learners toward a predetermined objective or encourages learners to design their own learning experience. The most successful learner will know the basic concepts and principles of human movement. The nondirective approach inspires creativity and forces students to assume responsibility for the skills they choose to use. This approach is particularly valuable as a means of safety in activities in which there is a wide range of skill (i.e., gymnastics and swimming).

In the nondirective approach the teacher interacts with students, providing feedback and identifying errors based on physiology, mechanics, choreography, and game strategy. Students are encouraged to work with others and to become experts in the observation of efficient movement. Video is used to guide students in the acquisition of knowledge essential in viewing personal performance and that of others.

In a learner-focused program, the teacher merely designates the subject area; learners are engaged in the design of experiences that will enable them to reach their objectives. This is used when students have sufficient knowledge of the underlying content that they are capable of designing their own learning experiences. When the learner-designed approach is used in an activity organization, an entire team will decide how they will sequence the learning of a particular strategy.

▶ Recommended Readings

Harris, Janet C., and Park, Roberta J. (Eds.). (1983). *Play, Games and Sports in Cultural Contexts*. Champaign, Illinois: Human Kinetics.

Underwood, Gordon L. (1988). *Teaching and Learning and Physical Education: A Social Psychological Perspective*. New York: Falmer Press.

Vickers, Joan N. (1990). *Instructional Design for Teaching Physical Activities, a Knowledge Structures Approach*. Champaign, Illinois: Human Kinetics.

Legal Liability and Documentation

Anyone can be sued and at any time. A teacher cannot prevent someone from suing him or her. A teacher can, however, plan and carry out work in such a way that there will be only a slim chance of being sued, and if sued, a good chance of succeeding or winning in a court of law. This chapter contains the legal theories directly related to instruction and suggests the selection of documents to be retained in the event that some aspect of the teaching or learning process is challenged in a court of law. Legal theories within tort and civil rights will be explained. Within tort, an understanding of negligence is important. Sex, race, and handicapped legislation are the concepts most often encountered under civil rights.

Teachers of physical activity are to be cognizant of the fact that many activities involve risk; injuries may occur and the cost resulting from injury and rehabilitation can be substantial. When the cost of the injury and rehabilitation is beyond what a person can pay, that person will search for someone who could be considered responsible for the injury. The teacher is often that individual.

Physical activity professionals are fortunate in that suits filed against them will usually be prepared by an attorney who works on a contingency fee basis. A contingency fee plan means that the attorney prepares the case at the attorney's expense and receives pay only after the case has been settled. Although the contingent-fee attorney may obtain a fairly large percentage of a winning fee, a loss results in no fee. Attorneys are not inclined to take cases they do not believe they can win. Society's notion that many claims are frivolous needs to be questioned in this regard. An analogy to the physical activity field would be paying coaches' salaries only after winning a game or a championship; losing coaches would work the season for free. Given this fee structure, would coaches continue to represent teams that did not win? For the same reason, attorneys are not inclined to accept a case without merit. Therefore, when a claim has been filed against a teacher, the teacher needs to figure out what the attorney views as merit.

▶ Negligence

Negligence is the legal theory most often faced in physical activity lawsuits. Conduct that falls below a standard established by law to protect others against unreasonable harm is negligence. Elements of negligence are:

1. legal duty of care
2. breach of the legal duty
3. breach of the legal duty is the proximate cause of the injury
4. substantial damage

Negligence may be described in degrees and includes negligence, gross negligence, and willful, wanton, and reckless misconduct. The instructor may use the defenses of contributory negligence, assumption of risk, and comparative negligence. Remedies used in settling the typical negligent claim are compensatory, punitive, and injunctive. Compensatory relief covers medical expenses and loss of work. When the damage results from an outrageous event, punitive damages are awarded. Injunctive relief occurs when the court orders that the action be stopped. This is used most often in civil rights cases.

Legal Duty of Care

The instructor of physical activity has a legal duty or responsibility to possess specific knowledge relating to the use of skills, strategies, and rules; the ability to assess the readiness of each performer to engage in activities; and the capacity to organize learning experiences in a safe manner. Many professionals, particularly those associated with the medical profession, have standards of care to which all professionals in the field are expected to adhere. As of 1991, most physical activity professional organizations have not established a standard of care for professionals; some, such as sports medicine and physical therapy, have standards that can be interpreted as a standard of care.

The merit of a profession establishing a standard of care is open to debate and beyond this chapter. The difficulty of monitoring a standard of care, once created and accepted, is another issue dealt with elsewhere. When a standard of care does not exist, the parties engaged in a suit are forced to look to persons in the field, identified by contemporaries as experts, to establish the standard. These experts provide attorneys, juries, and judges with statements identifying what they believe the minimal standard of care is, given the conditions stated in the case.

In light of the fact that a standard of care does not exist, the instructor should establish his or her own. The standard is to be in writing, carried out on a day-to-day basis, and documentation of its existence and execution must exist. Numerous texts and many institutes and courses designed to prepare teachers can be used in creating the standard of care. This text has been designed to enable the instructor to arrive at a standard of care and to be able to explain that standard if required to do so by a court of law. Part I provides information on skill development for use in creating a standard of care; Part II lists the minimal knowledge that a teacher of physical activity should possess.

Breach of the Legal Duty

The question that will be asked during an investigation of an accident is whether the standard of care was breached? An instructor who has carefully thought through the standard of care and used that standard in the learning environment is in a more comfortable position to deal with a discussion of a breach of the standard than a professional who does not know what a standard of care means.

Even though a standard of care has been established, it does not mean that the standard was in use on the day of the accident. There could be a time in which a professional establishes such a standard, but realizes that she or he was in breach at the time of the accident, thus admitting fault, and pays or requests his or her insurance company to pay damages. Insurance companies tend to advise against the latter behavior.

Breach of the Legal Duty Is the Proximate Cause of the Injury

A complaint must clearly connect the breach of the legal duty to the injury. Even though a legal duty, such as the use of a sequence in teaching a backward roll, has been breached, the neck injury may be a result of a previous accident that the performer failed to share with the agency or teacher. It may not relate to the failure to use the sequence in teaching the backward roll.

Substantial Damage

Substantial damage means that the person has sustained incapacitating physical or mental injury. Questions concerning whether the injury is substantial usually go to the jury.

▶ Gross Negligence

Gross negligence is "failure to exercise even that care that a careless person would use" (Keeton et al. 1984, 212).

▶ Willful, Wanton, and Reckless Misconduct

Willful, wanton, and reckless misconduct is "an intentional act of an unreasonable character in total disregard of human safety" (*Restatement of the Law of Torts* [Second] 1965, 587).

▶ Defenses

Defenses encountered in physical activity are contributory negligence, assumption of risk, and comparative negligence.

Contributory Negligence

The concept in contributory negligence is that the injured person is responsible in total or in part for the injuries sustained. Contributory negligence exists when a participant's behavior falls below the standard that a teacher would expect from a participant or below a standard to which the injured person would be expected to conform for his or her own protection. (*Restatement of the Law of Torts* [Second] 1965, 597). Horseplay, one of the chief causes of contributory negligence, has been accepted by some courts as contributory negligence and denied by others. A learner's consistent unwillingness to follow instructions or to reveal information about serious previous injuries may constitute contributory negligence.

Assumption of Risk

Assumption of risk means that the learner has full knowledge of the risks and has assumed personal responsibility. The assumption may be express or implied. Express means that the client has, in advance of the accident, given written consent to relieve the instructor of an obligation and has agreed to take the chance of risk of an injury. Implied consent means that the client has full knowledge of the risk and by virtue, for example, of paying a fee, has assumed liability.

Whether an assumption of risk form or the payment of a fee will hold up in court is influenced by many factors, a discussion of which is beyond this chapter. No minor can be held to an assumption of risk signature on a form because the form is a contract in the eyes of the law and minors cannot be held to contract. All assumption of risk paper documents are to be prepared by a professional and/or an organization's legal counsel and/or an insurance company advisor. Documents are to be created with full understanding of federal and state law and of the results of court decisions in the locality.

Comparative Negligence

Comparative negligence is a system for allocating fault for an injury by percentages, with, in this case, a percentage going to the instructor and a percentage going to the injured victim. This is a fairly new concept that has rapidly become popular throughout the United States. Prior to comparative negligence, when fault was allocated at fifty-one or more percent, it was treated as total fault. Comparative negligence fault systems may open the gates, making teachers and others just a "little bit at fault" in cases that previously did not render the teacher at fault.

▶ Civil or Constitutional Rights

Teachers preparing the learning environment need to consider the equal protection clause of the Fourteenth Amendment to the Constitution and the various federal and state statutes that deal with similar individual rights. The Fourteenth Amendment, Equal Protection Clause states: "No state shall make or enforce any law which shall . . . deny to any person within its jurisdiction the equal protection of the laws" (U.S. Constitution, Amendment XIV, 1). An equal protection legal challenge must show that a group of people is being treated differently than the total population. There is no adequate justification for the difference in treatment. Groups for whom treatment in the past has been different include age, race, sex, and handicapped (Clement 1988, 132).

In addition to the Fourteenth Amendment, attention should be given to federal statutes, including but not limited to Title IX of the Education Amendments of 1972 and the Restoration of Title IX Act of 1989; Public Law 94-142; the Americans with Disabilities Act of 1990; and the Civil Rights Act of 1964. In addition, many states have civil rights statutes in one or more of these areas.

Title IX states: "No person in the United States shall, on the basis of sex, be excluded from participation in, be denied the benefit of, or be subject to discrimination under any education program or activity receiving Federal financial assistance" (Education Amendments of 1972).

An easy way for the person who is new to these statutes to learn what they mean is to substitute within this phrase

- "No person in the United States shall, on the basis of *sex*, . . ." by replacing the word "sex" with each of the following: *race, ethnic origin, age,* or *disability.*

Then read the entire statement, eliminating the final phrase ("receiving Federal financial assistance"). The latter concept differs from one statute to another; all other concepts are the same.

What should the statement "No person in the United States shall, on the basis of _____ , be excluded from participation in, be denied the benefits of . . . be subjected to discrimination . . ." mean to the teacher of physical activity? It means that every goal and objective selected for the learning environment is appropriate for every person participating in the program. It means, in Title IX for example, that every student is challenged to maximum capacity. It does not say that physical education classes have to be integrated. Best professional thinking has arrived at the conclusion that the only way to challenge the highly skilled female is to provide sex-integrated classes.

Replace the word sex with handicapped. It means that the goals and objectives are to be applied to all handicapped persons. Each handicapped person is to be able to achieve to his or her maximum physical and social capacity. Handicapped individuals are to be treated as equal with all other people.

Schools have been working diligently to design programs that will provide opportunities for persons who have not had these opportunities in the past. Public-owned sport facilities and facilities that provide sport and entertainment to the public will be affected measurably by these statutes in the next few years. Full integration of golf facilities by race, sex, age, and disability will be a major focus for the 1990s.

Civil rights litigation differs from tort litigation in that perceived violations can be filed with an Office of Civil Rights or taken to a court of law. They also differ in that most people request only an injunction or that the behavior be stopped. It is expected, however, that requests for money damages will be part of future litigation in civil rights.

▶ Documentation

If a legal complaint is filed, the instructor's defense is that he or she had maintained the appropriate standard of care and is able to document that it had been maintained. Recommendations are provided in an effort to assist the professional in creating his or her own recordkeeping system; this is not a system to be copied. Every employment agency has a number of unique characteristics that should be incorporated. Areas in which specific documents can be organized and retained are:

Goals and Objectives

1. Content selections based on the goals and objectives of the learner.
2. Proof of prohibition of horseplay.
3. Balancing system used to make decisions about risk activities. The value of the activity is weighed against the magnitude and potential for risk. (See Clement 1988, for details.)

Content and Progression

1. Progressions, sequences of learning, lessons, units, and dance routines are retained.
2. Frequency and use of conditioning and warm-ups are recorded.
3. Methodologies employed for instruction would meet peer scrutiny.
4. When specific safety equipment, spotting techniques, or the matching of participants is required, the procedures are noted in planning documents.
5. Evidence is recorded that referees are used when official games are played.
6. Evidence is recorded that students are informed of risks that could be encountered in activities.

Assessment

1. Baseline information sufficient to identify skill level and to prepare the next lesson are available.
2. Grades and/or written statements of achievement given to learners are based upon objective criteria. Copies are retained.
3. Information exists and is adequate to document that the learner is ready for an advanced skill.
4. Many fitness clubs and corporations use computer programs and checklists to monitor participant progress and document readiness to move to more difficult activities.
5. Teacher has full knowledge and understanding of the ramifications of all learners' medical conditions.

Facilities and Equipment

1. Condition of facilities is assessed routinely.
2. Repair requests and follow-though orders are retained.
3. Equipment is maintained according to manufacturer's specifications. Cleanliness is monitored.
4. Equipment is designed to provide safety and fits properly.
5. Instructions and warning about equipment have been passed on to students.
6. Equipment used in competitive sports meets standards established by the sport.

Instructor Concerns

1. Emergency/accident procedures exist and the teacher understands the role the teacher will play at the time of an accident.

2. Accident forms record a true picture of the scene at the time of the accident. An objective statement has been made by the victim, and if possible, by two or more witnesses and the instructor. All of this occurs within an hour of the accident. Incidents that are brought to an instructor's attention sometime after an accident are also documented.
3. Accident reports are retained over the time frame recommended by legal counsel.
4. Instructors understand the parameters of personal and agency liability insurance.
5. Instructors understand the nature of their employment relationship and its effect, if any, on their responsibilities and obligations.
6. Instructors know their legal rights and are free to enforce them.

▶ References

Clement, Annie. (1988). *Law in Sport and Physical Activity*. Carmel, Indiana: Benchmark Press.
Education Amendments of 1972, 901, 20 U.S.C. 1681 (1976).
Keeton, W. Page, Dobbs, Dan B., Keeton, Robert E., and Owen, David G. (1984). *Prosser and Keeton on Torts* (5th ed.). St. Paul, Minnesota: West.
Restatement of the Law of Torts (Second). 1965.
United States Constitution. Amendment XIV, 1.

Bibliography for Activity Organizations

▶ **Placement**

Badminton

Bloss, Margaret Varner, and Hales, R. Stanton. (1990). *Badminton*. Dubuque, Iowa: Wm. C. Brown.

Davis, Pat. (1988). *The Badminton Coach; a Manual for Coaches, Teachers and Players*. London, England: Ward Lock Limited.

Dugas, Edmond A. (1989). *Badminton Made Simple*. Dubuque, Iowa: Eddie Bowers.

Krotee, March L., and Turner, Edward T. (1983). *Innovative Theory and Practice of Badminton*. Dubuque, Iowa: Kendall-Hunt.

Poole, James. (1982). *Badminton*. Glenview, Illinois: Scott, Foresman.

Racquetball

Collins, Ray, and Hodges, Patrick. (1985). *The Art and Science of Racquetball*. New York: Tichenor Publications.

Fabian, Lou. (1986). *Racquetball: Strategies for Winning*. Dubuque, Iowa: Eddie Bowers.

FitzGibbons, Herbert S., II, and Bairstow, Jeffery N. (1979). *The Complete Racquet Sports Player*. New York: Simon and Schuster.

Fleming, A. William, and Bloom, Joel A. (1973). *Paddleball and Racquetball*. Palisades, California: Goodyear Physical Activities Series.

Francher, Terry. (1984). *Racquetball 1, 2, 3*. North Palm Beach, Florida: The Athletic Institute.

Garfinkel, Charles. (1982). *Racquetball for the Serious Player*. New York: Atheneum.

Norton, Cheryl, and Bryant, James. (1984). *Racquetball: A Guide for the Aspiring Player*. Englewood, Colorado: Morton Publishing Co.

Sheftel, Chuck, and Shay, Arthur. (1978). *Contemporary Racquetball*. Chicago, Illinois: Contemporary Books.

Sylvia, James. (1985). *Racquetball for Everyone; Techniques and Strategy*. Englewood Cliffs, New Jersey: Prentice-Hall.

Table Tennis

Die, Ding Shu, Fang, Wang Lian, Zuo, Zhu Quing, and Lu, Yuan Hai. (1981). *The Chinese Book of Table Tennis*. New York: Atheneum.

Hammersley, Jill, and Parker, Donald. (1984). *Top Class Table Tennis*. Sterling, England: E.P. Publishing.

Tennis

Braden, Vic, and Bruns, Bill. (1980). *Vic Braden's Tennis for the Future*. Boston: Little, Brown.

Braden, Vic, and Bruns, Bill. (1988). *Vic Braden's Quick Fixes*. Boston: Little, Brown.

Bryant, James E. (1986). *Game, Set and Match: A Beginning Guide*. Englewood, Colorado: Morton Publishing Co.

Bunker, Linda K., and Kotella, Robert J. (1982). *Mind, Set and Match, Using Your Head to Play Tennis Better*. Englewood Cliffs, New Jersey: Prentice-Hall.

Elliott, Bruce, and Kilderry, Rob. (1983). *The Art and Science of Tennis*. New York: Saunders College Publishing.

Groppel, Jack L. (1979). *Proceedings of a National Symposium on the Racquet Sports*. Champaign, Illinois: University of Illinois.

Gutman, Bill. (1990). *Go For It! Tennis for Boys and Girls*. Freeport, New York: Grey Castle Press.

Meinhardt, Tom, and Brown, J. (Eds.). (1984). *Tennis Group Instruction II*. Reston, Virginia: AAHPERD.

Murphy, Chet. (1984). *Tennis for Thinking Players*. West Point, New York: Leisure Press.

Murphy, Chet, and Murphy, Bill. (1975). *Tennis for the Player, Teacher and Coach*. Philadelphia: Saunders College Publishing.

Plagenhoef, Stanley. (1970). *Fundamentals of Tennis*. Englewood Cliffs, New Jersey: Prentice-Hall.

Sullivan, George. (1981). *Tennis Rules Illustrated*. New York: Simon and Schuster.

Tantalo, Victor, and Tantalo, Anne Brown. (1986). *USA Tennis Course*. Orlando, Florida: USA Publishers.

United States Professional Tennis Association. (1984). *Tennis, A Professional Guide*. New York: Harper and Row.

USTA School Program Tennis Curriculum. (1986). Princeton, New Jersey: United States Tennis Association.

Volleyball

Banachowski, Andy. (1983). *Power Volleyball; the Women's Game*. Palm Beach, Florida: Athletic Institute.

Bertucci, Bob. (1987). *The AVCA Volleyball Handbook*. Grand Rapids, Michigan: Masters Press.

Brown, Michael. (1988). *Volleyball Rules in Pictures*. New York: Putnam Publishing Group.

Fraser, Stephen D. (1988). *Strategies for Competitive Volleyball*. Champaign, Illinois: Leisure Press.

International Volleyball Federation Coaches Manual. (1974). Ontario, Canada: Runge Press.

Kluka, Darlene A., and Dunn, Peter J. (1989). *Volleyball.* Dubuque, Iowa: Wm. C. Brown.

Lucas, Jeff. (1985). *Pass, Set, Crush; Volleyball Illustrated.* Wenatchee, Washington: Euclid Northwest Publications.

Nicholls, Keith. (1986). *Volleyball, the Skills of the Game.* Marlborough, Wiltshire: The Crowood Press.

Scates, Allen E. (1988). *Winning Volleyball.* Boston: Allyn and Bacon.

Slaymaker, Thomas. (1983). *Power Volleyball.* Philadelphia: W. B. Saunders.

▶ Convergence on a Goal

Basketball

Barnes, Mildred J. (1980). *Women's Basketball.* Boston: Allyn and Bacon.

Cooper, John M. (1987). *Basketball: Player Movement Skills.* Carmel, Indiana: Benchmark Press.

Paye, Burrall. (1984). *Basketball's Zone Passes: A Complete Coaching Guide.* West Nyack, New York: Parker.

Pruden, Vic. (1987). *A Conceptual Approach to Basketball.* Champaign, Illinois: Leisure Press.

Field Hockey

Barnes, Mildred J., and Kentwell, Richard G. R. (1979). *Field Hockey, the Coach and the Player.* Boston: Allyn and Bacon.

Cadman, John. (1989). *Hockey (Skills of the Game).* Crowood, United Kingdom: David and Charles.

Horst, Wein. (1977). *The Science of Hockey.* London, England: Pelham Books, Ltd.

Kostrinsky, David S. (1987). *Field Hockey Coaching Drills.* Ann Arbor, Michigan: McNaughton Gunn.

Soccer

Hopper, Christopher A., and Davis, Michael S. (1988). *Coaching Soccer Effectively.* Champaign, Illinois: Human Kinetics.

Thomson, William. (1980). *Teaching Soccer.* Minneapolis, Minnesota: Burgess.

Water Polo

Cicciarella, Charles F. (1981). *The Sport of Water Polo.* Boston, Massachusetts: American Press.

Cutino, Peter J., and Bledsoe, Dennis R. (1976). *Polo: The Manual for Coach and Player.* Los Angeles, California: Swimming World Publications.

▶ **Target**

Archery

Atkinson, Jim. (1988). *Archery, A Sport for All Seasons*. Bessemer, Alabama: Colonial Press.

Haywood, Kathleen, and Lewis, Catherine F. (1989). *Teaching Archery, Steps to Success*. Champaign, Illinois: Leisure Press.

Pszczola, Lorraine, and Mussett, Lois J. (1989). *Archery*. Dubuque, Iowa: Wm. C. Brown.

Bowling

Harrison, Joyce M., and Maxey, Ron. (1987). *Bowling*. Glenview, Illinois: Scott, Foresman.

Holman, Marshall, and Nelson, Roy G. (1985). *Holman's Bowling Tips and Techniques*. Chicago, Illinois: Contemporary Books.

Mackey, Richard T. (1987). *Bowling*. Palo Alto, California: Mayfield.

Martin, Joan L., Tandy, Ruth E., and Agne-Traub, Charlene E. (1986). *Bowling*. Dubuque, Iowa: Wm. C. Brown.

Strickland, Robert H. (1989). *Teaching Bowling, Steps to Success*. Champaign, Illinois: Leisure Press.

Fencing

Bower, Muriel. (1985). *Foil Fencing*. Dubuque, Iowa: Wm. C. Brown.

Lukovich, Istvan. (1986). *Fencing*. Debrecen, Hungary: Alfoldi Printing House.

Pitman, Brian. (1988). *Fencing*. Wiltshire, England: The Crowood.

Simonian, Charles. (1982). *Basic Foil Fencing*. Dubuque, Iowa: Kendall-Hunt.

Golf

Bunker, Linda K., and Owens, DeDe. (1984). *Golf: Better Practice for Better Play*. Champaign, Illinois: Leisure Press.

Cochran, Alastair, and Stobbs, John. (1968). *The Search for the Perfect Swing*. Philadelphia: J. B. Lippincott.

Ewers, James. (1989). *Golf*. Glenview, Illinois: Scott, Foresman.

Softball

Baker, Kianne I., and Cole, Sandra S. (1989). *Winning Softball Drills*. Nacogdoches, Texas: Winning Softball Enterprises.

Houseworth, Steven D., and Rivkin, Francine. (1985). *Coaching Softball Effectively*. Champaign, Illinois: Human Kinetics.

Johnson, Connie Peterson, and Wright, Margie. (1984). *The Women's Softball Book*. New York: Leisure Press.

Linda, Karen, and Hoben, Robert G. (1985). *Girls' Softball: A Complete Guide for Players and Coaches*. West Nyack, New York: Parker.

Meyer, Gladys C. (1982). *Softball for Girls and Women*. New York: Charles Scribner's Sons.

National Softball Coaching Certification Committee. (1979). *Softball Coaching Manual*. Vanier, Ontario: Canadian Amateur Softball Association.

Potter, Diane L., and Brockmeyer, Gretchen A. (1989). *Softball, Steps to Success*. Champaign, Illinois: Leisure Press.

▶ # Self-Dominated

Dance

Aerobic Dance

Greene, Leon. (1989). *Sport Specific Aerobic Routines*. Dubuque, Iowa: Eddie Bowers.

Jacobson, Phyllis. (1989). *Aerobic Dance*. Glenview, Illinois: Scott, Foresman.

Kan, Esther, and Kraines, Minda Goodman. (1989). *Keep Moving! It's Aerobic Dance*. Mountain View, California: Mayfield Pub.

Mazzeo, Karen L., and Kisselle, Judy. (1987). *Aerobic Dance, A Way to Fitness*. Englewood, Colorado: Morton.

Minton, Sandra Cerny. (1986). *Choreography, A Basic Approach Using Improvisation*. Champaign, Illinois: Human Kinetics.

Polley, Maxine. (1983). *Dance Aerobics, Two*. Mountain View, California: Anderson World Books.

Stoll, Sharon Kay, and Beller, Jennifer Marie. (1989). *The Professional's Guide to Teaching Aerobics*. Englewood Cliffs, New Jersey: Prentice-Hall.

Wilmoth, Susan K. (1986). *Leading Aerobic Dance, Exercise*. Champaign, Illinois: Human Kinetics.

Educational Dance

Laban, Rudolf. (1960). *The Mastery of Movement*. New York: D.B.S. Publications.

Laban, Rudolf. (1963). *Modern Educational Dance*. London, England: MacDonald and Evans, Ltd.

Russell, Joan. (1961). *Modern Dance in Education*. New York: Frederick A. Praeger.

Russell, Joan. (1965). *Creative Dance in the Primary Schools*. New York: Frederick A. Praeger.

Modern Dance

Adshead, Janet. (Ed.). (1988). *Dance Analysis, Theory and Practice*. Cecil Court, London: Dance Books.

Blom, Lynne Anne, and Chaplin, L. Tarin. (1988). *The Moment of Movement, Dance Improvisation*. Pittsburgh, Pennsylvania: University of Pittsburgh Press.

Cohen, Robert. (1986). *The Dance Workshop*. London, England: Gaia Books, Ltd.

Guest, Ann Hutchinson. (1983). *Your Move, A New Approach to the Study of Movement and Dance*. New York: Gordon and Breach.

Hinkley, Carolie. (1980). *Creativity in Dance*. Chippendale, Sydney: Alternative Publishing Co-Operative Limited.
Minton, Sandra Cerny. (1986). *Choreography, A Basic Approach Using Improvisation*. Champaign, Illinois: Human Kinetics.

Science of Dance
Clarkson, Priscilla, and Skrinar, Margaret, eds. (1987). *Science of Dance Training*. Champaign, Illinois: Human Kinetics.
Laws, Kenneth. (1984). *The Physics of Dance*. New York: Schirmer Books.
Peterson, Donna, Lapenskie, Garry, and Taylor, Albert W. (1986). *The Medical Aspects of Dance*. London, Ontario: Pear Creative Ltd.

Folk and Ethnic Dance
Adamczyk, Alice J. (1989). *Black Dance: An Annotated Bibliography*. New York: Garland.
Hall, J. Tillman. (1980). *Dance, A Complete Guide to Social, Folk and Square Dancing*. New York: Arno Press.
Harris, Jane A., Pittman, Anne M., and Waller, Marlys S. (1988). *Dance a While*. New York: Macmillan.
Parson, Thomas E. (1986). *How to Dance*. New York: Harper and Row.
Ross, F. Russel. (1984). *Multicultural Dance*. Cleveland, Ohio: Russel and King.

Gymnastics

Bowers, Carolyn Osborn, Fie, Jacquelyn Klein, and Schmid, Andrea Bodo. (1981). *Judging and Coaching Gymnastics*. Palo Alto, California: Mayfield.
Carpenter, Linda Jean. (1985). *Gymnastics for Girls and Women*. West Nyack, New York: Parker.
Carroll, M. E., and Garner, K. R. (1984). *Gymnastics*. New York: Falmer Press.
Dainis, Andrew. (1981). A model for gymnastics vaulting. *Medicine and Science in Sports and Exercise, 13*(1), 34–43.
George, Gerald S. (1980). *Biomechanics of Women's Gymnastics*. Englewood Cliffs, New Jersey: Prentice-Hall.
Gluck, Myke. (1982). *Mechanics for Gymnastics Coaching*. Springfield, Illinois: Charles L. Thomas.
Gula, Denise A. (1990). *Dance Choreography for Competitive Gymnastics*. Champaign, Illinois: Leisure Press.
Loken, Newton C., and Willoughby, Robert J. (1977). *The Complete Book of Gymnastics*. Englewood Cliffs, New Jersey: Prentice-Hall.
Mauldon, E., and Layson, J. (1965). *Teaching Gymnastics*. London, England: MacDonald and Evans, Ltd.
Noble, Darcy Kelsey. (1983). *Gymnastics for Kids Ages 3–7*. New York: Leisure Press.
O'Quinn, Garland. (1990). *Teaching Developmental Gymnastics, Skills to Take Through Life*. Austin, Texas: University of Texas Press.
Schmidt, Darlene Kraklow. (1980). *A Scientific Approach to Women's Gymnastics*. Salt Lake City, Utah: Brighton.

Smith, Tony. (1982). *Gymnastics: A Mechanical Understanding*. New York: Holmes and Meier.
Unestahl, Lars-Eric. (1983). *The Mental Aspects of Gymnastics*. Orebro, Sweden: Vegi Publications.
Wettstone, Eugene. (1979). *Gymnastics Safety Manual*. University Park, Pennsylvania: The Pennsylvania State University Press.
Young Mens Christian Association. (1987). *Progressive Gymnastics*. Champaign, Illinois: Human Kinetics.

Ice Skating

Harris, Rickey. (1980). *Choreography and Style for Ice Skaters*. New York: St. Martin's.
House, Marylin G. (1983). *Ice Skating Fundamentals*. Dubuque, Iowa: Kendall-Hunt.
MacLean, Norman. (1984). *Ice Skating Basics*. Englewood Cliffs, New Jersey: Prentice-Hall.
Petkovich, John Misha. (1988). *Figure Skating Championship Techniques*. New York: Sports Illustrated.
Ryan, Margaret. (1987). *Figure Skating*. New York: Franklin Watts.
Stamm, Laura. (1989). *Laura Stamm's Power Skating*. Champaign, Illinois: Leisure Press.
Sullivan, George. (1976). *Better Ice Skating for Boys and Girls*. New York: Dodd, Mead.

Skiing

Abraham, Horst. (1980). *Teaching Concepts*. Boulder, Colorado: Professional Ski Instructors of America.
Abraham, Horst. (1983). *Skiing Right*. Boulder, Colorado: Johnson Books.
Barnett, Steve. (1983). *Cross-Country, Downhill*. Seattle, Washington: Pacific Search Press.
Borowski, Lee. (1986). *Ski Faster, Easier*. Champaign, Illinois: Leisure Press.
Campbell, Stu, and Lundberg, Max. (1986). *The Way to Ski*. Tucson, Arizona: The Body Press.
Hall, William. (1983). *Teaching Concepts, Nordic*. Boulder, Colorado: Professional Ski Instructors of America.
Hall, William. (1985). *Cross Country Skiing Right*. San Francisco: Harper and Row.
Sanders, R. J. (1979). *The Anatomy of Skiing*. New York: Random House.
Wagnon, John. (1983). *Introduction to Teaching*. Boulder Colorado: Professional Ski Instructors of America.
Yacenda, John. (1987). *High Performance Skiing*. Champaign, Illinois: Leisure Press.

Swimming

Dickerson, Kim. (1985). *Fitness Swimming*. Princeton, New Jersey: Princeton Book Company.
Forbes, Margaret Swan. (1989). *Coaching Synchronized Swimming Effectively*. Champaign, Illinois: Leisure Press.

Gundling, Beulah O., and White, Jill E. (1988). *Creative Synchronized Swimming.* Champaign, Illinois: Leisure Press.

Krasevec, Joseph A., and Grimes, Diane C. (1984). *HydroRobics.* New York: Leisure Press.

Labarrabee, Jean G. (1987). *Coaching Swimming Effectively.* Champaign, Illinois: Human Kinetics.

Lundholm, Jean K., and Ruggieri, Mary Jo. (1976). *Introduction to Synchronized Swimming.* Minneapolis, Minnesota: Burgess.

Official 1991–1992 Synchronized Swimming Handbook. (1991). Indianapolis, Indiana: United States Synchronized Swimming.

Swimming and Aquatic Safety. (1981). Washington, D.C.: American Red Cross.

Thomas, David G. (1989). *Swimming, Steps to Success.* Champaign, Illinois: Human Kinetics.

Thomas, David G. (1989). *Teaching Swimming, Steps to Success.* Champaign, Illinois: Human Kinetics.

Thomas, David G. (1990). *Advanced Swimming, Steps to Success.* Champaign, Illinois: Human Kinetics.

Thomas, John A., and Clayton, Robert K. (1981). *Teaching Aquatics.* Minneapolis, Minnesota: Burgess.

VanBuskirk, Kim E. (1987). *Coaching Intermediate Synchronized Swimming.* Champaign, Illinois: Human Kinetics.

Track

Bowerman, W. J., and Freeman, W. H. (1990). *High Performance Training for Track and Field.* Champaign, Illinois: Human Kinetics.

Bush, Jim. (1978). *Track and Field.* Boston: Allyn and Bacon.

Carr, Gerry A. (1990). *Fundamentals of Track and Field.* Champaign, Illinois: Human Kinetics.

Gambetta, Vern (Ed.). (1989). *The Athletics Congress's Track and Field Coaching Manual.* Champaign, Illinois: Leisure Press.

Index